SMART & WISE:

A TRANSFORMATION

SMART & WISE:

A TRANSFORMATION

Florence Pittman Matusky, Ph.D.

Smart & Wise:
A Transformation

© 2012 Florence Pittman Matusky

cover by Jeanne Matusky
and Lucy Swerdfeger

All rights reserved. No part of this book may be used or reproduced in any manner whatsoever without written permission from the publisher, except in the case of brief quotations embodied in articles and reviews.

Published by

NEW EDUCATION PRESS

www.NewEducationPress.com

Paperback: 978-1-932842-7-22 — $29.95

E-Book: 978-1-932842-7-39 — $ 9.99

Printed in the United States of America

Dedication

To my father, Malcolm Pittman,
my mother, Elodie Frampton Pittman,
my brother, Edmund Malcolm Pittman.

Dad died at age 58 of cancer before my children were born. I regret that they missed experiencing his loving presence and wisdom. My mother died at 87 of heart and lung issues. Her two grandchildren were the center of her life. Ed died in 2011, after a long bout with heart and lung diseases; he had no children. He loved mine: Malcolm John Matusky and Jeanne Elodie Matusky.

Table of Contents

Preface		i
Chapter One	The Future Is In Us Now: Wake Up! It's The 21st Century Already Overview: Smart & Wise: A Transformation	1
Chapter Two	The Western Intellectual Tradition's Legacy: K-12 Public School Education: Flourish or Perish History and Foundational Principles	32
Chapter Three	Smart versus Wise: "Mind-Forg'd Manacles" Definitions: Smart; Wise; Wisdom	70
Chapter Four	Smart and Wise: Thinking Purple Whole-Brained K-12 Public Education	109
Chapter Five	America's Politicized Democracy: The Waters In Which We Swim - Familial, Cultural, Political, Economic Maximum Terms for all Politicians?	162
Chapter Six	The Politics of Beliefs: The Foundations of Western Civilization and The Western Intellectual Tradition — Five of the World's Religions with an Emphasis upon Christianity's Legacy	206

Chapter Seven	The Politics of Gender Violence against Women and Children	262
Chapter Eight	The Politics of Hidden History and Secret Societies, Financial System, Human Origins, Mythology	296
Chapter Nine	Who's in Charge? Cancer as Metaphor: Divided Selves, Society's Ills, and Transformation Process: America's best high school students versus 33 other modern countries, Current K-12 public vs. Whole-Brain Education, *Homo Sapiens'* Sustainability Manual, Transformation, Hope	339

Bibliography & References* 397
  *Bibliography and references are one. Referenced
  authors are alphabetized with numbers 1-354.

Index 416

Preface

> *No one can make you feel inferior*
> *without your consent.*
> —Eleanor Roosevelt

Freedom Love Joy Wonder Curiosity Fear Judgment Sadness Rebellion Free Spirit

I experienced those feelings long before I heard or knew the words attached to them. I lived them first, then I learned the words and to print my name, F-L-O-R-E-N-C-E. I yearned to print more words. My favorite spot in our two-story house was to sit on the kitchen table and look out the window. I could see Grandpop Frampton's house across the road on the large salt water Sound, the homes dotting the hill, and the school at the top. My mother's brother was the teacher/headmaster of that one-room schoolhouse. I cried to go to school. I did, at age three.

My first day of school, a dog barked outside, so I ran to the row of windows. Uncle Lin gently took my hand as he led me to my row seat and said, "You're in school now. You must sit still, listen, and practice your lesson. You must not disrupt the class" (grades one through eleven). I spent the next five years in that one-room schoolhouse, except for recess, lunch at home, weekends, holidays, and summers off. I learned the difference between the mind's freedom and the body's freedom. Physical discipline was a small price to pay then for the world of knowledge that opened up to me as I learned to figure things out by myself, make my own mind map of what and when I had to learn that made sense to me, so learning became natural. I also learned I could think what I wanted to think about even if I couldn't say it out loud, without being scolded in a British culture that practiced, *Children should be seen and not heard.* My imagination soared.

I know we humans are natural storytellers. The left-brain is a master at smoothing out life's wrinkles to invent a more palatable story line. Nevertheless, those years in that one-room schoolhouse are positively imprinted in my brain as the standard by which I evaluated my experience of my public school education to undergraduate, master's and doctoral degrees, teaching 7th grade English in public school, working with K-12 public school teachers in a master's program for ten years, with counseling psychology M.A. students for ten years and with doctoral students for over twenty-five years.

In retrospect, my early school years were spent on earning a self – "I am somebody" – and my next years were spent fending off cognitive assaults on my female self from left-brained-oriented familial, cultural, religious, and academic conditioning to be less than a somebody, a nobody. Those experiences reinforced my quest for knowledge beyond our Western society's "approved" knowledge: the bedrock of America's K-12 public school system also known as The Western Intellectual Tradition. [331]

In my first academic job of teaching 7th grade English in a public school, I became aware that students' themes ran the gamut from subjective details of personal interactions to objective observations and metaphors to express their ideas. Their differences appeared to be gender- and self-esteem-based. Then I noticed that during tests, some smart students appeared threatened and did not test smart at remembering what they had learned. I empathized with such students for, after my one-room schoolhouse experience, I spent a year in boarding school with self-contained grades.

I lived with my aunt-teacher who drilled me and expected me to know answers to her questions when my classmates did not. I felt conflicted: wanting to please her and not wanting to shame anyone or be the center of their negative attention. My inner conflict caused me to blush. Much later I learned that dissonance between the left- and right-brains' responses evokes the right-brain's body language: red face, smiling in sad situations, or defensive body stances. Perceived ego-threatening situations, such as tests, also mean that the ego's fear of failure or survival may submerge the left-brain's learned data, so there is little access to learned cognitive data during tests and reflected in poor grades.

But it was the verbal abuse experienced by some 7th grade students from their teachers and the physical and psychological abuse experienced by other students within their families that made me feel powerless to change their situation. I could relate to them with respect and empathy. For example, Dennis brought a jar of live butterflies to school. When the girls hovered around him, he pulled off the butterflies' wings; the girls screamed and fled. I learned his father used to beat him. A little girl wrote that she wanted to be a librarian. Her mother said she was too stupid so she guessed she wouldn't become a librarian. Parents, adults, and children's unresolved demons, fears, and ignorance may be unleashed upon those whose lives they touch, yet most victims prefer to stay with or protect their adult tormentors.

A 7th grader, whose father was on the K-12 public school's Board of Education, told me that by teaching them *Animal Farm* (George Orwell), I was teaching communism, and that his father could have me fired. However, I believed we can be in charge of what we do know and think, not what we don't know or what others' think. "Learn the difference!" became the theme of my approach to the 7th graders who feared threats to democracy or questioned, "Why should I study English when I've been talking it all my life?" as well as those who wanted to write creatively without paying attention to sentence construction, spelling, punctuation, or grammar. To learn how public education really works, I became the Board Secretary/Business Manager of a K-6 public school's Board of Education. I relearned that institutions (family units, schools/colleges/universities, religions) and organizations (corporations, businesses, foundations, etc.) are only as good as the people who people them, despite their reputations or status.

It was an undergraduate psychology class taught by a psychologist/hypnotist that piqued my interest in the human brain's functioning. The professor had been in the U.S. Army overseas; his job was to debrief soldiers who were sent on missions to locate buried land mines after they had consciously reported on the mines they had found. Under hypnosis, the soldiers described the locations where other mines were buried that were out of their conscious awareness. So we have conscious and unconscious minds in charge of our thinking, feeling, being, and doing. It's the unconscious mind that harbors unresolved traumas, negative experiences, and/or unexamined beliefs about religion, gender, politics, and race that are out of our conscious awareness yet impact our conscious decisions and lives.

Articles in Tuesday's Science Times of *The New York Times*, by Daniel Goleman on the human brain and references to Neuroscientist Joseph LeDoux's research at New York University, increased my interest in brain differences, the antecedents of personal and system power, and the power bases of self- and other-esteem. My prior studies of progressive educator John Dewey's learn-by-doing and person-centered psychologist Carl Rogers' early belief that the public education system was a jug (teachers) and mug (students) pouring and measuring process[285] led me to question the foundations of The Western Intellectual Tradition that are the underpinnings of the K-12 public school system.

But it was marriage to a civil engineer with many common values and beliefs that highlighted our two different ways of communicating that were diametrically opposed to the point that I kept asking myself, "What's wrong with me?" I learned that the rigid left hemisphere's world is a closed system of details, content, how things work, beliefs, values, rules, order, orders, roles, competition, judgments, comparisons, bigger toys, and little sensitivity. The right hemisphere's wide world of positive emotions – love, joy, respect, wonder, curiosity, intuition – and negative emotions – fear, hate, anger, judgment, shame, guilt – is the big picture, or context, and the domain of virtues that humanize us – honesty, responsibility, morals, ethics, compassion, altruism – and non-virtues that dehumanize us: narcissism, greed, lust, sin, violence. The right hemisphere acknowledges what the left hemisphere knows, but the left hemisphere discounts what the right hemisphere knows, says, and does by locking into its own point of view.

From exposure to his family members and culture, differences in our lived family dynamics became apparent. His gender issue and my quest to understand and accentuate the positive motivated me to research hemispheric differences. The Western Intellectual Tradition's continued legitimization of the left hemisphere only blocks the marriage of each human beings' two hemispheres, resulting in divided brains, divided hearts and minds, and divided relationships between people and nations.

When we are ready, a teacher appears. I discovered a nearby university's interdisciplinary Human Development master's program (psychology, physiology, sociology, and some anthropology). I was interviewed by Dr. Alice Z. Castner;[50] she had been mentored by Daniel Prescott at the University of Maryland. Her doctoral work included journaling; her case study of Jane appeared in Dr. Prescott's 1957 book, *The Child in the Educative Process*. Journaling to separate left- and right-brain information was the core of her university's Human Development program, augmented by courses in psychology, physiology, sociology, and other courses related to human beings' morals and ethics, values, belief systems, race, and gender. Dr. Castner hired me as an adjunct to work with M.A. graduate students when I graduated, so I enrolled in a doctoral program. A butterfly was the symbol of the Graduate Center for Human Development.

Journaling the left-right-brain way is composed of writing balanced positive and negative anecdotes of interpersonal communications. Anecdotes are recorded in a notebook with setting, date, time, participants involved, and a line drawn dividing the page into left and right sections. The direct study of another human being was recommended for the first year, two semesters, and then the study of self interacting with others for the second year. What actually occurs or happens in an interpersonal interaction, the objective data, the facts, are recorded on the left side of the page. The subjective data are recorded on the right side of the page: how we felt during the interaction, our assumptions, value judgments, or biases; what we would liked to have happen; what we would do differently in a similar future encounter, and/or what we learned from it about ourselves.

The initial Journaling process – collecting raw data – is the anthropological phase: choosing a person to study (with a pseudonym), weeks of careful observation, mining the mind to write it up, and logically recording what we saw and heard – the facts – on the left-side of the page. When we record our authentic feelings about the factual interaction, on the right-side of the page, we learn how we see the interaction, ourselves, others, and the world. Each time we make visible the other life going on inside of us, we learn that we see not with our eyes but with our brains. In the act of responding from our voiceless but feeling and intuitive right-brains, we teach ourselves something about ourselves, our brains' functioning. When we are ready, insight ensues from the recurring themes in our journaling.

"Who will read?" – the left, objective side only – meant classmates gave feedback to help improve observations, writing, and understanding so they could listen to the anecdote and "be there" without questions and answers to flesh it out. As a result of journaling, I learned to communicate the "funnel effect" way: the context – the big picture – then the content, the details. I also learned to be willing to be misunderstood, to realize how much is heard when no one is talking, and to acknowledge we do not see others as they are but as we are. For the first time, I saw, in black and white, that the hemispheres' right- and left-brains hold different worldviews with opposing priorities. I saw how easily the left- and right-brains' buttons are pushed, and that peaceful closure requires understanding and accepting – but not necessarily agreeing with – the objective or subjective views of what happened and why: the payoffs. The result? A higher tolerance for ambiguity and for differences. The objective? To be whole-brain thinkers and learners by integrating the disowned brain (either the left or the right) to use both our twin brains, as Nature intended, to be whole, healthy, fully functioning people with diverse talents and gifts to be developed.

I also learned that a society that promotes the left-brain as the epitome of intelligence and rejects the right-brain as moronic also produces a left-brained person who believes, "I'm right, so there must be something wrong with you." By default, our society also perpetuates a right-brained person who becomes anti-intellectual and rejects education as elitism or snobbery or as a threat to age-old, status quo beliefs, including faith-based beliefs that do not invite questions. True believers believe, "I'm right, so there must be something wrong with those who don't think or believe as I do."

Knowing the extreme differences and the priorities of rigid left- and rigid right-brain dominant people does not necessarily change relationships for the better, for there's no room for differences until both partners' twin brains are educated, formally or informally. But, the issues changed for me from "What's wrong with me or you?" to "What's right about you and me?" and "What's wrong with The Western Intellectual Tradition that promotes academic intelligence, not humans' full intelligence? Half-brained dominated students and adults may disown their other half brain and become anti-intellectual or anti-emotional, which exacerbates gender differences and worldviews. Yet, we think our brains are acting as one, a unified whole, and are unaware of the drama in the unconscious mind. Full intelligence and wisdom require the integration of the left- and right-hemispheres' intelligences, or whole-brained.

Unfortunately, the master's program in Human Development was phased out after nearly twenty years by a new Dean who cleverly changed a "cash cow" program into a costly one: figures don't lie, but liars figure. The Dean was not impressed by interdisciplinary education, even when several graduates were named Teacher of the Year in the State. Later, State Laws were changed to no reimbursement or advancement on pay scales for teachers' master's degrees not in their field. However, my ongoing mission has been to study the brain research, to do presentations on the brain, to study the history of Western civilization, religions, and The Western Intellectual Tradition, to glean data from scholars' and journalists' writings and national and global events, and to weave in my personal and professional learnings and experiences. All of which have culminated in a synthesis: *Smart & Wise: A Transformation*, by adding the right-brain's emotional intelligence and virtues, including the heart, gut and whole body to the current K-12 public education's curricula. Then academic intelligence is more available to those left- and right-brainers who have human development deficits that interfere with learning, retention, and test taking. Such deficits are: their sense of being respected and belonging, emotional resilience, and character building. Without heart consciousness in the K-12 public education system, there is no caring teaching-learning relationship, just heartless numbers, scarcity of As, and fear of failure that pervade most of our institutions and organizations that are information- and money-driven. Without a formally or informally educated right-brain, there is no wisdom, for wisdom is more right-brain-oriented than left-brain-dominated. Without wisdom, beliefs overrule decisions for the greater good.

Since our college and university systems of education produce the K-12 public education teachers, administrators, politicians, and other professionals in our society who perpetuate the status quo – *The way things are done around here!* – I interviewed two former college presidents. One had been president of a secular university and the other had been the president of several Christian colleges. Both were aware of hemispheric differences, but it was not translated into changing their traditional curricula; however, character was emphasized in the Christian colleges. Evidently, college and university presidents are so busy staying on top of what is going on – networking and maintaining their university's presence in their secular and academic communities, raising funds for endowments and scholarships, dealing with rivalry between departments of academic disciplines and recurring problems, and keeping their Boards informed and their students relatively happy – that there was no time for thinking or acting outside the status quo's box.

Then there's Michael Crow, President of Arizona State University! My son and I attended "Emerge" on Saturday, March 3, 2012, sponsored by the ASU Office of the President, ASU Herberger Institute for Design and The Arts, ASU Center for Nanotechnology in Society, The Prevail Project of the ASU Sandra Day O'Connor College of Law, ASU School of Sustainability, ASU Ira A. Fulton Schools of Engineering, and LightWorks, and the computer chip maker Intel. President Crow explained the choice of "Emerge" for the event and defined its two meanings: 1) move out and away from something, and 2) come into view.

Dr. Crow stated, in effect, that we are trapped in a bureaucracy that is overly methodologized to the point we have a lack of geniuses, boring and structured teaching, and "siloed" and routinized thinking. All of which are the rubble from which we can emerge to understand who we are, where we came from, learn a different way to move out and away from the old as something new comes into view, and conceptualize and reshape the future of learning and colleges and universities toward an interdisciplinary perspective of innovation and creativity.

Now we know that new ideas and innovation are more likely to emerge when left-brained knowledge of a field crosses over into another field, and the right-brain finds "the subtle connections between seemingly unrelated things."[204] Brain research has confirmed that neurons that fire together wire together, creating habits, but the plasticity of the human brains means the brain also changes itself[75] by its thoughts, feelings, and activities, so change is possible with effort.

Now we know that the right-brain can be studied and measured, but also nurtured and encouraged. The immaturity of the brain's prefrontal lobes until age 21 to 25 or later, so young people's ignorance gives them creative advantages, such as risk taking, and makes them innovative thinkers in most fields, from physics to music. At that time, youths are less jaded by the status quo and experience. Yet, adults, too, may be creative by maintaining an outsider's perspective. During prefrontal immaturity, young people's ability to assess the consequences of their actions is missing unless they have been taught at home, learned through personal experience, or educated at school to know the difference since their brains are not fully matured yet. That's another reason to add the cognitive left-brain's partner – the right-brain's intelligence – in the K-12 public educative process.

There is hope that breaking down the barriers between the left-brain and the right-brain and academic disciplines – science and engineering for example – will create undivided brains within and between students, professors, and other people to unleash their full human intelligence potential to learn to think integratively and innovatively. Intel and other corporations learn from science fiction writers, for example, what and how to build integrated approaches and processes, or according to Steve Jobs, "to read things that are not yet on the page"[165] to sustain themselves, seven billion people, and the Earth in the 21st century.

College students' enthusiasm for "Emerge" is contagious and sorely needed when a political candidate labeled America's colleges as "indoctrination mills" from which God-fearing Americans should "keep their distance." And "snobbery" is a term used to label those who urge young Americans to go to college.[68] An array of 2012 presidential candidates took "a hard right turn against education, or at least against education that working Americans can afford"¹⁹³ and women's rights.

"The right perceives a 'war on Christianity' and gears up for a holy war. The left perceives a 'war on women' and gears up for, well, a holy war"¹³⁷ at a time when the Middle East is clamoring against dictators' oppression for freedom and wanting more education for all and rights for women, but they are bogged down by religious rivalry. As a consequence, religious conflicts become a barrier to freedom, equality, and women's rights, even in America.

America's economic crisis began in 2007, and we are still in the throes of a Great Recession that equals the 1929-1939 Great Depression, except for safety nets instituted for the people after the 1930s, such as Social Security, Medicare, Medicaid, and limited unemployment benefits. Wall Streeters thrive at their clients' and the public's expense. Ongoing wars and tensions in the Middle East mean government budget deficits and less money for government programs and less money for retirees who were hurt by the stock market and workers who lost jobs. Jobs are being created in some parts of the private sector, layoffs continue in local governments, especially in public education, and large corporations' trillions are buried, just like Jesus Christ's parable in the Bible's New Testament, Matthew 25:14-30, about buried talents – a large sum of money – not being invested in their own and America's future.

Despite American colleges – Harvard, Yale, Princeton, for example – being founded upon Protestant principles, those principles have been modified from a) God's favors are gifts to be "converted into working and living on behalf of others"⁶⁸ to b) the Calvinistic/Puritan Work Ethic which was embedded in our culture's consciousness along with material success. "Success in material terms became, under Protestantism, a sign of spiritual prowess, the reward of God to his faithful."²²⁵ It may make sense to the rich to judge the unemployed and underemployed as undeserving of God's bounty or of any "socialistic" sharing. "Perhaps if our leading colleges encouraged more humility and less hubris, college-bashing would go out of style and we could get on with the urgent business of providing the best education for as many Americans as possible."⁶⁸ and to equally fund all K-12 public schools.

Some Americans are responding to a God-loving spirituality or the Golden Rule by emphasizing morality in business and relationships. Greg Smith, a former Goldman Sachs executive, publicly resigned his position in an Op-Ed article in *The New York Times* about a corporate culture that "values only one thing: making as much money as possible, by whatever means necessary."[240] On the other hand, Howard Schultz, CEO of Starbucks, "has been practicing a kind of moral capitalism...companies that earn the country's trust will ultimately be rewarded with a higher stock price."[240]

From my human development perspective, there is a message to be heard and learned here. We don't have to conform to the old German adage *Too soon old and too late smart*. Our Western Intellectual Tradition, specifically our K-12 public education system, has ignored the right-brain's negative emotions, human virtues, creativity, intuition, as well as the heart and gut's "knowings." As a results, we grow students to be adults who are academically smart with utilitarian approaches to life, work, and other people; they are focused on making money without heart consciousness. Since the 1960s, when our nation, families, churches, and role models changed, there has been little emphasis upon informally educating young people's character, honesty, morals, ethics, compassion, and altruism, so the me-generation's consumerism overrode America's equality principles and innovation. The K-12 public schools leave nearly 50 percent of its right-brained and nonwhite culture students behind. Usually, they do not match its left-brained teaching-learning styles, so they do not test smart in real or perceived threatening environments when the cognitive brain is hijacked and downshifts into the fight or flight protection mode so access to learned data is minimal. Public schools fail children, especially those in the underfunded K-12 public school system.

We learn that educators at the top have known since 1938 that academic intelligence without emotional intelligence, character, and virtues will override reason and that the freedom to teach and to learn will disappear, creating havoc in American society. And we also learn that Japanese children are as wise as Zen masters. Why? Their Asian written language includes aspects of the right-brain, so they have a content and context approach to learning; whereas, our written language does not. But we can teach children to be wise in our K-12 public schools.

Western civilization and The Western Intellectual Tradition are sustained by tradition and beliefs that are sacrosanct to people who believe in and support the status quo. Change is inevitable. Nothing and no one remain the same. Just as our nation's infrastructure has deteriorated, our society is steeped in violence, not peace. The morals, ethics, public education, diet, and lifestyles of our children and adults have deteriorated to the point that our K-12 public school and higher educational systems that set the curriculum content are long overdue for a paradigm shift.

With video games and Hollywood movies that desensitize young people to violence, children are also desensitized to killing human beings without a conscience or remorse. U.S. Army-type assault weapons are their choice when they go on killing sprees, as in Littleton and Aurora, Colorado, and in Norway, for example. It is evident that many young Americans and adults do not respect life or death either when heart consciousness and what humanizes them are sacrificed for grades and money. Their residual resentments, anger, traumas, and failures are daily reminders that they do not matter; they are of no significance. Alice Miller learned from experience that all human beings have a basic need to express their unique self, in word, gesture, or behavior.[229] When Human Development 101 at home or in public school, fails children their undereducated or damaged right-brains create knots within themselves that become illnesses to be played out as war on their perceived enemies or innocent people. They get their 15 minutes of infamy instead of a K-12 whole-brain education.

My friend Susan, an oncology psychologist and professor, and I attended a South Korean Shaman Seminar at the Asia Society in New York City. A common belief among the Korean lower class is that most people die with seven to eleven resentments. Resentments may be unfulfilled needs, wants, or desires, such as loving parents, loving relationships, good looks, good health, good education, rewarding career, financial success, and successful children. Shamans are hired at funerals to exorcise the resentments to facilitate the deceased to reach Nirvana. A shaman, whose family were shamans for 700 years, and his two female assistants performed a mock funeral on stage with long, enfolded strands of cotton "rope" tied with seven half-knots every 6 feet or so. Each knot represented a resentment. After each ritual of alternately drumming, chanting, or dancing, they would shake the rope, and a knot would untie. "Aha!" said Susan, "That's what I do! When I help my cancer patients to untie their knots, they don't have to die any more. Or they die in peace."

Some knots are tied by our culture's conditioning to behave according to society's stereotypes. I grew up with my mother's "What will people think?" She was the only one of her seven siblings who did not get some college education. At sixteen her mother died and she became the designated family caretaker until her father remarried. Before my mother died, at eighty-seven, she said to me, "If I had my life to live over, you'd be just like me, a housewife." Her comment was the first time she voiced her feelings over my life choices; I interpreted it as a tribute to her happy life as a housewife with my father. My unconscious "no" to her lifestyle had been a "yes" to me as a female who questioned conventional practices.

A good friend told me his father asked him, after graduating from college with a business administration degree and getting promoted for his performance in a corporation, "Couldn't they find someone else?" He is an astute businessman, with heart consciousness, and wealthy. Yet, he still ponders, "What will people think if I don't go to my younger brother's funeral?" when he is too ill to fly 1,000 miles yet has plane reservations to go. We don't need special police or religions to monitor our behaviors when our internal "colonizer" becomes society's enforcer of its norms.

I realized that my hope for using my human development experiences and studies to understand power, esteem, and education's inequities had transitioned into a quest when my aunt told me, upon receiving my doctorate, "You must be all-puffed up now!" Instead, my studies had taught me how much I don't know; it was a humbling, not a puffed-up experience. Now, though, I had the academic research tools and understanding of the larger world context to put hope into practice: a quest – a search to find answers to the many questions I had as a child. As a five-year old, I had resisted and insisted, "I am not a sinner!"

to my Grandpop's sermons in our Christian church and learned to count 1-2-3 and higher when I wanted to drown out negatives. My updated questions include, Why do many women, like authentic artists and the hopeless poor, exist on the fringes of society? And why do some people believe and practice that they are more equal than others? Those who have the gold and status have the choice and the power to be selfish and help create more Hell in America or to be stewards of our nation, like some billionaires, who by their good deeds, create more educational and workplace opportunities: Heaven in America for more Americans. To me, the answers to the divisiveness within our society are self-evident: the lack of K-12 whole-brain public education.

This book's chapters are written as stories with some paragraph headings where the flow is interrupted or when a point is illuminated. Stories are said to be best remembered and understood when they follow the preacher's retort when asked why people remembered his sermons; he said, in effect, first, you tell them what you're going to tell them, then you tell them, and then you tell them what you told them. I believe that stories we hear in our gut are more likely to get our attention than those that reach the head, yet I found myself telling more in different ways than showing more examples and using the word "recall" to repeat authors' words meaningful to me at that writing. I expect there will be readers who may agree with Nathaniel Hawthorne's characterization of his contemporary women writers who focused on education, women's rights, and slavery: "those damned scribbling women." Nevertheless, this book is an attempt to provide the foundation principles and the story of male history of how we become who we are as products and legatees of The Western Intellectual Tradition's K-12 public school system.

Essentially, the book is about transformation from Smart versus Wise, which is the legacy of The Western Intellectual Tradition, to Smart and Wise. It is also the story of one of my epiphanies. An epiphany is an appearance or manifestation of a god or supernatural being; whereas my epiphanies are a relationship, an accident, and cancer that have taught me lessons and are still teaching me lessons. I am responsible for ending my first male relationship, a platonic one, when I discovered he was a pathological liar, which his mother knew and hid to promote the relationship to "save" her son; I am responsible for daughter Jeanne being hit by a car in a parking lot; and I am responsible for ten years of multiple myeloma cancer. The body doesn't lie.

Cancer cells are normal cells that lose their genetic memory and become communication incompetent. They consume healthy cells to thrive while killing their support system. My cancer experience is giving me the opportunity and courage to write my story, my understanding of the foundational principles behind the current state of K-12 public education and people's condition when our whole, communicative selves and genetic humanness are neglected. People are expected to conform to society's norms and be consumers of outside-self things and money for their identities: Smart versus Wise. But, the divisive economic system as support system has failed Americans and America: the Great Depression, other economic downturns, and the ongoing Great Recession. Our money- and consumer-driven society is unsustainable. It is peopled with people who have lost touch with their humanity, so our society is dis-eased or cancerous: with crime, violence, wars, addictions, greed, and we-they confrontations, even in politics.

People who are whole, undivided selves – *Smart & Wise* – rely upon their inner resources and do not have to buy self-esteem or be obsessed with images, entrenched beliefs, money/wealth, and wars instead of authentic selves to thrive and share. Cancer as a metaphor for what's happening in our society may inspire us to grow fully intelligent, communication-competent human beings to balance those institutions and organizations that are more numbers than people-oriented. I propose that the transformational process of all energy systems, as theorized by Ilya Prigogene,[275] is applicable to human beings, except transformation appears to be a choice for us. His theory of dissipative structure is of behavorial patterns he observed in nature, which process he conceptualized and named as "perturbation." Perturbation is basically about upsetting the status quo of an energy system to transform itself into a higher state, or higher levels of consciousness in human beings. Just as a caterpillar spins a cocoon, the chrysalis stage before becoming a Luna moth (as on the book's cover) or a butterfly, we may perceive our transformation from smart to *Smart & Wise* as an example of the perturbation process as we come out of the dark into the light of new ideas and whole-brained ways of thinking, feeling, being, and doing.

The future is in us now. Will we settle for half-brained K-12 public education that divides and conquers us all? Will we settle for the status quo that exists today with our uncertain economic future? Will we settle for representation by career politicians who appear to have lost touch with Main Street and America's Four Freedoms and equality? Or will we be active participants in taking steps to change our todays and tomorrows? To be or not to be agents of change? What kind of future do you want for yourself, your children, and grandchildren? Your answers will influence your future and the many human beings whose lives you touch.

Florence Pittman Matusky
Scottsdale, Arizona
July 2012
www.drflorencem.com

Chapter One

> *We do not come from nowhere.*
> *We are embedded in a very deep*
> *biological and cosmological history.*
> —Robert N. Bellah, 2011, p. 83

The Future Is In Us Now:
Wake Up! It's the 21ˢᵗ Century Already

"Western rational thought is not an innate human characteristic; it is learned and is the great achievement of Western civilization."[165] Our ancestors' rational thoughts, beliefs, and practices were the bases upon which they established Western civilization and The Western Intellectual Tradition,[331] particularly K-12 public schools, to teach and pass on their knowledge to ensuing generations. They did not know that their heads housed two hemispheres with two different brains with different worldviews because a unified self's single stream of consciousness prevails. It was not known until the "mid-nineteenth century that the hemispheres were not identical, and that there seemed to be a clear asymmetry of function related to language, favouring the left hemisphere."[225]

Since our ancestors emphasized the left hemisphere's worldview only, our heritage is a society of institutions and organizations run by people with divided brains that need to cooperate. Instead, we are involved in power struggles that "explain many aspects of contemporary Western culture."[225] Neuroscientists' brain research of recent decades and scholars' writings tell a story "about ourselves and the world, and about how we got to be where we are now."[225]

We have two hemispheres for a reason: Nature provided us with two versions of the world – head (left-brain) and heart (right-brain and the whole body) – to be integrated. The two hemispheres of the brain seamlessly work together and separately in complex ways. Each hemisphere perceives differently and performs unique tasks. As Harvard neurosurgeon Richard Bergland[21] wrote in *The Fabric of Mind*: "You have two brains: a left and a right. Modern brain scientists now know that your left brain is your verbal and rational brain; it thinks serially and reduces its thoughts to numbers, letters, and words...Your right brain is your nonverbal and intuitive brain; it thinks in patterns or pictures, composed of 'whole things,' and does not comprehend reductions, either numbers, letters, or words."[21] In fact, the left-brain which is "the kind of mind modeled by cognitive science can...play chess very well, and can even be programmed to cheat. But it is not plagued with guilt when it cheats, or distracted by love, anger, or fear."[202]

Cognitive science is based on how the mind works with language, facts, and figures, not on how it works in unique individuals with unique life and embedded sensory experiences and with morals and ethics and the Golden Rule. Neuroscientist Joseph LeDoux illuminates the problem for society when a person's left-brain thinking is not modified by the right-brain's input and thinking: "The fact that emotions and motivation are not studied by cognitive science makes sense if cognitive science is regarded as a science of cognition, but is troubling if the field is supposed to be the science of mind."[202] Neuroscientists inform us that "thinking is not done solely by the brain, an organ housed in the cranium. Thinking is done by the mind, which is not an organ but a process that is distributed throughout the body and draws on every faculty we have."[254]

Neuroscientist Jill Bolte Taylor writes that the right brain-mind is depicted in our society as an "uncontrollable, potentially violent, moronic, rather despicable ignoramus, which is not even conscious and without whom we would probably be better off. In vast contrast, our left mind has routinely been touted as linguistic, sequential, methodical, rational, smart, and the seat of our consciousness."[325] The right-brain-mind is also conscious and the seat of human virtues and intuition beyond the positive and negative emotions.

When one hemisphere, the right, is not formally or informally educated or legitimized, there is greater reliance upon the left hemisphere's point of view where the ego is primary, and paper is a symbol of human beings' word, worth, power, and performance: contracts, rules, regulations, money, today's financial derivative products, and evaluations of human beings. Such paper replaces, abuses, and motivates people. Some people behave as if they value paper's symbols of wealth more than people. In the left hemisphere's world, people are dehumanized when experience is virtualized, knowledge is politicized, and power and control are bureaucratized, in the hands of the few. Divided brains produce divided people, so imbalance occurs spilling onto the world's stage: win-lose wars, divisiveness, violence, crime, addictions, greed, poverty, wealth, and humans' ongoing inhumanity to men, women, children, and animals.

In our culture, we used to be culture- and gender-conditioned, consciously and unconsciously, to prefer the left- or the right-brain. Boys were given chemistry sets, sports equipment, and toy guns and continue to be encouraged in math, logical analysis, and competition. Girls were given dolls and tea sets and are encouraged to be nurturing and cooperative. Girls are allowed and expected to cry; boys are seen as sissies if they do.

There are no census figures; it is estimated that 50 percent of America's population are left-brain dominant and the other 50 percent are right-brain dominant. Despite the stereotyping that all men are left-brained and all women are right-brained, women may be left-brain dominant and men may be right-brain dominant. Right-brainers have easy access to their left-brains. After all, they learned to read, write, and compute, so those with few mental hangups may learn to crossover and play the education game more wisely. Right-brainers, though, may be less competitive, more inquisitive, persevere, and/or have context/contemplative learning styles. Left-brainers, though, have direct access to the right-brain's anger and discounts the right-brain's broader view of humanity and the world.

Because of these intriguing differences between the two hemispheres' skills, many writers and thinkers today characterize two distinct worldviews or personality types in terms of the two hemispheres. People who are referred to as "left-brained" prefer to think in ways that are analytical, linear, rational, logical, verbal, and objective; whereas, people who are referred to as "right-brained" prefer to think in ways that are synergistic, wholistic, intuitive, metaphorical, nonverbal, visual, and subjective. Left-brained people prefer to focus on details and content; whereas, right-brained people prefer to focus more on context, process, emotion, and relationships. It is said that left-brained persons are more "I" oriented, and right-brained persons are more "we" oriented. The right-brained person is also often characterized as compassionate, altruistic, and spiritual; whereas, the left-brained person is more interested in rules, regulations, laws, money, status, and power.

Instead of exploring hemispheric differences, some psychologists have rallied around five personality traits that appear to represent dimensions of personality: Extroversion, Neuroticism, Agreeableness, Conscientiousness, and Openness.[298] Extroverts are socially warm; Introverts are reserved; Neurotics are generally emotionally vulnerable versus emotionally stable; Agreeableness denotes trust and empathy as opposed to meanness and arrogance; Conscientious people are methodical, achieve established goals; those low in consciousness may be more impulsive or disorganized. The duality of those personality traits may fall within the realm of the left and right hemispheres where they are modified by inherited genes, lived experiences, relationships, life events, the environment, and education.

Brain research of past decades indicates that we use both brains simultaneously, so most of us feel we are unified as a self and in control of our thoughts and actions. Thus, few people experience themselves to be hemispherically out of balance. Because the two brains work so well together, we feel we are a seamless self who is in charge of our choices and decisions. Why? The brain is a complex system."The common characteristic of all complex systems is that they display organization without any external organizing principle being applied."[116]

For the past 2,500 years, Western civilization has been an evolving achievement of the left hemisphere's thought and creation. Western civilization now needs to correct itself to finally include the right-brain alongside the left-brain in the K-12 educative process because the uneducated right-brain's uncivil and passionate aspects are being played out in our society and destroying ourselves and our nation from within.

Without the formal and informal education of the right hemisphere's intelligence, we may override the left-brain's reason and become "socially and emotionally insensitive, and have an impaired understanding of beauty, art, and religion...Yet the pursuit of self-interest has not left us happier"[224] and others' self-interests have left the majority of us poorer: physically, mentally, emotionally, socially, economically, and spiritually.

This book's purpose is to tell the rest of the story: what we need to learn and unlearn to go beyond where we are now. We cannot undo the past, what was said and done that negatively affected us by those who were indoctrinated by The Western Intellectual Tradition's left hemisphere and who were not exposed to informal education of their right hemisphere's emotions (love and respect for all God's creations), virtues, and the Golden Rule: Do unto others as you would have them do unto you. As a result of being parented as their parents were parented, being taught as their teachers were taught, and being conditioned by their inner and outer environments, many left-brainers are blind to their own blindness and don't even know they don't know how to treat and be with others, except with objectivity, selfishness, or anger. With a black or white, right or wrong, or locked-in attitude toward its own point of view, there is no room for differences.

Father, forgive them, for they know not what they are doing (Bible's Luke 23:34), as Jesus Christ said when he was taken to the Cross for crucifixion, is a way for us to let go of the negatives in our lives (especially childhood memories and negative experiences that we continue to nurture after age 21), forgive ourselves for being so innocent or naïve, reframe intense memories to empower ourselves, not our transgressors, and begin to live the life we want to live. It's easier for me to write those words than to live them, as it may be for most of us. However, we are empowered to reinvent ourselves from a whole-brain perspective when we entertain new ways of perceiving, knowing, doing, and being on this Earth. Let the healing begin!

I used to wonder why, in democratic America, some established scholars and seasoned professionals were content to teach or repeat one year twenty-five times over and over and rarely entertained a new idea or an interdisciplinary perspective. And why some scholars/professionals were near retirement age before acknowledging their interest in "outside the box" topics or initiated responses/solutions to situations/problems beyond our society's "approved" knowledge.

Then I learned that knowledge in all academic disciplines that is "inconsistent with what is already known," via the scientific research method, is not legitimate in our left-brain-run society. So, our society encourages conformity and objectivity. New knowledge, ideas, and academic and health care practices that do not have America's status quo seal of approval are ridiculed, not funded, and its creators may be subjected to character assassination. The Western Intellectual Tradition's status quo – The way things are done around here! – reigns in America's higher education systems; they define what K-12 public schools teach and what it means to be an educated individual.[322]

Our left-brained-run society's definition of new ideas/knowledge was succinctly described by senior vice president of the Andrew W. Mellon Foundation, the sociologist Harriet Zuckerman, when she stated, "We know people have ideas beyond the mainstream, but if they want funds for research they have to go through peer reviews, and the system is going to be very skeptical of ideas that are inconsistent with what is already known."[48]

"Contrary to conventional expectations, science is actually not about a pre-given, hidden, microscopic world existing completely independent of us, but it is about what we can know through experience and reason"[254] and direct observation. Dr. Janet Davison Rowley, 85, is the matriarch of modern cancer genetics whose contributions to her field were gleaned through observationally-driven research. She said, "That's the kiss of death if you're looking for funding today. We're so fixated now on hypothesis-driven research that if you do what I did, it would be called a 'fishing expedition,' a bad thing...I keep saying that fishing is good. You're fishing because you want to know what's there."[83]

Nobel prize winner Albert Szent Gyorgyi related his understanding of seeking National Institutes of Health (NIH) grants for research projects: "NIH...Now write up exactly what you will be doing during the three years of your grant...research means going into the unknown. If you know what you are going to do in science then you are stupid! This is like telling Michelangelo or Renoir that he must tell you in advance how many reds and how many blues he will buy, and exactly how he will put those colors together."[323]

Our Western society is still enmeshed in the left-brain's self-invested version of how things and people should be in this world, without being grounded by our "knowings:" observations, experience, intuition, interdisciplinary exploration, and our interconnectedness with all creation. Coming to our senses means we break through to the knowing that is "based on direct experience, to see with eyes of wholeness, to practice awareness of the mind as if our lives depended on it – because... 'in virtually every way that has any meaning, literal or metaphorical, they surely do.'"[254]

For centuries, the left-brainers have dominated our culture's policies, laws, practices, K-12 public educational systems, and most of our institutions and organizations. The right-brain's virtues and inherited and experiential data stored in our brains from inception in the womb on are not part of the formal K-12 public educative equation. So emotional intelligence, which humanizes us, is part of the invisible curriculum; whereas, the left-brain's cognitive intelligence – the world of ABCs and 123s and logic – is sanctioned and deemed to be the epitome of being human and human intelligence. It is academic intelligence instead.

With evidence of rampant corruption, greed, poverty, addictions, and violence today, it has become more evident that Western man "has created chaos by denying that part of self that integrates [right-brain] while enshrining the parts that fragment experience [left-brain]...we in the West value one of these ways above all others – the one we call 'logic,' a linear system that has been with us since Socrates [469–399 BC]. Western man sees his system of logic as synonymous with the truth"[139] and is the basis of The Western Intellectual Tradition that produced the K-12 public school system.

To venture beyond The Western Intellectual Tradition, to embrace scientific brain research of past decades, is a challenge. Encountering resistance to change, "neuroscience has returned to the necessary and unimpeachable business of amassing findings, and has largely given up the attempt to make sense of the findings, once amassed, in any larger context."[225]

For me, to make sense out of life through narration originates from an unconscious but motivated quest. First, I experienced how long it takes for some of us to be aware of and overcome years of familial, gender, race, cultural, political, economic, academic brainwashing, and personal mistakes. We may ask ourselves "Who's in charge of me?" and "Who's in charge of us?" before reconnecting with our essence, our wholeness.

Reconnecting starts with our human brain's right and left hemispheres, or neural structures, which are connected by the corpus callosum. Now I understand that the ongoing growth of white matter (myelin) in the corpus callosum was long neglected by science. Like fingerprints, each brain is different, but the white matter represents "a vast network of fibers connecting neural structures. The way in which the brain processes information is dependent on how these fibers are connected ...Using DTI [diffusion tensor imaging] we have found that the way one person's corpus callosum is hooked up may be very different from someone else."[116] The accumulation of myelin throughout the hemispheres accounts for "middle-aged wisdom," according to a Harvard scientist.[160]

Then there's the brainwashing problem that starts in childhood, thanks to our ancestors whose thinking. without having knowledge of human brain differences and functioning, created Western civilization and The Western Intellectual Tradition to inculcate their views. In preliterate times, the right-brain's intelligence was more integrated with the left-brain's intelligence since the right- and left-brains develop independently but in harmony. Over five thousand years ago, our ancestors evolved from an oral tradition to one driven by alphabets and numbers, which are the left-brain's forte, when they learned to read, write, and do math.[307; 225] Thereafter, the left-brain dominated Western civilization, except for artists and writers' works and those who learned to be whole-brained through their own efforts.

Formal schooling originated in Europe for wealthy, elite males to be educated in the past's classics, languages, and living and to continue to rule the masses through "the divine nature of authority."[271] For eons, left-brained scholars taught that rationality, logic, and objectivity were the defining characteristics of humans and science and that the mind and body were separate entities. Today's scholars inform us the mind and body are interconnected, thoughts are mostly subjective and often unconscious and metaphorical.[199] Emotions and feelings "because of their inextricable ties to the body... pervade our mental life."[63] Yet, "the guardians of perceived wisdom, for the so-called 'lack of scientific evidence,'"[297] retain the status quo in K-12 public education and in disciplines dealing with human nature[75] and human bodies.

Mass education led to a left-brained focus on disseminating information. Education's founders with left-brained perspective required a curriculum based on certainty, the explicit and the literal, focused on fragmented details, and dealt with data that are already known. Our ancestors believed their mechanistic construction of the world, sheared of complexity, was the only one with validity; they believed they knew everything when they did not. For example, 17th century Rene Descartes' "I think, therefore I am" denied the more primitive, "I feel, therefore I am" since "Feeling came, and comes, first, and reason emerged from it."[225] However, the separation of mind, emotions, and body prevailed. Isaac Newton's 18th century mathematical, left-brained-entrenched way of thinking dominates today's academic institutions, despite quantum physics, and dismisses the right-brain as a nuisance and female, despite scientific brain research to the contrary.

Charles Darwin[65] affirmed brute force – the physically fittest – as survivors, not the mentally, psychologically, or spiritually fittest, just the strongest from his study of ants and animals; he made inferences from his research and applied it to human behavior. His inherited beliefs, mindset, and inferences were Biblical dominance: top-down authoritarian rule in the family, institutions, nation, and over the Earth and its resources. Systems of domination "require insensitivity, cruelty, violence, and destructiveness because rigid top-down rankings – be they man over woman, man over man, race over race, religion over religion, and so forth – cannot be maintained otherwise. So our human capacities for caring, empathy, and consciousness have to be suppressed or fragmented for a domination system to be imposed and maintained."[91]

The foundations of Western civilization and The Western Intellectual Tradition are left-brain dominated and divinity-inspired. Thus, the right-brain's attention – to the wholeness of human beings not machines, new information and ideas, personal and social experiences, our interconnectedness, and what is intuitive, visionary, and embodied – has had no legitimate place in The Western Intellectual Tradition for centuries. Yet, we have decades of scientific research about the human brain and the fact that early childhood experiences, including in utero, have a great influence upon brain development and how we learn and relate.

All fetal brains look alike in utero until the eighth week when a testosterone wash turns a unisex brain into a male one. Some cells in the male brain's communication centers are killed off to grow more cells to enlarge its sex and aggression centers.[27] The female brain retains its larger than the male communication center. Relationships become paramount for right-brainers, not left-brainers.

In essence, we human beings are born into this world with fully activated, sensory-driven right-brains and with stored genetic inheritances, instincts, and experiences in the unconscious brain-mind. The brain stem or reptilian brain begins its function in the first trimester of gestation. The reptilian brain provides us with an awareness of our outer sensory world. The right-brain's limbic system begins developing in the second trimester. The limbic system (amygdala, hippocampus, hypothalamus, for example) provides us with an awareness of our interior, subjective world. The left-brain or neocortex begins developing in the third trimester,[260] but it is not active. The neocortex, or verbal-cognitive left-brain, is the language and cognitive thinking center. The left-brain begins its growth spurt around the second year of life. Thus, the right-brain is more active in children during the first three or four years of their lives when intelligence is principally a function of the right hemisphere. [225] The fact that all human brains' prefrontal lobes do not fully mature until age 21 to 25 or later is not generally acknowledged. The prefrontal lobes are believed to turn our brains (reptilian, limbic, and neocortex) into one civilized mind. [260]

In the 1970s, prevailing thought held that people's thinking was generally rational, logical, and sound. Daniel Kahneman's research on thinking informs us that human beings' two minds – 1. fast, intuitive, and emotional and 2. slower, more deliberate, and more logical – drive individuals' thinking. Mind #1 has no voice; it uses body language to communicate its agreement or disagreement with the left-brain's communications. For the right-brain, reading others' body language is automatic, so a viewer quickly combines seeing and intuitive thinking. Mind #2's slower thinking requires effortful mental work, from multiplying 17 x 24 to "the conscious, reasoning self that has beliefs, makes choices, and decides what to think about and what to do"[172] and thinks it is in charge.

Neuroscientist Roger Sperry, in his 1981 Nobel lecture, presented the prevailing view of the right hemisphere when he began studying it: "not only mute and agraphic but also dyslexic, word-deaf and apraxic, and lacking generally in higher cognitive functions."[204] Now we know that the world is so complex that Nature's brain has to process it in two different ways simultaneously: to see the forest and the trees, but it's the right hemisphere that helps us to see the forest. The right hemisphere solves problems by insight, which happens unconsciously, but the left hemisphere's forte is analysis, which takes much longer. However, both hemispheres are involved in the experience of writing and reading poetry.

The poet John Ciardi taught students how to read a poem by focusing on its adjectives and metaphors. He emphasized *How Does A Poem Mean?*[55] rather than what a poem means or its subject matter. Dr. Ciardi stated that "A poem is some sort of living performance; it comes out of live sources in us. And everyone has these live sources...The feeling is there, yes, but the communication of the feeling is a skill—a way of doing...Every good poet educates your eyes because you don't see with your eyes; you see with your brain. The eyes are just windows letting in impulses...anything significantly looked at is significant...a thing is significant that teaches us something more about ourselves."[54] It takes an educated right-brain to translate metaphors, to understand meaning from the whole brain, including the Bible. The left hemisphere, though, focuses on the literal definition of words.

"We have discovered something in the left brain, another module that takes all the input into the brain and builds the narrative. We call this the interpreter module."[116] We humans are storytellers, but the left-brain "confabulates stories that try to make sense of what the unconscious mind is doing of its own accord"[33] or to whitewash one's history. The left-brain's conscious mind believes it is in charge of what it thinks, feels, says, and does. When the desires of the conscious mind conflict with the unconscious mind's early programming, the unconscious mind wins. That's why we can repeatedly say positive affirmations, such as we are lovable, cancer-free, or will find a rewarding job, but if, as a child, we heard we are unworthy, sickly, or stupid, those negative judgments of us may be out of our conscious awareness but are etched in our unconscious mind and will undermine efforts to change our lives[208] – until we cognitively and emotionally change the messages because human beings manifest what is in mind.[144]

David Hawkins, a psychiatrist, calibrated energy levels of human consciousness (and of man-made things and entities), from 0 to 1,000 with his knowledge of kinesiology.[144] The right-brain's emotions are divided into negative (shame, sin, guilt, apathy, hatred, fear, anger, and pride – which are anti-life and calibrate under 200 each) and positive ones (peace, joy, love, respect, and acceptance – which support and nurture life and calibrate over 200 each). The uneducated right-brain's negative aspect, fear, is the means by which governments, corporations, politicians, priests and preachers, and other authority figures control public perceptions and freedom by encouraging low levels of consciousness, beginning in the K-12 public school system.

We have two brains for a reason: Nature's wisdom. Scientists inform us that hemispheric specialization evolved to do an efficient job of processing two diverse kinds of information at the same time. Birds and chickens, for example, narrowly focus their attention on finding food with the left hemisphere while globally focusing attention on guarding against predators with the right hemisphere,[214] which is a simplified version of their hemispheric differences. When each hemisphere is developed relatively independently, but in harmony, there are few inner and outer conflicts, within human beings, to spill over onto the world's stage, which we have today when divisiveness surrounds us and violence, terrorism, and wars engulf us, and the Almighty Dollar controls us.

Left-brain thinking and intelligence have come to dominate individuals and our American culture. Our status quo society deems the right-brain to be women's domain and unworthy of formal education, yet it's the right-brain's emotions and virtues (respect, love, honesty, morals and ethics, justice, intuition, altruism, and compassion) that humanize people and our society while the right-brain's seven deadly sins – pride, covetousness, lust, anger, gluttony (including greed), envy, and sloth – are rampantly expressed in and destroy our society from within. Another reason the right-brain may not be formally educated: the right-brain's virtues and intuition or the heart's consciousness are not measurable on tests like the left-brain's True/False and a, b, c, or d tests.

Tests alone are not the measure of an individual's intelligence, character, or future performance. Also, few educated professionals (including teachers, principals, and administrators) have the self-knowledge, intercultural literacy, and empathy to holistically work with developing human beings whose basic needs for survival may not have been adequately met. Most educated, left-brain professionals are unprepared for the world of work beyond the left-brained world of ABCs, 123s, and defined roles, unless they have invested in self-knowledge and have self-educated their right-brains or learned from their experience.

Our political climate, though, discourages disseminating what is already known about brain development processes, brain differences, and applying what is scientifically known today in K-12 public education systems to understand "something taking place inside ourselves, inside our brains, and played out in the cultural history of the West"[225] and in our daily lives with those we love, work, and relate.

Now we know that reasoned thinking is often lacking in normal people's Mind #2 due to faulty or lack of data, biases, prejudices, irrational beliefs, values, perceptions, overconfidence, and media priorities. Now we know that Mind #1's intuitive impressions may be flawed, that unresolved emotional issues, and lack of self- and other-esteem may hijack reasoned thinking, and that wisdom depends more upon the right-brain's intelligence (Mind #1) than the left-brain's logic (Mind #2). Thus, our thinking, decisions, actions, and wisdom are shaped by the interaction between the data in our two hemispheres' brains (left and right) and in our two minds (conscious and unconscious) and especially by the embedded data bank we have accumulated from in utero onward. We may learn to recognize our own unexamined beliefs, biases, and judgments or unresolved emotional issues when we experience an averse reaction to someone or something. Our disowned self and unexamined issues are more recognizable in others' behavior than in ours, so our negative reactions are opportunities to learn more about ourselves and resolve them toward whole-brain thinking.

Since only the left-brain's intelligence is welcome and educated in public schools, there is a tendency for left-brainers to be predictable, mechanistic thinkers, to believe they know everything when they do not. They disregard data from the right-brain's broad context, new experiences, new ideas, relationships, and the big picture – the world – in their decisions. "We tend more and more to see the world as a heap of intrinsically meaningless fragments."[224]

Until the 1960s, the right-brain used to be informally educated in many families so left-brain goals were more integrated with right-brain virtues. Then, with the devaluing of traditional institutions (the family, religion, public education, role models) and with organizations (corporations) becoming more left-brained, more performance- than people-oriented, more profit-oriented, and paying huge salaries and perks for CEOs, our society became more left-brain- and money-dominated. Too many American families need two paychecks each week to keep a roof over their heads and food on the table. Earning money to stay alive dominates most Americans' time and energy, leaving less room for family, friendships, and involvement in the public schools or our communities.

The right-brain's intelligence is not welcome or educated in K-12 public schools, except for art and music which are the first to be cut in budget crises. Positive and negative emotions and feelings, intuition, imagination, vision, honesty, morals, ethics, compassion, altruism, perseverance, and the emotional resilience to learn from mistakes are part of the invisible curriculum that is now left to chance.

Public education's K-12 curriculum is geared to left-brained excellence in programming a Watson (IBM's smart robot) to compete on TV's "Jeopardy!" not to educating a human being for whole-brain thinking, understanding, loving self and others, parenting, working, and living. Thus, The Western Intellectual Tradition is not a viable educative approach, without the right-brain-mind, for America and for all Americans to flourish. The Western Intellectual Tradition enslaves more people with Poet William Blake's "mind-forg'd manacles" than it frees.

There are multiple intelligences.[114] Intelligence is one of the definitions of being smart, implying clever, capable, witty, and shrewd or sharp, as in one's dealings by taking advantage of others. The so-called smartest students (meaning those with strong by-the-book, left-brain attributes that match left-brained tests based on our dominant white culture and excerpts from fragmented texts) are judged to be highly intelligent. Such students get the high IQs, high grades, and scholarships for their Logical-Mathematical Intelligence, or academic or cognitive excellence.

Those skilled in Bodily-Kinesthetic Intelligence, the sports athletes, are recruited with cash and perks, so "intercollegiate athletics is undermining the integrity of our institutions."[255] For example, "between 1985 and 2010, average salaries at public universities rose 32 percent for full professors, 90 percent for presidents, and 650 percent for football coaches."[255] One way of asserting "balance between athletics and academics...[is] elevating academic standards for athletes."[255] Reining in college sports may not be possible because "the dollars are simply too attractive, the pressures from outside too great."[255] American "kids have grown up with the idea that sports are really a major part of American society and something they should care about."[255] The evidence shows that "fandom carries an academic price,"[255] for male students' grades and learning suffer; they study less, drink more alcohol, and party more.

An antidote to the perception and reality that some athletes are undermining the intellectual integrity of our colleges and universities would be to take Grand Valley State University (Michigan) Professor John Kilbourne's suggestion and create academic degrees/majors in football or basketball,[239] for example.

Some sports figures are good role models for America's youth, but today many of them are not when they use drugs, abuse women and animals, or break laws. Due to their media visibility, they command huge salaries and perks, without the benefit of higher education, and they are perceived as role models. "The modern sports hero is competitive and ambitious...He is assertive, proud and intimidating...His identity is built around his prowess...His primary virtue is courage—the ability to withstand pain, remain calm under pressure and rise from nowhere to topple the greats...This sporting ethos pervades modern life and shapes how we think about business, academics and political competition."[32]

Today, Darwin's "survival of the fittest" translates into doing whatever it takes to win, including targeting the competition's previous injuries. The early Roman Empire's Gladiator Games" (264BC- 483AD) perfected the art of violence toward people as entertainment, but today's violence in sports is more about winning money and fame. What sports, businesses, academics, and politics have in common is competition. Competition is a left-brainer's forte. Competition implies scarcity: our culture promotes winners versus losers; smart students' A and B test scores in academia are balanced by judgments of not-so-smart students' C and D test scores. Plotting class test scores on a parabola or bell curve avoids administrative censure for too many As or too many Ds. Religions compete for members when Seventh Day Adventists, Mormons, and other Christian missionaries are sent forth to convert the "heathens." Businesses are about making money, whatever the human and environmental costs. Sports are about glory, victory, supremacy, beat the competition, and avoid defeat. The practice of politics is about egos, charisma, money, seduction, lies, history, philosophy, and ideology.

"The moral ethos of sport is in tension with the moral ethos of faith, whether Jewish, Christian or Muslim...The religious ethos is about redemption, self-abnegation and surrender to God,"[32] which ethos appears to be at odds with the me-first competition for grades, votes, sales, status, money, and power inherent in academia, politics, and financiers and capitalists as well. David Brooks avers that "the two moral universes are not reconcilable,"[32] that Earth's first man, Adam I, epitomizes "the part of us that creates, discovers, competes and is involved in building the world" and that Heaven-oriented Adam II epitomizes "the spiritual individual who is awed and humbled by the universe as a spectator and a worshiper."[32]

While many Americans believe that religions' essence is to fear and obey God, some Americans believe that spirituality's essence is to love God and become God-like with Divine consciousness, which appears to be more congruent with Jesus Christ's teachings than religions that instill fear and Thou Shalt Nots to control sexuality and obedience to its dogma. Extreme religionists, fundamentalists, and fanaticists believe their path only leads to God and Truth. Truth is not found in a single religion, Bible, Torah, Veda, or Koran. Life and the human brain-mind-body-soul are more complex but unified than the terms, words, and left-brain-made practices that perpetuate divided human beings' brains and lives.

The academic and athletic stars have access to prestigious universities and professions, and often do whatever it takes to attain power, status, and money – if they ignore or are deficient in emotional intelligence: right-brain virtues such as respect, honesty, empathy, and compassion, or if they value things and money more than people.

We know that "modern America is prodigiously good at producing sports stars...And yet the same excess does not apply to other kinds of talent."[204] We encourage our kids to participate in sports when they're young; mothers and fathers drive them to practice and watch their games. Exposure to sports develops kids' talent and allows coaches to identify those with natural ability. Plus, we celebrate athletic success with trophies, parades, newspaper coverage, scholarships, and community esteem. We could learn lessons from the Penn State sports coach who tainted the whole university and ruined young boys' sex lives and minds. Again, at the highest levels of the institution's administration, money, power, and status proved to be more important than students' welfare.

If a nation ever needed a course correction, America needs one right now before we hit rock bottom. Not just in the sports field but, more importantly, in the public education and the financial fields. We could concentrate on and publicly celebrate smart and wise students' talents, beyond Spelling Bees and Science Fairs, not just those who excel at sports. Yes, "it's possible to create more geniuses...The first meta-idea we need to take seriously is education...We do an excellent job of lavishing gifted athletes with attention and scholarships, but too many of their peers are forced to attend failing schools with high dropout rates."[204]

How do we get to perform at Carnegie Hall? Practice, Practice. Practice. How do we get to be gifted athletes in a game? Practice. Practice. Practice. How do we get to be smart in academia? Study. Test. Study. Test. Study. Test. Tests are not practice when they are used to label us. If The Western Intellectual Tradition used tests to determine what students need to study and learn, then tests as practice, not performance, would make more sense than they do now: label students' left-brain academic intelligence, not their overall intelligences.

John Dewey's learn-by-doing is not part of the public educative equation; students are not given the tools to discover knowledge or to find solutions to real problems, or to cope with complexity. "When students are given explicit instructions, when they are told what they need to know, they become less likely to explore on their own. Curiosity is a fragile thing."[204] The Western Intellectual Tradition is holding them back. "We've become so obsessed with rote learning, with making sure that kids memorize the year of some old battle. But in this day and age that's the least valuable kind of learning. That's the stuff you can look up on your phone!"[204]

Researchers compared the cognitive development of four-year-olds in an unstructured play preschool with those in a structured preschool where they were taught phonics and numbers. After one year, the play-based school kids scored better on the skills that are linked to academic and real-world achievement: cognitive, self-control, attention focus, and working memory.[204] Learning is fun, not a chore. Homework is work. Learning is what we do all the time, whether we are aware of it or not. Perception is all.

Worldviews change when existing solutions do not work, except when a new worldview conflicts with the old worldview held by those in power. Giordano Bruno, 1548-1600, preferred burning at the stake to recanting his hypothesis that the Earth orbited the Sun. Galileo Galilei, 1564-1642, avoided the stake by publicly bowing to the Roman Church's worldview that the Earth was flat, but he whispered, "It's round!" The flat Earth view prevailed for centuries even though Nicolaus Copernicus, 1473-1543, a Polish astronomer, promulgated the theory that the Earth and the planets moved about the Sun before both Bruno and Galileo were born. The Mayan calendar dates back to 5th century BCE, indicating a sophisticated understanding of the cosmos. It has taken many centuries for Western civilization to attain some of the knowledge that the Mayans knew and practiced in pre-Columbian Mesoamerica.

The facts remain that the Earth pivots around the Sun and is round, whether people believed or disbelieved what the Roman Church taught in earlier centuries, so people's knowledge was limited. Similarly, the mind and body are one whether we believe it or not. The two hemispheres of the human brain are involved in all human processes, especially our intelligence and wisdom, whether we believe it or not.

Cultural conditioning whereby people prefer one brain over the other produces one-dimensional human beings whether we believe it or not.

Since The Western Intellectual Tradition's K-12 public schools educate only one of our two brains, the right-brain also must be educated, formally or informally, to attain full human intelligence whether we believe it or not. Not only is people's knowledge limited by The Western Intellectual Tradition's policies, but people's human and humane development and lives are compromised by the neglected and abuse of the right-brain's negative emotions. Unresolved feelings of anger, fear, shame, guilt, greed, desire, envy, lust, despair and even pride override reason, forcing recognition, unwittingly, of their undereducated states and desires.

Basically, The Western Intellectual Tradition fails the majority of its right-brained students and rewards the by-the-book smartest, me-first students, who ace left-brain tests. They are the winners on Wall Street, at the public's expense, and the elite leaders who command obscene salaries for their slash and burn expertise as they sell off companies' assets and ship jobs overseas to look good for the short-run's roll of the dice. While some of America's industries were unprofitable and needed to be upgraded and some complacent workers and unions needed a wake-up call, many Chambers of Commerce were outsourcing advocates/business advisers. They led the way for more profits and higher salaries and perks to capitalize on the global market's human capital, often enslaving them in their own countries. Most CEOs' reputations and financial traders' investment skills are based on their left-brain's overconfidence in their abilities, so people judge their comments, decisions, and actions more favorably than they deserve, known as the halo effect.[172] Dr. Kahneman examined "the illusion of financial skill...The results resembled what you would expect from a dice-rolling contest, not a game of skill,"[172] just luck. Nevertheless, the deeds are done and CEO's and financiers' high compensations reign with political opposition to the elites' paying their fair share of taxes. Is it now unAmerican to say that there's nothing modern about capitalism, just old-fashioned capitalists whose narrow worldviews are ever thus: I, me, my, mine? Is it also unAmerican to advocate for whole-brained K-12 public education to widen people's worldviews so they don't become capitalists' economic slaves?

The Western Intellectual Tradition is sustained by its left-brain orientation and the proponents of historical traditions. The dominant left- and right-brainers are culturally and educationally conditioned to focus on details, the content, not the larger picture, the context. To demonstrate that fact, I would hold up a U.S. $1.00 bill in my classes and ask, "What do you see?" Rarely would the left- or right-brained American students report seeing my fingers holding the bill or the background, but many Asian-Americans did. We have been conditioned to see and attend to details, not the big picture. Asians' language/heritage includes aspects of the right-brain, so they perceive content and context: a whole-brained perspective. The Chinese language consists of "logographic symbols that also activate sections of the right-brain."[181]

A misuse of the uneducated right-brain occurs when many parents, teachers, preachers, and other adults use its negatives – anger, fear, and shame – rather than its positives – love, joy, and respect – to influence young minds and their behavior. What adults may not know is that using the right-brain's negatives as threats, evoke unresolved issues, such as conscious and unconscious negative memories or flashbacks – trauma, physical, verbal, or sexual abuse – which hijack or limit access to the left-brain's cognitive learnings, especially during testing.

What we are learning is "Love becomes essential to survival because it is necessary in the tolerance of painful affects"[198] since love encompasses all our feelings experienced from the cradle to the grave. "Just as white light contains all the colors of the spectrum, so love encompasses all the feelings reflecting our living process."[198] Psychiatrist J. M. Dorsey understood by experiencing that "every emotion is made of nothing but love. All pathology is merely physiology struggling under stressful ordeal. Anger, or grief, or jealousy, of whatever painful emotion, is merely inhibited love struggling under stressful ordeal. Hate is hurt (hindered) love, deviltry is hurt (hindered) divinity, doubt is hurt (hindered) belief, fear is hurt (hindered) safety, guilt is hurt (hindered) innocence."[198] The hindrance of a positive emotion evokes its negative, often unconscious, aspects: fear, shame, hate, anger, greed, or ego survival at all cost.

Yet, centuries ago, in 1519, Niccolo Machiavelli[212] advised *The Prince* it was safer to be feared than loved. Fear may work for princes and dictators, but it impairs children's overall development, especially in faith-based institutions that practice, "Spare the rod and spoil the child," which is a short form of the King James Bible, Proverbs 13:24: "He that spareth his rod hateth his son, but he that loveth his son chasteneth him betimes." That kind of love breeds hate, and is another example of the left-brained, cold-hearted, power-hungry men who disenfranchised women from the Roman Church's hierarchy because they disowned loving themselves and renounced women who symbolized love to them. According to Psychiatrist Henry Krystal, "the affect most dreaded is not aggression, but love, particularly in adolescents."[198]

Many men do not rise above the adolescent stage of emotional development when their right-brains are not formally or informally educated. Seeking power over people, including beating children and taking advantage of people financially because they can, is like a genetic disease, the misuse of love, that gets passed down from generation to generation and separates us from our genetic humanness. The Roman Church's focus upon Original Sin, that all Christians are sinners, is not a healthy inner climate for loving oneself or others. Instead, self-negation is a sin: "This sin consists of the refusal to love oneself well, the refusal to celebrate both one's dignity and one's responsibility. When people sin in this way, they become suckers for hero-worship, for projecting onto others their own dignity as images of God."[103] Money is a surefire panacea for the felt lack of love.

America was ripe for unrestrained capitalism in the 19th century to repudiate the traditional Calvinism/Puritanism ideals of poverty and simplicity and to accelerate its ideals of industriousness and production into capitalism Protestant evangelists, Dwight L. Moody, Russell H. Cornwall, and Billy Sunday were friends with capitalist barons, such as John Wanamaker, Cornelius Vanderbilt II, J. P. Morgan, John D. Rockefeller, and Andrew Carnegie who coined the term "The Gospel of Wealth" and believed in the divine law of economics: the sacredness of private property, open commercial competition, unrestrained accumulation and any constraints were the devil's work. Moody preached the gospel of wealth; he correlated Biblical teachings with individualism, free enterprise, and unlimited material accumulation. Cornwall preached that "financial success was a reflection of personal righteousness while poverty was a mark of God's punishment." Billy Sunday was a friend of Rockefeller who supported him as a "police measure – as a means of keeping the lower classes quiet."²³² Now we understand how political economics and religion were fused and used to undermine our democracy in 1929-1939, Great Depression, and our current Great Recession.

Our society's evangelistic institutions are places – besides Hollywood movies and TV's game shows – where the right-brain's positive emotional expressiveness is welcome and sanctioned, creating a community of like-minded, enjoyable friendships, and redemption for sins, which has been granted to many fallen/sinful preachers. Seeking wealth is the Holy Grail of some American church members and non-members, not the Golden Rule, not to be an instrument of a cause that is larger than self, unless it is a tax sheltered foundation, for example, or a church. Churches with charismatic pastors or preachers attract members and tithed financial support, and many own radio and TV stations to increase their donations, membership, and power bases.

The robber barons appeared to perceive such churches to be a means of keeping the Christians focused on being saved from sin to go to Heaven and on keeping them unaware of elites' financial goals: to use religious beliefs and their institutions as leverage for their own unrestrained, tax-free enterprises without sharing with "undeserving others." Karl Marx's "Religion is the opium of the people" is taken out of context: "Religion is the sigh of the oppressed creature, the heart of a heartless world, and the soul of soulless conditions. It is the opium of the people." We do live in a heartless world with soulless conditions that are sanctioned by The Western Intellectual Tradition's institutions and organizations that separates our hearts from our heads. Religion is the one place where we integrate our heads and hearts, sing, listen to music, pray, and believe that God's in his Heaven – All's right with the world! ⁴¹ Then when we leave Church, reality may hit us: all's not right with the world.

Money-dominated, emotionally illiterate people may enjoy power over others. Bereft of compassion, persons with low self-esteem seek other human beings to dominate to make them feel superior and potent. Such "control freaks" may dominate other men, women, children, or animals in a society that has condoned such behavior from the ancient past, while giving lip service to their victims' rights. People with self- and other-esteem issues believe they have the right to treat their financial-dependents with name-calling and "Do as I say or else!" as they mete out conditional love. Abusers reject feedback and use it for more abuse. With a self-fulfilling prophecy operative, children and spouses pivot around their acquired toxic memories, which thwart learning and optimum functioning and compromise humans' immune systems.

Toxic memories are similar to undigested food that causes stomach upsets and headaches until resolved. Memories are reconstructions of remembered memories, not actual snapshots. Nevertheless, memories are etched in the brain because they contain intense emotional data, such as viewing the effects of the international terrorists' strikes on 9/11/01. Events that are perceived as threats to one's ego survival stand out as the remembering self versus the experiencing self.[172] Despite the experiencing self having positive memories, as in a long-term marriage, they may be overridden by the remembering self's negative memories. Focusing on the accumulated negative memories, interferes with relationship functioning. Most negative memories may be examined to find the lessons to be learned or may be reframed to remove the victim stance and to empower the self. Many rigid left-brainers have selective and massaged memories; they habitually whitewash themselves by blaming the victim for their actions or justifying the abuse by dehumanizing their perceived "enemies."

The key to how children and adults react is based in power. "A person with low self-esteem...will generally feel anxious about losing power and will habitually use power-over people for ego-protection, ego-building, or bullying.[5] Victims of bullying who commit suicide or become violent are judged, but their bullies may just choose other victims. However, bullying persists and its underlying cause is not understood by academics and parents as the result of uneducated or undereducated right-brains at home or in the K-12 public school system.

"A person with high self-esteem will generally use power gracefully and will not let the trappings of position seduce him or her into dependency on them in order to feel significant and potent."[5] Two of America's Republican presidential candidates in 2012 – Donald Trump and Mitt Romney – publicly stated that they like to fire people. To be in a position to have and enjoy power-over people to fire them, for whatever reason, represents a power-hungry individual who is insensitive, callous, and deficient in right-brain virtues. Corporate CEOs may not admit to a power-over others trait, but they justify firing employees to save money, which makes them look good or maintains their halo effect, for the short-run, and to satisfy investors.

In primitive times, in lieu of power, it made human development sense for Nature to rely upon the expression of hormones to create equilibrium between primitive men (testosterone for aggressiveness and sex) and primitive women (oxytocin for relationships and trust). When the two sexes harmonized their diverse functions, they survived hardships, saber-toothed tigers, and passed on their genes. Past cultures and the Holy Bible, though, have elevated males to dominance over females and the Earth. Historically, human beings inherit "a great river of knowledge."[33] If that knowledge is flawed, consists of rigid beliefs or is overconfident or underconfident and if those human beings have unresolved emotional or self- and other-esteem issues, then their levels of consciousness may be under 200[144] and they may be blind to their own blindness, and their leadership abilities and wisdom are suspect.

From an empirical study of 533 people, aged 20-89 from diverse educational and socioeconomic backgrounds, and probably white. German researchers Baltes and Staudinger predicted the "world record" in wisdom may be held by a man in his 60s.[16] Wisdom is equated with age, even by Western psychologists and human developers. However, wisdom is rare among older and retired individuals whose health and money worries distract them from questioning the status quo: why they cannot thrive in our democracy. Instead, the system appears rigged to empower and enrich the few. Too many seniors have bankrupted themselves and sold their homes just to pay hospitalization bills and purchase prescribed, expensive drugs. A society that devalues its senior citizens and professionals and individuals who cannot deal with death are not humanity-based or wise. A friend's wife was dying of cancer and in hospice care at home, yet a well-intentioned neighbor intervened and had her hospitalized via ambulance. Nearly $50,000 was spent in her last 24 hours of life to revive her; her surviving husband nearly lost their home to pay the hospital bills.

Erik Erikson's life cycles include "a generational principle which would tend to perpetuate a series of vital virtues from hope in infancy to wisdom in old age."[95] For Erikson, wisdom consisted of "ripened 'wits' to accumulated knowledge, mature judgment, and inclusive understanding."[95] Since wisdom is more right-brain-oriented than left-brain-dominated, the inclusion of the right-brain's virtues in The Western Intellectual Tradition would balance out our out-of-kilter hemispheres and increase the fibers in the corpus callosum. With access to our innate sense of fairness and justice, wisdom could be exercised at a much earlier age. In Japan for example, children's wisdom is on a par with Zen masters' wisdom.

A research study of wisdom, involving 186 Japanese and 225 Americans, by Igor Grossmann, University of Waterloo, Canada,[132] found that Japanese children are Zen masters' equals almost from the beginning. While Americans get wiser with age, wisdom does not vary with age for the Japanese. Dr. Grossmann's results suggest that, "at face value...Japanese learn wisdom faster than Americans,"[132] but a paradox may exist: America is an individualistic society where social or intergroup skills are required for wisdom to manifest; whereas, Japan is a collectivist society where individual or interpersonal skills are required. A factor also is language; Asian languages engage both the right- and the left-brains; whereas, our language is left-brained only.

Money is a panacea for wisdom; it compensates for right-brain deficits, especially lack of love for self and of people who are different or unlike oneself. Many Americans believe that people with lots of money are super intelligent, very smart, and to be emulated, whatever the source of their wealth. The Smart versus Wise are unbalanced people who favor things/money over people. America has been brought to its economic and moral knees by financial and religious agendas of those with schizophrenic behaviors or rigid positions that indicate the "right hemisphere is not functioning normally...an imbalance in favour of the left hemisphere occurs in schizophrenia."[225]

Our society's ills, from wars, violence, crime, bullying, rape, abuse, poverty, greed, corruption, and addictions to unemployment and a ripe climate for corporate profits, are fallout from not formally educating the right-brain and focusing on the left-brain only in The Western Intellectual Tradition. Few educators acknowledge the fact that the brain's prefrontal lobes (the wisdom lobes) do not fully mature until age 21 to 25 or later.[260] Then we may have the brainpower to consider the consequences of our actions. During prefrontal immaturity is the prime time to educate the right-brain, when children have the ability to be open to truth,[124] curiosity, imagination, new ideas, and new learning and to avoid blindly following unexamined beliefs and negative habits.

Children thrive on adults' unconditional love and respect, established limits, character building, and emotional resilience. Their emotional intelligence is undermined by adults' physical/verbal/sexual abuse, permissive or laissez-faire caretaking, being treated as if they are entitled to be the center of the universe, or when money and material things are substituted for parents' face time. Emotionally illiterate, character-deficient children become adults who pass on their ego deficits to their children, unless they unlearn what they lived.

Why aren't all Americans thriving? America's unlevel and unequal educational, living, and working fields have become more visible in past decades. The equal opportunity claim that has defined America since its founding in 1776 was resurrected in 1945 when one of the benefits for World World II and later veterans was a free college education. The resulting surge in college-educated Americans led to yesterday's prosperity and a huge middle class.

The failure to achieve equal opportunity in today's America starts early. Inequality in K-12 public education is so blatant that high school students' SAT scores may be predicted by zip code. We know that richer neighborhoods in America's cities collect more real estate taxes and spend more money on education than other zip codes in poor neighborhoods within the same cities. Low income families and their children are more likely to suffer from poor nutrition and inadequate health care in dangerous neighborhoods with underfinanced public schools, parental uninvolvement in their children's formal learning, and teachers' low expectations for impoverished students.

Presidential 2012 candidate, Rick Santorum, dubbed President Barack Obama's vision of college for all America's young as snobbery. As a former U.S. Senator with a law degree and anti-abortion Christian beliefs, Santorum also favors home schooling children over "liberal" public education. Home schooling requires stay-at-home, educated moms who do not have to help earn a living for the family to survive. Listening to biased left-brained politicians' rationalizations of their ideology, from a wealth perspective, is a prelude to America's future when the cost of attending college, secular and religious, is already prohibitive for middle and poorer class students. Without scholarships for skill or IQ, "smart poor kids are less likely than dumb rich kids to get a degree."[194] Education-bashers are reminiscent of the early Roman Church's Bishop Athanasius (293-373 AD) whose vision of a monk was "an illiterate and simple man,"[252] not Anthony of Egypt, a renowned monk who stressed "living the 'angelic life:' 'whosoever harms his neighbors harms himself...but whoever knows himself knows all things...and whoever is able to love himself loves all.'"[252]

America is headed back to the Dark Ages where schooling was designed for snobs, the wealthy elites, if the American Dream of education as a means of upward mobility is totally destroyed. As it is, the financial economy (business: insurance, banking, finance, medicine, law) is amply rewarded and the moral economy is not (right-brain, heart and soul work: K-12 public school teaching, pre-school teachers, some nursing, clerking, housekeeping, and waitressing).The devaluation of moral values reflects the status of children, the elderly, women, and the right-brain's morality and compassion in America.

Today, America's politicians claim they believe in equal opportunity for citizens, yet they slash funds for the poor's nutritional programs, poor K-12 public schools, teachers, Pell grants which help low-income students go to college, and attach "socialism" to any guaranteed health care that is taken for granted in other modern nations. But politicians' free health care, the best available in America, and guaranteed lifetime pensions are examples of America's inequality when politicians take care of themselves, not all citizens' health, education, and welfare.

The Western Intellectual Tradition has done and is doing a wonderful job of educating America's students who match public education's teaching-learning styles and/or those who experience master teachers who transcend The Western Intellectual Tradition and students' limitations. Generally, academically smart students, not wise, fit the system. Academic intelligence is not human intelligence, which requires an integration of data from both the left- and right-brains: heads and hearts. Most of the academically smart students go on to colleges and universities, expand their horizons, and become America's leaders. Because their K-12 public education led to their higher education and material success, many leaders and politicians believe the education they received is America's best form of public education. They may think that the fallen executives of Enron, FreddyMac, and Wall Street are anomalies, not hollow men. T. S. Eliot's poem, The Hollow Men,[92] is apropos to apply to those leaders who are empty of right-brain virtues, such as compassion and ethical standards, and driven by financial rewards, without heart consciousness.

There are about 99,000 - 100,000 public schools in the U.S. About 90 percent of America's youngsters go through them.[150] Public education is an investment in students and America's future. Too many public school students take public education for granted and many do not like and are bored in school. Business guru Peter Drucker believed "Businesses are not paid to reform customers; they are paid to satisfy customers"[84] or go out of business or reform their mission to satisfy customers/students.

Steve Jobs' approach to business was not to give the customers what they think they want: "Our job is to figure out what they're going to want before they do. I think Henry Ford once said, 'If I'd asked customers what they wanted, they would have told me, 'A faster horse!' People don't know what they want until you show it to them. That's why I never rely on market research. Our job is to read things that are not yet on the page."[165] That's not the current job of K-12 public schools or higher education: "College campuses are seen as the source for the newest thinking and for the generation of new ideas, as society's cutting edge...Yet undergraduate education changes remarkably little over time,"[322] and so does the K-12 public education system.

"Our nation has a huge human development deficit!"[319] and has an epidemic of brain robberies because the public schools have failed to develop students' intelligence potential. The K-12 public schools are doing a wonderful job of pouring facts into test-smart but are ignoring what it takes to educate students to be smart and wise. Teachers can do a wonderful job of educating all children to be smart and wise when the right-brain's attributes are finally introduced into the public educative process to produce whole-brained, fully intelligent students and adults.

Drawing out and nurturing each student's talent builds students' self-worth and capitalizes on their uniqueness. Current bureaucratic-imposed curricula are ends in themselves with a teach-and-test approach that results in predetermined, temporary rather than long-term knowledge. A relevant curricula "invites inquiry...raises questions... encourages investigation and digs deeper for connections between what is already in one's brain and the new material."[319] It's the right-brain that recognizes patterns in the left-brain's disparate data. Inquiry activates curiosity, generates more potent intelligence, and restores the joy of learning.

America's status quo keeps its elites in charge of knowledge disseminated to the public and K-12 public schools in our culture, so new knowledge that is inconsistent with what is already known is considered quackery, and the perpetrators are ridiculed. Knowledge is power. However, if that knowledge is a left-brain construct to seduce people through economics, ignorance, dogma, propaganda, beliefs, or secrets, without integrating the gut and heart's knowings, the right-brain's virtues, and self-knowledge, then the ensuing knowledge is flawed and not worthy as the basis of education and wisdom.

Many elders and enlightened people know that Western civilization needs outside the mainstream knowledge to focus our whole-brain intelligence on the struggle for the body, mind, emotions, and the soul of humanity. To survive and thrive, we wake up, link up with others, speak up, and expose those who would not only divide us through mind-forg'd manacles but also those who believe their hereditary superiority means their genes are better than the average American's gene pool when nurture is also a factor in human development, not just inherited genes or nature. While some people perceive themselves to be more equal and entitled to more money, power, and status than other Americans, without the right hemisphere's input, they are, "Effectively autistic, we have no sense of the broader context of experience."[224]

Pundits report that the next generations of American retirees will not have the cushion of social programs of my generation, if anti-government, free enterprise politicians continue to widen the gap between the rich and the poor. When corporations are a) anthropomorphized into "people" by presidential candidate Mitt Romney and others, when b) America's corporations' power and international reach define our foreign policies and our financial lives, when c) weapons of mass destruction/deception (WMDs) lure us into costly wars, d) when political language is used to conceal more than it reveals, when e) women's procreative and equal rights are ongoing religio-political issues, when f) a small percentage of America's population, the wealthy, is thriving and a huge percentage of salaried and paycheck-to-paycheck employees endures unemployment, poverty, or underemployment, and when g) politics overrides basic economic foresight that austerity in the midst of recession is a bad idea,[296] then "the forces of fundamentalism, sectarian racism, intolerance, etc. [are] at work,"[174] not democratic principles.

"Human nature has not changed much in the past 100,000 years, except now we have nuclear, chemical, and biological weapons to settle old scores,"[174] if politics without principles, cave man violence, and human ingenuity fail to achieve desired negative outcomes against those perceived to be enemies, less than human, or undeserving.

While scholars' pleas in the past for academia to include the right-brain's knowledge and virtues along with the left-brain's knowledge bases are ignored, who knew that out-of-kilter human hemispheres would lead to out-of-kilter Americans and America? Whole-brain thinkers – Daniel Prescott,[273] Carl Sagan,[294] John Sarno[297] and Iain McGilchrist[225] – know we have to educate the right-brain that Nature provided to make full and creative use of our human intelligence embedded in the two hemispheres, the heart, gut, and the body. Dr. Prescott learned from experience that unbridled passion submerges reason, creates havoc in society, and destroys the freedom to teach and to learn.

Left-brained thinking in America is akin to "the divine nature of authority"[271] that keeps dictators empowered in the Middle East. All uprisings must be crushed, just as the right-brain's virtues are dismissed as the preference for feelings at the expense of thought. As Albert Einstein, 1879-1955, informed us, *The world we have made, as a result of the thinking we have done thus far, creates problems we cannot solve at the same level of thinking at which we created them.*

Each of us is one-of-a-kind, unique human being. We may acknowledge that we are all interconnected and have the human right to whole-brain, equal education, and truthful knowledge that does not divide and conquer us. Over thousands of years, the left-brainers have constructed and dominated our Western civilization. Our history attests to people's inhumanity to men, women, children, and animals to the point that powerful people appear to have rigged even our democratic system to perpetuate inequality, especially income inequality.

It is time to upgrade to the 21st century's knowledge explosion and to concentrate on processing and using information dynamically instead of disseminating status quo information to maintain passive learning. "A paradox of American higher education is this: The expectations of leading universities do much to define what secondary schools teach, and much to establish a template for what it means to be an educated man or woman."[322] Educating both human hemispheres at the higher education level in America appears to be a prerequisite for change at the K-12 public school level. However, I know there are many master teachers in the K-12 public school system who are equipped to begin the transformation process toward whole-brain public education.

Since the Mayan Calendar ends in December 2012, now is a time for truthful knowledge from individuals' initiatives and for higher levels of consciousness to reign on Earth. From a numbers perspective, there are more of us who want truth and freedom than those who would seduce us with tradition, money, fear, deceit, and secrecy. With minds open to knowledge's heartfelt truth, we do not conform to conventional wisdom.

With a whole-brain perspective, we acknowledge the personal power unique to each human being, gain the inner freedom to confront our man-made fears, to honor our human right to not only survive but thrive, and to make thriving happen in collaboration with other human beings, like and unlike ourselves. The most recent warning about the left-brain's dominance in creating Western civilization – yet its continued dominance when a correction is necessary portends disaster – was the topic of an essay in *The Wall Street Journal* by Iain McGilchrist, a psychiatrist and former Oxford University literature professor. He summarized Western civilization's plight with left-brainers in charge: "The left hemisphere ever optimistic, is like a sleepwalker whistling a happy tune as it ambles toward the abyss. Let's wake up before we free-fall into the void."[224]

Chapter Two

> *By academic freedom I understand the right to search for truth and to publish and teach what one holds to be true. This right implies also a duty: one must not conceal any part of what one has recognized to be true.*
> –Albert Einstein (1879-1955)

The Western Intellectual Tradition: Flourish or Perish

Once upon a time there were no K-12 public schools or colleges and universities. Europeans had not yet discovered the Americas. Men ruled for the gods by "the divine nature of authority"[271] and people's accumulated knowledge was transmitted orally from generation-to-generation. For thousands of years, masses of people were illiterate, poor, and part of the Divine Chain of Being or natural order, according to those priests and kings who ruled for the gods through rituals and ceremonies.

In early times, the bulk of humankind was agrarian and craft-oriented with intact families who toiled as a unit on the land or in their homes. With population growth, most of the people lived in villages with traditions based on work and beliefs. People were ruled by the gods, priest-kings, or monarchs, and there was an aristocracy of warriors and landowners. Below them were the wealthy merchants with special privileges. Below them were the toiling peasants whose powerful rulers dispensed punishment, demanded obedience, and kept them at a subsistence level until they died at young ages.

Formal schooling was established by and for the elites, the sons of the wealthiest. Those schools were designed to transmit the ruling class's culture to the next generation of young elites to perpetuate their ruling the masses through the divine nature of authority. The young elites were educated in the past's classics, languages, and living. They agreed to be disciplined, to learn subjects, such as Latin, medieval history, and theology, because the rewards of success were obvious: high professional office and status.[271]

The education of human beings evolved over the centuries from foundational historical and intellectual concepts based on the divine nature of the elites to rule and control the peasants, what was worth being taught, who was worth educating, and who was not. The Western Intellectual Tradition[331] evolved from those principles, adapted from the Roman Church and elites' historical governance, into today's standardized approaches to transmit, to all students, America's "approved" knowledge and methodologies.

Although there was no or little knowledge of the human brain's left and right hemispheres in earlier times, without interventions or favoritism each hemisphere apparently developed relatively independently and in harmony. Therefore, in preliterate societies, according to Leonard Shlain, the right-brain's virtues may have been more integrated with those of the left-brain.[307] Evidently, 30,000 years ago wall paintings in France's caves pictured animals in pairs, male and female; figurines of images of women; and in the next stage of evolution, Neolithic, female goddesses were featured. "The archaeological research demonstrates that these early cradles of civilization conformed more to the partnership configuration: they were more peaceful, gender balanced, and equitable."[91] Human beings, men and women, needed and used both versions of their hemispheres' takes on the world to survive.

Then, over 5,000 years ago, alphabets and numbers were invented by creative people for oral languages.[307; 225] Reading, writing, and numbers created social memories that were more reliable than oral traditions and individuals' memories. Writing and numbers are the forte of the human brain's left hemisphere and symbols of power, laws, and orders to control, manipulate, influence, or teach people. Thus, the left-brain achieved dominance over the right-brain. History affirmed the divine nature of authority, religion was taught as truth, and education was more than learning a skill; it was a means to sustain life, society, and universal truths from an elite perspective. Robert Bellah informs us that "although literacy goes back as far as 3000 B.C.E., it is true that it remained largely a craft literacy, confined to small groups of scribes until well into the first millennium."[19]

Since formal schools and universities in Europe were established by and for the elites, those secular and religious schools were designed to transmit the ruling class's culture to the next generation of elites to rule the masses. Therefore, we look to history for the foundational principles upon which Western civilization and The Western Intellectual Tradition were founded. Over the past 2,000 years, Christianity has defined the Western civilizations of Europe and eventually America and has influenced its public educational systems as well as public and private lives. Ancient records show that most religions appear to have Jewish roots. which, in turn, have other ancient roots in the Mesopotamian and Babylonian cultures and oral traditions from around 10 BC to 1 BC. Although Jesus Christ may have been born in 4 BC, little is known of his life until 26 AD. Christianity was founded by followers of Jesus Christ, a Jew. Since Christianity has evolved over the ages, it is examined as a key foundational principle of America's K-12 public education system and society.

The Roman Church flourished when Emperor Constantine became a Christian in 313 AD and endowed himself with divinely inspired authority. He insured his and the Church's power and control by incorporating aspects of pagan and other religious sects to attract worshipers and defuse the rivalries between Christian sects. Christianity was sanctioned as the Christian Church in 380 AD with tenets, original sin, and women's equal status with men was abolished. Western civilization emerged from the Dark Ages, part of the Early Middle Ages, that began in 476 AD, when a barbarian deposed Roman Emperor Romulus Augustulus. The Roman Church's Christianization of the barbarians spared the Roman church when they overran Rome. With the fall of the Roman Empire in the 5th century, there was an era of backwardness: anti-intellectualism, book burnings, barbarous ways, torture, Muslim conquests, and religious faith as education until the Crusades began in 1095 AD.

In centuries prior to the Dark Ages, the Greco-Roman civilizations were pagan, although gods and goddesses were common to both and the Roman and Orthodox Churches were consolidating their power and members. Both civilizations evolved to the importance of leading a virtuous life, being a good citizen, and ushered in the classical world of humanistic ideals and art. In ancient Greece, art of the human face and body reflected empathy, tragic drama reflected human emotions, and poetry was rich in metaphor.

By Socrates' era, 5th century BC, "Greek language and thought... favored abstraction...what is purely conceptual is real."[225] Socrates pursued wisdom with "rational discourse"[225] as the way to truth. Reason requires cognition, left-brain, and seeing things in context, right-brain, but rationality is context independent; whereas, "Rationality imposes an 'either/or' on life which is far from reasonable."[225] Thus, in Socrates' era, the balance between the two hemispheres implied in reason was replaced with rationalism. Although Socrates could not read or write, Plato was his follower and it was "his association with Socrates that impressed on him the need to forsake poetry for dialectic"[225] or logical argument. "Plato's influence on the history of logic, mathematics, and moral and political philosophy cannot be overestimated, despite the fact that his works were lost from view for over a thousand years [Dark Ages] until the Renaissance, available only in partial reports and commentaries translated into Latin via Arabic."[225]

Prussian Philosopher Nietzsche's, 1844-1900, "view that Socrates, far from being the hero of our culture, was its first degenerate, because Socrates had lost the ability of the nobles to trust intuition."[225] For example, Socrates met "a prominent Athenian politician – 'a man with a high reputation for wisdom'...[he] lured him into a classic Socratic trap."[139] Socrates said he was wiser for he was aware of his ignorance, whereas the politician thought he knew what he didn't know. Socrates discounted the politician's intuition as a factor in his wisdom, so Socrates may have been smarter, not wiser, than the politician.

By "the time we reach the fourth century BC, each of the changes that had taken place in written language favoured a shift of balance inexorably towards the left hemisphere. In this way the history of writing recapitulates the history of language generally: originating in the right hemisphere, but translating itself into the left."[225] As writing "became established as a means of controlling society,"[225] namely, the uneducated masses, there is "no doubt that it is ultimately the left-hemisphere version of the world that Plato [in his Republic] puts forward, for the first time in history...so strongly that it has taken two thousand years to shake it off."[225]

Jerusalem was conquered by the Turks in 1065, which led to the Roman Church's Crusade in 1095 and to nine Crusades over 200 years, until 1291 when the Kingdom of Jerusalem fell into the hands of Saladin, a Muslim. The Crusades had some effects on Western civilization: they influenced the wealth and power of the Roman Church, created social and material effects and knightly orders, such as the Knights Templar, promoted intellectual development, commerce, feudalism, and led to voyages of discovery and trade routes which spread diseases from China's Gobi Desert to the European continent.

The Roman Church, in the 14th century, was corrupt. The papacy lived in palaces, and sin was rampant. Indulgences were freely given to kings, lords, and those who could pay. In the midst of a corrupt Church and a hundred year war between France and England, the Black Plague broke out, in 1328; it was the worst plague in history and claimed millions of lives. While people lived in a Roman Church world mixed with alchemists, astrologers, diviners, conjurers, healers, and witches, the emotional climate was such that people openly wept, for death was a constant, the work ethic suffered, and so did their Christian faith when the plague also decimated the clergy.

In the 15th century, a peasants' rebellion due to the effects of the Black Plague, dissatisfaction with the Roman Church ensued. During the Renaissance of the 14th through 16th centuries, the cooperation of the hemispheres was evident in plays, scientific discoveries, and explorers' new worlds. The arts flourished but gave way to rigid thinking, increased bureaucracy, the codification of laws, and Roman architecture benefited from the invention of concrete from volcanic ash. A shift occurred favoring the left hemisphere: the left-brained Reformation and Industrial Revolution spread across Europe and to America.

In the 16th and 17th centuries, some scientists in Western Europe believed they knew as much if not more and had achieved more than our ancestors. Their thinking, though, was based on ancients' beliefs in the separation of the human mind and body, the supremacy of logic, mathematics, rationality, and women's role as servant to man. The left hemisphere pushed for "a renewed emphasis on symmetry and stasis.

Ambiguity was no longer a sign of richness, but of obscurity. Imagination was mistrusted and metaphor became a lie. Rationalism came to replace the humane balance implied in reason. As Descartes said, things can be seen clearly only if they are seen singly, one by one. The world was atomized"[224] and ready for the Industrial Revolution's machine age.

The result of the Industrial Revolution's technology – from about 1760 in England – was to affirm the centuries-old mind-body split but to also split the human brain into two parts, the head or the heart. Then the world became: "the hard, masculine, and objective world of machines, and the soft, feminine, and subjective world of emotions."[307] Such dichotomies are totally compatible with scientific objectivity: the removal of human experience from the scientific worldview!

The left hemisphere's world is a closed system: predictable, focuses on details, isolates what it sees, manipulative, literalistic, sharply delineated and certain, locks into its own point of view, limited to doing things it has always done, and rule-bound. The right hemisphere is an open system: sees things in context and as interconnected, "at ease with ambiguity and the idea that opposites may be compatible."[224] "Without the right hemisphere, we are socially and emotionally insensitive and have an impaired understanding of beauty, art and religion. Effectively autistic, we have no sense of the broader context of experience. Meanwhile, without the left hemisphere, we struggle to bring detail into focus. If a culture were ever to rely excessively on one take [of the world] alone, there would sooner or later need to be a correction."[224]

For the past 300 years, people have been treated primarily as machines. We have inherited scientific objectivity from Newtonian engineered-thinking of the Industrial Age. Scientific objectivity, methodologies, and thought patterns break knowledge into separate disciplines and fragmented subjects, organize people into roles and the specialization of labor, gather extensive numerical data, and make decisions using complex mathematical formulas to treat people and their work as engineering problems. Thus, in traditional Newtonian science, the human body and the human brain are considered to be similar to a machine with replaceable parts, but destined to wear out with old age. It was assumed that human beings were born with "x" number of brain cells and that they did not regenerate. Not so.

Before "the twentieth century only a small percentage of mankind could read and write."[271] America established The Western Intellectual Tradition, the public school system, to educate America's youngsters for citizenship; it was modeled after the factory system of the Industrial Revolution, which was modeled after the Prussian Army's strict discipline and the Roman Church's hierarchy. As in Europe, America's public schools were originally intended as a privilege for middle to upper class males, for boys of the elites, to make gentlemen out of young boys by secular and religious institutions.

In Colonial America (1620-1776), there were various kinds of schools. In a dame school, women taught neighbors' children for a fee. In a town school, the community hired a teacher and paid either tuition or taxes. In the Latin Grammar school, Latin and Greek were taught to boys only to prepare them for college. In New England, the Puritans held local governments responsible for teaching all children to read the Bible to defeat Satan. The original New England School Primer was published in Boston between 1688 and 1690. The Primer became America's staple textbook for over 150 years. Many of wealthy families' boys were sent to Europe for their college eduction. Before the 1776 Revolution, Harvard and eight other colleges were founded primarily for training clergymen.

In America (1776-1840), our Founding Fathers believed that every citizen should have a good education. They feared the tyranny of central authority, so they left the control of schools to individual states and omitted education from the Constitution. However, in 1787, Congress distributed federal lands to encourage education through building schools.

By the 1880s, children sat at individual desks, often bolted to the floor. Boys sat on one side of the room and girls sat on the other. All faced the teacher in a teacher-centered learning environment, for the teacher was the classroom's sole source of instruction and discipline. Attendance at school, though, was based upon farmers' needs for their children to work the fields in the summer. Cities' schools followed suit in the mistaken belief of the era that too much schooling damaged children's brains, especially girls and young women's brains. For years, women were denied admission to colleges in America because of male perceptions of their fragile brains and menstrual cycles.

Mass education led to a left-brained focus on disseminating information for regurgitation on tests to separate the smart from those who would dropout and learn a trade. By the beginning of the 20th century, public schools' 19th century political purpose – to educate the citizens of a democracy – changed to an economic one. Parents perceived that high school graduates got most of the good jobs, so they started a movement to demand free, public high schools in their communities. The 1929 "Middletown" sociological study of life in Indiana equated education with religion: a means of salvation for a large segment of the U.S. population. The U.S. Great Depression years of 1929-1939 meant many teenagers could not attend school; they had to work full-time to help their families eke out a living.

Nevertheless, the spread of high schools by 1940 meant half of U.S. teenagers were earning a diploma. The U.S. had been accused by European intellectuals of over-educating its masses. However, population surveys show that the American K-12 public education system paid off handsomely. President Roosevelt's re-election in 1936 was fiercely opposed by objections to government spending. But America's recovery from the 1929-1939 Depression continued to the point that American resources, industries and educated people had a huge role in defeating Germany's Adolf Hitler's eugenic dream of conquering the Western world, and in our re-creating the American Dream after the war, despite our huge debt from World War II.

When World War II began in Europe in 1939, and in America in 1941, our industries were ready to supply England and ourselves with the necessary factory-made defense materials. Thanks to public education, high school graduates were employed as white collar workers by General Electric Company (founded by Thomas Edison) and by John Deere, for example. White collar workers utilized their broad base of skills to help their employers become global corporations. Blue collar workers with a high school education were more likely to enter more technologically advanced industries.

When Japan attacked Pearl Harbor, Hawaii, U.S.A. on December 7, 1941, we were drawn into World War II raging in Europe since the late 1930s. If the Japanese had not attacked us, drawing us into World War II, it is possible that our at-home isolationist and anti-spending politicians would have prevailed and the Nazis would have overrun

Europe, including England. Instead, democracy and prosperity prevailed. Our formal entry into the war meant American males were drafted into the armed forces, so women and 4-F men took over their jobs in education and industry. World War II was a brain drain upon America's public educational system as administrators, teachers, and professors were drafted into the armed services. Many substitute teachers were not well-educated, proficient, or qualified to teach subjects or children, but many of them remained in the teaching profession after World War II.

Our nation mobilized around winning World War II, but our public education system continued to emphasize a business-as-usual, mechanistic approach to learning whereby people were treated as machines. Students' performance continues to be rated by the numbers. It was unthinkable in the 1940s and 1950s to question teaching and learning styles or authorities' decisions. After the long Depression years, many Americans were happy to have an assembly-line job, a roof over their heads, and food on the table than to worry about the philosophy of education. They, too, were products of The Western Intellectual Tradition.

Traditionally, the K-12 public educational system used to prepare the young to obey bells and whistles, to sit at rows of desks that match production lines, and to progress through the grades by age, while urging them to stay in line from the cradle to the grave. Public educational systems are primarily about logical doing: downloading an incredible volume of information or details into children's left-brains to be book smart and to test smart, not to think for themselves or to be creative or wise.

The right-brain's wider view of life is overlooked, but the right-brain's negative emotions (fear, sin, shame, guilt, anger, and sometimes violence) were and are utilized by adults to maintain discipline and by peers to bully the vulnerable. "Without the right hemisphere, we are socially and emotionally insensitive."[224]

Before America's entry into World War II, in 1941, the American Council on Education commissioned a state-of-education-report from Daniel A. Prescott at the University of Maryland. In Dr. Prescott's 1938 transmittal letter, he placed the U.S. public school's left-brained approach to education within a global context:

> World political developments [wars in Europe], new devices [radio] for swaying the emotions of entire nations...emphasis on   blind mass fervor [Adolf Hitler's toxic but charismatic rants, propaganda as truth, scapegoating Jews, gypsies, the physically and mentally challenged, and others he deemed to be nonAryans], impatience with the scientific approach [objectivity] to national problems [the Depression], all have driven home the lessons that the job of education is not done when knowledge is disseminated and increased. If the scholar, concerned with his primary business of knowledge, fails to deal with the whole man, particularly with the control of passion and the guidance of desire, he may properly be charged with contributory negligence when the democracy   becomes either a mob or a regimented army, when freedom to   learn or to teach disappears, when the neglected emotions submerge the life of reason, and so force recognition of their claim to share in the lives of men.[351]

Not only was Dr. Prescott's 1938 American Council on Education Report, about educating the right-brain alongside the left-brain, ignored in 1938, it was filed away in Washington, D.C. during World War II. It is still available for around $2.00. Then the Report was ignored after World War II ended in 1945 when public school structures, not students, became priorities. Rebuilding America spawned Levittown-type tracts of homes far from cities and huge K-12 public school systems on the outskirts of towns. Shopping and transportation were solved with more cars, school buses, shopping malls, trucks, and new roads that eventually made most of our railroads obsolete Most Americans, not just the elites, focused on money and consumerism to make up for the harsh 1929-1939 Depression years. The building blocks of human flourishing, outlined by Daniel Prescott, are not the same prerequisites for America's left-brained elites to financially flourish.

Essentially, America changed from depressive economic times in the 1930s and war times in the mid 1940s to "Big is Better" boom times in the 1950s, to social upheavals in the 1960s, and to the 1970s without changes in how children were taught and treated, except children with special needs. But problems in America's secondary schools in the 1950s were outlined in James B. Conant's 1959 *The American High School Today*. A return to education's "basics" was seen as part of the solution at the high school level, while phonics was seen as a solution to reading in public elementary schools. *Equality of Educational Opportunity* by James

S. Coleman (1966) helped lead the forced racial integration of America's schools and transportation in the 1970s.

The 1960s was a favorable time in public education for Special Education students. I took extra college courses and was involved in creating a Special Education class in a K-6 public school and was the substitute teacher for the class. Prominent politicians – from John F. Kennedy and Hubert Humphrey to Nelson Rockefeller and Winston Churchill – had family members with special needs or had experienced learning problems, or were dyslexic themselves. Those prominent people helped to dispel popular beliefs that mental disabilities indicated witch-like, satanic tendencies, or occult powers and to accommodate such students within the K-12 public school system.

In addition to those students who have mental challenges and are labeled Learning Dysfunctional/Disorder, LD; Attention Deficit Disorder, ADD; or Attention Deficit/Hyperactive Disorder, ADHD, some girls and boys with right hemisphere dominance or maturation delays tend not to do well in K-12 public schools' threatening, testing, and pressured environments. They may be allotted one of the foregoing labels. Since many students cannot sit still for long periods of time without time out for some exercise or socialization, such students get graded on their behavior, not their minds, and may end up in Special Education classes. Misdiagnoses are not uncommon. Today's solution for those disorders are to drug the students into submissive behavior, which stresses the human brain, diminishes learning capacity, halts emotional development, destroys creativity, and impairs making and living a good life. There is more concern for being politically correct with labeling students than about drugs with side effects that the children are forced to take to attend public school.

The K-12 public school system fails all students when they are labeled, warehoused, and sentenced to a slow-track high school program when administrators do not take into consideration any delayed physical or psychological maturation processes. For many labeled students, their public education ceases during their adolescence. So they are not prepared for higher education or for an independent future. Education, though, is not a valued commodity in some American minds.

With society's approval of legal drugs for problematic children, we have been growing passive citizens. Genius is disappearing as medications for all disruptive behaviors shut down children's right-brain imagination and creativity. Public schools appear to favor instilling passive behavior more than cultivating genius. Unfortunately, students with psychic pain or plain boredom are also using drugs to get high in our drug-oriented culture, and dumbing themselves down too. Many young girls focus on our culture's obsession with youth, looks, image, fashion, and neglect their minds when they become teenagers because boys don't prefer intelligent girls. Bright young girls at age eleven or twelve, become not-so-bright as teenagers as they focus on relationships, dictated by hormones and their relationship-oriented female brains.

It was in the 1960s that Richard Hofstadter found that it was widely believed, in America, that intelligence is tantamount to being clever, sly, or diabolical and that intelligence is anti-democracy and defies egalitarianism.[157] Hofstadter's findings hold true for today as well when left-brained intelligence is primarily anti-emotional and when anti-intellectual voices are popular in politicized 2012 America. The 1960's cultural, social, moral, and business changed toward individual's self-indulgence and disregard for education or for others' welfare. All negatively impacted the respect for the K-12 public school system, its teachers, and our democratic principles.

The 1960s was the tipping point for America as the desires of individuals overrode their reason, as predicted in 1938. The 1960's legacy is the ever-widening gap between the rich and the poor, since the 1980s, with a diminishing middle class whose 1950s growth had been exponential, due to free government education for veterans. Why the 1960s happened makes sense. Many Americans had suffered much deprivation during the 1929-1939 Great Depression and the 1941-1945 World War II's sacrifices. Our veterans' overseas experiences with different lifestyles collided with our social submissiveness, so boom times in the 1950s unleashed hedonistic impulses and ideas in and around them. Colleges were centers of protests and debates as students rebelled against the conservative 1950s. Women's rights, black's rights, gay's rights, the Earth's rights were accompanied by sexual freedom, street drugs, and rock 'n' roll. Simultaneously, the culture changed in the businessworld, despite the McCarthy Anti-Communist Era to a libertarian philosophy supported by Ayn Rand's 1957 *Atlas Shrugged* and her celebration of selfishness. Capitalists and like-minded politicians applied her and their own philosophy to shoot down any social changes that seemed like socialism which, in their view, would have a negative impact upon their status, money, and power. Who knew that the pursuit of greed-is-good and sharing-is-bad philosophy was also supported by our left-brained, K-12 public education system's emphasis upon testing and competitiveness to separate winners from losers?

Beginning in the 1970s, K-12 public education became an administrative bureaucracy. Administrative and custodial personnel often outweigh the number of certified teaching personnel and aides. Public education's K-12 teachers, principals, and administrators have become organized, professionalized, and legitimized by The Western Intellectual Tradition's Federal and State Education Boards. Most of them hide behind their roles and expertise as they heartlessly relate to the students whose lives they touch. One result of the public school becoming so professionalized is teachers are products of an academic bureaucracy where even Albert Einstein would not not be welcome as a teacher or professor.

"Science has never been organized in a way that is friendly to seers."[313] Who are the seers? "They are by definition highly independent and self-motivated individuals who are so committed to science [or their field] that they will do it even if they can't make a living at it."[313] "Because they think clearly about the foundations of their subjects, they are often good, even charismatic teachers. Nothing inspires students like a seer on fire. Because they are not competitive, they are good advisors and mentors. After all, isn't the main business of colleges and universities [and K-12 public schools] to teach?"[313] There's no room for such teachers in our regimented public educational systems; they don't have the required, State-approved K-12 teaching credentials and, with a professionalized system, they don't have any power to deviate from the norms. Public schools have graduated from being a community's responsibility, except for financing them and their local school boards, to one controlled by state and federal government bureaucracies, testing materials, and textbook sellers.

Another result of The Western Intellectual Tradition becoming so organized and professionalized at the K-12 level is public school is boring for most of today's five and six year-olds who are technology literate. They've been raised on entertainment television, their visual sense is highly developed, and they've developed physical, mental, and behavioral habits to the point that their schooling beyond the second grade plays a minor role in reducing their educational and performance gaps, for K-12 public education does not respond to their human development deficits. The Western Intellectual Tradition assumes that young children are ready for the outer world of ABCs and 123s when they pass standardized readiness tests (correct age and deportment) without attention to brain dominance or to their inner world: conscious and unconscious self-and intergenerational information that is stored in the brain in the womb, lived experiences since birth, and ongoing experiences at home and at school.

Little attention is paid to or acknowledgment of the 20th and 21st centuries' neuroscientists' findings that we have two brains to educate for human beings' full intelligence. The left-brain is usually unencumbered by emotions or virtues, so rote learning becomes easier. The right-brain, though, without formal or informal right-brain education, is encumbered by its embedded data, unless resolved or unless the data stimulates them. Otherwise, embedded data are waiting to be triggered in threatening situations, such as tests; then the brain downshifts into survival mode and access to left-brain academic learning is diminished. Teaching bureaucratic-designed curricula for testing – to separate smart students from the not-so-smart ones on tests – ignores the human need to have a map of what is to be learned, to belong and voice our fears so we may master them; to learn how the human brain works and its fuel for fully functioning intelligence; and to love ourselves as capable but unique human beings with gifts to be developed and shared. Plutarch's, 46 - 120 AD, a Greek historian and Roman citizen, had prescient advice for educators: The mind is not a vessel to be filled, but a fire to be kindled.

Over seventy years since the 1938 Education Report informed education's top administrators what was needed to educate students for a sustainable democratic America, our society is still reaping the negative fallout of not teaching whole brains' full intelligence.

Left-brained, K-12 smart students are revered and many not-so-smart, by left-brain standards, fail, are labeled, sidetracked, or dropout. Educators rarely check the tests to see what's wrong with the test or the system; instead they assume there's something wrong with the students whose test scores are low. K-12 public schools affix the blame to failing students and institute "back to basics" instead of fixing the problems of The Western Intellectual Tradition. Some K-12 charter and private schools, though, are providing students with a more humane approach to their individual educational needs.

Haven Academy, a charter school in the South Bronx, New York, for children from broken families and foster care, acknowledges that "kids don't show up ready for the three R's. There's no amount of math that a kid can be ready for if you saw your mother beaten, if you were beaten or if you are constantly dealing with turmoil."[226] When the inner lives of students are ignored and allowed to simmer, their inner data interfere with learning, studying, retention, testing, and relating. Bullies are grown, not born; they live what they learned at home, in their neighborhoods, and how they are treated at school by teachers and their peers. Every child needs affirmation of his or her significence.

At the high school level, relevance is an issue. What students are taught by teachers – from textbooks to testing materials – and what they should be able to do on tests are set by Federal and State Boards of Education, textbook publishers, and local boards of education without input from students, educators, and brain scientists' findings about how the human brain works and learns. Textbooks are designed for teachers to dispense information a little bit at a time, in an analytic, sequential but fragmented way. The human brain works when an overall picture or global view of what to expect is presented, for the brain perceives wholes, and it simultaneously processes disparate data Scientists, scholars, teachers, and students do not set The Western Intellectual Tradition's basic curricula. America's K-12 public school systems are run primarily by left-brain administrators, principals, and unqualified school board members, with personal or ideological agendas, to maintain tradition in a world that has changed and so has the average child's technology experiences with TV shows, video games, and computer skills. But, public schools are burdened with expensive quick-fixes, tenured or unionized administrators, teachers, and custodians, and mind-numbing curricula devoid of inquiry. Antiquated teaching-learning methods and tests are used to inculcate learning; instead, it often instills students' fear of labeling and failing. The Federal government's No Child Left Behind, NCLB, educational testing mandate is a costly left-brained war on the freedom to teach and to learn.

Our society's ongoing obsession with test scores has also corrupted the educative process. The left-brain's ability to crunch numbers and data in record time is the epitome of linguistic and logical-mathematical intelligence, of being smart as measured by tests, IQ, CAT, SAT, GRE, PSAT, and PISA. However, there are multiple intelligences.[114] Many of those intelligences, beyond logical-mathematical, are difficult to assess on standardized tests. But, utilitarian short-cuts, which happen to favor left-brain processes, such as true/false and multiple-choice answers, are easier and faster for students to complete and for teachers to correct than essays or other methods of assessment. Facts without relevance or context are harder to remember, so learning is shallow and soon forgotten. An emphasis upon testing is contributing to students' academic failure and inhibiting long-term learning and integrative thinking, especially when the right-brain's attributes are missing from the curriculum.

Students' curiosity and imagination are squelched when unmotivated to conform to one size fits few.[246] Drawing out and nurturing each student's latent talent is not part of traditional education, nor is building on their uniqueness. Teachers teach top-down imposed curriculum as ends in themselves instead of as tools of inquiry.[319] The smartest students are judged to be highly intelligent, very smart. They get scholarships, gain access to prestigious universities and high paying professions, and often do whatever it takes to attain power, status, and money – if they ignore or are deficient in right-brain attributes, such as context, morality, creativity, empathy, and compassion.

With due respect for left-brainers' positive attributes – learning to read, write, and do math – which all of us learn and appreciate, rigid left-brainers are not usually hindered by right-brain input or context, so it is easier for them to be book smart and ace tests in K-12 public schools where most do not learn how to think or to integrate what they learned. With direct access to anger to justify their processes, many left-brain dominant students are not sidetracked or bogged down by feelings, empathy or compassion, the heart, or the gut; nor do they consult the right-brain for a moral and ethical view of a situation. Therefore, it is easier for them to recall abstract data and regurgitate it on standardized tests. "It is not generally realized that intelligence [cognitive] is not everything, that an intellectual genius may be an emotional baby or a monster."[297]

Despite the 7 billion people on Earth today who have been exposed to some form of education, "No matter how intelligent and smart we think we are, we constantly display signs of basic animal behaviour that can lead to the decimation of our kind in the blink of an eye"[327] with nuclear war or poisonous chemicals. It's possible that animals' survival behaviors are motivated more by basic physical needs for a territory's prey, not by humans' more basic psychological survival needs and deficits, which are brain-based inheritances or caretaker-caused, and ignored by The Western Intellectual Tradition.

It is not generally recognized that inadequate nutrition to fuel the brain or that life's accumulated little traumas are magnified when children perceive themselves to be helpless or hopeless in ego threatening or humiliating situations, such as being judged by tests, teachers, or classmates. Those students who do not absorb, regurgitate, and pass tests are usually those students whose lack of brain fuel or ready access to negative experiences and unresolved traumas get in the way of their learning and retention. At those times, many of them are disenfranchised, labeled, and sidetracked in our K-12 public school system when they are perceived not to conform to society's left-brain testing standards.

Test scores quantitatively measure the content of what a student has yet to learn. Test scores based on top-down, bureaucratic-imposed curricula cannot reveal students' and teachers' uniqueness, experience, knowledge, talents, multiple intelligences, motivation, and promise. The problems with testing are the perceptions and motivations behind the testing: Are the tests used to teach what a student has yet to learn, to stimulate them to learn? Or, are the scores being used to label students and teachers as misfits, to remove them from The Western Intellectual Tradition? Flourish or perish?

To become an integrative thinker and wise is a rare option in K-12 public schools today where left-brain test scores are valued more than character and substance. Character-building used to be part of the invisible curriculum of family, religion, and positive role models. Since World War II, character has become less visible and its absence more apparent in our society and in human development, for the majority of our population has become self-invested, divisive, violent, and money-driven.

Once upon a time in America, left-brain goals were more integrated with right-brain virtues when families, preachers, and teachers emphasized character and modeled positive human behavior, so the right-brain was informally educated. In the early 1800s, President Jefferson warned Americans to become educated. He knew that nobody's liberty is secure if a large group of us became incompetent or negligent of our civic responsibilities. He didn't know that, in the 1960s and 1970s, the K-12 public school teaching profession would become disrespected in our society (because they don't make a lot of money?) and would be required to teach and test top-down, bureaucratic curriculum primarily. He didn't know that the right-brain's compassion, morals and ethics inculcated by families, public figures as role models, and religious institutions would be overridden by selfish interests. He didn't know that the traditionally intact American family would become a rarity.

As a consequence of the gradual demise of the invisible curriculum that encompassed the informal education of the right hemisphere, we and our society are out of balance. Psychologist Robert E. Ornstein warned, "the development of a purely logical, rational science, unbalanced by a perspective born of intuition, can proceed, if unchecked, close to the point of self-destruction."[248]

For past decades, because emotional literacy has not been and is not considered a public school responsibility, emotional illiteracy and negativity are passed down from generation-to-generation, but are not confined to families where physical survival and living by their wits are primary and inequality pervades the public school system. Inequality in America's K-12 public school system begins before kindergarten with living and performance gaps between rich and poor students. Low income families and their children are more likely to suffer from poor nutrition and inadequate health care in dangerous neighborhoods with underfinanced public schools, insufficient textbooks, inadequate teaching materials and workbooks. For teaching my 7th graders, I used to purchase books and materials to flesh out the required text as well as Italian and Spanish dictionaries to communicate with immigrant children when English as a Second Language (ESL) was a dream. In addition, with parental uninvolvement in their children's formal learning or attendance at parent-teacher conferences, teachers' perceptions may lead to low expectations for underperforming students.

Public education is underwritten by State and Federal Funds, but county, town, or city property taxes and sales taxes are the primary source of K-12 public school funds. Therefore, quality education depends on the resources of local real estate and sales tax dollars to spend more on its schools. School board members are elected on their popularity in the community or by their axes to grind, not on their academic expertise. Retired voters or voters who send their children to private schools may vote down public school budgets since the public schools don't benefit them anymore.

A Stanford University poll indicates that "68 percent of adults believe parents deserve heavy blame for what's wrong with the U.S. education system – more than teachers, school administration, the government or teachers unions."[23] Yes, parents may be blamed or praised for the quality of their children's physical, mental, and emotional selves by preparing them for learning and by monitoring their progress, but not for what's wrong with and what's right about America's K-12 public education system.

Public education, Kindergarten through Grade 12, is America's most important domestic job/role today and will be in the future. "More than 90 percent of American youngsters go through the public schools."[150] An educated population is an investment in America. A number of students either do not learn within or dislike public school, its products and processes, so they get poor grades, disrupt classes, bully their peers, and about 25 to 30 percent of them don't finish high school. Despite the thousands of dollars spent annually per student, many students try to get the least out of their K-12 educational experience. Why?

The 99,000-100,000 public schools in the U.S. were decentralized, in the past, without a relevant or challenging academic curricula. Today, while the curriculum titles may remain the same throughout diverse public school systems, the content of the courses vary to conform to the expectations and ideology of individuals who run local K-12 public school systems. Some public school boards have banned literature, prefer revised history, and denied scientific theories or philosophical ideas that conflict with their religious beliefs. The direct consumers of education are not consulted; nor are renowned educators. Even today's education panels' recommendations seek approval from the States' governors whose political ambitions and financial woes may override their wisdom. They may be aligned more with staying in power and their future than with making waves that benefit the "little people" today and tomorrow for America, so "Back to Basics" is their answer.

Most adults, teachers, administrators, and politicians/governors do not respect or value children's wisdom, but surveys of students' perceptions of teachers' effectiveness are more reliable than administrators' superficial impressions or fellow teachers' protectiveness.[69] Students are experts at sizing up their teachers on a daily basis. Students recognize good teaching that piques their imagination, motivates them to learn when they experience it, and questions what they learn at home. It is their direct knowledge of what works in the classroom that could drive education reform. Although, parents' attitudes, beliefs, and biases about K-12 public education's content rub off on their innocent children.

With a narrow view of intelligence and humans' potentialities, "The public school system, which was created to put muscle into democracy, ended up by becoming the closing fingers of the long arm of the state"[313] and the Federal government's bureaucracies. While teachers are not in charge of the curricula, the textbooks, or the selection of national tests, teachers have some control over how they teach and behave in their classrooms, but they are judged by their students' scores on isolated information-based texts and tests.

Many K-12 public educational systems have been failing its students for decades, yet from The Western Intellectual Tradition's perspective the students fail, not the system. When will the education business learn from business guru Peter F. Drucker's and Apple founder Steve Jobs?

Drucker believes "Businesses are not paid to reform customers; they are paid to satisfy customers"[84] or go out of business or reform its mission and teaching-learning processes to attract customers/students.

On the other hand, Steve Jobs believes, "Our job is to figure out what they're going to want before they do...People don't know what they want until you show it to them...Our job is to read things that are not yet on the page."[165] Students and parents cannot know today what the future holds, so providing the basics in a non-threatening, whole-brain-oriented environment plus what's not yet "on the page" prepare students for the future that is in us now. I believe that K-12 public schools are the places for most Americans to reinvent themselves to reinvent America and that public schools would graduate more students if the right-brain's emotions and virtues were included in the K-12 educative process.

For years, Microsoft's Bill Gates [115] has publicly stated that the American high school system is obsolete and was never designed to provide high-quality education for all of its students. He added that America's high schools are behind the times and are ruining the lives of millions of young Americans every year. Furthermore, he avers that many of our high school graduates are undereducated and unemployable in his computer field. How does the majority of the governors of our states respond? Back to basics, more rigorous testing, and cut out the frills, from music to art as well as recess: the mental and physical exercises that developing minds and bodies need to enhance learning.

Traditional K-12 public educational systems are fragment-oriented and linear, demanding that a student's brain "meekly put aside its mighty resources and go step-by-step down one path is to cripple and inhibit it."[143] And to use only the left-side of the brain's two hemispheres as well. Education as a cultural and political process for educating the left half of the human hemisphere means the other uneducated right half is the means by which authorities' perpetuate power, control, status, and fear and the uneducated perpetuate violence, crime, and chaos in society. Failure is a rationale for blaming and oppressing people whose actions are right-brain-dominated, and/or are economically or mentally challenged, or they are perceived to be less than human for not being members of the dominant white culture or race — even that is changing at conscious levels in America.

With our K-12 public school system failing those students who do not measure up to its left-brain standards — or students who succumb to the siren call of illegal drugs or owning a car — high school dropouts are a problem for a society that has become technology- and information-oriented. Blue collar jobs have been outsourced to cheaper labor in Asia and India. The students and graduates who have the skills, motivation, and financial access to the technology, which has changed all of our lives for the better and for the worse, are thriving.

If America's best students who ranked 23rd in Science, 17th in Reading, and 32nd in Math,[70] on an international test in 2009, are the cream of our high school crop, then even the best students from the best public high schools are average compared to the 33 other developed nations' schools. Imagine how mediocre the majority of our K-12 public schools are! Overall, America's K-12 public schools are in a sorry state, but fixable. To be educated on a par with top students from other nations who don't spend an equal amount or more money on wars that we do, America's priorities have to change toward peace, not permanent war,[14] and K-12 equal, well-financed education in every public school. If we want students not to fail or drop out, then our public educational systems may introduce more responsible freedom to teach and to learn. That would offset the fact that we are conditioned by our culture, language, and numbering systems to be myopically left-brained without context or heart consciousness.

Many high performing public high school students have a utilitarian view of education as a vehicle for them to become financial manipulators and to do whatever it takes to be a millionaire by age 40. American K-12 public schools' obsession: test and produce smart students (but not-so-smart by 33 other modern nations' standards). Such narrow-minded students' views toward education and life deprives them of their humanity, so many students do not have a sense of civic responsibility to others, just themselves, or to our democracy either. Finland's educators are respected on a par with doctors, they do "whatever it takes" so students learn with their long-term memories, not their short-term memories as in America. Their 15 year-olds scored 2nd in Reading, 3rd in Science, and 6th in Math[141] without all the teaching to the test and pre-testing that goes on in America.

Since the late 1960s, the higher education boom has slowed. Up until the 1990s, students' attainment of bachelor's degrees rose to 32 percent only, and many of those graduates were women. In the past two decades, it seems that young men are not more educated than their fathers.[206] The median male worker in the U.S. is about as educated as he was 30 years ago and makes about the same hourly pay, until our ongoing Recession and layoffs occurred. Female workers are more educated than they were 30 years ago and make 30 percent more than they did then. "On the most basic level, education helps people figure out how to make objects and accomplish tasks more efficiently. It allows companies to make complex products that the rest of the world wants to buy and this creates high-wage jobs,"[206] at least until manufacturing jobs were sent overseas to maximize profits and corporate reinvestment ceased.

So the last thirty years, when education gains slowed markedly, have been years of slower growth and rising inequality, including income inequality, in our society. In fact, the wealth of the paper-pusher-financiers and America's off-shore manufacturers have increased dramatically, while the income of America's middle and lower classes has declined. It is also a fact that more educated people are a nation's assets; they tend to be healthier, live longer, and make more money, which means they usually pay more taxes.

The two most affluent and educated immigrant cultures in America today are Asian-Americans and Jews: Jewish-Americans. As a group, those families value their cultural identities and education, so their students work harder, instead of coasting on their IQs, and have access to their cultural networks. When students have a good sense of belonging to a valued culture, their identity and self-esteem are not dependent upon being accepted by the popular, dominant white culture. Those attitudes make a huge difference in how they are perceived by peers and in the freedom to learn. When students belong to a disvalued culture or race, it is more difficult for them to affirm and integrate themselves into our dominant white culture and to succeed in the K-12 public school system.

Our materialistic, get-rich-quick culture does not value education as the primary route to success or value public school teachers when their college educations and salaries are not on a par with other professions, such as medicine, science, and law, sports, or entertainment. Traditionally, some of our universities' disciplines have looked down their noses at K-12 public education and educators and perceive prospective teachers as intellectually inferior.[93] Based on that perception, it was my choice to attain a B.A. in Literature rather than an education degree. The cost to society of not choosing teachers for their character, not educating teachers well, and adhering to unionized, professionalized, and bureaucratized curricula are borne by children who do not conform to one size fits all.[246]

Some poor families don't value their children's education; teachers can be their children's educational surrogates and rescue them from failure. The first step is to get colleges and universities to upgrade their education programs with rich resources and intensive admissions processes. If colleges and universities required prospective teachers to love teaching, like children, and be smart (maintain a 3.5 GPA: Grade Point Average) and wise with access to their whole brain's intelligence, emotionally and interculturally literate with a wider worldview, and a caring sense of humor, then they have teacher material. That's what I learned about master teachers in working with K-12 public school teachers. I also learned that some teachers like the hours, the summer and holiday vacations, and their pensions, but not their jobs or children. Their negative attitudes and lack of enthusiasm permeate their classrooms and Teachers' Lounges.

So far, The Traditional Western Tradition is being usurped by independent educational innovators. For example, Wendy Kopp, founder of Teach for America (TFA), which was the topic of her thesis from Princeton University with a B.A. degree in 1989, has worked, sustained, and taught teachers to grow her organization. In the 2009-2010 school year, about 7,300 TFA members taught in our country's poorest communities. They reached more than 450,000 students. There are about 17,000 Teach for America alumni. KIPP is a Knowledge is Power Program that may be best-known and the most successful network of charter schools in the U.S. The TFA and KIPP programs are producing inspiring teachers who make a difference by changing children's learned beliefs that they can't learn by instilling confidence and know-how so they will succeed academically.

The psychology field's research primarily deals with psychopathy: what's wrong with children and adults and its "cure" is pharmaceutical drugs and talking therapies. We have after-the-fact programs for youth and adults aimed at curbing drug use, violence, suicide, teen pregnancy, and other behavioral and social problems that originate with emotional illiteracy and boredom. Missing are preventative or positive psychology programs in the K-12 classroom whereby children and adolescents are motivated to learn and become optimistic about the future, socially competent, compassionate, and psychologically and physically healthy. Young people's boredom, alienation, and disconnection from meaningful challenges are not signs of psychopathology; they are signs of deficiencies in positive development: what's right about children and adults.[200]

The signs of passion submerging the life of reason are everywhere. Dear Abby's syndicated newspaper column is a national barometer of our Western culture's unresolved socialization and multicultural issues. An Arizona high school male freshman voiced the interpersonal problems that affect young people today when the top echelon of society's priorities of money, status, and image trickle down and define a human being's worth:

> My problem is so many of my schoolmates judge others by their possessions -- cell phones, iPods, laptops, etc. It matters what brand of clothing you wear and how much money you have. If you don't have those things or your parents aren't rich, you're treated as an outcast. Character and talent don't matter, apparently -- only money. This has started affecting my self-esteem. What do you advise?[67]

Dear Abby advised him:

> You will be better off, and lead a happier life, if you stop looking for acceptance from shallow, immature kids who belong to tight, judgmental little cliques...

Those shallow kids of the entitlement era represent not only their families' beliefs but also their own unresolved emotional issues and demons, so they become terrorists – terrorizing themselves and their peers. A left-brainer's raw, uneducated ego becomes a predator, an anti-emotional one, so does a negative right-brainer, especially those who are anti-intellectual. Both are guilty of engaging in a competitive process known as pseudospeciation. That term was defined by Erik Erikson as an individual or "A group driven to dominate its rival as though it were a different species, less than human, therefore not deserving normal human consideration."[176]

Our recent history is rife with the inhumane results of left hemispheric views of humanity, from Germany's Adolf Hitler and his Nazism in the 1930s and 1940s to America's Joseph McCarthy's witch hunt for Communist sympathizers in the 1950s. America's infamous torture techniques used against "terrorists" in its Guantanamo prison since 9/11/2001 have shocked most Americans. Such anti-human behavior is yet another result of a left-brained-run nation and its "military industrial complex" that former General and President Dwight D. (Ike) Eisenhower warned us against in the 1950s.

Yale University Psychologist Stanley Milgram's (1933-1984) 1960's experiments on obedience to authority figures showed the willingness of participants in the study to obey orders, override their conscience, and inflict pain on other participants as directed by authority figures' orders, not knowing that the participants in the pain/torture exercise were actors. Psychological studies also show that the U.S. Government's sanction of the torture of alleged terrorists involved in the 9/11/2001 terrorist attack on America is an ongoing example of Western society's left-brained narrow worldviews that some people don't deserve humane treatment for reasons beyond national security.

While there are some people who blindly follow authority figures' orders, when they think they have no choice and have learned to do as they were told, there are many more people, including right-brainers, who inflict pain and suffering on others, even loved ones, to satisfy ego deficits or to do unto others what was done unto them, without learning any lessons from their experience about how it felt to be victimized.

There are cold-blooded people in our environment, K-12 public schools, and prison systems. Like psychopaths, they lack empathy, lie, and manipulate others without regret as they whitewash themselves. They have no moral conscience or emotions and feelings. They are good at masking their deficits with charm to appear as normal human beings. Evidently, they do not do well in group therapy for they are very good at sensing and exploiting others' weaknesses. Intensive, one-on-one decompression therapy for youthful offenders with psychopathic tendencies, by Michael Caldwell in Madison, Wisconsin, focuses on ending punishment for bad behavior since punishment inspires more bad behavior.[44] Public school personnel could learn not only how to draw out students' gifts but how to handle behavior without punishment that leads to more bad behavior, labeling, and dropping out of public school.

Emotional illiteracy and the lack of love are the roots of violence and bullying, which are major concerns throughout our nation's K-12 public school systems. "Social skills are necessary for school success...they affect how you do on the playground, in the classroom, in the workplace."[178] A rude child becomes a rude student and a rude adult. Behavior is public, and children's and adults' rudeness means no one has taught them manners or compassion or they have found that their bad behavior is a "safety" feature, for it advises others: "Don't mess with me!" That attitude also works for emotionally literate people when confronted with negative behavior.

Entertainer Lady Gaga has formed The Born This Way Foundation to ease the trauma of adolescence.[185] She said, "I was called really horrible, profane names very loudly in front of huge crowds of people, and my schoolwork suffered at one point...I didn't want to go to class. And I was a straight-A student...I just couldn't even focus on class because I was so embarrassed all the time."[185] Lady Gaga was invited to Harvard by Dean Kathleen McCartney of the Graduate School of Education "to address bullying as a neglected area of education – and a human rights issue. As many as one-fifth of children feel bullied, she said, adding: 'If you don't feel safe as a child, you can't learn.'"[185]

Violence and bullying are major concerns in America where disrespect for differences has surfaced in public places and in our K-12 public schools. A fifteen-year-old girl, an immigrant from Ireland, was the object of classmates boys' and girls' relentless taunting and bullying for months in 2010. She committed suicide by hanging to end her plight at her public school in Massachusetts. Only then did she draw attention by the media and the public at large, except for those who had bullied her. They exhibited no compassion for their victim or guilt for their own behavior. No public school children should be exposed to peers' or teachers' rudeness and negative comments about their personal selves, but they are.

Physical brutes have been replaced in our society by verbal brutes. The old adage, "Sticks and stones may break my bones, but words/names will never harm me" represents left-brainers' ongoing denial of the legitimacy of the right-brain's feelings and emotions. Physical pain is acknowledged but mental pain is not, despite the proliferation of verbal abuse, bullying, and hate speech. Free speech is not free, nor a debate for those who have no intellectual recourse but to "grin and bear it," as the U.S. Supreme Court justices ruled on March 2, 2011. Hateful speech – slander, propaganda, lies, and ideology – is protected under U.S. free speech laws, until the hate manifests as physical violence. The inclusion of the right-brain in the K-12 public school curricula will protect us from others' hate. We will recognize it as their projecting onto us their problems, unresolved life issues, negative self-esteem, envy, jealousy, and lack of respect for themselves or just plain meanness. We do not have to collude in their crazies or to give power to their venom personally when we recognize they are coming from positions of insecurity and fear.

When students' left-brained studies do not satisfy their emotional and creative needs, many young students unconsciously rebel and seek drugs, legal and illegal, alcohol, and sex to temporarily numb their felt deficits. The "Why?" of people's illegal drug usage in this country, especially in America's K-12 public school students, has its underpinnings in emotional illiteracy. Illegal drug usage needs more attention and funding that addresses individual prevention through emotional resilience rather than upon the extinction of the source of drugs. The failed War on Illegal Drugs may change our nation's policies since today America's drug problem is shifting to the abuse of pharmaceutical prescription painkillers. In 2008, there were about 36,000 overdose deaths; 20,000 of them were prescription drugs, indicating a decrease of demand for illegal drugs, in a plentiful supply market.

The U.S. laws on illegal drugs, from marijuana to cocaine, have fueled a drug appetite in the U.S. population. In turn, the drug scene has funneled billions of dollars to drug lords in Mexico, Afghanistan, and other countries. Those exported dollars do not include the U.S. government's spending on eradicating drug crops or on sustaining an anti-drug workforce with drug czars. Nor does it include the cost of increased incarceration in our prisons or of U.S. public and private drug rehabilitation programs. The Mexican government is under siege by the wealthy drug cartels who can afford weapons of mass destruction (purchased in the U.S.) to kill and kidnap and the cash to bribe and intimidate government officials, policemen, soldiers, women, and children.

Instead of our government's War on Drugs having a curtailing effect, the opposite is true. Drug abuse is a problem in all K-12 public school systems. We have an unprecedented U.S. prison population due to drug dealing or using. Americans' demand for Mexico's and other countries' illegal drug supplies masks the felt deficits of people's uneducated right-brains. As in economics, an ample supply feeds the demands and keeps the prices lower, but government's emphasis upon decreasing the supply, not upon Americans' demand is not part of the War on Drugs; that's prevention which is also not part of our disease-care insurance policies.

By not acknowledging that outlawing drugs for forty-one years has not worked, just as Alcohol Prohibition's 1920-1933 era didn't work either, it seems that the War on Drugs' priority is the preservation of the bureaucratic fiefdoms that have ensued and proliferated at a hefty cost to taxpayers. The left-brained committee members who created our War on Drugs and our huge State and Federal prison systems appear not to have the integrative thinking necessary to dismantle them, just too big to fail, like corrupt banks. Over the past forty years, our government has spent over $1 trillion on its War on Drugs. America, with only 5% of the world's population, has about 2.3 million incarcerated people, representing 25% of the world's prison population. The War on Drugs has not deterred illegal drug usage and trafficking[227] when our overpaid white collar financiers, Hollywood and TV personalities, and sports idols are users and role models for gullible teenagers. Our government drug agencies are bureaucratic fiefdoms for the politically connected and are averse to any program that could make their bureaucratic agencies obsolete. With the highest per capita prison population in the world, primarily drug related, it's about time to stop fixing the blame, not the problem and easing out the fiefdoms.

All failed laws and practices, especially the current anti-drug laws and K-12 public education's missing pieces (self-control, emotional resilience, and responsibility for self and to others are just three of the traits that are equated with emotional intelligence). All would benefit from understanding how the human brain works and how it can be re-educated. Money to "fight" wars on drugs would be better spent on prevention. Prevention begins with acknowledging that addictive drug usage, bullying, failure in the K-12 public school system, and post-traumatic stress disorder are symptoms of human development deficits in a society that ignores teaching whole human brains for full intelligence.

Left-brained decisions that impact children's and adults' present behaviors and future may be found today in people's psyches. Since World War II, urban sprawl in America has led to suburbs becoming bedrooms of larger cities. With the American belief that "bigger is better," large complexes of schools have been built on the outskirts of towns with less open and shared community spaces, such as parks, community centers, or outdoor meeting places so popular in European cities or in old-fashioned, established American towns. Forced isolation was a setting ripe for children's demands for television, video games, computers, and cell phones as they coped with being unable to socialize themselves: to develop relationships or self-reliance in the midst of thousands of other children. The bigger the school, the more alienated students become and the more possibilities for their becoming bullies or to be bullied in person or succumbing to cyberbullying. Technology has connected us, and it has diminished face-to-face relationships.

The Western Intellectual Tradition, TWIT[334] and TWITTER

We Americans have changed, and not necessarily for the better, as the Internet dominates our lives. "Computers keep getting smarter, while we just stay the same."[217] Artificial intelligence people have built computers that "can see and hear, respond to questions, learn, draw inferences and solve problems."[217] This generation of America's smart computer hackers, engineers, and programmers believe that such computers will be able to build better computers and robots that are self-aware and with superhuman intelligence.

We may not be remaining the same. When we spend considerable time working with computers, the computers may rewire our brains. Overwhelming the brain with information may lead to an inability to discriminate between what is important or truthful or wise. Relying upon sound bites, instead of in-depth data, to make decisions is often based upon GIGO (garbage in, garbage out).

Our left-brain society's passion for left-brain information was ripe for Twitter when it was created in 2006 by Jack Dorsey of the podcasting company Odeoin. The desire to capture the physical sensation or feeling (right-brain) of buzzing friends led to choosing the word Twitter with a definition of "a short burst of inconsequential information." Left-brained and a maximum of 140 texted characters, Twitter is free to subscribers; it is an informational networking, microblogging service. Access may be restricted to a circle of friends (known as followers) or, by default, texters have open access to all subscribers to the Twitter website.

A market research firm analyzed 2,000 tweets over a two-week period that originated from the U.S. in English. The firm divided them into six categories: 1. News, 2. Spam, 3. Self-promotion, 4. Pointless babble, 5. Conversational, and 6. Pass-along value (Mainstream news, Emergencies, and Relief Efforts). They found that 40.55% of the tweets were pointless babble and 37.55% were conversational. Children, adolescents, and teenagers are Twitter and Facebook users. They post the most mundane and inane data about their lives, such as the day's underwear color, and other personal details that could put them at risk for predators and/or haunt them when they enter the professional world. What their Twittering reveals is the shallowness of their lives, interests, and unthinking with no attention to the consequences of their actions because the brain's prefrontal lobes do not fully mature until age 21 to 25 or later, but they don't know that.

Technology and computer literacy are requirements of the 21st Century's Information Age. IBM is touting that this is the "decade of smart...Building a Smarter Planet."[164] It is indeed the decade of smart. Technology's smart devices are people's extensions of themselves to be high-tech smart but not high-touch wise or communication competent, interpersonally or intrapersonally. Many of smart technology's smart users lack the qualities that humanize them, like robots. Violent video games desensitize some smart people to be more emotionally illiterate and to kill innocent human beings in our public schools and on campuses. While IBM technology is smart, it is not contributing to building a smarter planet. If IBM plans to build a smarter planet, then it needs to be peopled with smart and wise users. Artificial Intelligence needs to be partnered with Artificial Emotional Intelligence, beginning with empathy.

Computers and other communication devices are great teaching and learning tools; however, by jumping from one piece of information to another on a screen is distracting, consumes energy, and creates an inability to discriminate; hence, the rush to decision-making is premature and without the depth of reflection.[59] Children are becoming smart, not wise, as they become more technology-literate, technology-dependent, interpersonally illiterate, morally-deficient, and culturally unaware without heart consciousness.

Information Technology requires computer literacy. Computers are wonderful teaching and learning tools for all, including children. Certainly, the Internet is a source of all kinds of knowledge that not only makes us more productive but also gives us the opportunity to become smarter. Do you think K-12 education's purpose is to cram our brains with information as fast as possible? That's what the Internet does. That appears to be the modus operandi of K-12 public school systems when timed I.Q. tests and examinations to regurgitate disparate data are the current way human beings' academic intelligence is determined. Or, "do you think intelligence means stepping back from that information, thinking about it, and drawing your own conclusions in a calm, thoughtful way?"[59]

The word intelligence derives from the Latin word intelligo, meaning to select among. Gathering information, stepping back from it, thinking about it, and drawing conclusions in a thoughtful way is more in line with the original meaning of intelligence and the route to wisdom. Recall that Intelligence is one of the definitions of being smart, implying clever, capable, witty, and shrewd or sharp, as in one's dealings by taking advantage of others.

There is research evidence that consistently using the Internet by jumping from one piece of information to another and clicking on hyperlinks is similar to settling for distracting sound bites on TV or newspaper headlines. Training our brains to gather information the way the Internet supplies it, quickly and efficiently through a computer screen which alienates us from direct sensory contact with Nature, teaches us "to substitute symbols of reality for reality itself."[59] That process lessens our ability to concentrate while reading books, for example, and not to be reflective or contemplative.

Arnie Cooper cited Gary Small's research at UCLA whereby he found different brain activity patterns between the experienced and inexperienced Internet user groups. The scanned brains of the inexperienced group, while using the Web, showed activity in the "language, memory, and visual centers of the brain,"[59] which is the brain activity similar to reading a book. However, the experienced group, while using the Web, "had more activity in the decision-making areas at the front of the brain."[59] However, with increased usage, the inexperienced Internet users "began to match the activity of the experienced Web users."[59] What is the difference between the two groups, experienced and inexperienced Internet users?

"Neurology experiments demonstrate that decision-making consumes a lot of your mental resources, leaving less available for other modes of thinking...reading a book while simultaneously working on a crossword puzzle. That's the intellectual environment of the Web."[59] The intellectual environment of students is rapidly becoming the Internet as more college courses are undertaken online. Overwhelming the brain with information overload may lead to an inability to discriminate between what is truthful or to make wise decisions. Wisdom involves weighing data from both brains, many sources, and concentrating deeply and reflectively. The experienced Web surfers in the study who bypassed language, memory, and visual centers of the brain meant the rush to decision-making activity was premature and without depth or reflection.

Technology, from cellphones, iPads, and BlackBerries to TVs, video games, computers, and the Internet seem to dominates our lives. Thus, all Americans would benefit from becoming educated about the Internet, its implications, and the fact that computer services outside of

America are "running important parts of our economy."[59] Our country's "competitiveness and wealth are going to be tied up in this network, and there's going to be geopolitical tensions over who controls it and how it works,"[59] so computer services are becoming a political issue as well as a wisdom issue. Foreigners' ability to hack into our institutional, organizational, and government's computers is also a political issue. Insiders who hack into government's computers to access "sensitive" diplomatic and international data are often the sources of Internet services' leaks to the general public.

Secrets have a way of managing Americans' perceptions, keeping us uninformed, unable to make honest decisions, and, thus, harmed. So, "outing" secrets may do more good than harm by making the keepers of secrets more accountable. Actually, the Internet is now one of our freedoms with global equal opportunities; therefore, we have to resist any attempts to control the Internet and its users, except for its abusers.

The WikiLeaks storm has its pros and cons. Julian Assange, an Australian, founded WikiLeaks in 2006. In 2010 he published classified data about our wars in Afghanistan and Iraq; then in November, he published secret U.S. Diplomatic cables, which the U.S. government considers espionage and seeks his extradition as a "high-tech terrorist" from London after extradition from Sweden where he was held on bail in a sexual assault charge, which he denies. Allegedly, he also holds incriminating financial data on U.S. banks, which publication could lead to management resignations. Our financial industries need a visible-to-the-public overhaul since their financial machinations have affected most poor- and middle-class Americans and have led to job losses, market losses, and poverty during the ongoing Great Recession.

Whistleblowers are enemies of national and international financiers who feel threatened when data of their dealings are released for public consumption and decision-making. Similarly, Assange's release of U.S. government documents has a possible beneficial effect for the public: we can become informed about corruption, corporate access to legitimate government agencies, services, and other facts that fearmonger bureaucrats would prefer kept secret. Whistleblowers are perceived by governments as conspirators to reveal its secrets. When everything is labeled "secret" and disseminated information is micromanaged, then democratic transparency is missing and U.S. citizens cannot make informed decisions at the polls.

Harvard Psychologist Steven Pinker[270] writes that "Twitter, e-mail and PowerPoint aren't making us stupid...Far from making us stupid, these technologies are the only things that will keep us smart,"[270] if smart is preferable to being smart and wise or having wisdom. He also states that "The solution is not to bemoan technology but to develop strategies of self-control, as we do with every other temptation in life. [Except the many who do not.] Turn off e-mail or Twitter when you work, put away your Blackberry at dinner time, ask your spouse to call you to bed at a designated hour...Knowledge is increasing exponentially; human brainpower and waking hours are not."[270]

Self-control has proven to be a huge problem for some Americans, as we know. So managing Internet usage is another challenge to add to the list for some of us, but fragmented information via the Internet overloads the brain. However, it does not necessarily mean decreased brainpower; the process is similar to multitasking where none of the tasks are done well, if we settle for just doing a good enough job. Brainpower is enhanced when technology is used not as entertainment, or as an end in itself, but as tools to gather ideas for in-depth research. Self-control, though, appears to be losing to addiction to cellphone usage and texting mostly about trivia.

Not only parents but public educational systems have to teach unsuspecting students how to protect themselves from being exploited by predators or exploiting themselves by revealing too much data in their blogs. Thus, with the inundation of information via the Internet, educators need to train children to use it wisely, make sense out of it, and identify what may be trusted and what is suspicious in order to avoid becoming a victim.

Eighteen-year old freshman Rutgers University student, Tyler Clementi, committed suicide by jumping off the George Washington Bridge on September 22, 2010, after asking his dormitory roommate for the room until midnight. The roommate, Dharun Ravi used his webcam to record Tyler in a gay relationship and broadcast it over the Internet. Rutgers launched a project to teach (and practice?) civility and attention to bullying in the use and abuse of technology.[101]

Smart technology – from television, computers, video games, cell phones, Twitter, Facebook, ipods, Black Berries, and robots – is proliferating and reinforcing a left-brained society – when high-tech (machines) are preferred over high-touch (people). Emotional illiteracy has reared its ugly head on the Internet as young bullies have gone digital. Facebook is a popular site for students to cyberbully by posting false data, invading others' privacy, assassinating character, and making fun of the handicapped or differences. Perpetrators' bad behaviors and immaturity have roots in their negative human development experiences, so raw egos grasp any straw to feel better about themselves. Parents' lack of practicing the Golden Rule becomes visible in their children's behavior. Parental monitoring of their children's Internet activities would be a 24/7 job; however, serious abuse cases must be reported to the school's principal, the police, and Internet providers. Offenders' telephone numbers may be blocked. There are several Web sites to contact: ConnectSafely.org,

Stopcyberbullying. org, and Commonsensemedia.org.

Online education transmission began in 1989 by The University of Phoenix. Today, most colleges and universities have embraced the Internet for online education, including Harvard and Massachusetts Institute of Technology. One of the doctoral students I mentored – with an extensive background in teaching and in clinical psychology has an entertaining way of establishing rapport with students. She completed a dissertation on creativity. She is now in charge of a university's online psychology department program. She is immersed in not only the rigors of curriculum and testing but equally concentrating on how to establish the online student-teacher-relationship, charismatic teaching skills, and ways for students to absorb the information, reflect upon it again and again, think about it, test it against other theories, and organize all into a synthesis on paper of their learning processes. Even online, learning can be a rich social and emotional process when master teachers are in charge. Online quality teaching-learning is a way to educate more people, nationally and globally. It may also lead to traditional master's and doctoral programs' addressing not just their academic intelligence but their full intelligence to turn graduate students into scholars.

Making connections to the outside world with more sophisticated technology is part of our future. Making connections to connect disparate things in our brains is the process that lets us "understand cause and effect, learn from our mistakes, and anticipate the future."[130] However, "imagining the future involves brain processes similar to, but distinct from those involved in conjuring up the past."[130] It's a whole-brain process.

The close relationship between the right and left hemispheres is not acknowledged in The Western Intellectual Tradition, so the importance of having an intrapersonal relationship with oneself is not acknowledged either. Yet, our relationship with ourselves is the basis of the quality of our intimate relationships, interpersonal relationships, and relationships with those who are unlike us. The quality, not the quantity, of our connections to the world outside ourselves will humanize us in a technology world that is currently dehumanizing. The Internet is the only network or organization freely available to our and other nations' people to communicate with each other. It is a perfect site for grassroot organizations to unite Americans toward a united America.

❧ ❧ ❧

Education is the common denominator of all our lives, whether we are educated by academia, experience, or the Internet. From an academic perspective, we are not a nation at educational risk any more. We are a nation in overall decline educationally and democratically as a result of teaching half-brains, reaching half the students, living with diseases, addictions, and violence; saddled with the financial and human ruins of left-brain wars; and subject to symptom- and BigPharma-oriented disease-care insurance instead of a prevention option toward health care.

Most of us are unaware that we are experiencing the physical, mental, emotional, and social consequences of ingesting the chemicals and toxins from our industries that negatively affect the quality of our own and our nation's future. Few educators are aware of the consequences of the uneducated right-brain's unexamined data. Mental and physical health is influenced by what we think, feel, eat, drink, and inhale and how we think, feel, breathe, exercise, rest, and socialize.

What we think and how we think may be more important to our overall health than we know.[233] We would have a more harmonious, communicative nation if The Western Intellectual Tradition acknowledged that we are whole people who require whole-brain education and whole foods for optimum brain functioning.

Education is jokingly referred to as what remains after we've forgotten everything we've learned in school. When the heart, gut, and right-brain's emotions and virtues are included in K-12 public school student's education, "Long after they forget the content they learned, who they become will endure and determine much of the character and quality of their contribution to society and the personal satisfaction they take in life."[254] Mind-forg'd manacles are not a solution for 21st century human beings or America!

Chapter Three

I wander thro' each charter'd street,
Near where the charter'd Thames does flow
And mark in every face I meet
Marks of weakness, marks of woe.
In every cry of every Man,
In every Infant's cry of fear,
In every voice, in every ban,
The mind-forg'd manacles I hear.
—William Blake

Smart versus Wise:
Mind-Forg'd Manacles

Left-brained-dominated scientific, intellectual thought and faith-based Christianity's Church of England prevailed in 18th century England: a source of America's early immigrants and foundation principles for establishing a new country and its institutions and organizations. Reality was based in material objects, similar to America today where materialism, wide gaps between the rich and the poor, and left-brainism thrive. William Blake was one of the English Romantic poets who, when he walked the "charter'd" or mapped streets, saw despair in people's faces. He was concerned that organized society's emphasis on rationalism, not reason, and on religion's array of Thou Shalt Nots meant human imagination would disappear along with their connections to themselves, other human beings, and with Nature. Since reason requires cognition and seeing things in context and rationalism is context independent, Blake intuited that the nation would become left-brain dominated.

Blake's metaphor, "mind-forg'd manacles," represented to him the negative effects of educational and belief systems on English minds. To him, imagination was a surer guide to truth than rationalism. He recognized that societal and self-imposed intellectual limits deprived people of experiencing their wholeness, their connection to Nature, their human spirit, and their relationships with others with heart consciousness.

Centuries later, our left-brained K-12 public educational system has neglected not only students' imagination, but the intelligence of their right-brain, heart, and gut is missing in the teaching-testing-learning-living process. This fact has led to school dropouts whose education ends in adolescence and to left-brain-educated teenagers and adults whose human development deficits direct them to numb their felt insignificance through addictions, crime, violence, and greed as they create havoc in our society for the majority of Americans. When stressed by life's circumstances or perceived threatening situations, individuals with undereducated or underused left-brains' reason and uneducated or overused right-brains' passion collide within themselves. Raw egos emerge to survive by living by their wits or at someone else's expense when there is no respect for human beings' rights. Until they actually physically harm another human being, they may escape incarceration or remediation for a left-brained dominant, society-caused mental dis-ease. When emotional resilience, character building, and the Golden Rule are not taught and practiced at home, in school, or in the media, logic and reason may be overridden by passion and desire, people revert to the jungle's "survival of the fittest" behaviors. Even educated to be smart left-brainers are prone to believe they are above the law, from using drugs and dissing others to questionable financial dealings and immoral and unethical behavior, when they do not have access to or ignore civilized society's human virtues.

A fable by Prussian Philosopher Nietzsche, 1844-1900. characterized for Iain McGilchrist, a British psychiatrist and former English professor at Oxford University, the left-brain's total domination of Western society over the past five hundred years. The fable was the inspiration for his 2009 book's title: *The Master and His Emissary: The Divided Brain and the Making of the Western World.*

Nietzsche's fable is about a right-brained spiritual master, the ruler of a realm, devoted to his people. He nurtured and trained an emissary or vizier as his dominion grew beyond his capacity for his personal attention. The left-brained emissary betrayed his master's trust in order to "advance his own wealth and influence. He saw his master's temperance and forbearance as weakness, not wisdom, and...became contemptuous of his master...the people were duped, the domain became a tyranny...as the Master, the one whose wisdom gave the people power and security, is led away in chains...At present the domain – our civilization – finds itself in the hands of the [left-brained] vizier, who, however gifted, is effectively an ambitious regional bureaucrat with his own interests at heart."[225]

The emissary is an example of left-brained, emotionally illiterate people who take advantage of those whose kindness – a right-brain virtue – they mistake for weakness. Power, status, money-oriented, and lacking the right-brain's virtues, the emissary is socially and emotionally insensitive to others, self-interested as he exploited his master and his people. He was locked into his own point of view by ignoring new ideas, avoiding new experiences, repeating what worked for him in the past, taking advantage of a situation, and discounting the importance of the right-brain and the humanities as exhibited by his master.

Whole-brained people are more integrated in that they are non-violent except when they have to protect themselves or others from harm. They are peace loving but warriors when they have to be, their kindness is not confused with meekness but from a position of strength, and their sensitivity softens their hypermasculinity. Both sides of their brains serve them as needed, so they may not be taken advantage of, like the master by the emissary. Similarly, a country is peace-oriented by being fully prepared to defend itself. But war is the last possible resort, not grandstanding by war hawks' deficit egos that are fulfilled by winning wars.

Dr. McGilchrist's assessment that today's ambitious bureaucrats, with their own interests at heart, are running and ruining our Western civilization appears to be true when power over citizens' lives, their financial security, and K-12 public education systems are out of citizens' control. Nietzsche's parable about a left-brained vizier/emissary who duped his master's people into subjugation is apropos for our democratic republic today when income inequality, job opportunities, and health insurance are concerns of America's citizens while the ultraconservative politicians want to reduce the budget deficit, cut services, layoff more employees, diminish women's rights, and eliminate any reasonably priced health insurance for the uninsured, while they have the best health insurance our taxpayer money can buy for them.

The result is we now live in a dehumanized society with rigid left-brain, bureaucratic mentalities who are obsessed with protecting America's richest 2 percent from tax increases. Those politicians are exploiting a fiscal opportunity with our budget deficit to side with the 2 percenters to break America's and Americans' backbone that visibly began with the election of Tea Party governors. The rich have money; they want more money; they have power, but that is not enough; they want to own America and run it as their own cash cow monarchy. They've been behind the scenes for too long and want to be acknowledged, crowned, and revered as America's royalty. And it all began with our K-12 public education system that splits human brains in two and discards what makes humans humane and integrated toward self-fulfilling lives not based upon status, money, and power. It is vital that our two hemispheres work together as partners – not consistently log onto one brain – to have access to our full intelligence to be whole, fully functioning people, if we want to preserve our human dignity and our freedom in America.

Beliefs about hemispheric hierarchies have been etched into Western society's popular consciousness. The left-brainers believe their perspective is the truth. Those beliefs are not as cut-and-dried as right- or left-brain functioning appears. It's an oversimplification that suggests the two cerebral hemispheres operate independently when, in fact, they specialize and also work together as they process incoming stimuli in unique ways, so we are exercising our right-brain all the time. Events, situations, and people trigger our emotions involving unresolved life experiences and our hardwired instincts that color our thinking and responses. "In reality, both hemispheres are crucially involved in reason, just as they are in language; both hemispheres play their part in creativity...there is, literally, a world of difference between the hemispheres...two different modes of experience; that each is of ultimate importance in bringing about the recognizably human world...that the hemispheres need to cooperate, but...they are in fact involved in a sort of power struggle."[225] But the inner power struggle gets played out on the political and the world's stages.

We Westerners have been brainwashed to accept learned duality as a result of cognitive decisions made thousands of years ago by ancient philosophers, monarchies, religionists, and other powerful white men who considered themselves to be the epitome of intelligence and wisdom. They made decisions about the legitimacy of the left-brain, separated the mind from the body, and denigrated women's bodies, minds, and value. Those decisions became practices and beliefs that have been handed down to us, from generation to generation and have influenced The Western Intellectual Tradition and today's politics in America.

Traditionally, the hemispheres' two brains, the neocortex, have been labeled male, left, and female, right. We Westerners have devolved to the point that the neocortex is culturally and gender-divided into "the mother of invention [right-brain] and father of abstract thought [left-brain].[158] The left-brain is the seat of cognition with direct access to the limbic system's hippocampus (memory) and the hypothalamus (pleasure/rewards). "And it also turns out that the capacities that help us, as humans, form bonds with others – empathy, emotional understanding, and so on – which involves a quite different kind of attention paid to the world, are largely right-hemisphere functions."[225]

Left-brain dominance is wrongly presumed to be the sole domain of men and right-brain dominance to be women's domain. Although not all men are left-brained, nor are all women right-brained, both genders may be raised to prefer their right- or left-brains to dominate or be whole-brained. There are no census statistics on left- versus right brain-dominance; it is estimated to be 50-50, which correlates with ongoing results from *Mindex: Your Thinking Style Profile*.[6]

Cultural conditioning may or may not reinforce males' preferences for their left-brain's attributes and females may or may not prefer their right-brain's aspects. Also, before birth, the quality of in utero experience and the quantity of testosterone and other hormones experienced there may be factored into an individual's preference for right- or left-brain dominance or whole-brainism. Most of our before-

and after-birth experiences are out of our conscious mind's awareness and are buried in our unconscious mind for later retrieval.

Although, people are said to be left-brained or right-brained, those labels go far beyond what research of neuroscientists and psychologists tells us about brain function and personality. However, the use of these two categories – left-brained and right-brained – is a simplified, meaningful, and colorful way to encompass and express two fascinating worldview differences that correlate (to some degree) to the brain functions of the left and right hemispheres.

Thinking, Fast and Slow, is Daniel Kahneman's tour of the human mind that informs us we have two separate systems that drive the way we think. System 1 represents the right-brain; it is fast, intuitive, and emotional; whereas, System 2 represents the left-brain; it is slower, more deliberative, and more logical. Kahneman simply explained the difference between the two systems by 1. picturing a woman's facial expression that most of us would intuitively know she is angry – fast thinking – and by 2. presenting a mathematical problem – 17 times 24 – that most of us would have to use pencil and paper to arrive at an answer – slow thinking.[172] Yet, most of us have a "strong sense of being seamlessly unified into one self and feeling in control of our actions,[116] even though we have competing multiple dynamic mental modules for control of our responses.

As it locks into its own viewpoint, the left-brain is hard-nosed, rational, realistic, and exclusive of the intelligence of the right-brain, the heart and the gut. Whereas, the right-brain is emotional, compassionate, and intuitive as well as creative and inclusive of the left-brain's intelligence. The right-brain complements the left-brain's action by adding nonverbal communication and instincts or gut feelings. The right brain "evaluates the more subtle cues of language including tone of voice, facial expression, and body language."[325]

The descriptive difference between each brain is much more than a few adjectives or nouns, for both serve different aspects of language, imagery, reason, and emotions, even though each brain has a different perspective of the world. Referring to right- brain and left-brain may be less clear-cut as to location than to function. To be a fully functioning human being, we integrate both brains' data bases to access our full intelligence by prioritizing our inherited, educated, experienced, beliefs, and emotions' modules to make informed, wise decisions based upon our whole brain's data bank. Below is a partial list of the diverse worldviews experienced by those who are left-brain dominant and by those who are right-brain dominant:

Left-Brain Dominant	**Right-Brain Dominant**
Characterized as Male	Characterized as Female
Linear	Nonlinear
Cognitive	Heart, Emotions, Intuition
Cognitive Intelligence	Emotional Intelligence
Thought: Analytical, Rational	Feelings, Imagination, creativity
Thinks in Words	Thinks in Pictures
Narrowly focused attention	Global attention
Deals in Parts/Specifics	Deals in Wholes/Patterns
Language	Nonverbal Language
Mathematics, Logic	Expressive Art
Number skills	3-D forms
Quantitative	Qualitative
Objective	Subjective
Literal	Metaphorical
Short-term view	Long-term view
By-the-book	Experiential
Task-oriented	People-oriented
Short-run decisions	Long-run decisions
"What's in for me?"	Group focus
(I-centered)	(We-centered)
Detail-oriented	Big-picture-oriented
Content	Context
Concrete facts	Visionary
Locus of conceptualized data	Embodies intuitive perception
Analysis	Synthesis
Cooler toward People	Warmer toward People
Systematizing	Empathizing
Cold-hearted	Warm-hearted
Sex: Expression of biologic need: lust; or romantic love	Sex: Expression of romantic love; or physical needs
Sex as Weapon: Power Over	Sex: Victim of Power Over
Competitive	Collaborative
Impersonal	Personal
Resistance to admit ignorance	Comfortable with "I don't know"
Doing Consciousness	Being Consciousness

Head Consciousness	Heart Consciousness
Depends on the right hemisphere	Needs the left hemispheres
Exclusive of the right-brain	Inclusive of the left-brain
Looks out for its own hemisphere	Looks out for both hemispheres
Controls the Right hand	Controls the Left hand
Conscious/Unconscious Minds	Conscious/Unconscious Minds
Yang	Yin
Color: Blue (Metaphor)	Color: Red (metaphor)

Relationships

With few clues to who we are but many ideas about what we want, we make decisions and hope for the best. I asked counseling psychology master's students: "Most of us are either left- or right-brain dominant. How may we integrate our neural centers to complete ourselves, to have full human intelligence?" "Get married?" MaryBeth said with a tentative smile. We laughed, as many a true word is said in jest. We are attracted to polar opposite partners as if endowed with inner radar systems to guide us toward integrating our left and right hemispheres. Relationships are opportunities to identify, learn lessons, and grow whole selves. Will we make smart short-run or wise long-run choices to learn, grow, and be happy with ourselves?

Biologically, male brains receive a testosterone wash at eight weeks in utero that eliminates some relationship/communication areas in the brain to make room for a larger sex and aggression area. Without education to compensate, communication issues, verbal and/or physical abuse, and negative memories, recur in negative encounters between partners who are wedded to opposite hemispheres with two distinct worldviews. The two are a) left-brained – those who are head- and I-oriented, literal, mechanistic, focused on details or content, unrealistically optimistic, insensitive, future-oriented, rationalize behavior, and have a narrow worldview with direct access to the right-brain's anger and aggression – and b) right-brained – those who are gut, heart- and we-oriented, intuitive, metaphorical, creative, a holistic or big picture worldview, with direct access to positive emotions – peace, love, joy, respect, reason, acceptance, willingness, neutrality, and courage – and to negative emotions – pride, anger, desire, fear, grief, apathy, hatred, guilt, and shame.[114] In addition, left and right hemisphere dominant individuals with "Below consciousness level 200, there is a predominance of adrenaline and animal-instinct survival response: fight or flight, freeze or feign. In contrast, in consciousness levels over 200 and up, there is a release of endorphins, which is accompanied by feelings of pleasure and happiness."[144] Thus, those with high levels of consciousness have different brain responses.

Why do partners fight? Because "there is a tendency of the left hemisphere to perceive the workings of the right hemisphere as purely incompatible, antagonistic, as a threat to its dominion."[225] Instead of learning lessons, the left-brained person attempts to make the other think or behave as he or she does because the right brain is characterized as female, that is, inferior to the left-brain and not sanctioned by society. We allow a partner who is uncomfortable with intimacy to control our behavior when we stop saying "I love you," for example, if the automatic response is, "Thank you." We may question whether or not we said it to get a loving response or if we were truly expressing felt feelings. A right-brainer is more expressive, but the right-brain's ways are not sanctioned, even though an educated right-brain complements the left-brain, enhances learning, and improves behavior and relationships. So, the right-brained person in the relationship may experience constant negative feedback, which undermines self-esteem and overall health. Either partner may decide to move on and unwittingly repeat unlearned lessons in another relationship, stay put and lead lives of noisy or quiet desperation, or one partner may learn from, accept, understand, and integrate the other's worldview and be grateful for a higher level of consciousness and a fully functioning whole-brain.

Each of us has an inherent drive toward wholeness that may be blocked due to in utero conditions, beliefs, childhood experiences, and cultural conditioning, so mindsight is a skill to lead us toward integration when we perceive our negative reactions as part of our own disowned self. There are many other relationship ways, from career, religion, cults, gangs, and sports to causes, for people – singles, couples, or groups – to satisfy the need to belong or to make sense out of or to balance their lives. All human endeavors and encounters are opportunities to learn and grow, or not.

MaryBeth's response to my question about integrating both hemispheres was, "Get married?!" That's the traditional way most people are drawn to complete themselves. Romantic love is said to be blind, for the heart usually chooses the soul mate. However, it is likely that our level of self-esteem and consciousness also influences our choice of partners. In Newtonian science (based upon atoms) opposites attract or like attracts the unlike, unconsciously. However, people's learned beliefs and uneducated right-brains foster a conscious dislike for the unlike – the disowned parts of the self – so many are consciously attracted to those like themselves, reinforcing shared biases, stereotypes, and brain dominance.

Many left-brainers don't learn lessons in opposites-attract partnerships. Instead, they may verbally abuse or deny the validity of the right-brain's way of thinking, doing, and being. Left-brainers' refusal to understand, accept, or acknowledge two distinct worldviews becomes an inner power struggle that often ends with contempt for the different other, war, or broken vows and homes, which take a huge toll on children's lives.

Relationships could be simpler and more satisfying if all we had to do was to integrate the positive attributes of the left- and right-brains to guide our behavior. The left-brain's conscious self, the voice of our thoughts, thinks it is in charge when, in fact, it may be hijacked. "Although many of us think of ourselves as thinking creatures that feel, biologically we are feeling creatures that think,"[325] so feelings influence our behaviors, whether we believe it or not. The unconscious mind is preprogrammed by intergenerational genetics, in utero, and by early life experiences, parents, peers, teachers, the media, and our culture, which "may not support the goals of our conscious minds. The biggest impediments to realizing the successes of which we dream are the limitations [in the unconscious mind]...These limitations not only influence our behavior, they can also play a major role in determining our physiology and health."[208] The left-brain person rationalizes his or her behavior[276] when behavior succumbs to habitual, no-brainer responses, instead of to the here-and-now.

In a wisdom-oriented society, we nourish our lives toward wholeness and empathy for different others, so we marry ourselves first before we marry another unique individual. In the new science of quantum physics (based upon subatomic particles), wholeness attracts wholeness. Two whole people make one whole relationship, and ensuing generations may be raised with unconditional love, less fear, and healthier living, learning, and working relationships.

"Our 'free' choice of a mate is, in the end, a product of our unconscious, which has an agenda of its own."[153] If love is not our primary guide in our intimate relations or if we get married to fulfill a felt deficit, a biological need for a child, or ego's desire for love, status, money, and power, we may be presented with life's lessons through conflicts or other crises as opportunities to learn, grow healthy, and be smart and wise – later on in life. If children are involved while we are emotionally or physically unavailable to them, they suffer the "sins" of their parents. Not necessarily the seven deadly sins of pride, covetousness, lust, anger, gluttony, envy, and sloth, but "the refusal to love oneself well, the refusal to celebrate both one's dignity and one's responsibility"[103] and "the refusal of humans to become who we are."[102]

When we do not love ourselves, it is harder to love and be totally responsible for babies who require 24/7/365 attention. Sin, in its deepest depth. is the common practice of making oneself the center of the universe, believing everything is ownable and "mine." As Khalil Gibran wrote in *The Prophet*, "Your children are not your children. They are the sons and daughters of Life's longing for itself. They come through you but not from you, yet they belong not to you."[119] In essence, children are only lent to us for a little while, so our stewardship of ourselves will reflect our stewardship of our relationships with developing and developed human beings and all life.

Instead of addressing the roots of social and physical diseases and maladies in our society and population, the left-brained response is to rely upon its accepted doctrine and practices or address their symptoms by declaring a War on Reading, a War on Drugs, a War on Poverty, and a War on Cancer, for example. Symptoms are not the enemy; they are messages to inform us that wars are not a solution; it's the half-brained, fragmented approaches that do not attend to whole individuals and our whole society that are the problem. Our left-brained society's inequalities, inequities, and unhealthy environments affect us all.

Adversarial positions exist in our left-brain-dominated nation when cognitive intelligence is educated and emotional intelligence is excluded as a partner in the education equation. Many people are conflicted within and divided against each other when anti-emotional and anti-intellectual forces are the result of our inherited, absurd beliefs and practices that the left-brain is legitimate and superior to the right-brain or that the left-brain is male and the right-brain is female and inferior.

The K-12 public education system does not emphasize the inner mind – "the unconscious realm of emotions, intuitions, biases, longings, genetic predispositions, character traits, and social norms. This is the realm where character is formed and street smarts grow."[33] Today it has become more evident that Western man "has created chaos by denying that part of self that integrates while enshrining the parts that fragment experience...we in the West value one of these ways above all others – the one we call 'logic,' a linear system that has been with us since Socrates. Western man sees his system of logic as synonymous with the truth."[139]

The left-brain dominant students, who are unencumbered by negative labels, emotions, morality, or compassion, are empowered by cognitive science. Cognitive science is based upon how the mind works with facts and figures, not upon how it works in unique individuals with unique life and embedded sensory experiences and in unique-to-them situations.

Left-brain dominant people are more anger- than fear-oriented (but fear talk hooks more people), for left-brainers' direct access to the right-brain's anger[225] is aligned with the left-brained worldview that is I-focused. Left-brainers are smart, serial thinkers who reduce thoughts to emotionless numbers and words to control people and events. They make decisions based upon the bottom-line, money, without attention to any fallout of their actions, from no jobs to no benefits and no future. Their fear, though, is the fear of the loss of job, status, money, and power in society and of the loss of control in love, intimate, and committed relationships. Such left-brainers are not driven by a quest for truth or equality, just entitled to be powerful in a culture that promotes their narcissism, consumerism, greed, and hate speech.

The Western Intellectual Tradition's legacy: emotional intelligence is sacrificed for cognitive intelligence and no full intelligence. Ignorance of our academic and human development deficits will continue until we stop projecting onto others our hindered love's opposites: fear, hate, doubt, anger. Society's angry ones are primarily the rigid left-brainers with uneducated right-brains who may not love themselves. For some, their emotions are unavailable, or alexithyymic, while others' emotions may be repressed or expressed cruelly. Their apparent uncomfortableness with acknowledging or positively expressing their emotions and feelings makes them talk about things, how the world works, sports, work, and money or joke about sex and women instead.

"Since 1983, we've reformed the [K-12] education systems again and again, yet more than a quarter of high-school students drop out"[33] in America. "The failures have been marked by a single feature: Reliance on an overly simplistic view of human nature...And they will continue to fail unless the new knowledge about our true makeup is integrated more fully into the world of public policy."[33] And, unless The Western Intellectual Tradition discontinues focusing upon producing smart students at the expense of their wholeness and wisdom, our society as a whole will continue to dumb down.

Smart versus Wise

Smart

The present U.S. K-12 public school student population is estimated to be 50 percent left-brained and 50 percent right-brained. Smart is an adjective applied to left-brainers, primarily, who score high on standardized tests; they receive the honors and scholarships and are positioned for success. However, left-brained-dominant students are not automatically smart. While they match K-12 public education's teaching-learning styles, I.Q. alone does not lead to being smart or not smart. Motivation and perseverance are two factors that influence success in school. An added advantage of being left-brain-dominant is the ability to concentrate and be cognitive without being encumbered by any interference from the heart, gut, or the right-brain's emotions, empathy, or compassion.

Many left-brain-dominant people may not be the "kind modeled by cognitive science" and their emotions may interfere with acing tests and being smart; however, there are many left-brainers in our society, especially those in powerful and well-compensated positions, who demonstrate their lack of character: the Golden Rule is passé for them and is not factored into professional relationships. Their modus operandi is infected with cunning and conning as they demonstrate their need for obedient subjects and to overkill differences since they know what's best. Some left-brainers are alexithymics. Alexithymics are people who are "not accustomed to recognizing their feeling states...the diminished ability to recognize, name and use their emotions as guides to self-monitoring results in an overdependence on and overutilization of reasoning"[198] and what worked in the past.

Smart is a popular adjective in our educational, personal, professional, advertising, social, and political worlds. Smart originated from the Latin mordere, meaning to bite, sting, and is defined by *Webster's New World Dictionary* as 1. causing sharp or stinging pain. 2. sharp or stinging, as pain. 3. brisk; vigorous; lively. 4a) intelligent, alert, clever, capable, witty, etc. 4b) shrewd or sharp, as in one's dealings. 5. neat, trim, spruce. 6a) in keeping with current fashion; stylish. 6b) characteristic of or used to those who follow the current fashion. 7. impertinent, flippant or saucy. 8. Quite strong, intense, numerous, etc. Smart is self-oriented, from body pain to mental alertness. "She looks smart" is a physical compliment, meaning "She looks good." "He is smart" is a mental compliment, meaning "He is intelligent." Note the stereotyping: physical commentary for women and mental attributes for men. Cognitive intelligence does not include emotional intelligence.

Thus, smart is defined as sting, irritation, mental distress, pain; intelligent, alert, clever, capable, witty, and shrewd or sharp, as in one's dealings. Today, smart is a left-brain construct for book smarts or academic intelligence, which has evolved to be devoid of any interference from the heart, emotions, morality, ethics, intuition, creativity, respect, compassion, altruism, or experience. In other words, robotic.

We've witnessed cognitively intelligent people displaying their ego deficits and disloyalty by self-destructive to their reputation forays into illicit sex. They stretch their wives, families, and the public's capacity to understand their thinking, from former U.S. presidents to State governors, politicians, and business executives. Symptoms of being smart at the expense of the emotional, social, and moral bonds are amorality, greed, character deficits, and disrespect for the common good and democracy.

Today, the definitions of some words in our language are changing or are being upgraded. The Internet's Wikipedia has a Wiktionary. With Old English and Germanic roots, Wiktionary defines smart (an adjective) as: 1. Exhibiting social ability or cleverness. 2. Exhibiting intellectual knowledge, such as that found in books. 3. Good-looking. 4. Cleverly and/or sarcastically humorous in a way that may be rude and disrespectful; 5. Sudden and intense; and 6. Intense in feeling, painful. Nevertheless, being smart implies a person who is good-looking or a good dresser and ego-oriented. He or she learns from books, not necessarily from experience, and is willing to outsmart others or "sting" them with smart remarks, if necessary, to win, indicating the use of the right-brain's negative aspects. In essence, the meaning of smart has remained the same over time: more social image- and externally-oriented and clever to the point of being disrespectful and taking advantage of others.

Our Western society's preoccupation with the self means those who are smart are perceived as savvy, as having the qualities that are valued to get ahead: competitive and do whatever it takes to win. And they do, based upon the shrewd financial dealings that have enriched those who play by their own rules, such as New Yorker Bernard Madoff, master of the Ponzi scheme, corporate lobbyists, and economic hit men whose financial interests outweigh the greater good of all Americans and America.

Smart is a left-brain society's short-cut to intelligence. While a student's preference for right- or left-brain dominance may be innate – Nature – or conditioning – nurture – all students are conditioned to "see" what is taught, instead of the context, as demonstrated by my holding up a dollar bill to my class. Critical thinking is also missing when taught to focus on content instead of the larger context.

Left-brain dominant people are less influenced by their right-brain's feelings, except for anger; whereas, right-brain dominant person may be overwhelmed by feelings – fear, threat, or failure – so access to left-brained learned data to regurgitate on tests or in oral reports is compromised. Current public K-12 educational systems fail students who do not test well so self-esteem and expectations are negatively affected, making it more difficult for them to achieve their academic goals. Students' high test scores are judged to be the epitome of being smart and intelligent in our public schools; character as moral strength and self-discipline is not part of being smart on paper or in life where a good character may be a drawback to achieving financial goals.

"Character is what you are. Not what you pretend to be to yourself or others. It is what you do over the years when you think no one is watching you. Or, What you would do if you knew you would never be found out. It is the totality of what you are, your thoughts, your word, and especially your behavior. It is living by quiet example. It communicates you. Character complements honor and integrity and are gifts you give yourself. It is a consistency of all the other good qualities you have, especially, a positive attitude...Choosing not to respond to a criticism about you shows character. Only you can damage your character."[288]

Smart is an appropriate term to describe the majority of America's successful people whose feelings do not impede their learning and whose high opinions of themselves, often at others' expense, allow them to be be shallow characters, so narcissistic and greedy that they take advantage of or outwit those who are not so smart, too trusting, or gullible. The not-so-smart often refuse to believe that if a deal is too good to be true, it is, or are blinded by the perpetrator's reputation and the opportunity to make easy money. Even a mild form of greed makes them gullible. Smart also defines those with street-smarts who live by their wits and take advantage of others' trust or naivete and those whose book-smarts have provided them with theories but no practical experience. In life, smart is more about pride, the antithesis of wise, than being humble.

Wise

Adding the right-brain's attributes to the left- brain's cognition does not automatically result in Smart and Wise. Both brains have to be educated or seasoned to be wise. However, most left-brain dominant people have disowned their right-brains to be smart, and right-brain-dominant people may have disowned their left-brains by not valuing education. Many right-brainers' unresolved feelings, negative emotions, and negative living experiences tamper with their learned academic intelligence abilities when, under test conditions for example, the left-brain may downshift into the fight, flight, freeze, or feign syndrome for physical or ego survival. To be wise requires that the right-brain and the left-brain work together. Being wise or having wisdom slows down the automatic, emotional, knee-jerk response. Essentially, wisdom is a process whereby neural activity is more emotionally balanced, intuitive, and context-related than content-related and logical to arrive at a dynamically balanced outcome for the greater good.

Wise is defined by a Webster's dictionary as 1. Having or showing good judgment; sagacious; prudent; discreet. 2. Prompted by wisdom; judicious; sound. 3. Having information; informed. 4. Learned; erudite. 5. Shrewd; crafty; cunning. Wise is defined by *Webster's Encyclopedic Unabridged Dictionary of the English Language* as 1. having the power of discerning and judging properly as to what is true or right; possessing discernment, judgment, or discretion. 2. characterized by or showing such power, judicious, or prudent: a wise decision. 3. possessed of or characterized by scholarly knowledge or learning...4. Having knowledge or information as to facts, circumstances, etc.

Of interest, *homo sapiens* is the scientific name for the only living species of the genus Homo (modern man, mankind, human being). Yet, sapient is the Latin word for full of knowledge, wise, sagacious. If *homo sapiens* have innate wisdom, our educational systems squash it. We need whole-brained education to draw it out in our Western society. The word education derives from educere, meaning to draw out.

Wise is an adjective; the noun is wisdom. Wisdom is defined by a Webster's as 1. the quality of being wise; power of judging rightly and following the soundest course of action, based on knowledge, experience, understanding, etc.; good judgment; sagacity. 2. learning;

knowledge; erudition [the wisdom of the ages]. 3. wise discourse or teaching. 4. a wise plan or course of action. Wiktionary's definition of wisdom: Wisdom is knowledge of what is true or right coupled with just judgment as to action; sagacity, discernment, or insight. It is an ideal that has been celebrated since antiquity as the application of knowledge needed to live a good life. Beyond simply knowing/understanding what options are available, "wisdom" provides the ability to differentiate between them and to choose the one that is best. What this means depends on the various wisdom schools and traditions claiming to foster it. In general, these schools have emphasized various combinations of the following: knowledge, understanding, experience, discipline, discretion, and intuitive understanding, along with a capacity to apply these qualities well toward finding solutions to problems. In many traditions, the terms wisdom and intelligence have overlapping meaning. In other traditions, they are arranged hierarchically, with intelligence being necessary but not sufficient for wisdom.

Positive psychology researchers define wisdom as the coordination of "knowledge and experience" and "its deliberate use to improve well-being."[226] With the foregoing definition, wisdom may be measured using the following criteria: "A wise person has self-knowledge. A wise person seems sincere and direct with others. Others ask wise people for advice. A wise person's actions are consistent with his/her ethical beliefs."[266]

Studies of wisdom are rooted in ancient lore and eclectic explanations, ranging from the practical and moral to the scholastical and mystical. It was Howard Gardner who wondered why Western society perpetuates the ancients' narrow view of intelligence. His *Frames of Mind* is the result of his research studies of prodigies, gifted individuals, brain-damaged patients, idiot savants, normal children, normal adults, experts in different lines of work, and individuals from diverse cultures to formulate his multiple intelligences theory. Gardner's intelligences are Linguistic Intelligence, Musical Intelligence, Logical-Mathematical Intelligence, Spatial Intelligence, Bodily-Kinesthetic Intelligence, and Personal Intelligence (the developmental stages of sets of selves). Bodily-Kinesthetic Intelligence includes muscular, sensory, respiratory, and nutrition intelligence for whole-brain intelligence.[114] It was Daniel Goleman who added *Emotional Intelligence* in 1995. Creative, Intuitive, and Wisdom Intelligences have yet to be included in human beings' multiple intelligences. Jonas Salk defined wisdom as equilibrium, as natural wisdom. He proposed the naturalness of equilibrium and how equilibrium promotes synergy.[295]

Many scientists (Albert Einstein and Otto Loewi, for example) reported being immersed in their unsolvable scientific problems, fell asleep, and dreamed solutions. Visionary leaders are known to weigh all the data and to trust their gut in making decisions. While some creative ideas and solutions to problems emerge full-blown, the wisdom process demands an individual's active participation in its inquiry, dictated by intelligence and intuition. Thus, wisdom may be perceived as intuitive and creative processes. All human beings have the capacity for gaining and asserting wisdom, yet what may be wise in one culture may be unwise in other cultures. Wisdom is measurable by behavior, by what we do rather than by what we think or say we do, and by what we believe to be truth, which influences our knowledge, emotions, morality, and compassion.

There appears to be a hierarchical aspect that pervades our culture regarding faith and wisdom. Religion has been around longer than science in Western civilization. For eons, religious figures have asserted control over science and scientists who disputed the Church's beliefs or dogma. While Roman Catholic Church's Pope Benedict has accepted evolution as an explanation for humankind's origins, the Church's Christian cousins, the Fundamentalists, have not as they press for creationism and anti-women rights. Even today, many people look to religion for wisdom, not to science.

"Wisdom" is mentioned 233 times in the Bible, 180 times in the Old Testament, and 53 times in the New Testament, according to Fred Hafner's The Mustard Seed Project. He also reported that "wise" is mentioned 183 times in the Bible, 144 times in the Old Testament, and 39 times in the New Testament.[135] Wisdom and wise appear to be emphasized less in the New Testament than in the Old Testament. Could it be that wisdom and wise became the property of religion's elites while religion or faith was relegated to the masses? Today, many people seem to believe that "Scientists and academics are smart, but religious leaders are wise,"[251] which implies that being religious is wiser than being smart.

Nevertheless, scientists' quests for answers are based upon "curiosity, doubt, humility, tolerance,"[251] which are wisdom-directed. Today, scientists and religionists need to upgrade their reputation and character. Some religious figures have been involved in the sexual abuse of young children and some scientist have published fraudulent or biased research or adopted their graduate students' findings as their own: Nobelist Selman Waksman of Rutgers University, for example.

A survey by the Pew Research Center for the American Association for the Advancement of Science (AAAS) that polled 2500 scientists and 2000 members of the public, found that "at least two-thirds of Americans hold scientists and engineers in high regard...85 percent of the science association members surveyed said public ignorance of science was a major problem...Alan I. Leshner, chief executive of the science association, said scientists must find new ways to engage the public."[66]

In many American and Canadian Indian cultures, elders enjoy great respect. The Inuits of western Canada consider wisdom to be the result of aging well. Wisdom for them reflects "the individual's function as a repository of cultural knowledge and his or her involvement in community life by interacting with younger people and talking to them, teaching them about 'traditional cultural values.'"[57] They are also respected for their oral traditions that teach the young about their ancestors' experiences, history, and beginnings.

A much older educational tradition has existed in America for eons: A Native American elder was asked how she had become so wise, happy, and respected. She said, "In my heart there are two wolves: a wolf of love and a wolf of hate. It all depends on which one I feed each day."[142] None of us can afford a preponderance of negative thoughts, if we want to be physically, mentally, psychologically, socially, and spiritually healthy.

Wisdom is equated with age, even by Western psychologists and human developers. Erik Erikson's life cycles include "a generational principle which would tend to perpetuate a series of vital virtues from hope in infancy to wisdom in old age."[95] For Erikson, wisdom consists of "ripened 'wits' to accumulated knowledge, mature judgment, and inclusive understanding."[95] Although Robert Sternberg's concept of wisdom appears not to be age-related, his concept is about applying tacit knowledge to achieve a common good through balancing multiple vested interests (intrapersonal, interpersonal, and extrapersonal) within the context of environmental conditions.[317]

Research by Richard E. Nisbett of the University of Michigan found that older people may not have knowledge about computers or be a source of factual knowledge, but they have social wisdom. Older people had an advantage over younger ones for settling social disputes. "The study concluded that economic status, education and IQ also were significantly related to increased wisdom, but it found that 'academics were no wiser than non-academics' with similar education levels."[301]

Carolyn Heilbrun stated, "Most of my young friends are smarter than I am...which is not to say wiser."[152] Her assessment of young people's wisdom correlated with the Canadian research study comparing Japanese and Americans' wisdom. Dr. Grossmann found that young Japanese are as wise as Zen masters; whereas, Americans get wiser with age.[132]

Daniel Pink informs us that we are moving from the Information Age to the Conceptual Age, just as we progressed from a farmer society to a society of factory workers and then to a society of knowledge workers: the Information Age.[269] The Conceptual Age will thrive if we have Smart and Wise students and adults. For young and older Americans to participate in the Conceptual Age of innovation and creativity, there's a connection, an ability, that gives us a completely different view of what our and America's future may look like and be like. That connection is wisdom. "One way to define wisdom is the ability to see, into the future, the consequences of your choices in the present."[7]

When our educational leaders include educating the right-brain in the K-12 curricula, they will discover that whole-brain learning and functioning correlates with increased intelligence, improved learning, enhanced moral reasoning, and psychological stability and emotional maturity.[136] That's the "right stuff" for Smart and Wise to prevail and for our democracy to survive and thrive for all, not just for the self-anointed and smart few.

K-12 Public Education's Legacy

Many Americans appear to be stuck in an unacknowledged Ignorance Age due to education beyond public school not being a priority for too many Americans and poor segments of our society. K-12 public school systems' fail poor students and they fail themselves when they do not have the support system to rise above their impoverished circumstances, so that their attending college, or even attaining a high school diploma, may not be an option. The College Board reports that the U.S., which used to lead the world in the proportionate number of young adults with college degrees, has dropped to 12th place[189] The cost of public and private colleges and universities has become prohibitive for high school graduates. Those who did go to college and incurred student loans are only finding part-time jobs in 2012 to repay as much as $900 a month or more on their college loans. Many college graduates have had to move back home to survive.

Colleges and universities are also constrained by The Western Intellectual Tradition. They are slow to innovate, integrate arts and science courses, and lead the way toward wisdom. What is broken cannot be fixed when few educators acknowledge that our K-12 public schools feed into college and university educational systems that have to deal with dumbed down students with high test scores but require remedial courses in the basics before undertaking colleges' 101 courses.

Some Americans appear to have capitalized on the Information Age and now are in their own Narcissistic Age. The K-12 system is undermining the American Dream of upward mobility through education when people's whole brains are not educated. Chasing the American Dream without wisdom has spawned industries whose owners' practices have demonstrated they value money over people's health and well-being. Graduates of the K-12 system become adults who, if they are right-brain illiterate without heart consciousness, are less likely to consider the consequences of their actions in their business dealings. Profit is the bottom line in most commercial undertakings, which is necessary to stay in business, but when their profit is due to ignoring the research that their products are harmful to human life, all living things, and the Earth's natural resources, and hire lawyers to dispute or delay change, then they value money more than people. They are greedy capitalists.

Despite living longer, our immune systems are under siege, sleep problems, inflammatory and autoimmune diseases are rampant. Heart disease is #1 and Cancer is #2. America may be the most advanced country in the world, but human bodies work the same way as they did in our ancestors' bodies. Our near future medical bill is projected to be "20 percent of the country's earnings."[244] Why?

Since World War II ended in 1945, we have experienced an explosion in technology. We are exposed to positive charged electromagnetic (EM) devices – from TVs, video games, cellphones, and computers to the latest communication wireless technologies – and have simultaneously disconnected ourselves from the negative ion charged Earth that grounds us, thereby minimizing the effects of positive charged ion technologies so many of us are sensitive to electropollution. Human beings have evolved from living and working in caves and sleeping on deer skins to "Our bare feet, with their rich networks of nerve endings, rarely touch the ground. We wear insulating synthetic-soled shoes. We sleep on elevated beds made from insulating material."[244] And we breathe polluted air, eat manufactured salty foods, and drink sugared water. Not optimum fuel for fully functioning brains!

The overall health of our nation is at risk when we are not educated to know the difference between moderation and abuse. We abuse our usage of technology and go along with Big Businesses' practices of using chemicals and abusing the Earth's water, air, and soil. Hippocrates, the ancient Greek father of medicine, stated, "Illnesses do not come upon us out of the blue. They are developed from small daily sins against Nature." When enough sins have accumulated, illnesses will suddenly appear. Sins are foods that contain pesticides, chemical drifts from spraying, flavorings, shelf-life chemicals; polluted air and water. By valuing money more than people, we have not only disconnected from our human nature but from Mother Nature as well.

Add agribusiness farming methods since World War II, and human beings are bombarded with hormones, antibiotics, pesticides, herbicides, fertilizers, and 86,000 "approved" chemicals in the air we breathe, our food supply and in animals that we eat. Only a small percentage of those chemicals have been tested for health effects. Animals are slaves and are treated as human slaves once were and still are in some areas. Farm animals do not graze on the land; they are given manufactured feed from corn and animal by-products and/or fishery products. A huge percentage (about 80 percent) of manufactured antibiotics are administered to farm animals. "No one, rural or urban, is untouched by chemical drift. The Centers for Disease Control and Prevention estimate 89 to 100 percent of fetuses in the United States are exposed to pesticides in utero and 95 percent of the population has measurable pesticides in their urine."[161]

We shape our farming methods to preserve food and feed huge populations throughout the world and our farming methods shape us and impact our health and animals' welfare. Changing to a vegetarian diet would save our health care system about 84 billion dollars a year, according to the Center for Science in the Public Interest.[52] A vegetarian diet would also save human beings from the exponential rise in heart disease, cancer, Type 2 diabetes, arthritis and the need for addictive painkillers, obesity, and many other chronic and lifestyle diseases. Not only are 9 billion animals slaughtered for human consumption in the U.S. each year, the air and soil pollution from such operations are prime sources of greenhouse gases. The animals barely move in overcrowded conditions prior to their deaths. Most of us remember the horrid odors emanating from such feedlots. Compassionate people tend to become vegetarians because they do not want to collude in animals' suffering at the hand of inhumane livestock businesses. When we help others, we help ourselves.

Big lumber companies in Oregon, for example, "apply chemicals [Atrazine and 2,4-D] by helicopter and ground applicators on clear-cut timberland over mountainsides, often spraying right up to their [neighbors'] property lines. Helicopter blades create enough air turbulence to blow a chemical fog over nearby property...a ground applicator sprayed pesticides right up to the grounds of the Triangle Lake School, 60 feet from classroom windows."[161] The manufacturers of Atrazine, Syngenta, aver that Atrazinbe has safely passed multiple reviews by the EPA, with low birth defects in areas with high Atrazine usage. However, independent scientific research of Atrazine "found that that counties with high pesticide use had higher birth defects [and] that counties with lower pesticide use had lower rates of birth defects."[161]

The Director of Neonatal Care at an Indianapolis hospital "reported disproportionately high rates of birth defects for children conceived between April and July, the peak period of Atrazsine applications."[161] In another study, a researcher "measured the school performance of 1.6 million children in Indiana in grades 3 through 10 and found significantly lower scores on statewide standardized tests in math and language for children conceived in months of peak pesticide and nitrate use."[161]

Since the majority of people's right-brains are not being educated informally or formally today, advertising determines the fuel for the brain and body. Children get fat on the way to adulthood obesity. Obesity is a problem in America for children and adults. Eating habits are usually learned in families and associated with love or soul food. Fast foods are popular with poor and busy families. Seductive food advertising on TV becomes "Tell your mother to buy..." Our politicians pander and give subsidies to the food industry; they rubberstamp government bureaucrats' actions that contribute to the nation's obesity.

A *New York Times* article, by Michael Moss about the U.S. Department of Agriculture's Dairy Management helped Domino's Pizza lagging sales by adding 40 percent more cheese and allegedly paid $12 million for its marketing campaign, became an Internet sensation. Bloggers called the partnering an example of corporate welfare and a bailout. With conflict existing within the USDA's dual role as agricultural products marketer and America's nutrition police, a social media specialist responded that Domino's Pizza had been one of his clients and that it didn't get any government money, that Dairy Management collects a fee from dairy farmers/manufacturers from the milk they produce, and that DM's purpose is to promote new products with more cheese. Whatever, Domino's sold more pizza and the farmers sold more cheese; both were happier, but one slice of Domino's Pizza now contains two-thirds of the recommended daily intake of saturated fat, more calories mean kids get fatter, and saturated fat is linked to heart disease in adults. The dairy farmers have to charge more to consumers when they pay the so-called fee to DM for its spending sprees.

Government's subsidizing agribusiness means cheaper, high calorie fast foods are more available to the poor while unsubsidized healthy food is expensive by comparison. Dr. Martha Grout calls America a "Hay Belly Nation:" Bales of hay are stored in barns to protect them from rain, which washes out the hay's nutrients. When cattle eat nutrient-deficient hay, "their bodies signal them to eat more of it than usual in an effort to get a full quota of nutrients. Their bellies get really big – what farmers call hay bellies. It is a sign of poor quality food."[133] A huge percentage of Americans are obese; many of whom are emotional eaters due to unresolved and ongoing issues that are right-brain-based.

Telemarketing's scams or get-rich-quick schemes separate people from their savings. Divisive politics and religions dominate America's popular culture and manipulate the right-brain toward its own purposes. Few money/power-oriented left-brainers are interested in educating children's and adults' right-brains to be less vulnerable to their practices and products that compromise people's health.

It is smart and wise to be conscious of and in charge of what we think believe, eat, drink, breathe, experience, and behave for the benefit of our overall health and well-being. Not only are human hemispheres divided into a left- and a right-brain, the body's autonomic nervous system is divided into the sympathetic (protection) and parasympathetic (growth, healing) modes, and our physical and mental states vary in response to our thinking, habits, and behavior. Our negative thoughts, emotions, and perceived threats to ego and physical survival spark physiologic changes and release cortisol to prepare the body for the fight, flight, freeze, or feign response (sympathetic mode), which impairs thinking, increases blood pressure, and shuts down the body's growth, repair, and healing responses (the parasympathetic mode).

The sources of discontent or disease that disturb our comfort zone and put us into the sympathetic mode may be examined for our blind spots, disowned or disengaged selves, and for ways to control our left brain's chatter, to relax, by breathing exercises that influence the vagus nerve, which influences the autonomic system. What we think and feel, who we are, and how we react are limited when we primarily use only one hemisphere, or half our brains, as espoused by The Western Intellectual Tradition's K-12 public school system of mass education.

Research indicates that when fear or anger, for example, is activated, the left-brain's ego's desire to survive at all costs reverts to the fight-fight-freeze-or-feign syndrome in the brain stem. Chemicals flood the body to energize the sympathetic autonomic system to protect us from real or imagined threats. The parasympathetic autonomic system shuts down digestion, left-brained thinking, and the immune system's healing abilities. That's what happens to students who fear tests and do not test well: their emotions temporarily override their left-brain knowledge. For adults, it's similar to white-coat high blood pressure at the doctor's office.

Thus, negative thoughts, memories, and emotions not only engage the body's defense physiology but under stress, anxiety, and unstable situations, the right-brain becomes dominant, both protective and defensive. Calming upset people whose left-brains have been hijacked in order to focus on problem solving requires a well-functioning corpus callosum to resolve disputes. Since the right-brain is sensitive to non-verbal communications – tone of voice, facial expressions, eye contract, and hand gestures – those factors may be more important than words to effect change.

I recall the news reporting of a chaotic scene at New York's JFK airline terminal. A passenger had gotten upset with his carrier and was jumping up and down, yelling incoherently, creating a scene, and disrupting airline service. Attempts to get his attention did not work until an airline employee joined him and jumped up and down with him, which caught the passenger's attention: "What did they do to you?" At that point, the airline employee had the passenger's attention and was able to refocus his attention, calm him down, and disperse the gathered crowd.

Conventional wisdom holds that we make choices based on conscious, informed thoughts from weighing the pros and cons of issues. Research indicates that unconscious negative views of prior experiences or associations with race and gender enter the decision-making process, despite conscious beliefs to the contrary.[113] We cannot, if we value our lives, agree to be pawns in the game of life. When we place our trust in politicians, the food and pharmaceutical industries, and the pharmaceutical-oriented medical field, we will be at risk for betrayal if we do not remain alert, informed, and vote for ourselves from a whole-brained perspective.

Government agencies may go along with industries' claims that what is good for their businesses is good for the country when it is not good for the American people. Industries' practices enrich the few, but government agencies, such as the FDA, USDA, and U.S. Department of Education and the politicians who are entrusted with its citizens' health, welfare, and education neglect their civic responsibilities when they are more responsive to Earth's new people (corporations) than to the real people, We the People, who are the unwitting recipients and consumers of The Western Intellectual Tradition's legacy: The K-12 public education system.

Passion Submerges Reason

The public asks, "Why did intelligent men, political figures such as Dominique Strauss-Kahn, Arnold Swarzenegger, Eliot Spitzer, Bill Clinton, and Newt Gingrich and many known and unknown others risk their reputations, careers, and marriages and families to pursue illicit sex?" It appears that their left-brained intelligence was overridden by the uneducated right-brain's raw ego's love of money, power, status, and lust (not love of women), or by rape fantasies or feelings of anger against or power over women – expressed through aggressiveness, violence, and/or sexual assault when a woman's "No" is a man's consensual yes.

It's not about left-brain cognitive intelligence; it's the lack of right-brain emotional intelligence. Male human beings' egos instinctively seek to survive and procreate. As you know, biologically, until eight weeks old in utero, male and female brains look alike. Then a testosterone wash turns a unisex brain into a male one. Cells in the male brain's communication centers are replaced by a larger sex and aggression center. As testosterone takes over the male brain, "boys grow less communicative and become more obsessed about scoring – in games, and in the backseat of a car."[27] Raw egos/predators thrive when the right-brain is not educated, so women become the means for some men to feed huge egos or satisfy primitive urges without guilt. Some women in power positions in the workplace have exhibited similar tendencies by preying upon men. Other women have stalked male celebrities. Sex and power may be inextricably intertwined for both genders.

Human beings have moral instincts, too, and ancient parables to guide human behavior. However, when emotions are uneducated, women are fair game. When entrenched power-over beliefs and opportunity collide, rape ensues. Rape is a global violence issue. In some men's mindsets, females are saints, mothers, or whores. Many rigid left- and right-brainers are culturally conditioned to believe women are unequal to males and disposable goods. Some men may perceive their wives as legal prostitutes, not partners. It's as if they live by the creed, "any woman can do for me what you can do," so their relationships with women may be more physical and financial than special, just lust. When the underlying belief is the "grass is greener" elsewhere and practiced, there is no emotional commitment to spouses or the family unit. If you think women's rights are a non-issue today, why haven't America's primarily male lawmakers passed the Equal Rights Amendment? Inherited beliefs about women's status are difficult to change, especially when Pope Benedict XVI is adamantly opposed to any changes in the Roman Catholic Church's established dogma or to acknowledge that the ban on relationships with women does not eradicate men's sexual urges, which priests have played out on young boys in the Church, nuns, and other women.

While left-brainers may satisfy their unengaged right-brain's sexual urges, without guilt or fear, on the weak, I propose that the fear-oriented are primarily the rigid right-brainers whose uneducated right-brains, undereducated left-brains, and conscious and unconscious minds direct them to seek a cause or construct a narrative, a story, to resolve or compensate for felt human development deficits, especially unconditional love.

The lack of integrative thinking and anti-intellectualism, are factors that make one susceptible to ideology. Most rigid right-brainers are we-oriented, their "we" includes those like themselves, not the unlike, so they tend to be anti-intellectuals in response to their own or others' negative experiences in the K-12 public school system or anti-everyone who doesn't agree with their beliefs or "shoulds" and "oughts." They're not driven by a quest for truth either, just to feel good, look good, and be heard. And the more people they attract to their cause or ideology, the more they can believe in it.

Self-knowledge is not a mainstream topic for it appears to be tainted with a left-brained slur of "touchy-feely." How can we, then, uncover any unconscious knowledge, traits, beliefs. biases, goals, and feelings that influence our behavior? Most of us, and often the most outspoken among us, do not know ourselves very well, our character, why we feel the way we do, and why we say what we say and do, although our left-brain conscious mind assures us it reveals truth. Not so! However, knowing the difference between our inherited self and our examined self makes a huge difference in whether the choices we make are ours, not others' choices for us. We who are *Strangers to Ourselves* [346] may become our own loving friend.

A way to understand the nature of our hidden data bank is by looking outward, not inward, at our own behavior and by listening to others' reactions to us. When we learn to carefully observe others' behavior, instead of wanting facts only (a left-brained attribute) to make up our minds, then we will be in a better position to observe our own behavior, record it in a right-/left-brain journal, and learn from it. When we change toward love, collaboration, and wisdom, and are able to globally accept (not necessarily agree with) others' ideas, beliefs, and behaviors, then we are living integrated, whole selves as Nature intended and other species practice naturally.

Sovereignty

Researchers, such as "geneticists, neuroscientists, psychologists, sociologists, economists, anthropologists, and others have made great strides in understanding the building blocks of human flourishing. And a core finding of their work is that we are not primarily the products of our conscious thinking. We are primarily the products of thinking that happens below the level of awareness."[33] The conscious mind focuses on reason and analysis, the power of the ego self, and hungers for status, money, power over people, and applause. The unconscious mind focuses on passions, perceptions, relationships, the invisible bonds between people, and hungers for peace and wholeness when our human development processes include: "Self-reverence, self-knowledge, self-control – These three alone lead life to sovereign power."[329]

America's and Americans' sovereignty depends upon a united, sustainable, and flourishing America. Instead, we are a nation of divided citizens. We are trapped in a left-brained society that cannot save itself with the same old thinking that leads to conflict, wars, and world-wide, left-brained economic and technology disasters. We have a top 1% elite, our "royalty,' class that owned (in 2007, on the cusp of the current Recession) 34.6% of privately held wealth and paid less taxes. Overall, the top 20% owned 80%, leaving just 15% of the wealth for the bottom 80%.[348] Federal/State tax laws, in 1984 under Ronald Reagan's reign, allowed "dynasty trusts" to perpetuate America's aristocracy.

Five of the top hedge funds chiefs who pocketed huge sums in 2011 are: Ray Dalio, Bridgewater Associates – $3.9 billion; Carl C. Icahn – $2.5 billion; James Simons, Renaissance Fund – $2.1 billion and two of his co-chiefs pocketed top dollars; Kenneth C. Griffin, Citadel, – $700 million; and Steven A. Cohen, SAC Capital Advisors – $585 million.[61] "Elites not masses govern America,"[86] not "We the People."

Left-brained thinking in America is akin to the divine nature of authority that keeps dictators empowered in the Middle East. All uprisings must be crushed, just as the right-brain's emotions and virtues are dismissed as the glorification of feelings at the expense of cognitive thought. As Albert Einstein (1879-1955) said, "The world we have made, as a result of the thinking we have done thus far, creates problems we cannot solve at the same level of thinking at which we created them." It will take a broader form of thinking and doing for America and Americans to flourish: whole-brained, innovative thinkers who are responsible for self and to others, instead of narrow-minded thinking of left-brainers, right-brainers, or no-brainers.

Each human being has instincts to learn and grow and talents to be identified and developed, but the human brain needs novelty and relevant content to be stimulated, not draconian teaching-learning methods geared to the left-brain while fear, shame, and/or anger are directed at the vulnerable right-brain. Our K-12 public schools have failed many students and America, yet students and teachers are blamed, not the status quo's antiquated public school system. Without an educated right-brain, our vulnerable emotions are exposed to – often subliminally – seductive and fear-inducing advertising by food manufacturers and pharmaceuticals. When we acknowledge the choices we have by using both sides of our brains, we are more in charge of our decisions and actions. Wisdom requires authentic knowledge and authentic individuals. The key to America's future is the wisdom of its citizenry for, as George Bernard Shaw said, "Democracy is a device that ensures we shall be governed no better than we deserve."

Our Founding Fathers believed America would flourish if everyone was educated and if they substituted the tyranny of a pure democracy's majority rule for a constitutional republic of a democratic nature. Instead, left-brained K-12 public education works for half our citizenry; the other half is experiencing the tyranny of our democratic republic's rigidly left-brained representatives. Our Founders also feared the tyranny of central authority if they opted for a nationwide K-12 public school system, but individual States have proved to be financially punishing toward poor public schools. Today, it seems, some of our elected representatives are no better educated than the citizens who elect them; nor do they have the vision or wisdom to perpetuate our Founding Fathers' 1776 legacy.

The evidence for whole-brain thinking, doing, and being is in plain sight. In addition to Drs. Prescott and McGilchrist, Cosmologist Carl Sagan wrote: "The coordinated functioning of both cerebral hemispheres is the tool Nature has provided...We are unlikely to survive if we do not make full and creative use of our human intelligence."[294] John Sarno, M.D. wrote: "It is not generally realized that...an intellectual genius may be an emotional baby or a monster."[297] Editor/writer Jonah Lehrer concluded, it is the "lack of emotional management that brings incivility to our homes and streets and a lack of caring in our interactions with others."[295] Differences and "disagreements can only be solved by entering a domain of co-inspiration, in which things are done together because the participants want to do them"[221] for the greater good of all. The Western Intellectual Tradition's status quo is not justifiable in the 21st century.

Historically, ingenious human beings have given themselves authority and power to attract followers to gain control over the uneducated masses by depicting God as fallible with negative emotions of revenge, hatred, wrath, pride, and vanity, not the God of Truth that Jesus Christ represented, the God of mercy, forgiveness, love, and peace.[146] Today's ingenious human beings have the gold to attract followers and to gain control of and power over others. They are fallible, too, and an educated population will frustrate and defeat them when we unlock our mind-ford'd manacles and opt for the truthful, nonviolent, human dignity way toward love and peace.

Heresy

Culture is defined informally as "the way things are done around here," the status quo represents the preservation of the existing state of affairs in our society. Heretics are those church members who have beliefs opposed to church dogma. The Roman Catholic Church employed heresy to keep people in line, killed, or burned heretics at the stake and to destroy historical records that conflicted with their dogma. Heresy may be defined as

1) the rejection of a belief that is a part of church dogma;
2) any opinion (in philosophy, politics, etc.) opposed to official or established views or doctrines;
   the holding of any such belief or opinion.

Traditionally, heresy was invoked when voiced/written opinions or acts were at variance with the establishment's ways of thinking, being, and doing to punish the perpetrators. However, today, heresy, in the form of character assassination, "socialism" labels, and alleged "death panels" in health insurance for the elderly, is used by those who are bankrolled by entrenched businesses and financiers. Without health insurance, we have Death Sentences, and we have bankruptcy. Wealthy financiers and insurance, banking, oil, agribusinesses, and pharmaceutical corporations have the money to re-elect some politicians, to ostracize other politicians, and to buy gullible voters' votes through SuperPac advertising money to vote against their own interests because of their belief systems. Universal health care is a given in other modern nations, and in Germany since 1880.

When men made the rules thousands of years ago, they defined, consolidated, and perpetuated their philosophical and ideological power without a vision of the future which was beyond their imagination as they laid claim to the present. Enough women and men have already been burned at the stake for heresy and witchcraft by religious beliefs without changing societies for the betterment of humankind.

As Nature's wisdom intended, when both our brains are educated and cooperate toward being whole-brain, integrative thinkers and doers, we may experience more of Heaven than Hell on Earth The labels won't disable us when we have truth, peace, and love on our side.

Resistance to Change

Resistance to acknowledging that within each human being there are both hard and soft hemispheres, or so-called masculine and feminine sides, is expected in a somewhat hypermasculine, homophobic culture. There is evidence that both men and women have been culturally conditioned at pre-verbal stages to believe that hierarchies are natural in favor of white men. There is also evidence in our culture that ignorance is the new norm. To perceive intellect as "a form of distinction that defies egalitarianism."[341] is the antithesis of the American tradition that education is the path to upward mobility. Using labels, intellectual or elite imply liberal, to influence or appeal to others' baser human instincts and emotions to join him or her in attempts to assassinate an individual's or a politician's character, are the earmarks of bullies and cowards who have unresolved personal and emotional issues, not political sensibilities.

America's public educational hierarchy is resistant to change, as demonstrated years ago when educational organizations objected to changing to the universal metric system. Canada changed, not the U.S.A. There is also resistance in a left-brained society to teaching courses that cannot be measured, for our K-12 public school's emphasis upon competition requires winners and losers. "Whether on the field, in a classroom or at work, rivalry changes more than our body chemistry...it also sways our minds, changing how we think and believe during competition...also can disrupt rational thinking, bias memories, and encourage unethical behavior."[166]

The powerful teachers' unions are resistant to ridding the schools of nonperforming, tenured teachers and of rules that limit teachers' access to students on school property. The lack of standard performance evaluations is unions' rationale for not policing themselves. Tenure also means that innovative young teachers are subject to unions' last hired, first fired syndrome. K-12 teachers' right to a paying job for life without keeping current and reinventing themselves amounts to ruining children's motivation to learn when complacent and unimaginative teachers are boring and students are bored. Some teachers are addicted to drugs, alcohol or food and are often "protected" by fellow teachers. Poor teachers are a blight on developing children's curiosity, imagination, and their right to a positive role model for learning and emulating. Children learn best from those they love, respect, and admire.

Albert Einstein believed, "Imagination is more important than knowledge." For knowledge is limited to all we now know and understand, while imagination embraces the entire world, and all there ever will be to know and understand. Historically, imagination was assumed to be separate and different from other kinds of thinking. "Until we understand the set of mental events that give rise to new thoughts, we will never understand what makes us so special"[204] and how we imagine. It's a matter of educating both the left- and right hemispheres so they may collaborate, "making sense of the whole, seeing not just the parts but how they hang together."[204] That's the freedom to learn!

Evidently, the resistance to change in academia is rampant and is not confined to K-12 public education. Lee Smolin in his *The Trouble with Physics* writes, "How Do You Fight Sociology?" It boils down to "Who has power over whom, and how is that power exercised? The sociology of science...refers to the influence that older, established scientists have over the careers of younger scientists."[313] Smolin avers, "Universities stopped growing in the early 1970s, yet the professors hired in previous eras have continued to train graduate students... Despite the fact that quantum physics superseded Newtonian mechanics eighty years ago, most colleges and universities in North

America still postpone quantum mechanics until the third year of study."[313]

Human development courses that teach whole people how to live with themselves, others, and differences are judged to be "touchy-feely" by those left-brainers who are strangers to themselves, their minds and bodies, and most do not question why they feel uncomfortable with intimacy and more comfortable with machoism. Many educators do not differentiate between the love of humanity, lust, and romantic love and/or confuse entrenched beliefs with critical thinking. Their inauthenticity becomes apparent even to their young students. Yet, K-12 public schools' administrators and unions encourage teachers to get master's degrees in their subject, not in human development, when combining both may lead to a boon for their students and Teacher of the Year awards.

In an age of personal expressiveness that is way beyond satire, civility is missing. Today's human behaviors border on blasphemy and perpetuate untruths. There is no personal accountability or morals and ethics either. It's the epitome of a myopic left-brain with unexamined beliefs and direct access to the expression of anger – or of an uneducated or misused right brain – to vent its rage for not getting what it wants or for getting the visibility it wants. All are similar to the learned bad behavior of a two-year-old who has an immature prefrontal cortex and permissive parents who want to be loved more than instilling self-esteem with limits in their child. The left hemisphere is subject to paranoia, and a left-brainer's resistance to change is just another word for maintaining the status quo where winning at all costs is part of the money, status, and power game of life.

Psychiatrist Iain McGilchrist suggests that damaged [or unused] right-brains manifest a range of clinical problems similar to schizophrenia. He states,"If this is what happens in individuals, could a culture dominated by the left hemisphere modes of apprehension begin to exhibit such features?"[225] "Contrary to popular misunderstanding, the term 'schizophrenia' does not refer to the multiple personality syndrome [or Jung's "when the dream becomes real"], the Greek etymology of the word actually means 'broken soul' or 'broken heart.'"[321] For a fully functioning right-brain, "it is the left hand, the servant of the right hemisphere, that contains the ever-living striving for truth."[225]

Americans' rights to knowingly speak untruths, use propaganda, and promote character assassination are forms of injustice to truth and a laser beam for like-minded ideologists who gravitate to those whose dislike of the unlike unites them.

Back to The Center?

Smart and Wise: A Transformation is an invitation to explore the making of our Western hemisphere's civilization and our own hemispheres' historical conditioning from thousands of years of records of domination by one of our two hemispheres of the brain: the left! We have come a long way from when the majority of Western society's people could barely sign their name. The nation we inhabit today, though, requires whole-brain K-12 public education to make a course correction toward humanity's higher nature and away from humanity's baser nature.

New thinking, learning, and behavior reshape our brain's anatomy and that means we can become smart and wise by reshaping the fact that currently "All of the humanities, social sciences, and physical sciences, insofar as they deal with human nature, are [negatively] affected, as are all forms of training."[75] The left-brain's rhetoric of power, wealth, and status does not work in personal, professional, national, and international relationships or in working with our new enemies since our post-9/11/01 wars in the Muslim world. Wisdom honors what it means to be fully human with enlightened levels of consciousness with respect for fellow human beings, both friends and foes.

All of us are part of Nature and part of the mystery that demands a spiritual engagement to find our reason to be, or meaning, on Earth that is larger than self. We can be the change that results in societal changes that are aligned with the spirit of democracy: "seek the benefits of the many rather than the comfort of the few."[139] Clinging to the status quo or our horse-driven past does not acknowledge that the past is a guidepost not a hitching post.

In America's past, many formally and informally left-brain educated people also mastered the invisible curriculum, or the right-brain attributes, through self-education, life experiences, family, organized religion, and social causes to become whole-brained. To truly educate Americans, the missing right-brain's attributes would be included in academic curricula. Otherwise, we will continue to be a nation being influenced by talking heads who behave more like "pimps" who control the money and control and use others as "ho's"[39] to actualize their dreams of status, money, and power with no consideration of the ho's dreams.

Our left-brain dominant Western society has created Heaven and Hell here on Earth. Fear, arrogance, and power over others nourish Hell on Earth. Love, respect, and power shared with others nourish Heaven on Earth. Each of us has experienced both at some points in our lives. Many of us have accessed and mastered the invisible curriculum. The invisible curriculum includes the talents and gifts we were born with that are unique to us that reside in the right hemisphere but need the left-hemisphere to make them visible. Until the right-brain's talents are integrated with the left's. we have the personal power, whether or not we know it or own it, to trust our innate wisdom and our hunches or intuition and to enlist our right-brain to complement our left-brain in exercising emotions and wisdom for ourselves and others.

The speakers at the Memorial at the University of Arizona in Tucson, on January 12, 2011, for those harmed and those killed by Jared Loughans on January 8th were not only emotionally but morally-oriented. President Barack Obama's 2011 eulogy was personal and universal, reminding us that:

> Scripture tells us that there is evil in the world and that terrible things happen for reasons that defy human understanding... and we have to guard against simple explanations... We should be willing to challenge old assumptions in order to lessen the prospects of violence in the future... But what we can't do is use this tragedy as one more occasion to turn on one another... sudden loss causes us to look backward, but it also forces us to look forward, to reflect on the present and the future, on the manner in which we live our lives and nurture our relationships with those who are still with us. We may ask ourselves if we've shown enough kindness and generosity and compassion to the people in our lives... We recognize our own mortality, and we are reminded that in the fleeting time we have on

this Earth, what matters is not wealth, or status, or power, or fame but rather, how well we have loved, and what small part we have played in making the lives of other people better.[243]

A nine-year-old girl, Christina Taylor Greene, born 9/11/01, was one of the six killed in Arizona on January 8, 2011 by Jared Loughans. She was a student council member at her public school and was interested in politics. She saw public service as something exciting and hopeful. President Obama continued, she "was off to meet her congresswoman [Gabrielle Giffords], someone she was sure was good and important and might be a role model. She was all this through the eyes of a child, undimmed by the cynicism or vitriol that we adults all too often just take for granted. I want to live up to her expectations. I want our democracy to be as good as Christine imagined it. I want America to be as good as she imagined it. All of us, we should do everything we can to make sure this country lives up to our children's expectations."[243]

We reap what we sow.

Chapter Four

> *But strange that I was not told*
> *That the brain can hold*
> *In a tiny ivory cell*
> *God's heaven or hell.*
> —Oscar Wilde (1854-1900)

Whole-Brained K-12 Public Education: Thinking Purple

In 19th century London, Irish poet Oscar Wilde thought it strange that he wasn't told that Heaven or Hell existed within human brain cells. Who teaches us that we have choices, within our brain-mind, between hellish or heavenly lives right here on Earth? The Western Intellectual Tradition's K-12 public schools do not teach us that. They program us with the ABCs and 123s to be regurgitated on tests to label us, not inspire and empower us to think outside "mind-forg'd manacles" or to believe our destiny lies not only in our hands but in our positive-thinking brain-minds.

Australian Rhonda Byrne's books, *The Secret* and *The Power*, are based on the "law of attraction: whatever you experience in life is a direct result of your thoughts" and have sold millions of copies. Cognitive psychologists Chabris and Simons[53] ridiculed Byrne (and Oprah Winfrey for plugging both books on her show) for her "pseudoscientific concept" and "absurd physics behind the law of attraction" as "a sort of intellectual virus" and branded the books with the psychological label, "illusory correlation."[53] They reportedly spent time and energy on negatively training their students to resist/attack/label Byrne's clinical psychology fallacies. A more positive psychology approach would have been to acknowledge her books' contribution to humans' apparent innate need to think/feel/believe they have some power and control over their lives.

The Chabris-Simons critique of Byrne's books attracted my attention although I was not as invested in her writings as I would have been had they similarly critiqued, say, Arntz's *What the Bleep Do We Know* and the movie.[12] "Why," I questioned myself, "is their overkill of Byrne and the so-called law of attraction relevant to this chapter on smart and wise?" After all, Norman Vincent Peale's *The Power of Positive Thinking* sold millions of copies too. That book was based on thinking the kind of thoughts that lead to fuller lives and satisfying success and on the faith-based "formula 1) PRAYERIZE, 2) PICTURIZE, 3) ACTUALIZE."[259] I hypothesized that they perceived Byrne's foray into their cognitive turf as a) competition, b) "unapproved" status quo knowledge, or c) a threat to their cognitive psychology profession's "approved" knowledge and their reputations. Then I realized that threats evoke the fight or flight response. Therefore, c) may be interpreted as a metaphor for The Western Intellectual Tradition's ongoing resistance to formally educating the right-brain as the equal partner of the left-brain's cognition in diverse academic educational fields.

Metaphors are the right-brain's forte. With implied comparisons, they allow us to see beyond all aspects of ourselves and our world that transcend the man-made Newtonian mechanistic perspective of the status quo's approved knowledge, rules, separate disciplines, and control issues, for starters. An illusion is a distortion of the senses or a misinterpretation of a stimulus. Physical and ego threats, real or imagined, are felt in the body as fear and give rise to stressful thoughts in the mind. Stressful thoughts in the mind evoke a flood of hormones in the body to prepare it for a fight or flight response. The fight-flight response means the blood vessels to the digestive tract are constricted and ongoing growth processes are inhibited to nourish the tissues of the arms and legs to fight or flee. Thus, the stress hormones prepare the body for the self-protection mode at the expense of ongoing maintenance and cellular growth of the entire organism.

The cost to the mind of the body's fight-flight mode? The left-brain processes are repressed with reduced access to cognitive intelligence. That's the emotional illiteracy process some students endure when fear of failure or judgment overwhelms their academic intelligence. Prolonged protection stances may not only affect the quality but quantity of life on the human level and of the possible irrelevance of some disciplines at the educational level. Reaffirming a religion's dogma or defending a discipline's parameters by assassinating heretics' or dissidents' character or excluding them from membership is not confined to the Roman Church when the fear of change reigns in America's left-brained institutions, especially academia, and organizations, especially the disease-oriented medical profession.

The traditional medical profession thinks it is under siege when people spend as much money on alternative medicine as they do on allopathic medicine, so they engage their "big guns" in an attempt to further limit the public's access to vitamins or supplements, such as iodine and borax for example, and holistic practices. Prevention is a political and moral issue when people's health is perceived as competition for business. Similarly, it seems other disciplined fields are threatened when "outside the box" or new ideas may afflict those who could be disempowered by changes in the status quo. When the fight syndrome engages protecting one's discipline from "intellectual viruses," which may be a pseudonym for "ideas that are inconsistent with what is already known,"[48] then there's less time and energy to spend on reinvigorating and growing one's discipline. Smart versus wise!

Bruce Lipton writes, "The simple truth is, when you're frightened you're dumber...Fear Kills."[208] The international terrorists' attacks on 9/11/01 were experienced by New Yorkers and the nation as a threat to survival. People "shifted from a state of growth to a state of protection. After a few days of this heart-stopping fear, the country's economic vitality was so compromised that the president had to intervene."[208] President George W. Bush advised the nation, "America is open for business: go shopping!" Lipton advised the nation, "we should look more carefully at how our fear of future acts of terrorism is undermining our quality of life... the terrorists have already won since they have succeeded in frightening us into a chronic, soul-sapping protective mode."[208] He also reiterated President Franklin D. Roosevelt's words when our nation was in the midst of the Great Depression and World War II was looming: "We have nothing to fear, but fear itself." It's harder to let go of our fears when we don't understand how the brain-mind works and "authorities" use it to control people's thinking and behavior.

In *The Invisible Gorilla* by Psychologists Christopher Chabris and Daniel Simons, they teach us to not be so sure of or have faith in our thinking processes, that our illusions lead to infallible minds that mislead or trick us into confidently thinking that we see, know, and intuit more than we actually do. They pinpoint what is going on in half the brain, the cognitive mind, that may not have input from the right-brain's intelligence. What is invisible in our society is the missing right-brain's curriculum that complements the left-brain's cognition, which is sad, not humorous. In *Thinking, Fast and Slow*, Dr. Kahneman demonstrated that Wall Street traders' auras and confidence are boosted by perceptions of their abilities when, in fact, their decisions were scientifically proven by him to be no better than a roll of the dice.[172]

Optimism, according to Mayo Clinic, is the belief that good things will happen to you and that negative events are temporary setbacks to be overcome. It's not about positive thinking so much as being motivated to pursue a healthy lifestyle, to cultivate healthy relationships, to seek rewarding careers where money is not the sole name of the game of work, and to keep reinventing oneself by integrating education and experience with lifestyle.

If it's an illusion to think there's a relationship, a connection, a correlation, or causation between what we think/feel and what we experience, then, for the illusionists, there's no such thing as the self-fulfilling prophecy, stage fright doesn't cause poor or no performance, and there's no correlation between reliving, I'm in a life-or-death situation AGAIN! and PTSD (post-traumatic stress disorder). The illusion is rigid thinking where results must be immediately visible. But, thinking is an invisible process. It is not confined to the left-brain's worldview that thinks it is in charge of its thinking and is not responsible for outcomes of its overall thinking. The fast-acting unconscious mind often overrides the slow-thinking conscious mind!

We are not taught that the unconscious mind's data and mental processes "are inaccessible to consciousness…[yet] influence judgments, feelings, or behavior."[346] Thus, embedded but out-of-awareness emotional, experiential, and cognitive information are data in our unconscious mind that initiate a response without the conscious mind's knowledge and is a what that we experience in the now or portends an event likely to occur in the future, from a self-fulfilling prophecy to a health or career outcome. In addition, a negative- or a positive-focused conscious thought or a belief with accompanying emotional relevance is also likely to result in what we experience in life, for we create our own reality. In essence, the effects of the conscious mind's thoughts, emotions, and beliefs on behavior may or may not be directly perceived by us or correlated with outcomes, for it is in our unconscious mind "where most of the decisions and many of the most impressive acts of thinking take place."[33]

What we experience in life is directly influenced by how we react (positively or negatively) to what we experience beyond our individual control, such as war, terrorism, earthquakes, hurricanes, tornadoes, a national or international economic recession, or a traffic delay. "Illusory correlation" is thinking and believing that our left-brain's conscious mind is in charge when our unconscious mind, with its storehouse of embedded data that connect the dots between now and early life experiences, beliefs and prejudices, may be in charge of and running our lives.

The Western Intellectual Tradition's age-old, man-made split between the head and the body is revived when thinking is perceived to be disembodied and the body's feelings are discounted as stimulus and partner in the thinking process. "As neuroscientists such as Candace Pert [*Molecules of Emotions*] have told us, thinking is not done solely by the brain, an organ housed in the cranium. Thinking is done by the mind, which is not an organ but a process that is distributed throughout the body and draws on every faculty we have."[254]

Brain structures are contained in the skull and are part of the body. While each hemisphere complements the other with different abilities, it appears that "experience has to occur in something that is greater than the body and its sensations, its sensory mechanisms, and that is mind itself. It is because of mind that one is aware of what is going on within the sensations."[144] The word mind derives from the Greek word menos or spirit force. Psychiatrist David Hawkins informs us that human beings manifest [in their bodies and lives] what thoughts, beliefs, and experiences are in their minds, especially in the unconscious mind.

The human mind, though, draws upon the quality of its brain structures' functioning and stored and incoming data from the whole body to do its thinking.

The brain's two hemispheres are asymmetrical (normally, the left side of the body is controlled by the right-brain; the right side of the body is controlled by the left-brain). The hemispheres are separated by and connected to each other by the corpus callosum, known as "the Bridge." Our ancient ancestors did not know the human head was divided into two separate brains and that people are asymmetrical. In fact, it was not until the mid-19th century that the we learned that the head houses two different brains with functional asymmetry. The ancients valued the right hand, which is borne out by language. The word left in French is gauche, which means crooked; warped; lacking grace, especially social grace. The Latin for left is *sinistre*, meaning left-hand or unlucky. We use sinister in English to mean evil or misfortune. There used to be a built-in societal stigma against left-handedness. Today, while being ambidextrous is valued, whole-brainism is not – yet!

The human brain, with an estimated one trillion cells is an electrical conductor of one hundred billion neurons or nerve cells with about one hundred trillion connections in the brain to the heart and to our inner and outer worlds as thoughts, sensations, signals, movements, behaviors, and actions are translated into electrical pulses and energy. Thus, thoughts are energy and energy follows thought. "Neurons make up only 15 percent of our brain cells. Glial cells make up the rest... Glial cells interact with neurons, control them, work alongside them... and play a central role in learning... Most neurological and some psychological disorders involve glia."[9] "The speed of electromagnetic energy signals is 186,000 miles per second...while the speed of a diffusible chemical is considerably less than 1 centimeter per second. Energy signals are 100 times more efficient and infinitely faster that physical chemical [hormones] signals."[208]

Quantum physics researchers of recent decades reveal that "'invisible forces' of the electromagnetic spectrum profoundly impact every facet of biological regulation."[208] We are more than a collection of tissues and organs that are treated by K-12 public educational systems as clean slates or by traditional medicine from a biochemical, pharmaceutical perspective. The heart, brain, nervous system, muscles, and immune system are "prime examples of electrical subsystems operating within your 'bioelectrical' body...We all live and function electrically on an electric planet."[244] "A human being is a complex organization of electrical fields. The body is about 70 percent water with a high mineral content making it highly electrically conductive. The human body has some 60 trillion cells...cells know when to divide by vibrating. Although Western medicine has been focused on chemistry for the past century, electricity is what drives our biology."[133]

There is evidence that the physical structure of the brain changes based on an individual's life experiences.[299] In the brain, new "connections are formed between neurons based on life experiences... [and] new neurons may be formed and existing neurons may be discarded based on the nature of life experiences."[299] Conditioning is the result of unconscious learned behaviors, beliefs, and attitudes, such as innate gender/brain preferences, familial values, and cultural mores. Human beings' conditioning becomes unconscious knowledge. "Such unconscious knowledge constitutes the primary source of learning and behavior, not only in animals but also in human beings."[299] Human beings also have a rich template of hardwired genetics and instincts; however, "life experiences and environmental influences may alter the degree to which the expression of those genes occurs"[299] and whether instincts are honored.

Due to past decades' scientific discoveries and technologies, we can observe the human brain at work when it makes connections among its three brain structures: 1. hindbrain (reptillian or brain stem), 2. midbrain (limbic systems' amygdala, thalamus, hippocampus, hypothalamus), and 3. forebrain (neocortex: left-brain's cognitive cortex, the right-brain's emotional cortex, and the right and left lobes of the prefrontal cortex. The three brains, actually four with the prefrontal lobes' maturation, operate as interconnected biologic systems. However, each has its unique architecture, subjective intelligence, memory, and hindsight, insight, or foresight, respectively.

Even with functional magnetic resonance imaging (fMRI), "One cannot assume that the areas that light up are those fundamentally responsible for the 'function' being imaged, or that areas that do not light up are not involved."[225] What is not currently observable with technology is the mind at work when the powers of the conscious and unconscious minds, including the heart, gut, and body are harnessed and processed to arrive at states of consciousness.

The unconscious mind processes about 20 million environmental stimuli per second, whereas about 40 environmental stimuli are interpreted by the conscious mind in the same second.[208] A later estimate in *Strangers to Ourselves*[346] is 11 million environmental stimuli per second for the unconscious mind and the same 40 for the conscious mind. "What happens to the other 10,999,960?" Wilson asked.[346] Much of it resides in our unconscious mind which may retrieve the information beyond our conscious awareness or may be brought to consciousness through hypnosis. My psychology professor in college was also a hypnotherapist. In the U.S. Army, his job had been to hypnotize soldiers, after they reported on their conscious search for land mines, to ascertain where the rest of the mines were hidden.

"Consciousness takes time, but it arrives after the work is done."[116] Neuroscientists have found that there are time lapses between the stimulation of one's hand and of being conscious of the sensation. That is just one of the many examples where the unconscious mind operates faster than the conscious mind. Then the conscious mind makes up stories to justify what was said or done. A simplified definition of consciousness belies the complexity of what goes on behind the scene to produce awareness: "Consciousness is nothing more than integrated information."[332]

Our conscious mind is the one we know and live with; the one that can conjure up positive or negative thoughts which may be changed by our unconscious mind. "If the desires of the conscious mind conflict with the programs of the subconscious [unconscious] mind, which 'mind' do you think will win out? You can repeat the positive affirmations that you are lovable over and over or that your cancer tumor will shrink. But, if as a child, you heard over and over that you are worthless and sickly, those messages programmed in your subconscious [unconscious] mind will undermine your best efforts to change your life."[208]

The unconscious mind is "an emotional and an enchanted place"[33] and flourishes "when the affections and aversions that guide us every day have been properly nurtured, the emotions properly educated."[33]

The unconscious mind is the storehouse of stimulus-response tapes of genetic inheritances, instincts, in utero, after birth lived experiences, and learned information, beliefs, and biases. As we now know, the unconscious mind's neurological processing capacity is "millions of times more powerful than the conscious mind."[208]

Brain research proposes that the lack of interaction between an individual's left- and right-brains and the conscious mind's lack of access to the unconscious mind lead to duality within all human beings, including in children. Dr. Sarno writes: "Those traits that reside in the unconscious that we consider the most troublesome, like childishness, dependency, or the capacity for savage behavior, are the products of an old, primitive part of the brain, anatomically deep, just above the brain stem. Evolution has added what is called the neocortex, the new brain, the brain of reason, higher intelligence, communication, and morality. There appears to be an ongoing struggle between these two parts of the brain. Sometimes reason prevails, and at other times the more childish, bestial part of human nature is dominant."[297]

Candace Pert teaches that the emotions unite the mind and the body. "All honest emotions are positive emotions."[263] "To suppress these emotions and not let them flow freely is to set up dis-integrity in the system, causing it to act at cross-purposes rather than as a unified whole. The stress this creates, which takes the form of blockages and insufficient flow of peptide signals to maintain functions at the cellular level, is what sets up the weakened conditions that can lead to disease."[263]

In 1933, Austria's Sigmund Freud, the father of psychoanalysis, named the three-part self: the id, ego, and superego with different personalities. It was Yale Neuroscientist Paul MacLean who described the three-part brain with different mentalities as the reptile brain, the limbic system, and the neocortex.[213] But it was Harvard Neuroscientist Jill Bolte Taylor who experienced and documented her left-brain stroke and her right-brain's intelligence and thinking mode in *My Stroke of Insight*.[325]

Dr. Taylor's documented, live account of her left-brain stroke went far beyond an fMRI's light show that pinpoints where things are happening or not happening, not what is going on. She experienced what was happening to her, almost moment-to-moment, and how her right-brain's ingenuity saved her life. Thanks to Dr. Taylor's inside-her-own-brain reporting, she gave voice to her nonverbal right-brain's ability to be in charge when her left-brain broke down. Her recalled observations have increased our understanding of how the brains operate independently and interdependently.

While Dr. Taylor's stroke was in progress, she actually experienced what it was like to alternate between two opposing brains' realities and then how it felt to cope with a voiceless right-brain only until she healed her left-brain years later. With access to her right-brain only, she could not talk or read; but she could think. Home alone, getting ready for work, and knowing she was having a left-brain stroke, she realized her lab's telephone number was programmed into her telephone and inaccessible to her right-brain. She could not recall the number, but, with concentration, the digits finally appeared in her mind's eye; she made left-hand squiggles with a pen of the images and matched them with the images on her phone pad. Her colleague answered; both sounded like Golden Retrievers to her. She intuited from the tone of his voice that he would help her.

During the time of her worsening stroke, Dr. Taylor experienced the decline in her left hemispheres' ability to overrule her right-brain. She discovered that the right-brain's feelings of peace and well-being are within our power to access when our left-brain's chatter and control issues are overruled. The human brain remains, "The most special thing in the universe."[158] Yet, many of us take our brain for granted by not educating it, ignoring its nutritional needs, or overwhelming it with negative thoughts and substances, so we may fail to own the power, love, and wonder of being fully human with access to our full intelligences.

Dr. Taylor's book is about the wonder of being human. Socrates, 469-399 BC, said, "Wisdom begins in wonder." Many of us wonder what happened when we are not aware of why we think, feel, and behave the way we do or understand what we experience. Both wonder and wisdom are missing in our institutions. Now we know that being wise or having wisdom requires neural activity that is more right-brain-oriented than left-brain-dominated.

Up until the 1960s, we were taught that human beings' brains were developed fully by early adulthood and each person received "x" number of brain cells; it was downhill thereafter. In Norman Doidge's book, *The Brain That Changes Itself*, he cites research that the human brain changes itself in response to its thoughts, feelings, and activities.[75] With the discovery of the plasticity of the human brain, science reveals that the brain regenerates itself, is able to respond to injury with amazing rewiring, and to even think itself into a new configuration. The plasticity of the human brain means our brains can change and grow new neurons ornerve cells until we die of old age. Neuronal stem cells divide and differentiate to become neurons or glial cells and that neurogenesis processes continue throughout life.

Neuroplasticity is not engaged through normal day-to-day activities; neuroplasticity is both positive and negative. "If you don't use it, you lose it!" applies to the brain as well as to other muscles. For positive neuroplasticity to occur, optimal stimuli must be present, and our hearts must be engaged in any brain fitness plan. Initial changes are temporary and must be reinforced, for "Neurons that fire together wire together!" creating habits. When we exercise our conscious mind's ability to overcome habits or addictions, for example, we find that "Neurons that fire apart wire apart" or "Neurons out of sync fail to link."[75] We have the power to change our brains for the better, but motivation and effort are keys in utilizing the brain's plasticity.

Prolonged plasticity of the developing brain until human beings' mid-20s or later represents a learning curve era – before the prefrontal lobes fully mature, not mental retardation. It appears that Nature has wisdom in prolonging the maturation process: if we get set in our ways of thinking too soon, we may end up dumber. "Troublesome traits and haste don't really characterize adolescence. They're just what we notice most because they annoy us or put our children in danger."[74] During human brain development, children get better at balancing impulses and self-interest with rules, ethics, and possibly altruism, but the process entails selfishness, idiocy, and taking reckless chances. Nevertheless, their openness to the new, new people, and the love of novelty actually prepares them to leave a safe home, explore unfamiliar territory, and establish new networks. That's the time when K-12 public education could make a difference in students' destinies.

Now that we know that the brain is capable of changing itself, we also know how vulnerable it is to negative programming by others' ambitions and manipulations and by its owners' undereducating both sides of their brains, resulting in lower levels of consciousness. Since "the human brain is as a lump of wet clay not only in infancy, as scientists have long known, but well into hoary old age,"[354] our curiosity and questions may be satisfied through lifelong learning.

Newfound evidence points to the fact that much of what we do results from unconscious brain processing and that our conscious mind justifies what we do by making up stories, or confabulations, to support a rationale for our decisions.[267] With the plasticity of the human brain, negatives may be consciously resolved and managed. The plasticity of the human brain means each of us has the brainpower to re-educate a divided, unbalanced brain to heal itself to be an agent of wholeness, goodness, and wisdom: the antithesis of The Western Intellectual Tradition but the essence of humane human development.

Like fingerprints, all human brains are slightly different with unique configurations; each solves problems differently, and brain scans do not provide evidence that a person is functioning normally or not. The education of whole brains from "a more complete scientific understanding of the nature of life, of brain/mind…of the magnificence of being human…to feel our own worth and the worth of others…We are people, not brains."[116] The process begins with demystifying the brain and acknowledging that "all of life's experiences, personal and social, impact our emergent mental system. These experiences are powerful forces modulating the end. They not only constrain our brains but also reveal that it is the interaction of the two layers of brain and mind that provides our conscious reality, our moment in real time."[116]

We have the power to change our DNA for the better through our thoughts, feelings, and actions. We have come a long way in understanding the human brain, but the knowledge is not translated into parenting or K-12 public school classes for growing humanly and humanely developed people. New teaching and learning styles, curriculum content, and new approaches to testing are needed to counter school failure and dropout rates and to also improve even America's best students currently being graduated from our best public high schools.

The story of how we became who we are and think today – head smart or heart wise or both – is accessible to us through knowledge of human history, the unconscious data stored in the brain – which may be triggered through memory or crises – and knowledge of the waters in which we swam. "If we change our heads about who we are – and can see ourselves as creative, eternal beings creating physical experiences, joined at that level of existence we call consciousness – then we start to see and create this world that we live in quite differently."[230] It's a matter of thinking differently, revising our stories, to produce a different future for ourselves and America.

According to Richard Bergland, "The mechanisms that drive thought are found all over the body and, wherever they live, they function at the highest level."[21] It behooves The Western Intellectual Tradition, our K-12 public schools, colleges, and universities, to counter the current political climate that discourages applying what is already known for decades about brain differences and acknowledging the right-brain's superior role to the left-brain's in wisdom and creative processes. One reason for teaching-learning processes that include the right-brain is Dr. Bergland's assessment that the right-brain's "pattern recognition is the highest form of thought."[21] As Nature's wisdom intended, when both our brains are educated and cooperate to be whole-brain thinkers and doers, we may experience more of Heaven than Hell on Earth.

Whether we experience living in Heaven or in Hell on Earth, families and academia's curricula "have largely neglected this central, if profoundly difficult task of learning to love, which is also the task of learning to live in true peace and harmony with others and with nature."[254] Just as the wise Native American Elder chose to feed the wolf of love, not hate, we too may choose, from a whole-brain perspective, to think and live a more loving, meaningful, purposeful, and flourishing life with a keen sense of interconnectedness with all life and grounded in Nature on a sustainable, flourishing Earth.

The importance of human, humane, and inhumane development begins before a child is conceived. *Making Babies: Stumbling Into Motherhood* by Anne Enright [94] is not to be stumbled into for the parents' genetic inheritances and physical conditions, psychological resilience, environmental circumstances, and exposure to toxins are factors that will determine an infant's potential mental and physical health. Now we know that the quality of the 9-month gestation period and the quality of nurturing for the first three years set the stage for developing a healthy child or a problem child.

"Psychologists now believe fledgling psychopaths can be identified as early as kindergarten. The hope is to teach kids empathy before it's too late."[171] There are so many variables involved in a developing fetus, including an expectant mother's peaceful or hostile environment, and in rearing a child that positive outcomes cannot be predicted when left to chance. However, education of the right-brain's emotions and virtues, including empathy, may address the "Stumbling Into Motherhood" syndrome that is prevalent, not rare, when the downside of pregnancy offsets the pleasure. Fathers or partners are not exempt from their role to love the expectant mother, especially during the pregnancy, making sure she is safe and not exposed to unnecessary marital or familial stressors that cause toxic chemicals to flood her body and the fetus, and to love and share the raising of the child with her.

Educating the right-brain alongside the left-brain early on in the nation's K-12 public schools would address current assumptions that children come to school with clean disks, ready to record verbatim. Each student has an embedded story that helps or hinders his or her human development and readiness to learn. It would also address children who may be impulsive, ADHD, autistic, or have delayed maturity and those who appear to lack humanity, display antisocial behavior, or do whatever it takes to get what they think they want to feel better about themselves. There's not a lot of joy and happiness in the problem child and in his or her parents, and administrators and teachers often exacerbate rather than understand or ameliorate their problems. With right-brain education for all, we honor our two brains for endowing us with the opportunity to have a cognitive presence and emotional empathy, for we need both to engage during trying times of our lives, as parents and as teachers, so we may teach by example. We learn from the human development foundational research that precautions may be taken before and after conceiving a child so parents-to-be may responsibly take charge of what they can prevent and what they can foster within themselves to grow healthy children who will thrive in the K-12 public school system.

The Story of Human, Humane, and Inhumane Development

Human fetuses swim in water in a mother's uterus for nine months or so before they are born. Today, many fetuses swim in toxic soup[277] due to environmental pollutants in the air, our food and water supplies, and the Earth's soil. All human babies arrive on planet Earth with inborn individuality. Why are we unique individuals? While most of us have visible similarities: two arms, ten fingers on two hands, two legs, ten toes on two feet, two eyes, two ears, one nose, and a head, every body part is unlike others' body parts. It's not just our fingerprints, voice-prints, footprints, brain-prints, and faces that make us unique, our nervous system is unlike any other. In fact, all human beings are distinctive, even the number and distribution of nerve endings (in the eyes, ears, nose, and mouth), which are the source of accessing data from our outer and inner environments, so the information we gather is unique to each of us.[345]

While we inherit some physical characteristics from our ancestors, we do not come into this world with blank slates. Less acceptable to many Americans is the growing awareness of an intergenerational predisposition to physical and mental health problems as well as gifts by way of genetic memories. Dr. Darold Treffert's study of savants' personalities, minds and abilities (specialized skills) revealed their gifts and the untapped potentialities of human minds. From his considerable experience with savant syndrome, autism, and Asperger's, he has found that "Genetic memory simply adds inherited knowledge and even certain specialized skills to those items than can be transmitted to offspring through a complex mix of genes and chromosomes."[333] Intergenerational traumas and conflicts of ancestors may be perpetuated by ancestors' genes that may impair or inform ensuing generations' intuitive "knowings," emotional literacy, and human development.

From medicine's history, we learn that the nine months in utero used to be considered a factor in a fetus's physical and mental health, until the medical field in England was purged of alleged superstition and old wives' tales. Dr. Robert Scaer's research for his book, *The Trauma Spectrum*, shows there is compelling evidence that "the fetus and newborn infant are sentient beings capable of processing information and learning through conditioning, perception of pain, and capable of interpersonal communication"[299] via their body language, including movement, kicking, then cries, smiles, and eye contact.

In mothers' wombs, all human fetuses grow into a right-brain first that has been dubbed the female brain. So, "every fetal brain looks female – female is nature's default gender setting... A huge testosterone surge beginning in the eighth week in utero will turn this unisex brain [into a] male by killing off some cells in the communication centers and growing more cells in the sex and aggression centers. If the testosterone surge doesn't happen, the female brain continues to grow unperturbed."[27]

Nature is not perfect when an egg is fertilized by a donor's sperm with genetic inheritances, including diseases, and lifestyles that are not perfect and when the expectant mothers' inner and outer environmental variables are not perfect, especially in the presence of stressors that flood the body and fetus with chemicals. Thus, differences from the expected "norm" for males and females may ensue during in utero growth spurts, including the testosterone wash as well as the birthing and their early and later experiences. In the procreation process, Nature adapts to "what is:" individuals' biological, psychological, cognitive, emotional, dietary, and environmental variables. Thus, human beings are co-creators of their lives and of other human beings.

"Mothers and fathers are in the conception and pregnancy business together, even though it is the mother who carries the child in her womb."[208] Nature provides a head-start program for the survival of an infant who will inhabit the same environment as its parents. Evidently. "Information acquired from the parents' perceptions of their environment transits the placenta and primes the prenate's physiology, preparing it to more effectively deal with future exigencies that will be encountered after birth."[208] "But no matter how 'good' one's genes may be, if an individual's nurture experiences are fraught with abuse, neglect or misperceptions, the realization of the genes' potentials will be sabotaged."[208]

If the environment that primes the prenate includes war, hostility, and abuse, will the ensuing child have a larger hindbrain (to fight or flee) to cope with such an environment? We learn that a warlike culture fosters warlike males within that culture.[299] We also know, from Allan

Schore's research, that "a mother who is emotionally mature, stable, loved, and feels secure gives birth to a child with an advanced forebrain...showing that an infant protected and nurtured has a larger prefrontal growth after birth...their foreheads extend beyond the tips of their noses...and maintains their growth during the toddler period if nurturing is unbroken."[260] Joseph Pearce believes the numbers of such children are increasing because more women are discovering their inner personal power so they are able to create peace and security for themselves, despite their outer world, and to practice natural birthing and breastfeeding. "A human nurtured instead of shamed and loved instead of driven by fear develops a different brain and therefore a different mind—he will not act against the well-being of another, nor against his larger body, the living earth."[260]

Recall that we human beings are born into this world with fully activated, sensory-driven right-brains and with stored genetic inheritances, instincts, experiences, and memories in our unconscious minds. The brain stem or reptilian brain begins functioning in the first trimester of gestation. The reptilian brain makes us aware of our outer sensory world. The limbic system begins developing in the second trimester and makes aware of our interior, subjective world. The left-brain or neocortex begins developing in the third trimester;[260] the language and thinking center takes longer to mature, so children's right hemisphere is more active during their first three or four years; thus, their intelligence is primarily right hemisphere-based,[225] although the left hemisphere begins its growth spurt around the second year of life.

A baby's brain weighs about 350 - 600 grams; whereas, an adult's brain today weighs between 1,300 and 1,400 grams. Sperm whales' brains weigh around 7,800 grams; elephants' brains weigh about 6,000 grams; bottle-nosed dolphins' brains weigh around 1,500 to 1,600 grams. The first Neanderthal skeleton was discovered in 1857, two years prior to Charles Darwin publishing *Origin of Species*. Now we know that the Neanderthal brain weighed on average between 1,200 and 1,750 grams. It seems that emerging scientific evidence indicates, supported by genetic and mitochondrial dating, that Homo erectus lived on Earth around 400,000 years ago with a brain weight of 800 – 900. Around 200,000 years ago, a new human species, Homo sapiens, our ancestor, appeared with a 55 percent larger brain.[327]

"Male brains are larger [than female brains] by about 9 percent,"[27] even when adjusted for body size; however, both have the same number of brain cells. The brain dictates innate gender differences that begin at eight weeks in utero when unisex babies destined (by the sperm donor) to be males receive a testosterone wash which narrows the width of their corpus callosum. However, the thicker the fibers within the corpus callosum, the more interactions, transfers of information, or integrations are possible between an individual's two brains. Yet, "the greater the asymmetry...the smaller the corpus callosum,"[225] and the "bigger the brain, the less interconnected it is."[225] The corpus callosum contains an estimated 300-800 million fibers; they increase with participation in the arts.

A smaller corpus callosum indicates less communication avenues between the right and left hemispheres. Neuroscientists have found that people, especially children, with smaller bridges have a harder time controlling their emotions or cannot solve problems when they are emotionally upset. Some such people were abused as children, may not have been exposed to environmental stimuli or left-brained skills, or have an extreme sense of entitlement.[326]

While certain traits, talents, skills, and cognitive abilities appear to run in our ancestral families, an important influence upon human life is our vulnerability to the conditions we experience as fetuses in utero. "For example, until surprisingly recently, many doctors and scientists were convinced that the fetus was a 'perfect parasite,' skimming the nutrients it needed from its mother's body, unaffected by the quantity or kind of food she consumed...the fetus is in fact exquisitely sensitive to its mother's diet."[257]

"In fact, we're learning the fetus inhabits the same world as adults—the world of alcohol and cigarettes, of polluted air and water, of industrial chemicals untested for their safety, the fetus's small size and immature state of development, as well as the permeability of the defense systems deployed around it by its mother, mean that individuals are more vulnerable to environmental toxins during the prenatal period than at any other time in their lives."[257]

Our medical establishment learned that fetuses are not sealed off from a mother's intrauterine environment and that fetuses are not just parasites. Mothers' alcoholism produces babies with fetal alcohol syndrome (FAS). There were disastrous effects, in the 1950s and 1960s, on fetuses in utero of drugs to address pregnant women's morning sickness or nausea. By treating pregnant women with thalidomide, that drug prevented fetuses' arms and legs from forming and most Thalidomide babies were born with heads and torsos only. By treating miscarriage with diethylstilbestrol (DES), that drug prevented miscarriage but led to aggressive cancers in the child as a result of exposure to DES.

The placenta's role in the womb is more than nourish a fetus with its blood vessels that deliver oxygen and nutrients from the mother, it shapes brain development. Researchers at the Zilkha Neurogenetic Institute, University of Southern California, report "it is the placenta – not the mother – that provides the hormone serotonin to the fetus's forebrain early in development. Because hormones play an essential role in brain wiring... placental abnormalities could directly influence the risk of developing depression, anxiety, and even autism."[175]

We are now more aware that much of what a pregnant woman "encounters in her daily life—the air she breathes, the food and drink she consumes, the emotions she feels, the chemicals she's exposed to—are shared in some fashion with her fetus."[257] "Cortisol is a hormone released when the body is under stress...the offspring of people with PTSD have low basal cortisol."[257] In addition, overweight but not obese pregnant women's offspring are more likely to have birth defects of the heart. Therefore, it seems that the mother's intrauterine environment is as important as genes. Her diet "can have lasting effects on her offspring."[257]

David Barker, a British physician, noted that the poorest areas of England had the highest rates of heart disease.[257] Armed with turn-of-the century birth records, he found that infants who weighed less at birth had higher rates of heart disease as adults in middle age. He published his findings in 1989, but they were not well received by his colleagues; he was ridiculed but he persevered with his "Barker hypothesis."[257] His rationale for heart disease is "When nutrients are scarce, they divert nutrients toward the really critical organ – the brain – and away from other organs, like the heart and liver."[257]

"There is also evidence that the mother's stress levels have a direct and significant effect on the health and brain development of the fetus."[299] From the research that continues to emerge from Harvard University's Project Viva and the National Children's Study by researchers from the National Institutes of Health, it makes sense that "the most effective antipoverty program might be one that starts before birth."[299]

Proper nutrition – "eating a diet of fruits, vegetables, beans, whole grains, nuts, seeds, and limited meat"[133] – is essential for a developing fetus and for up to three years of age after birth. However, it is one aspect of children's needs during their long maturation period. An infant's basic needs for food, water, warmth, and shelter are accompanied by safety and security needs, the need to be loved and to love, and to belong to a family or group. When an infant's needs are met, optimum growth is possible. Optimum development is blocked when needs are not adequately met, and the ensuing frustration stunts an infant's growth potential.

Babies' right-brains have no voice other than body language (gurgles, smiles, fidgeting, cries, and screams), so they are dependent upon adults for care for an extended period of immaturity. "This protracted period of immaturity is intimately tied up with the human capacity for change,"[124] which allows adaptation to different environments and promotes imagination and learning. However, babies' imagination and learning depend on the love of the people who care for them: "without mothering humans would lack nurturance, warmth, and emotional security."[124]

Brain scans indicate synchrony between a mother's brain and her child's brain. Daniel Siegal and Allan Schore of the University of California, Los Angeles, reported their discovery that not only does caretaking change a child's genes, it also influences how the genes express themselves as the child grows.[2] Does it also promote physical well-being? "'Scientific studies of longevity, medical and mental health, happiness and even wisdom,' Dr. Siegel says, 'point to supportive relationships as the most robust predictor of these positive attributes in our lives across the life span.'"[2]

Human beings in our lives rarely give us sufficient knowledge about and affirmation for our unique, lovable, and loving selves. We do not get How-To Manuals. Parents and caretakers rarely know how to care for their whole selves and, if they do, most learned it later in life.

Psychological wisdom holds that all we need is love, and we must love ourselves "as is" to love others. David Hawkins writes, "Loving is a state of being. It's a forgiving, nurturing, and supportive way of relating to self, others, and the world... Love emanates from the heart. It has the capacity to lift others and accomplish great feats because of its purity of motive."[147] Love is an emotion that is expressed by the heart and right-brain.

Foremost are the needs to respect self and be respected, to be feel secure and cared for, and to have human contact. The mother's face, particularly her eyes, and emotional expressions play a key role in the emotional development of her infant. Mutual gazing trigger high levels of endogenous opiates in the infant's developing brain.[302] Unconditional positive regard validates the essence of being in children and adults as they are in the now and not what they will be or do in the future. Parents' unconditional positive regard promotes children's faith in their resources, helps them function freely with effectiveness, and teaches them they are valuable in all respects. Unconditional positive regard, love, is the basis for optimum human and humane development and may prevent inhumane treatment of humans and animals.

Human attachment or bonding is about love. The process usually occurs within three months of birth between an infant and caregiver. Carl Rogers focused on the conditions necessary for the development of human possibilities and the characteristics of a helping relationship. He asserted that "if the parent creates with his [her] child a psychological climate ...then the child will become more self-directing, socialized, and mature."[287] Current brain research indicates that our fate is not determined by our genes alone but also by our lifestyle and our nurturance: "the quality of early maternal-infant bonding"[299] and our prebirth inheritances and experiences.

We come into this world with an active right-brain and the me-me stage, to get needs met. So, one of our instincts is to be self-centered or narcissistic, which is Nature's way for infants to survive. As newborns, we cry for food, changing, help when we hurt, and for attention. We smile and gurgle our appreciation. If we perceive that our early needs for love and care were not met by our parents or caretakers, we may remain narcissistic or obsessed with negativity. Narcissus, according to mythology, fell in love with his own reflection in the water when he did not see himself reflected in his mother's eyes. Hence, narcissism is a term applicable to those who are obsessed with themselves or are self-centered, possibly due to not feeling affirmed by a loving parent or caretaker so they are unable to affirm themselves as lovable and capable human beings. We learn to love from being loved, so self-love may be a late bloomer's avenue via a significant other or through earning a loving self.

While love is not all we need to flourish, its absence from the human development literature was discovered by Daniel Prescott at the University of Maryland. He concluded from his research that love is not rooted primarily in sexual or hormonal dynamics. Instead, being loved gives human beings basic psychological security and love must be perceived and experienced to love self and others.[274] Otherwise, we may remain narcissistic, for the right-brain only is operative before and after we are born. Our being narcissistic as babies is Nature's wisdom: to get our love and survival needs met.

Now that we know that human beings have innate senses of morality and fairness, that the hormones testosterone and oxytocin impel them to survive, procreate, and relate, and that love and nurturance are essential for affirming and inserting themselves into society beyond family, and egos emerge with a drive for power to compensate for felt ego deficits. Rollo May proposed a human development five level power base. Dr. May's first level of power is the power to be. Human infants depend upon a response to their crying and movement to get needs met; therefore, power is critical to their human development. If infants perceive through their own and others' actions and reactions that they are worthy and loved, then they feel affirmed by their parents or caregivers. May's second level is children's later ability to affirm self, to be separate, and to insert self into their larger society beyond family. Dr. May's third level, self-assertion, may take longer and used to be more applicable to boys than to girls.

If self-assertion is blocked, for whatever reason (abuse, bullied, gender, race, color, etc.), then a stronger form of self-assertion may be substituted: aggression. Dr. May perceives his fourth level as moving into power or prestige positions or into another's territory and taking it over. In this stage, if aggressive efforts are not effective, then violence erupts. In the fifth stage, passivity or impotence may be expressed as violence against self, including addictions, or others.[223] From the foregoing, we may understand the importance of parenting's role in an infant's self-affirmation process; otherwise, the process may take years, unless a significant other is available as surrogate or an individual earns a self through effort.

Narcissism and violence are ways to account for human beings' blocked self-assertion while gossip, bullying, addictions, greed, and learned helplessness and hopelessness are routes other children and adults may take when they don't have a good enough human development child-rearing experience. There is speculative evidence that "violence by male members of our species has at least a partly instinctive, genetic basis. The expression of that genetic behavioral substrate clearly is affected by the nature of the nurturing of the male infant within the context of the social/cultural standards of its tribe, society, or nation. A warlike, violent culture will foster the development of warlike violent males within that culture, enhancing the pleasure they experience from violent life experiences, including the waging of war, violent social behaviors, and violence in entertainment."[299]

Violence is a form of socializing children's behavior that is still popular in some segments of America. Many children's fables and fairy tales have plot lines of threats of violence for minor misbehaviors. Viewing violence on TV or in person begets violence; it also increases fear. In our Western left-brained society, children are taught to disbelieve their senses and their intuitive knowings when adults' "Don'ts!" control their early lives and feelings. Negative injunctions hark back to saber-toothed tiger times when obedience meant survival. Our ancestors lived to pass on their genes to us by paying more attention to the negative possibilities that could threaten their lives. Also, the brain detects negative data faster than positive information, and negative events usually get our attention more than positive ones. That inherited trait combined with early human development unresolved issues may account for individuals' predisposition to sabotage success in relationships and at work and to be hapless victims who feel morally superior to those who mistreat them. "Yet telling people they are the architects of their own misery doesn't go over very well."[106]

Since the prenatal period is the wellspring of an infant's health, well-being, and future diseases, pregnancy is not a waiting period but a crucial one, a staging period that is affected by the mother's inner and outer environments. "Until the mid-1980s, medical science...considered the preverbal period of human development to be one of a primarily reflexive, noncognitive state of awareness of the environment. Perception of pain, storage of memory, and processing of information were believed to be limited or absent."[299]

Researcher William Fifer and colleagues at Columbia University found that newborns between the ages of 10 to 72 hours old also learn while they are sleeping.[100] An infant "receives and understands the nonverbal language of touch long before it understands words."[290] "Newborn infants do not understand words; they hear the vocal tone and music of the voice. But they do understand experience and respond to the toucher's message and intention."[291]

Touch is crucial to healthy human development and to life itself. A study of Romanian orphans by Mary Carlson, a Harvard Medical School neurobiologist, documented the importance of human touching. The orphans' stress due to the lack of touch, attention, and care stunted the orphans' growth and negatively affected their behavior.[208] Early childhood trauma shrinks the hippocampus, the seat of memories, causing the release of the stress hormone glucocorticoid. That hormone kills cells in the hippocampus, thereby preventing synaptic connections in neural cells that make learning and memory possible for both boys and girls.

For years, researchers have known that "children whose mothers were chronically stressed during pregnancy—by famine, anxiety, the death of a relative or marital discord, for instance—show higher than normal rates of various psychological and behavioural disorders when they are adults."[134] Epigenetics is the probable answer.

"Epigenetics is a type of gene regulation that can be passed from a cell to its daughters [cells]...to inactivate the gene being methylated... Newborns whose mothers suffered from depression while they were pregnant are known to have more highly methylated glucocorticoid-receptor genes than others. The same is true of children who were abused when young."[134] Drs. Gunter, Meyer, and Elbert, University of Konstanz, Germany, examined children, aged 10 to 19, and 25 mothers and found that "women abused during pregnancy were significantly more likely than others to have a child with methylated glucocorticoid-receptor genes."[134]

Evidently, abuse of a mother before or after the pregnancy does not affect her child; therefore, gene methylation occurs in a fetus as a response to its mother's stress. The response by the fetus increases its risk after birth to obesity, depression, impulsiveness, aggression, and some autoimmune diseases. The cycle is repeated when males abuse the pregnant mothers of their children. Education and intervention to stop abuse are effective and intervention is recommended for the sake of mother and child.

Children thrive when they perceive they are under the protective umbrella of a mother, father, or caring adult. "The father's role and challenge, both before and after... is to support the mother right down the line and provide her with a safe space that is free of fear so that the child's safe space, first within the mother and later with her, is never in question. To force a mother to fend for herself after giving birth, as is too often the case in America, exacts an awful social price all of us must pay."[260]

Good fathers express love and affection for their pregnant spouses and to their sons and daughters. For good or for ill, a father's messages influence the positive or negative course of a son's life on into adulthood: what they do and become. A son learns from his father about the world, work, money, family, and relationships with women and other men. It's never too late for fathers to deepen their relationships with their sons and daughters, to bond, and to mutually respect one another for the common good of all. Some fathers may consider themselves good providers just because they support the family financially. Other fathers may contribute nothing to the health and welfare of their sons and daughters.

While the brains of males and females are not the same since male brains are 9 percent larger, 17th century scientists considered that to mean females had less mental capacity. However, both male and female brains contain the same number of brain cells, but female brain cells are more densely packed in the female brains. Babies' neural pathways in the brain are more highly connected than in adults' brains. However, as babies grow older their brains "'prune out' the weaker, less used pathways and strengthen the ones that are used more often."[124] Hence, the importance of loving care, diverse stimulation, including music and play, to maintain and prepare neural pathways for new learning.

Females' larger communication centers mean relationships, emotions, and social harmony are valued. Males and females have the potential for the same level of intelligence, including mathematical and scientific abilities. As estrogen floods female brains, their priorities may become more about connecting with others than about being perceived as smart and less desirable by boys. Nevertheless, both males and females have two hemispheres with left- and right-brains that are vulnerable to hormones and to familial, gender, cultural, and educational conditioning, but their brain size or weight is not a factor. Since baby girls' communication centers do not shrink at eight weeks in utero (but boys' communication centers shrink to make room for more sex and aggressiveness cells), their potential to communicate is better at birth than boys' potential. Baby girls are born with an interest in evoking emotionally expressive faces and connection, which may account for women's instinct that they'll get the reaction they expect or want when they go "after a narcissistic or otherwise emotionally unavailable man – 'if I do it right, he'll love me.'"[27] Baby boys, on the other hand, don't have social competence as a priority. "In fact, disorders that inhibit from picking up on social nuances – called autism spectrum disorders and Asperger's syndrome – are eight times more common in boys"[27] than in girls.

Children and young adults' intelligence – in both left- and right-brainers – is further complicated by the fact that the human brain does not end its growth until adulthood. The mature prefrontals are intended to balance the two hemispheres' diverse worldviews and to be aware that actions have consequences, but their job is to inhibit an inappropriate response, not to initiate an appropriate one.[203] By not educating the right-brain for self-control and emotional resiliency, children are judged, graded, and drugged for unacceptable behavior. An opportune time to teach emotional literacy and character-building is during prefrontal immaturity.

The brain's prefrontal cortex (right- and left- prefrontal lobes) develops rapidly after birth, it unfolds in two stages (primary: early and secondary: later). By age fifteen, the threefold brain is completed. Then

Nature's newest addition to the human brain, the prefrontal cortex, begins its secondary growth spurt between the ages of fifteen and eighteen, but the prefrontals are not completed until ten years or so later. "Because it was discovered only recently... this aspect of development has not yet been acknowledged on a broad academic level."[260] The prefrontals "are experience-dependent, shaped by the environment the child experiences."[260] So, "The caregiver's emotional state and the extent of nurturing and care an infant receives can actually affect the development of the prefrontals at the cellular level."[260]

In *The Philosophical Baby*, Alison Gopnik informs us that prefrontal immaturity gives children the ability to "remain open to anything that may turn out to be the truth...the prefrontal cortex is the most active part of the brain during childhood; it constantly changes throughout those years, and its final form depends heavily on childhood experiences."[124] Evidently, children's powers of imagination and new learning are the bases of prefrontal immaturity, providing adults with the tools to plan and control behavior. Harvard University's Howard Gardner of *Project Zero and Frames of Mind*, or multiple intelligences fame, developed intelligence tests for babies and tested older subjects as well. "The researchers found that up to age four, almost all the children were at the genius level, in terms of multiple frames of intelligence...spatial, kinesthetic, musical, interpersonal, mathematical, and linguistic. But by age twenty, the percentage of children at genius level was down to 10 percent, and over twenty, the genius level proportion of the subjects sank to 1 percent...'Where did it go?' It didn't go anywhere; it's covered over by the Voice of Judgment"[304] of our left-brain-dominated Western society and The Western Intellectual Tradition.

"The prefrontal cortex is especially involved in 'inhibition.' It actually helps shut down other parts of the brain, limiting and focusing experience, action and thought. This process is crucial for the complex thinking, planning, and acting that adults engage in."[124] The executive functions of our brain's prefrontal lobes are goal setting, judgment, strategic planning, and impulse control by making us aware of the consequences of our actions. However, the downside of delayed prefrontal lobes' maturation is many young people have already destroyed their own and others' lives by age twenty-one or have learned habits that direct them to the negative side of the right-brain, leading to conflict within and outside themselves.

The role of the prefrontals is believed to be to turn our brains (reptilian, limbic, and neocortex) into one civilized mind,[260] so we may exercise wisdom as adults when the prefrontals are fully mature, if our right-brain is educated, formally or informally. The human brain's prefrontals are informed by the human heart's intelligence of love, joy, compassion, and forgiveness in order to bring heart and brain into sync. When we open ourselves to the heart's intelligence, we can block the automatic "fight, flight, freeze, or feign"[222] reaction of our hindbrain, respond more positively to our daily stressors, and modify current triggers that activate our past traumas, resulting in emotional resilience. It appears that the fight-flight syndrome is a typical male response to stress. The freeze-feign syndrome is a more typical female response to stress. Hormones play huge roles in gender differences. Worldviews play huge roles in hemispheric differences.

Human beings have innate instincts. Paul Bloom and his wife Karen Wynn discovered that a one-year-old boy, after seeing three puppets play ball demonstrated an innate sense of fairness Two of the puppets would slide the ball back and forth to each other but when they directed the ball to the third puppet, he would take the ball and run away with it. Then two puppets (a game player and the non-game player) with treats in front of them were placed before the toddler. The toddler was asked to take a treat away from one puppet. The boy took the treat from the pile in front of the non-game player, the naughty one, and then smacked the puppet over the head. Bloom informs us that there is "A growing body of evidence...suggests that humans do have a rudimentary moral sense from the very start of life."[24]

There is also compelling data by Hamlin that pre-verbal infants, 6 to 10 months old, discriminate between individuals' actions toward others as appealing or aversive: "infants prefer an individual who helps another to one who hinders another, prefer a helping individual to a neutral individual, and prefer a neutral individual to a hindering individual."[140] Infants' preferences are not under their control, but their sensations, memories and experiences endure in their unconscious minds and run their young and adult lives. Our innate sense of justice and fairness is "rooted in a sense of fairness... such a sense is not the product of applying a rational deontological principle but rather results from emotional processing, providing suggestive evidence for moral sentimentalism."[139] Ernst Fehr, a Swiss economist and behavioral scientist at the Institute for Empirical Research at the University of Zurich, believes this innate discernment of what is fair, and how to enforce social justice within a group... must have evolved very early in the prehistory of the human race... that it emerged earlier than language in shaping the earliest human expression of social wisdom."[139]

We are born as innocents who believe what adults tell us. "It is out of lovingness and trust of its parents, its teachers, and the world of television, commercials, and society that the child becomes programmed."[144] A child's basic needs for loving care, nutrition, security, belonging, and respect are best met during his or her first seven years. Our pre-birth and early childhood experiences set the stage for later life: a) for loving relationships, positive self- and other-esteem, positive behaviors, and wisdom or b) for poor relationships, negative self- and other-esteem, negative behaviors, and stupidity. Even those children who had positive caretaking are at risk when exposed to traumas such as assaults on their dignity, gender, ethnicity, or core culture or to cognitive teachings promoting hatred, religious, racial, gender, or moral supremacy.

After birth, our opportunities and potentialities often get dampened by enculturation, hurtful experiences, and repressive relationships. Many of us are taught to be negative because we are raised by them and by the negative aspects of the right-brain's fear, anger, violence, guilt, shame, and sin. We are prone to negativity when constantly exposed to adults' negatives "for our own good." Today, we have become enculturated, not socialized, when negativity, from negative news to fighting cancer, poverty, terrorism, or wars, appears to be necessary for us to focus our attention.

It seems "good news" doesn't trigger the amygdala's alert system. What kind of self ensues from our culture's focus on negatives? A self prone to judge and be judged, to shame and be shamed, and to punish and be punished. "Being judged by someone offends us if the judgment is true and more so if it is false. When we accuse or judge another, it has the same effect on us as being judged ourselves."[260] Bad information about people and events carry more weight than good information.

Psychologist Allan Schore proposed that the effects of the negatives upon a developing child's transition, from a happy state to a depressed one, is "the fall of the human from grace into culture."[260] In our relationships, according to John Gottman, it takes about five positive interactions to offset the effects of one negative interaction.[260] We do not come into this world with blank slates either.

Humans develop a sense of self by the time they are eighteen months old or earlier, according to developmental psychologist Jerome Kagan. Antonio Damasio proposes that the self at that evolutionary point is autobiographical.[62] However, access to all of one's history from gestation to birth is usually out of conscious awareness, so the sense of the autobiographical self is at a basic level. "At its simplest and most basic level, consciousness lets us recognize an irresistible urge to stay alive and develop a concern for the self. At its most complex and elaborate level, consciousness helps us develop a concern for other selves and improve the art of life."[62]

"Consciousness is not conscience. It is not the same as love and honor and mercy; generosity and altruism; poetry and science; mathematical and technical invention. Nor...are moral turpitude, existential angst or lack of creativity examples of bad states of consciousness."[62] Consciousness is not the same as intelligence; "intelligence pertains to the ability to manipulate knowledge so successfully that novel responses can be planned and delivered"[62] Actually, "consciousness begins as a feeling."[62]

As we learn and grow, each of us re-constructs our sense of self, consciously and unconsciously, based upon "All of our memory, inherited from evolution and available at birth, or acquired through learning thereafter, in short, all our memory of things, of properties of things, of persons and places, of events and relationships, of skills, of biological regulations, you name it, exists in dispositional form [abstract records of potentialities] waiting to become an explicit image or action."[62] From the foregoing we learn the importance of knowing about our own and others' nature, our human and humane development, to our creating "a sense of good and evil as well as norms of conscionable behavior."[62] It is a truism that Children Learn What They Live, according to Dorothy Law Nolte[242] and often live what they learn until they are re-educated.

I will always remember Dennis, the physically abused 7th grader in my class who abused butterflies. It was a teachable moment that I missed. I could have related how lowly caterpillars become lovely butterflies and that while his wings were being clipped, metaphorically, by his father, it was his destiny to grow up and become a handsome and intelligent young man who did not make butterflies suffer for his anger but to use his anger to take charge of his education so he could be free like butterflies. The Russian dramatist, Anton Chekov, who noted the difference in the nature-nurture process between human beings and other species. "In nature, a repulsive caterpillar turns into a lovely butterfly. But with human beings, it is the other way around: a lovely butterfly turns into a repulsive caterpillar."[201] That's why elementary school teachers would benefit not only from Human Development courses but also from knowledge beyond their own specialty to recognize and act on teachable moments. Facts lose out to stories that show the depth and substance of a teacher's ability to reach children where they are and inspire them. A child's inherent nature-nurture process is thwarted by ignorant, half-brained adults and by heartless public education systems.

History is rife with cruelty to human beings and animals; it is also depicted in art. I shed tears whenever I hear of animals being abused by humans and see documentaries that appear to stage the animals or, at the least, to set them up for the kill. We receive four-legged love from our domesticated animals, and we utilize animals in therapy programs for both children and adults. Animals have right and left hemispheres too, like humans, and elephants weep. Fortunately, animal rights are public issues in America as many Americans are illuminating the plight of abused domestic animals and the abuse of our food supply animals: "80 percent of non-organic beef in the U.S, is slaughtered by four companies."[133]

While Charles Darwin drew his inference – "survival of the fittest"/strongest – from studying ants and animals, in the 1800s, now we know that nature is not so black or white as depicted. Not only domesticated animals but wild ones demonstrate more than survival of the fittest. Arizona has wild horses and rapid rivers. Recently, a witness with a camera recorded an event that ran on a local TV station: a young horse, a foal, attempted to join other horses across a river. The foal was swept downstream by the fast-flowing water, struggling to keep its head above the surface when an older horse raced to the foal's rescue. He or she used its head and neck to keep the foal's head above water until he/she found a way to safely guide the foal to shallow water. Anton Chekov observed the difference between animals' nature and nurture versus the nature and nurturance experienced by human beings. Until we acknowledge human beings' right brains as the left-brains' partner in the K-12 public school system, domination will prevail over caring, and violence and greed will prevail over compassion for all life.

The story of human, humane, and inhumane development is a work in progress. The left-brain's interpretative process is only as good as the credibility of the knowledge from the rest of the brain's modules. It synthesizes the knowledge into a story and rationalizes an action plan. Thus, our choices are only as good as our sources of knowledge. Personal and social responsibilities are hijacked when we compromise our normal brain's functioning to ignore our innate sense of fairness and knowing right from wrong action or behavior. A person with an abnormal brain is not automatically incapable of responsible behavior. "Responsibility is not located in the brain. The brain has no area or network for responsibility...the way to think about responsibility is that it is an interaction between people, a social contract...responsibility reflects a rule...and the hope that we share is that each person will follow certain rules"[116] "One of the main fears that men have of women...they won't abide by the rules."[183] One of the fears most of us have about our leaders is that their responsibility, as a social contract, will be broken by their assimilation into a hierarchical environment of power and self-interest.

While man's inhumanity to man exists as a political weapon, it is often exercised as a personal weapon as well. Most of us get good enough love and parenting or caretaking, but too many of us do not get good enough love or nurturing and learn to live by our wits, to outwit others, or to behave in self- or other-destructive ways, such as narcissism and violence. Children's lives without loving affirmation begin with polarities: either they trust or don't trust others and they love or don't love themselves and others. If, during early and ongoing development, the fear system is activated, rather than love and trust, "then the characteristic personality that begins to build...is one characterized by negativity and hopelessness rather than affection and optimism."[202]

Children are the last ones to be protected against the evils of professional power, control, and authority because inherited traditions, from patriarchal families and culture to religions taught that "Father knows best." "It's for your own good!" Children are also raised by the Don'ts, The Thou Shalt Nots, and by the negative characteristics of the right-brain (guilt, sin, shame, fear, anger, and violence: physical, emotional, psychological, and sexual abuse). Carl Rogers' humanistic writings influenced Thomas Gordon's thinking. Dr. Gordon created *Parent Effectiveness Training* and *Teacher Effectiveness Training* for he empathized with the mothers and fathers who undertake the most difficult job of raising their children without the self-knowledge, communication and parenting skills to rear productive and responsible citizens and with teachers who are charged with educating children's minds but have no power over what is taught.[125] Often, parents parent as they were parented. Teachers teach as they were taught. He concluded that parents and teachers who have problematic children or students must steer clear of the blame game: "You" messages. He taught, in effect, that to change a relationship requires those who hold the power to change first.[126]

We know that America has changed since the 1960s from intact families, communities, and values, but there are pockets in our society where children were and are raised with caring affirmation at home, in the community, and at school. Paul, a Marine veteran of the Vietnam war attributed to his intact family, extended family relationships in his community in North Dakota, and his K-12 public school teachers the fact that he had the emotional maturity, resilience, and character to survive in the jungle. He intuitively knew whom to trust to cover his back among the many Marines in his unit who succumbed to drugs, alcohol or lacked character, and he could handle the general public's negative perceptions of Vietnam veterans when he returned to America. But he is not as politically naive today as he was in his teens as a result of his Vietnam experience. He has become whole-brained.

However, many of us are among the walking wounded and are recovering from childhood and life's experiences and conditioning. We may have little faith in the power of the body-brain-mind-heart to change and heal itself, so we look up to authority figures to do our thinking for us. However, when we perceive that they are not living up to our expectations, to our innate moral sense of justice and fairness, then we become frustrated and lose faith in them and in our elected officials.

The human cost of the walking wounded due to our recent wars in Vietnam, Korea, Kuwait, Iraq, and Afghanistan is borne by today's veterans' PTSD, CTE (chronic traumatic encephalopathy), suicides, and physical disabilities and by the families of those who gave their lives for America's leaders' decisions. All wars are examples of not acknowledging the importance of educating our leaders' right-brained emotions, feelings, and virtues. Brute force decisions are last resort ones after exploring all the alternatives available to whole-brainers, not left-brainers. Only a left hemisphere-dominated society, a closed system, will continue to revere smart and remain blind and deaf to the compelling scientific research and experiential evidence that, without the harmonizing effects of the right hemisphere's virtues and wisdom, America and Americans will be held hostage by our status quo policies and practices that empower and enrich the few.

Now we know that human development begins before a child is conceived. Since World War II, Americans have grown up and live in a more violent and sicker world. What we think and how we think, though, may be more important to our health than what we eat, drink, breathe, and how we exercise and rest.[233] Until we learn to appreciate, educate, and integrate both sides of our brains' data, we will not learn to have faith in ourselves or others. The route to being smart and wise begins with K-12 whole-brained public school education.

Smart and Wise = Whole-Brain K-12 Public Education

The story of each child's human development, humane or inhumane, is embedded in his or her brain's right hemisphere without a voice. Even though children are not aware of the data bank hidden within themselves, when they perceive a real or imagined threat or unfamiliar situation to their physical or ego survival, they may exhibit behaviors that are clues to their past experiences that set off alarms in the present. Addressing a child's "history," beyond age and readiness indicators, to include an in-depth interview of the mother or caretaker, is an opportunity for the K-12, left-brain-oriented public school system personnel to provide future "teachable moments" rather than disciplinary ones that label and add another negative to a child's ongoing human development. Not only children, but adults, including teachers and administrators, have inner histories that may not have been addressed and lie fallow in their unconscious minds until triggered by a perceived threat to their professional selves, by a child, adult, or event.

Students' academic or cognitive intelligence is the foundational knowledge to build a self, relationship, community, society or career, but the quality of those endeavors is determined by whether or not they have developed their heart consciousness and humanity's virtues. It's how both hemispheres are consistently visible in human beings lives that makes the difference between a fully intelligent and fully functioning person and one with human development deficits that need to be resolved. Without full intelligence, human beings do not have access to their innate and learned intuition, creativity, and humanity's virtues for they are unconsciously run by beliefs, biases, and prejudices learned from their environment or by inherited and lived experiences in utero and during their first years of life when the right-brain only was active.

A K-12 public educational system that does not address the large body of data within each student when they come to school is negligent of its responsibilities to educate them for life, not throw them onto the streets when they do not conform to its man-made, left-brain standards or norms. It is the current K-12 public education school system that is failing its students, not the other way around, when 31 percent of them do not attain high school diplomas, and another 25 percent of those who do get high school diplomas are not even prospects for the U.S. Army or college. No attention is paid to why some smart students fail the standardized tests, for example, when "smart" is rigidly defined as cognitive intelligence only; often it is the smart ones who are without character or substance. The state of our crime-ridden, addictive, money-dominated, and violent society and nation is testament to the quality of K-12 education available to young people who become America's adults. They are primed to live what they were taught and not taught and to pass it on to the next generation through those whose lives they touch.

Some children come to school with no overwhelming histories that get in the way of their readiness to learn the ABCs and 123s and to enjoy being in school. Nevertheless, all children thrive in environments where they are not humiliated, criticized, or shamed by peers and some adults' negative, unschooled right-brain's emotions. They thrive when they are encouraged, justly praised, accepted, and feel loved or appreciated by adults' right-brain's positive emotions. They recognize adults with good or bad intentions and whom to trust and learn from, so children come to school with a knowledge base, not empty brains, and usually open to positive relationships.

To change a relationship from hierarchical to equality usually requires those who hold and wield the power to change first. The political power brokers outside and inside The Western Intellectual Tradition, Federal and State agencies, its administrators, staff, and teachers, may improve the curriculum of the K-12 public school, but the principal-teacher-student-relationship and the quality of public education may change by owning their personal power. Teachers with master's degrees in human development were able to turn their Teachers' Lounge from negative gossip fests into positive discussion arenas, which improved the teachers' attitudes and their classrooms.

Changing times, though, since the 1960s means the roles of parents, schools, religions, and our media/sports role models have changed and not necessarily for the better when violence as entertainment invades our lives, abuse of human beings and animals is rampant, and America seems to be perpetually warring within and outside its shores. Too many of today's children are raised by television, snack foods, and parents who have to hold down two jobs to keep food on the table and a roof over their heads with little face-to-face time for their children or involvement in their children's schools and their communities.

Adults with intact families, incomes, and communities who survived the K-12 public school system themselves and do not think changes to include the human element in the system are warranted are symptomatic of those hard-nosed politicians, professionals, and industrialists who believe "If it ain't broke, don't fix it!" Well, America's institutions and organizations are broken, even if they are making money, and our infrastructures are broken because the people who people them are broken as they try to maintain or sustain what they built with their left-brained, me-first mindsets. Does it take an Albert Einstein to remind us that we cannot solve problems with the same mindset that caused them? Or a William Shakespeare's Hamlet, when Marcellus sensed, "Something is rotten in the state of Denmark?" Something is wrong, not in Denmark, but in America when our K-12 public schools and democracy are working for the few, not the majority.

At a time when Arab nations' people are toppling their tyrants/dictators and demanding freedom, education, and jobs, we in America are experiencing a continuation of dismantling the safety nets we gained as a result of the 1929-1939 Great Depression. The eroding of those safety nets began in the 1980s during the Reagan presidency. In 2012, our democracy and our K-12 public school systems are in jeopardy when we have vocal politicians who, empowered by ideology and enriched by moneyed elites, are intent on reducing funding to the nation's K-12 public school systems and, by default, ending a future for an educated middle class by demanding tax cuts for the rich and less social services for the rest of us. They are politically motivated to cut out what they perceive to be welfare programs for "the undeserving poor" – Social Security, Medicare, universal health insurance, unemployment insurance, pension funds, and all social programs for the poor and middle classes – while advocating more clout and subsidies for the free enterprise system of the oil, agribusiness, and pharmaceutical industries and themselves under the guise of protecting their, not our, children from a mortgaged future they underwrote.

Our nation's future is already mortgaged by the trillions of debt dollars incurred by the 2000-2008 administrations' practices and wars in Afghanistan and Iraq that enriched the players in the military's industrial complex. For the scope of our spent and misspent taxpayers' dollars on "national security," not Americans' security, don't read the lips of the fiscally conservative politicians, read the researched words of Rachel Maddow's book, *Drift*,[215] and the lived experiences of John Perkins' *Confessions of an Economic Hit Man*.[261] There will be no future for the children of the middle and poor classes if the K-12 public school system is economically unable to function or to fully educate 90 percent of America's children.

There will be no higher education future for students to mortgage, based upon our nation's large number of college graduates who are experiencing the hollow promise of attaining the American Dream of upward mobility with higher education degrees. Some politicians are taking America away from young Americans, who have already mortgaged their future with educational loans, and are giving it to Big Businesses. People's little faith in Big Banks and Big Businesses to protect their interests and our Founding Fathers' little faith in a democracy's majority rule led to more faith in political representatives instead. Both are prime examples of misplaced faith: "the notion that bankers are rational creatures who wouldn't do anything stupid en masse."[34] Now we know that group's SuperPac money talks much louder than individuals' voices and that many politicians value money more than children, including those they "save" from abortion and then from so-called welfare. It is ironic that proposed Federal and State budget cuts harm the very children some politicians purport to protect from abortion or a mortgaged future by eliminating their health, nutritional, educational services, and future.

It is a truism that even smart human beings cannot compete with Big Blue's (IBM) Watson. What is Watson? Named after IBM's founder, Watson is a pre-programmed computer with left-brained information or artificial intelligence. Watson is not programmed with the intelligence of the human heart, gut, right-brained emotions or intuition, honesty, creativity, empathy, compassion, or altruism: an impossible task, so far. But, the engineers have programmed it with a form of concept recognition to connect the dots. Watson appeared on the TV show Jeopardy! Of course, Watson cognitively defeated its human competitors. The TV show's format poses a relevant answer, from a vast arsenal of data, to form a statement with an implied question. Rather than "Is there a statement in your question?" Jeopardy! expects a question to evolve from the statement or answer.

Dr. Abraham Verghese, a professor at Stanford University School of Medicine, and author of the novel, *Cutting for Stone*, suggested that "An answer that might have been posed on Jeopardy! is, 'An emergency treatment that is administered by ear.' I wonder if Watson would have known the question (although he will now, cybertroller that he is), which is, 'What are words of comfort?'"[336] If we are to experience more of Heaven than Hell on Earth, both brains, not just the left-brain's tool boxes, are needed for treating patients and teaching students with heart-to-heart respect, kindness, and empathy.

Although our nation's K-12 public education system has functioned under antiquated administrative-teaching-learning policies and practices that are sanctioned by Western society, today's K-12 public educational problems are fixable. Just as IBM's Watson is left-brained programmed to be smart on tests, so are our K-12 public school students. The K-12 public education system is failing about half of its students, and it is fixable by adding to its curriculum the missing half of students' brains – the right-brain's intelligence. – to not only humanize us but also evoke our creativity. Evidently, the right-brain finds "the subtle connections between seemingly unrelated things"[204] or recognizes patterns in the left-brain's disparate data.

For eons, Western society has accepted the inherited belief that only the left-brain should or could be educated and measured in our K-12 public school systems, although the right- and left-brains are complementary sources of intelligence that, when integrated, contain the future consequences of decisions. Using half of our brain, instead of our whole brain, is a root cause of most Americans' personal, professional, physical, emotional, social, and political issues today, including the presence of greed, violence, addictions, and the lack of peace, love, honesty, and morality in our lives. Those characteristics may not be measurable by left-brain quantitative standards but by the way we behave toward ourselves and others and by the lack of harmony in our society. Our left-brained society's growing inequalities, inequities, and unhealthy inner and outer environments affect us all.

Our negative emotions are our Achilles' heel; they are not welcome anywhere. Our unschooled emotions are seduced by fear and greed, primarily, so the leaders of our institutions and organizations maintain their beliefs underlying the status quo and their power by preying upon our fears and diminishing our access to wisdom. A reason for emotional intelligence to be taught as a partner of left-brain cognition: the right-brain's emotions are divided into positive and negative ones. Recall that David Hawkins' Maps of Consciousness show that positive emotions – peace, joy, love, acceptance – "support and nurture life." However, the negative emotions – shame, guilt, apathy, hatred, grief, fear, desire, anger, pride – may be considered "anti-life."[144] A few negative emotions, such as anger, fear, or guilt, may be the needed inspiration to work for positive outcomes for ourselves and/or the common good.

Now we know that the left-brain's knowledge is literal, content- and detail-oriented, rule-bound, narrowly focused, and manipulative within a closed system, so the left-brain uses the world to attain its goals and establish bureaucracies and order. The right-brain's knowledge is more complex, metaphorical, and wide-open as it pays attention to the world, so the right-brain perceives everything in context and as interconnected.[225] Synthesizing the two worldviews would result in moderating the polarizing policies and practices that currently influence all areas of America's institutions and organizations and American lives.

Divided selves conflict with Nature's intention that we be endowed with two hemispheres to serve ourselves and humanity, not to dehumanize or divide us. The right-brain is our defensive/protective brain, for it pays attention to threats in our environment. Also, the right-brain is faster-thinking than the left. In fact, the brain "contains mutually opposed elements whose contrary influence make possible finely calibrated responses to complex situations."[225] An educated right-brain would discern powerholders' hidden agendas and would be less susceptible to toxic charisma, propaganda, and ideology, so it's no accident that only the left-brain's intelligence is approved.

Applying human brain research has been plagued by behaviorism and determinism. "Should people be held accountable for their behavior?"[116] Neuroscience's DTI (diffusion tensor imaging) is introduced in the courtroom by lawyers to impact "responsibility, evidence, and the question of justice for the victim and the offender during sentencing."[116] Behaviorism teaches that humans come into this world with blank slates. Determinism teaches that the offender is blameless, so no blame. "Personal responsibility is a product of a normally functioning brain of the 'practical reasoner.'"[116]

However, things happen to a brain for a score of reasons, but DTI scans as evidence of brain lesions is not evidence of whether a person is functioning normally or not, for the scan "provides evidence of neither."[116] Dr. Gazzaniga argued: "We are responsible agents who should be held responsible for our actions, because responsibility is found in how people interact, not in brains."¹¹⁶ The Golden Rule is teachable, especially by example, and learnable.

When America is primarily run by left-brainers, it is natural to blame the underachieving students or the dropouts. Actually, students are victims of their circumstances, from their parents being labeled by our white culture's norms leading to disabling their own lives, living in ghettos or polluted neighborhoods, and underfunded schools with mediocre teachers to poverty and learned hopelessness which severely affect their self-affirmation process, so they cannot learn or have positive role models to emulate. No responsibility is taken by educators for their half-brained K-12 public educational system for failing students or failing their graduates either. K-12 professional administrators' wider view with broader job descriptions – versus teachers' limited job descriptions – are in professional networks that appear to be aligned with perpetuating powerless and hopelessness. Such students' feelings get translated into anti-social behavior and bullying. By ignoring the data generated in their school systems' test scores, incidents of violence, and dropouts that reveal the need for interventions, unwise professional educators "may properly be charged with contributory negligence," according to Danial Prescott.²⁷³

One of Stephen Hall's definitions of wisdom is, "It requires mediating, refereeing, between the frequently conflicting inputs of emotion and reason, of narrow self-interest and broader social interests, of instant rewards or future gains."¹³⁹ In addition to the foregoing, I propose a definition of wisdom as a knowledge- and experience-based process whereby intuitive, emotionally sensitive, and altruistic processes of the right hemisphere are required to temper, synergize, and elevate knowledge that is gained from the logical, analytical processes of the left hemisphere for the greater good. Thus, wisdom is a process whereby neural activity is more emotional than logical. Also, an individual's wisdom is similar to a sculptor who views his or her stone as if the stone has a soul waiting to be set free, and setting it free is a labor of love.²²²

The U.S. has had many wake-up calls to upgrade its K-12 public education since the Soviet Union's launch of Sputnik in 1957. There have been many calls for a back-to-basics curriculum and more rigorous testing, then a No Child Left Behind mandate led to teaching to the test.

Only a closed system perpetuates smart and remains blind and deaf to the compelling scientific research and experiential evidence that academia instills duality, not human's full intelligence. As it is, the K-12 curriculum reduces its students to the lowest common denominator for functioning in life, without the harmonizing effects of the right hemisphere's intelligence. The entrenched bureaucratic educational system is failing its students and America as the rest of the modern world's students surge ahead.

We can rise above any negative influences and emotions, if we are taught how to process the right-brain's negative emotions, then we will be more intelligent and perform better in school and at work. When we are not whole-brain educated, "Many youths do their schoolwork, comply with their parents, hang out with their friends, and get through the day, but are not invested in paths into the future that excite them or feel like they originate from within."[200] Questions arise: "How to light adolescents' fires? How to teach the skills needed to charge of their lives? Reed Larson believes initiative is a core quality of positive youth development in Western culture. He concluded from his research on boredom that "Western adolescent life does not provide abundant daily opportunities for the experience and development of initiative."[200]

Instead of inculcating their children with the big picture of education to create their own lives toward fulfillment, material incentives are given by parents to them to study, get As on tests, and do minor chores as if their childrens' education is for the parents' sake only. Teachers give gold stars to those who beat the competition and some school systems give students money just to stay in school, but those perks do not motivate students toward creativity, leadership, altruism, and civic engagement. In fact, "Children who learn cooperatively – compared with those who learn competitively or independently – learn better, feel better about themselves and get along better with each other."[182]

The Western Intellectual Tradition's myopic view of education has resulted in smart students who are amoral, average students with morals and ethics who are smarter than they test, and students who are smart but cannot learn because they are emotionally bankrupt and in need of love, respect, and remediation. Negative self- and other-esteem students need human and humane re-development in emotional literacy;

otherwise. they bully their peers, harm animals, create chaos in classrooms, or dropout of school as ways to offset their felt ego deficits and need for kind attention to their basic human rights. Ignored in academia is research that indicates the importance of emotion over rationalism, social connections over individual isolation, character over IQ, and emergent, organic systems over the idea that we have a single self.

To grow fully functioning, intelligent, and creative human beings, we educate young children in K-12 public school classrooms to know and appreciate who they are, that their ethnic and racial roots are equal to all others, how their brains work, the nutrition that fuels them, the toxins that damage them; how to manage their emotions, how to listen to their inner knowings and intuitions in their unconscious mind. Teachers can draw out their talents they wish to pursue. Students learn better in collaborative, non-competitive environments where initiative is encouraged, and their teachers have foundational knowledge of their subjects that elicit questions and answers not usually found in the textbook. Most students benefit from their welcomed acceptance into immersion in human development sessions. Children's minds, like adults' minds, take a while for them to disbelieve what they learned at home, at school, and on the streets about their worth and to believe that they are lovable and capable with future potentialities.

When students are under stress and in threatening or unstable situations, the right-brain becomes dominant. The fact that many children cannot control their passions, especially anger and fear, is demonstrated by students who bring guns to school. Anger and fear fuel each other. Negative life experiences and conditioned behaviors may be healed in K-12 public schools that integrate the 3Rs and science curricula with human development classes and left- and right-brain journaling. The need for including the right-brain alongside the left-brain has never been so important as today when violence pervades all our lives.

Conventional wisdom holds that it is not what happens to us that counts but how we respond to it and that suffering often leads to human greatness and creativity. That may be true for people who have had good enough human development, but it is not true for children with negative developmental processes. It is a left-brained rationalization for not educating the right-brain toward emotional literacy early on in K-12 public school and/or during parenting.

"Every year millions of children in America, from all walks of life, become victims of, or witnesses to, abusive or violent events that can result in long-lasting symptoms of distress. The events can range from sexual and physical abuse to involvement in a natural disaster, fire or serious motor vehicle accident."[28] Psychological and mental abuse as well as wars are distressful events too. The consequences of such events are often devastating: greater risk of developing behavioral problems, learning problems, failing at school, abusing drugs and alcohol, becoming bullies or violent. Without interventions, PTSD may persist into adulthood. Children who are abused or neglected are "39 percent more likely than those who were not victimized to be arrested as juveniles, 28 percent more likely to be arrested as adults, and 30 percent more likely to commit a violent crime. They also face much higher rates of teenage pregnancy and are likelier to abuse or neglect their own children."[28]

Traumatized children are visible in the classroom – unexplained injuries or bruises, undernourished, sleepy or lethargic, changes in behavior (aggressive or withdrawn), reluctance to go home, changes in school performance and attendance, lack of personal care or hygiene – and in their writings. Observant teachers report such children to the school's hierarchy; often nothing changes or they disappear from the classroom. Children in foster care are at a greater risk of being abused or neglected when money is adults' primary motivation for their care. Children are also at risk when hormones flood their bodies, they do not know how their bodies and brains work, and their prefrontal lobes have not matured so they feel and act out of control.

When the right-brain's attributes are included in the educative process, only traumatized children who are unable to function in a classroom would be referred to an intervention center. Just as we have English as a Second Language or ESL courses, Human Development courses provide the knowledge, experience, reassurance, and support to allow traumatic memories to be processed to diminish their negative effects, to be more resilient, and to be ready to learn and grow. Children can learn that emotions are transient when we don't give them energy. For example, we have ninety seconds when we experience our own or someone else's anger or fear to count to ten or higher in order not to let the emotion rule us.

Jane Brody also reported that professional, brief intervention programs for traumatized children are successful, such as developed by Dr. Steven R. Marans, professor of psychiatry at Yale and director of the Childhood Violent Trauma Center, and by Safe Horizon, child advocacy centers in New York City. Their experience results in healing victims who are less inclined to suffer from PTSD, to have feelings of depression, tantrums, helplessness or hopelessness, or sleep problems.[28]

Dr. Marans said, "When children are alone with and don't have words to describe their traumatic reactions, symptoms and symptomatic behaviors are their only means of expression...To heal, children need recognition and understanding from their caregivers...intervention inspires hope and confidence."[28] Students in K-12 public schools should be able to experience interventions for their currently uneducated right-brain problems so they can learn, pass tests, and reach their academic and human potential.

For the past forty years or so, education has been touted as a boon to those who work with their minds as opposed to those who work with their hands. Today, though, computers, clones of IBM's Watson, and telecommunications are manning white-collar information jobs, from medical diagnoses to legal research, thereby reducing the demand for left-brained, highly educated people without people skills. Education for cognitive and manual tasks may be executed by adhering to left-brained explicit rules. However, the right-brained people skills needed for building relationships between parents and children, students and teachers, health care workers and patients, and service workers and their clients are left to chance but can be taught in K-12 public schools. Our public schools could integrate the intelligences of both sides of our brains, smart and wise, to be whole-brained and less hierarchically-oriented toward current perceptions of work roles and money.

Acquiring higher educational degrees for dollars has been falling in America in recent years because a) students or their families incur hundreds of thousands of dollars in debt and b) and getting degrees for the sake of dollars has been failing America due to its underlying philosophy: the pursuit of the private good for personal gain instead of a public good for learning how to live healthy lives as educated citizens who think for themselves instead of expecting their representatives to do their thinking for them. Instead of promoting job descriptions that focus on personal interests, all job descriptions could include service to humanity to the best of the job holder's ability, if we want to have America work for all citizens.

That philosophy of pursuit of the private good for personal gain degrees requires instituting a whole new K-12 public educational curriculum to include the intelligence and virtues of the right-brain's human development. Thus, young Americans' love affair with higher education is undergoing a costly divorce. The American Dream was an accepted and proven truism: education was a key to human beings' upward mobility and economic success. That is a hollow promise today, so the mission and scope of K-12 public schools will have to change to educate most Americans for life, citizenship, and a career that utilizes their talents and gifts.

Educated, unemployed, and frustrated young men and women are not just represented by Arab regimes but also by Western societies. In the U.S., the unemployment rate fails to account for those graduates who are riding out the economic storm in graduate school or are working part time for lack of an alternative. In Italy, Portugal and Spain, about one-fourth of college graduate, under age 25, are unemployed.[179] In addition, at the K-12 level, over one fourth of America's students are not graduating from high school. The Occupy Wall Street Movement spread throughout the United States. Individuals' motivation for joining the Movement differed, from unemployment to frustration with partisan politics, but one theme unites them: anger over income inequality and lost job opportunities in America.

Today's hard evidence of anti-intellectualism in our society is a challenge to our K-12 public educational system to finally include the right-brain as part of the education equation so the head and heart may be re-united and evolve into wisdom. Instead, our K-12 public education system requires winners and losers, as in games and sports, but learning is not a short-term game, not a sport, yet games and sports require lots of practice before game time. The equally hard evidence of unequal K-12 public educational opportunities for all Americans is documented in a film, *Waiting for Superman*. When the young Geoffrey Canada learned that Superman was not going to rescue him from

Harlem's ghetto, his emotional resilience, self-confidence in his abilities, and support system were the foundations of rescuing himself from the ghetto by getting a scholarship to Harvard and becoming a beacon of success for thousands of Harlem school children whom he mentors.

Democracy, as experienced in America by its three-tiered class system, means "some are more equal than others."[249] Without emotional literacy, access to a democracy's best K-12 public school system, and a mental and physical support system, developing brains and lives are wasted. There are scientists, politicians, and academics' objections to applying current hemispheric specialization and brain asymmetry to confront historical and educational traditions that empower the left-brain and ignore the right-brain. Continuing to ignore decades of brain research and our individual, national, and international wars that result from using half a brain instead of a whole brain is an affirmation of Historian Henry Adams's learned observation, "Nothing is so astonishing in education as the amount of ignorance it assimilates in the form of inert facts."[14] Or, the amount of truthful knowledge it ignores in perpetuating historical and educational fallacies.

Where ignorance is bliss, 'T'is folly to be wise!"[129] Why aren't more of us happy? If ignorance is bliss? If it's folly to be wise in a society were ignorance reigns, then what we don't know can limit our innate potential. Why seek wisdom when we can settle for being smart? Smart is transient, for it is subject to changing times, aging, future trends; whereas, wisdom is transformative. Because wisdom is inside each of us waiting to get out, we don't have to look up to others for wisdom or happiness; both are hidden inside each of us and accessible when we participate in solving the mysteries of life. Helen Keller, who taught blind people to "see," observed that "The heresy of one age becomes orthodoxy to the next."

A search for truth is the search for freedom from mind-forg'd manacles. We begin by looking beyond the status quo's "approved" knowledge which may be based on incomplete or biased information manufactured to instill fear, divisiveness, and control. The control of seven billion people on Earth can only be accomplished through deceit and secrecy. Truths enable us flourish in a flourishing America that works for all. In the blurred vision of our founders, they distrusted the common people and considered their elected representatives to be "more consonant to the public good than if pronounced by the people themselves."[97] Instead, it is we the people who have to have the wisdom to regain "reason, justice and truth...[from being] misled by the artful misrepresentations of [self-] interested men"[97] and women. Smart and Wise works for us and for our nation.

To improve our economy and Americans' lives, we can improve the education, morals, and character of the majority of our current K-12 student population by making sure that they experience in public school that love is the antidote for fear, that imagination is more important than a test score but we do need knowledge to fuel creativity, that anyone who has never made a mistake did not try anything new, and that peace cannot be kept by force.

Equality and democracy are not the hallmarks of the current K-12 public education system in America. The mission of K-12 public education could be to educate all student to their potential for living, working, and citizenship. Citizenship is achieved through understanding that we are all Americans and entitled to an equal education with equal opportunities. Peace is achieved through understanding that we are part of a whole universe, that education doesn't have to be what remains after we've forgotten everything we learned in school, and that we can learn from and transcend what happens to us in the waters in which we swam for nine months and the waters in which we swim today.

More reasons for including the right hemisphere's intelligence with the left hemisphere's intelligence in the K-12 public school system are outlined in Chapter Nine. A few comparisons of the underlying differences between funding K-12 public schools, administrations' missions, assumptions, expectations, requirements, teachers' and students' roles, and future outcomes of a typical Left-brained K-12 classroom (The Western Intellectual Tradition: TWIT) and of a typical Whole-brained K-12 classroom are:

L-brained K-12 TWIT pub. school	L-&R-brained K-12 pub. school
Mission: TWIT's agent of status quo: Flourish or Perish! Life is linear.	Evoke/nurture both students' talents/brains. Life is organic.
Funding: The richer the neighborhood and State, the more money for teachers, per student, teaching materials/supplies and administrators and aides plus expenses.	Public schools receive the same amount of Federal funds per student, for teachers, and supplies with extra dollars for under-performing schools.

Desegregation: Only if neighborhood is mixed.	Open enrollment: Diversity is a plus for overall learning.
Assumption: Students are empty plates and mugs ready for the learning and testing the ABCs and 123s.	Students' have unique histories to be addressed while learning/integrating the ABCs and 123s.
Learning happens alone, by listening and reading in quiet but competitive relationships and classrooms..	Learning happens by practicing in often noisy, experiential and collaborative relationships.
Expectation: IQ determines grades;	IQ measures enculturation.
Knowledge: Textbooks; few or no field trips. Homework.	Texts; field trips; self-Knowledge. Home study.
Requirement: Curriculum is all; Tests measure learning capabilities: Numbers are indicators of a student's intelligence.	Curriculum is a tool of inquiry; Tests identify what has yet to be learned until students "get it."
Texts: By-the-book, out-of-context facts are memorized, not integrated into long-term knowledge, not as building blocks.	Foundations of subjects are presented to understand why learn for the long-term.
Teacher: bureaucracy-controlled, the jug to fill mugs and disciplinarian via threats of punishment or poor grades.	Teacher is facilitator, mentor; guides students' learning and self-discipline.
Students' left-brains are valued only.	Both brains are valued; Inter-dependent Thinking/Learning: Encouraged and practiced
Educational: Learned Thinking: Follower! Conformity. Endure vs. Enjoy.	
Culture: The Arts: Low Priority; (Competitive) Sports: High Priority.	The Arts: High Priority; Diet/Exercise: High Priority.
Psychological: Unrealized potential.	Develop self's natural resources.
Consciousness: Conscious Mind rules; Oblivious of the Unconscious Mind.	Knows of both operative Minds: Conscious and Unconscious
Social Outcome: Power; Inequality.	Freedom and Equality
Economic Forecast: Unfair.	Caring and Fair.
Higher Education: Winners in K-12 and the rich gain access to Ivy League schools, get high-paying jobs, and often do whatever it takes to get richer.	K-12 whole-brain students love their personal and professional lives where money and people are valued.
Political: Authoritarian	Democracy

There are studies indicating that about 95 percent of children's learning, or "structural knowledge," comes not from formal education but from their interaction with their environments. The waters in which we swim after birth and the powerful belief systems we absorb condition us to unlearn that we are part of the whole of all things, all life. We can rediscover that knowing when we integrate the authentic knowledge of both sides of our human brains to be whole-brained thinkers, to think purple.

Thinking Purple

During election times, we hear a lot about America being divided into red and blue states – according to the number of American voters registered as Republicans or Democrats, not Independents – with obvious divergent political and worldviews. Metaphors for the right- and left- brains are red and blue, respectively. Red and blue states are the media's way to differentiate between the two political parties in America: Republican (red) and Democratic (blue). Our political party affiliations are usually inherited from family tradition or chosen. However, emotions play a huge part in our party of choice, so our choice may not be concurrent with our brain dominance or whole-brainism.

Right-brain dominant people are usually heart-oriented or emotional and are considered to be warmer (red) toward people and left-brain dominant people are usually head-oriented or cognitive and are considered to be cooler (blue) toward people. However, the uneducated right-brain is divided into positive and negative emotions; therefore, while right-brain dominant people are generally warmer toward people, both right- and left-brainers are prone to allowing their beliefs, fear, anger, or passion to override their common and uncommon sense and to react illogically, ideologically, or reasonably.

While the colors red and blue are used to differentiate between human beings' right and left brains, colors as metaphors appear to have a relationship to the human body's chakras. The ancient Indian seven chakras, or energy system, are color-coded with attention to the light and dark sides of each chakra that make all the difference in having positive or negative attitudes as adults. Blue is associated with the fifth chakra (communication), the throat and the expression of one's choice, truth, and wisdom. The shadow side of the fifth chakra is the "need to control relationships and events."[235] Red is associated with the first chakra, the base or root chakra (ground to Earth, groups, or churches). When our groundedness is in balance, "we feel secure, alert, full of active energy, stable and warm"[102] When we are not, our shadow side excludes others, prejudice is operative, and illusions of superiority are present.[235] Also, when our emotional buttons (red) are pushed, the limbic brain's amygdala reacts as if we were two-year-olds, unless we have learned to differentiate between incoming data in the now from data from the past, and to consciously seek data from the left-brain. Thus, we learn from ancient color codings of the chakras that human beings have positive and negative positions that are lessons to be learned. Therefore, blue denotes communication and control issues; whereas, red denotes a base that may exclude others and prejudice may be operative. It is not uncommon for us to think red in one area of our lives and to think blue in another. Such responses may be situational or a preference, determined by what brain module emerges. However, the unconscious mind often makes decisions for conscious minds when we have unexamined belief systems or unresolved negative experiences. Thinking purple is a choice that takes effort, from analysis to synthesis.

Communication problems and security bases within self arise when we are stuck in one or the other brain and cannot integrate our twin brains to be fully intelligent and fully functioning human beings. An Eriksonian therapist, Steven Gilligan, related at one of his seminars in Connecticut that when he was living in his Peace mode, he attracted all sorts of negative people and events to himself. So he reintegrated his Warrior side and owned both sides of the archetype; then he was in balance again. Similarly, when we disown any parts of ourselves, including the attributes of either the left- or right-brain, we are unbalanced and may be stereotyped as red or blue, for example. Our negative emotional reactions to people and their worldviews are symptoms of our own disowned aspects of self that need to be acknowledged and integrated. We don't see things or people as they are but as we are.

Since our K-12 public education system directs us to owning only the left hemisphere, not only are we Americans divided within ourselves, divisiveness surrounds us. We live in fifty U.S. red and blue states. The ultimate goal is to integrate our brains and to integrate red and blue to achieve purple states and be the United States of America. To accomplish those goals, we could begin with examining the content of our brains' hemispheres that keep us from uniting ourselves before we can become whole-brained, to think purple.

When we mix the colors red and blue together, we get purple. Thinking purple is a metaphor for human intelligence and whole-brained thinking. Whole-brained thinking is desirable for humane functioning and wisdom. If people were taught to walk by-the-book, as we are taught the 3Rs in K-12 public school, many of us would be in remedial walking as a teenager.

In earlier centuries, purple dyes used to be rare and expensive and were available to elites only. It is no accident that, throughout the ages, royalty and religious hierarchical figures have worn purple robes. The mantle of wisdom was placed on their shoulders as well. Wearing purple symbolized the divine nature/right to rule the masses, not necessarily wisely when they were left-brain dominant. It is not enough just to wear purple but to live purple: thinking purple unites our divided brains, selves, and society; it is everyone's destiny in America.

A friend, Nancy, asked why – if the color red signifies being warmer toward people and the color blue signifies being cooler toward people – the red and blue metaphors for America's political division of states did not work for her within the political/financial context that divides us as well. From a Smart versus Wise perspective, the colors, red, blue, and purple are metaphors, and metaphors are tools to ground and understand abstract concepts that are tied to our lived experiences and possibilities. For example, the color blue may be perceived as left-brained in the educational and communications domain as reason, calm, cool, and collected, organized, and more task- than people-oriented. Similarly, red may be perceived as right-brained, big-picture-oriented, and warmer toward people, but the right-brain is divided into positive and negative feelings and emotions and prejudices; therefore, red also signifies succumbing to negative emotions and ideology.

In addition, we have belief systems and other modules as iterated by Neuroscientist Michael Gazzaniga [116] that influence our thinking toward reasoning or emotions. Thus, each human being may have a preference for the left- or right-brain's attributes, but we are a hybrid of both when both are not equally educated. Then the embedded and often learned biases, prejudices, and unexamined beliefs in the unconscious brain-mind make decisions for us. Researchers inform us that politics is no exception. Liberals – blue – are said to seek information beyond their beliefs, based upon reason; whereas, conservatives – red – are said to seek information that confirms their beliefs, including the man-made Puritannical/Calvinistic beliefs that became the gospel of wealth for not sharing with those who are poor as God's punishment, which undermines Jesus Christ's teachings from his heart consciousness.

It is unAmerican today for Americans to be anti-emotional (anti-right-brain) or anti-intellectual (anti-left-brain) or to be content- versus context-oriented. Each of us has the capacity to encompass both: to view all sides of situations, events, or people to form a reasoned decision. For Nature to endow each human being two complementary brains and then to educate one and not the other is not smart but stupid. Scientific research informs us we need both sides of our brain for optimum human functioning, just as animals do. We will be divided within ourselves and divided as red and blue states until we integrate and use both sides of our brains – think purple – to respond situationally rather than automatically.

Thinking purple is every American's right in our democracy, yet our K-12 public educational systems are anything but democratic or in sync with human nature. The scientific brain research of current and recent decades is ignored, so the left-brain continues to reign as it has for thousands of years, and the relationship brain – the right-brain – has not had much attention from researchers until a few decades ago.

An American Association of Retired People's (AARP) television advertisement, in the fall of 2008, showed a blue donkey and a red elephant running toward each other, clashing, rolling into a ball, and emerging as a purple-donkey-elephant creature: a new, united entity. The message was "Divided We Fall."

Our human condition does not have to be comedy or tragedy, or Heaven or Hell on Earth. We can choose to be Smart and Wise, to think purple, and not to succumb to others' coercion to be fearful, believe others' prophecies or expectations, or adhere to left-brained developmental norms or guidelines. Just write it off to their human development deficits. Our right-brain encompasses our intuition. Intuition is our wisest adviser until it is educated out of us as louder, authoritative voices drown it out. Wisdom may emerge as an emotion or physical sensation in the body. The emotional centers in the brain, the neurons in the stomach (the gut), and the heart have no outer voice, just an inner voice, and that "knowing," not logic, helps us to navigate the waters of life.

Chapter Five

An old New Yorker cartoon is a metaphor for many Americans who find themselves adrift: A person is drowning and yelling, "Help! Help!" A man, briefcase in hand, standing on a wharf, yells back, "I can't swim! Would ten dollars help?"

America's Politicized Democracy: The Waters In which We Swim

America's sovereignty and its political parties' processes are under siege in 2012 by divided Americans who are products of The Western Intellectual Tradition. Culture, power and politics, economics, religion, gender, and race appear to deeply estrange us from one another at conscious and unconscious levels. However, our two brains are the primary source of our estrangement when one brain is not formally educated in K-12 public schools or informally at home, leading to our being divided selves and citizens with opposing worldviews, instead of being integrated, fully intelligent human beings. As a result, the unlevel K-12 public educational system has divided Americans into heads who are anti-emotional and hearts who are anti-intellectual, public schools that separate the upper, middle and lower classes from cultural and economic opportunities, and partisan politics that paralyze government's and the president's ability and desire to solve America's problems that are in plain sight and visible to the world.

America's Founding Fathers were not of one mind, they were educated individuals, pragmatists, and committed to debating and integrating their ideas to stitch together 13 colonies of diverse populations and religions into a democratic republic. Their concern for the welfare and cohesion of the new republic led to banishing religious intolerance and granting religious freedom, for they worried about religious wars and political disputes whose intensities could mimic religious passion. They desired to create a nation where people could offer unconditional loyalty to the republic while compromising their disagreements over economic and political matters.

They were fearful of the tyranny of central authority and of majority mob rule, but they had more faith in people's elected representatives/politicians to honestly vote for "We the People" than in the majority of uneducated people's decisions to ensure a flourishing nation. In our Founding Fathers' times, Alexander Hamilton voiced what the other Founders believed – except Thomas Jefferson who probably believed: "man is neither utterly wicked nor naturally virtuous" – "that honest, competent administration was needed to maximize the chances of virtue prevailing."[88] The Founding Fathers presumed that educated representatives' worldviews, like their own, would include the greater good of all citizens and unconditional loyalty to the nation. However, Thomas Jefferson urged citizens to become educated, which does not include humanity's virtues. In his era, virtues were learned in the family, at church, or from revered role models. He knew that even in a democracy nobody's freedom is secure when segments of the population do not exercise their civic responsibilities.

Today's our future is not secure when the financial tension between self-interest and America's and others' interests changed since 1776, so capitalists' left-brain goals have not been balanced by right-brain virtues or by loyalty to our republic. America's corporations, industrialists, wealthy elites, and politicians learned from the Great Depression (1929-1939) that financial manipulations work: those who took their money out of the 1929 stock market contributed to its crash, and had the money to later buy up undervalued properties for a song to become wealthy.

From the 1980s onward, lobbyists representing the financial elites have secured politicians' votes to dismantle regulations or safety nets instituted in the 1930s to ensure a more sustainable economy for everyone. With déjà vu all over again in the ongoing Great Recession, the rich elites made money and the corporations that didn't were bailed out by government, not ordinary and retired Americans who lost over 40 percent of their assets, homes, and pensions. And jobs, over the past decades, have been outsourced to cheaper labor overseas. The financiers' timing was perfect with political collusion. America was in huge debt from oil-inspired wars by war hawks and the military-industrial-complex and by profit-inspired worthless paper products requiring corporate bailouts to Wall Street, not to Main Street. The majority of elected politicians played their hand to put a stranglehold on democracy and loyalty to our republic in favor of the financial elites who have the gold: the source of SuperPac money to win friends, influence people's votes, and ensure campaign money for re-election in the 2012 November election. Their political priorities became shrink government, focus on budget cuts across the board, women's rights, and ignore the sagging economy for the majority of Americans' future.

Our nation was founded as a republic, a constitutional republic of a democratic nature (one person, one vote), not as a democracy where the majority's voices/votes rule. The Founders of our republic had little faith in the character, judgment, and ability of uneducated people to have the time, wisdom, or level-headedness to make complex, political decisions. To ensure a flourishing America, they constructed institutions, laws, and regulations to improve people's character, guide their judgment, and limit their power by a republican form of government whereby people choose representatives who, in turn, make decisions on their behalf. Those safeguards were intended to protect Americans from the tyranny of democracy's majority rule so people's excesses based on irregular passion and illicit advantage could be mediated by people's elected representatives/politicians who are presumed to embody reason, justice, and truth. Instead, today, the people need protection from those politicians whose self-interest and their understanding of the U.S. Constitution and the country's needs conflict with Americans' and America's common good.

Believers in the democratic nature of our constitutional republic have more faith in the character and judgment of people as a voting group and believe that safeguards are needed to also protect America and its people from the possible lack of character and judgment of their representatives/politicians, people who run corporations, and from modern robber barons.

Today, the political differences between Republicans (small government, free enterprise, big businesses, tax the middle class, not the wealth-oriented elites) and the Democrats (big government, tax everyone equally or fairly: income-oriented professionals, blue collar hourly workers, financial elites, and the wealthy) have created irreconcilable policy differences and character assassinations that border on ideology and classic racism, not political compromise. In practice, believers in a republic tend to favor things (left-brain goals: money, business profits, and enterprises free of government oversight) more than ordinary and uneducated people (right-brain's emotions and intuition, our soft versus our hard sides that humanize us, and humanity's virtues: respect, civility, morals and ethics, empathy, and compassion).

One of America's Founders James Madison's rationale for establishing a republic versus a democratic form of government for America was a fear of pure democracy. He and other founders believed that elected representatives' "wisdom may best discern the true interest of their country and whose patriotism and love of justice will be least likely to sacrifice it."[97] Instead having to contend with the fear of pure democracy's majority, we have inherited a system whereby representatives/politicians and vocal minorities are smart, but their "wisdom" is not consonant with loyalty to our country or the public good.

"As every American youngster has been taught, one thing that Washington, Jefferson and all the founders did believe in was religious freedom. They were appalled by the fusion of religious and political power, epitomized by the divine right of kings."[88] "Regardless of their own views on the spiritual, people like Madison, Washington and Jefferson were intensely concerned for the welfare and cohesion of the new republic. They worried not only about religious wars as such but about political disputes which were 'religious' in their intensity... ponder the words of Jefferson in his first inaugural address: 'Let us reflect that, having banished from our land that religious intolerance under which mankind so long bled and suffered, we have yet gained little if we countenance a political intolerance as despotic, as wicked, and capable of as bitter and bloody persecutions."[88] Who knew that out-of-kilter human brains' hemispheres would lead to out-of-kilter Americans and America's society?

In politics, politicians may be egotists not leaders, charisma is not character, and a magnetic personality is not an indicator of a caring heart. In reality, America's economic success and moral foundation are at risk when a Pentagon culture of "permanent war"[14] and government corporate welfare are priorities, not all Americans' welfare. Just as both the left- and right-brains need to overlap to make smart and wise decisions, the concerns for America and all Americans by both political parties need to overlap to reform the military, corporate, and public welfare states. Decision-making is not a win-lose contest between left- and right-brained intelligences. Wise decisions are situation-dependent and a finely tuned blend of both hemispheres' input: Smart and Wise!

Since the 1960s, anti-intellectualism and divisiveness have been gaining momentum in America to the point that e-mails flooded the Internet in 2011-2012 loaded with fear, anger, and untruths as truths about Democrat President Obama. After all, they knew that President John Kennedy wore a back brace and that President Harry Truman played the piano, but President Obama...? It's as if President Obama doesn't fit any "facts" that they associate with their assumptions about blacks or half-white and half-black Americans. It's as if those under the anti-Obama spell are questioning their own perceived intellectual, cultural, or genetic superiority and economic entitlement with anger and fear at being usurped by the democratic voting process. It's as if their way of thinking is right and the truth and it's up to them to save America for themselves. Closed minds? Liberals are open to conservative views; conservatives are interested only in what echoes their own views[192] without regard for loyalty to America or people's equal rights.

The Waters In Which We Swim

The waters in which each of us swam for nine months or so in utero are beyond our control during our prebirth and after birth experiences during our helpless, dependency period in our family. Our gestation experience determines how well we can navigate the waters we encounter en route to adulthood. "Imagine water flowing downstream, prenatal influences might dig a canal, so to speak, making it easier for the water to flow one way rather than another."[257]

Armed with knowledge of the waters in which we swam and swim today, we may "add another layer to our understanding of who we are and how we got to be this way."[257] The choice is ours a) to blame our parents for "failed gestation" and for the familial, cultural, and economic waters in which we were reared; or b) to take responsibility for our total health and human condition by learning how to master the turbulent waters.

The waters have gotten murkier and more turbulent for many Americans since the late 1970s when Anthropologist Edward Hall wrote about the waters in which all Americans swim, known as culture,[138] but also known as politics and economics. Americans' experience of the impact that culture, politics, and economics has upon their lives depends upon the waters in which they swam in utero, whether they are members of the lower, middle, or upper classes, and whether or not they become aware of their divided hemispheres that, with effort, they may become whole-brained. Education in America used to be the path to swim toward upward mobility. Today it is more likely to be a means to label, track, and dumb down our potential.

Americans are divided culturally, politically, and economically. *The New Yorker* cartoon, "I can't swim! Would ten dollars help?" epitomizes the philosophy of roughly half of America's population today who feel a moral obligation to financially help those in need for democracy's failed past policies and practices. So, half of our population wants the government to jump-start the economy with new business ventures and needed infrastructure replacements, not just save the financial and industrial systems and spend money on wars, but to help those who are out of work with no jobs in sight, poverty stricken, undereducated, or overeducated.

Individuals who don't wait for government intervention and provide jobs and services for those in need are sprinkled throughout America. Social research indicates that students work harder when scholarship money is accompanied by personal interaction, a relationship with providers. Similarly, workers would personally benefit if unemployment insurance and disability, and social welfare dollars were accompanied by re-education, job training, or self-help living skills. *The New Yorker* cartoon dramatically emphasizes the futility of throwing money only at a drowning person when interventions to get them back on shore, on their own two feet, are necessary before they get into trouble.

America's other half's beliefs consist of moral outrage at the thought of sharing their income/wealth with the less fortunate or even paying their fair share of taxes. They would undo basic security for the unemployed whom they perceive as idle or undeserving: "Pull yourself up by your bootstraps, as I did!" some wannabe politicians and elites say, without acknowledging the direct and indirect roles government and ordinary people played in their accomplishments. "Blame Yourself!" said Republican presidential candidate Herman Cain, "not Wall Street! Get a job!"

In Elizabeth Warren's 2011-2012 bid for a U.S. congressional seat from Massachusetts, she asks wealthy business owners to pay their fair share of taxes. In past decades, income inequality, manufacturing jobs sent overseas, the disparity between hourly workers and CEOs and financiers also mean elites pay 15% taxes and less due to loopholes. The rest of us pay much more as the rich get greedier and richer and the poor get poorer. Warren stated:

> There is nobody in this country who got rich on his own. Nobody. You built a factory out there, good for you. But, I want to be clear: you moved your goods to market on the roads the rest of us paid for. You hired workers the rest of us paid to educate. You were safe in your factory because of police forces and fire forces that the rest of us paid for. You didn't have to worry that marauding bands would come and seize everything at your factory and hire someone to protect against this because of the work the rest of us did. Now look, you built a factory and it turned into something terrific or a great idea. God bless. Keep a big hunk of it. But part the underlying social contract is you take a hunk of that and pay forward for the next kid who comes along.[25]

Elizabeth Warren didn't mention the fact that manufacturers in this country use, pollute, and overload our common air, ground water, waterways, and public water and sewage systems (paid for by taxpayers' money) with industrial toxic wastes hazardous to public health. Some politicians prefer to perceive Elizabeth Warren's democratic position as class warfare, as envy. Envy is one of the Bible's seven deadly sins, so we are sinners if we object to elites' free rides. insider trading, 15% tax rates, off-shore stashed wealth like Biblical talents, and unequal education and opportunities. If that anti-Elizabeth-Warren attack doesn't work, there's always her Native American heritage, real or family lore, to be Swift-boated.

The Occupy Wall Streeters' protests that began October 2011 and spread throughout the United States have diverse motivations: income inequality, no jobs, frustration over partisan politics, loss of the American Dream, academic dollars owed for over-rated education, corruption, policies, and tax loopholes that enrich the top two percent of American society. The protesters. may not change America's politics or direction. "Yet, the protests have already elicited a remarkably hysterical reaction from Wall Street, the super-rich in general, and politicians and pundits who reliably serve the interests of the wealthiest hundredth of a percent."[195]

Evidently, the economic system is rigged to benefit wealthy Americans. "This special treatment can't bear close scrutiny – and therefore, as they see it, there must be no close scrutiny. Anyone who points out the obvious...must be demonized and driven from the stage... So, who's really being un-American here? Not the protesters, who are simply trying to get their voices heard. No, the real extremists here are America's oligarchs, who want to suppress any criticism of the sources of their wealth"[195] or to identify them as donors to SuperPacs.

In his 2007 book, *Words That Work: It's Not What You Say, It's What People Hear*, Frank Luntz, a political pollster, shares how he uses written and spoken language to manipulate public perceptions and opinion and to craft words that conceal more than they reveal.[211] All U.S. political parties engage such pundits to get their messages across, but some messages are more underhanded and distorted than others. It seems that a lie broadcast at least three times becomes truth to some ears. Often those voters who are influenced by emotionally-charged propaganda, and vote accordingly, will find they have voted against themselves.

President Thomas Jefferson, in the 1800s, warned Americans to become educated. He knew that nobody's liberty is secure in a democracy if a large group became incompetent or negligent of its civic responsibilities. In Jefferson's time, the right-brain was educated in the home, modeled at school, learned at church or through experiences. However, they believed that women and Blacks were the property of white men and had no civil rights other than accorded to them by white men, so slavery, racism, and sexism co-existed. Today, many wannabe politicians are proof that ignorance is fashionable in America.

Politicians and citizens who want to make a positive difference in our society would play the education card to expose those who, under the guise of freedom of speech, inflame the uneducated egos and passions of the vulnerable. They would stop shortchanging our K-12 public school students by providing an education that prepares whole-brainers for college, work, citizenship, and life.

Instead, America appears to be undergoing a social revolution. The majority of aging politicians are trapped in a 20th century mindset. There are few 21st century evolved institutions to lead the transition toward resolving the current "conflict between an ancient system of institutions struggling with…a totally new economic life-style"[271] where income inequality is greater than when Franklin D. Roosevelt engineered the New Deal in the 1930s.[210] It is K-12 public education where the left-brain is empowered, so smart is revered, yet mainstream Americans trust the heart more than the head. The social revolution is affecting our nation's children who are learning what they live.

The Fall from Family into Culture

Something happens to children in America's upper, middle, and lower classes on the way to adulthood. Over the past decades, more families are sustained by two careers or two paychecks, or by single or divorced parents. Their children may spend hours socializing in day care, with nannies, other children, or alone, watching TV, playing video games, or on the Internet. Parents who feel guilty about their absence may buy more material things to compensate and be more permissive or indulgent. Many children develop a sense of entitlement, believe they are the center of the universe, become materialistic, or are socially irresponsible. They learn what they live, and they will live what they learn.[242]

Nevertheless, most adults parent as they were parented or not parented. Parents may suppress emotional expression and the human spirit or not know how to cope with emotions or overindulge their children to compensate for what they themselves did not get. It's possible that parents' Don'ts may overpower the rare Do! "Don't fall!" (When learning to walk). "Don't cry!" (When feelings erupt or the body hurts). "Don't make waves!" (Conform to society's norms!). Don'ts are intertwined with You-messages: "Sit still!" "Listen to me or else!" "You're stupid!" "You won't amount to anything!" "Thou Shalt Not..." is the basis of religion and laws and "the source of all legal systems, prisons, war, and our downfall."[260] Psychologist Allan Schore proposed that the effects of the negatives upon a developing child's transition, from a carefree state to a depressed one, is "the fall of the human from grace into culture"[260] with its gender, racial, ethnic, and class stereotyping in America, despite legislation, which doesn't affect unexamined beliefs in unconscious minds.

The rearing of upper class children may be relegated to nannies, expensive private or boarding schools, extra immersion in after-school activities, tutors, reserved admission to parents' alma maters, world travel, possible little face time with parents, and intact networks, so their fall into culture may be one of the ease of entitlement.

The rearing of lower class children – depending upon the parent or parents' human condition – may be one of love and caring despite poverty or consist of physical and mental, neglect; children may end up raising themselves and their siblings, and be successful if they attend or graduate from high school. Poor children of poor mothers who were malnourished, under stress which reinforced smoking, drinking, and using drugs, means their nine months in the womb led to low birth weights and at risk for mental disabilities and later heart problems, so their fall into the dominant white culture may be one of low expectations, unless they are lucky enough to have a relationship with a significant other and/or motivate themselves.

The rearing of middle class children crosses the lines between the upper and the lower classes; thus, many get a taste of both, but their fall into culture is usually more direction-oriented. Most have been raised by human development role models. Girls used to be raised to be dependent upon relationships for their identity; boys used to be raised to be independent; they are actually dependent upon careers for identity. Today, many boys and girls are being raised to be interdependent, to integrate both dependent and independent roles.

What equalizes the classes? The fact that they were born in America where each individual may take advantage of opportunities to learn, grow, and become who they were meant to be, if they are emotionally literate and motivated. However, the research shows that poor schools in poor neighborhoods are the worst in the nation and are the antithesis of democratic principles. Money overrules the U.S. Constitution's promise. Educational opportunities are more available to those in high quality K-12 public schools and are raised with loving care or have mentors or significant others who take a special interest in them. Thus, the elite kids may be raised with what money can buy instead of loving care, so disdain of others and arrogance could be a mask to elevate self-esteem. Disenfranchised kids may mask their negative self-esteem by bullying others or dropping out of schools where they do not feel good about themselves.

What deters individuals from the three classes to develop to capacity? K-12 school systems that do not teach them how to cope with their unresolved life and ego deficits or the emotional resilience to learn from mistakes, so some students may drop out while others may take longer to mature. In any event, equality in America is highly overrated. Only whole-brained K-12 public education can level the human development field for the disparity America's young children experience, both upper, middle, and lower classes, from being born and raised in unequal circumstances. Fatalistic attitudes, though, need to be addressed: Learned helplessness may be unlearned through whole-brain K-12 education.

Some young people's negative experiences and negative aspects of the right-brain's cultural conditioning overwhelm them when they are emotionally illiterate. Our society expects young people (late teens through the 20s) to follow its "norms" of settling into a career when the ongoing Recession means there are no jobs and the human brain's prefrontal cortex is not fully mature until at least 25 years of age or later.

During prefrontal immaturity, before college, young people could volunteer or seek internships to gain experience beyond their upbringing or intended careers, seek adventures through travel, or work service jobs to save for college instead of relying on student loans. Without emotional literacy and sanctioned time out to delay society's expectations, young people rarely become all they could be or, if they bloom, they may be late bloomers. With a combination of brain (prefrontal cortex) immaturity and the onset of adulthood is happening later in our society, it is an opportunity for our country to invest in its young people when they are most open to perspectives that allow them to anticipate different futures and/or the long-term consequences of different choices. It's a matter of choosing to live, work, and relate with more Heaven than Hell on Earth.

The human brain responds to changing times, and all young people in their late teens and early twenties are not in the traditional lockstep march toward adulthood. Yet, puberty is happening earlier, primarily due to the use of hormones and antibiotics in our livestock's food supply and discarded hormones in our water supply. Psychological and physical processes are not in sync with traditional human development theorists. Since the 1990s, many young Americans have not been moving along the human developmental path from "adolescence" (age 11 to late teens) to "young adulthood" (late teens or age 20 to 45), as outlined by Erik Erikson.[95]

Since Americans are living into their nineties, it seems logical for young people to delay commitment choices that they would have to live with for fifty years or so, especially in view of the fact that human beings' brains mature later than the human development theorists knew. The fact that today's young people are taking longer to grow up has led to the need for an in-between stage in the human development cycle: "Emerging Adulthood."[11]

In prosperous times in America, young people used to follow their parents' example: entered young adulthood by starting their careers, became independent of their families, committed to relationships, had children, worked in one or two companies, and eventually retired. Many of those young people ended up regretting their early decisions or not wanting to repeat their parents' lives, so they divorced, negatively impacted their children, or endured mid-life crises, changed careers, or moved back in with parents. The ongoing Recession means that after college many young people in America have had to move back in with their parents or never left their parents' home after high school so, by default, they are participating in the Emerging Adulthood phase of human development.

The Emerging Adulthood stage for young men and women is not universal in practice because some young people skip the stage. But, in theory, a timeout period is essential for young people to explore their options and entertain new ideas before they settle down. Young people in their 20s have different issues, less experience, and immature brainpower than those adults in their 40s with whom they are currently lumped in human development theories.

Too many young people are emotionally immature: unfocused, adrift, into substance abuse, have eating disorders, are mentally depressed, or cannot commit to a permanent relationship. Many are overwhelmed by familial and society's demands that they grow up. K-12 public schools and colleges could prepare rites of passage for students' Emerging Adulthood era with Fulbright-type scholarships, stipends for volunteering in domestic Peace Corps programs in America, or mentoring opportunities with inner-city youths, for example. Such programs would make their first year of college less wasteful or playful.

A phenomenon in our American culture is the number of young people and adults who are not motivated to earn a self through good deeds, just be millionaires. Compare many young immigrants from Europe and Asia who see opportunities to work hard, become successful, and give back to other Americans too. If we can't grow our own geniuses to save America then we have to admit educated immigrants or educate the ones here, for many immigrants have proved themselves to be the lifeblood of America and loyal to America's democracy. Friend Keith is a contractor; recently he told me about an Iranian immigrant who works hard in his own contracting business and is financially rewarded. He is so happy to be in a free America; he believes in giving back, so he does pro bono work for the poor and retired who cannot afford his services.

Our popular culture's values have shifted away from its traditional focus on industrial and technical enterprises with a skilled working or blue-collar class. Instead, many Americans prefer consumer lifestyles and less product-oriented fields, such as professions that are considered more genteel: law, finance, consulting, and nonprofits.[36] It's as if hardworking, practical Americans climbed the left-brain ladder after creating the nation's wealth, prosperity, and fulfilling their American Dreams, but they wanted more for their offspring to experience what they may not have attained: education, status, and respect. It seems our culture does not value blue collar workers or those in the helping professions, from teachers and nurses to mothers. But K-12 public school systems fail those who are unmotivated or fail left-brain tests, so more undereducated students, unskilled workers, and emotionally illiterate people are populating our society and engendering disrespect.

Current emphasis upon public service versus corporate careers means, as David Brooks wrote, "America may become more humane but less prosperous."[36] However, at the lower class level, "A gigantic slice of America's human capital is vastly underused, and it has been that way for a generation."[36] Undereducated is a more appropriate term for students in poorly funded, failing public schools. They are labeled. unmotivated, bored, and disrespected; they aren't taught education's 3Rs, the basics, until they "get it" (as in Finland), so they are cast out to be picked up by other social agencies, especially the prison system.

According to anthropological research, "culture is a body of knowledge concerning learned survival strategies that are passed on to our young through teaching and modeling...It becomes the living repository of our species' survival ideation and is at the root of every issue of survival."[260] People who grow up in a bi- or tricultural setting are aware that everyone does not share the same cultural patterns or privileges, especially in America.

America was built upon the backs of poor people, immigrants and slaves, and most of our financial elites had humble beginnings, yet hierarchical work status attitudes and practices prevail. "How do you do?" is often replaced by "What do you do?" and what we do determines whether or not we are worth talking with at cocktail parties or conferences. To register at a 5-day Tavistock conference at Tufts University, I naively listed my occupation as housewife/student. The list was circulated, minus names, to the fifty or so participants. "Who's the housewife here?" someone demanded to know. I waited, expecting one of the few women to stand up; no one did, so I identified myself and was told, "You don't look like a housewife!" "What are you doing here?" "You're here under false pretenses!" I was in the company of a group of lawyers, psychiatrists, and other academic and corporate professionals who wanted the Tavistock leader to tell us what to do; most were adrift without their left-brained rules and regulations. One psychiatrist actually lost his cool and left, yelling, "I know what you're trying to do..." Yes, to unlock the "mind forg'd manacles" that keep us from exploring and experiencing alternatives to traditional leadership-followership role models, to use not just our heads' intelligence but our hearts' intelligence, and to examine residual stereotypes or assumptions that emerge in large groups. It is difficult to let go of hierarchical roles we absorb in our culture's pecking order: top leaders versus managers versus white collar workers or blue collar jobs, rich versus poor, and, today, the 2% financial elites versus the rest of us.

Most people who work with their hands also work with their heads and hearts, such as carpenters, cabinet/furniture makers, artists/poets, craftspeople, writers, and other pleasurable activities, like knitting or stained glass. Those occupations and activities are opportunities to integrate both sides of the brain. To value what we do for a living, even if someone else does not, is rare in most jobs where the left-brain's rules are operative and job satisfaction is in the money earned, so we learn to value our own and others' worth by how much our services are worth. Our ongoing Recession has ruined people's financial base, from jobs to retirement funds, but it has taken an extra toll on our cultural identities, psychologically, mentally, and emotionally. Cultures are the yin and yang of being human. "There is no self except in interaction with a culture, and no culture that is not made up of selves."[138]

Psychiatrist, Darold Treffert, an expert in savant syndrome, proposes that, in savants, the right-brain compensates for damage to the left-brain. Yet, many attributes of the right-brain, such as empathy, are absent and many attributes of the left-brain, such as focus on details and organization, are present.[333] Psychiatrist Iain McGilchrist proposes that damaged right-brains manifest a range of clinical problems similar to schizophrenia.[225] Both views indicate the overlapping of the two brains within each of us. He questions,"If this is what happens in individuals, could a culture dominated by the left hemisphere modes of apprehension begin to exhibit such features?"[225] Culture and its institutions and organizations mold us, just as our families and genetic inheritances do, so few of us acknowledge that "The trouble I have with him or her is me" has culture as a root cause.

An European immigrant, Albert Einstein, famous for his quotes, said, Too many of us look upon Americans as dollar chasers. This is a cruel libel, even if it is reiterated thoughtlessly by the Americans themselves. In our culture, the money chasers have gotten more active since 1955, when Einstein died, and they are practicing greed and corruption to the point that our current economic downturn has affected all of us. Cultural and social injustice prevails.

When we pay attention to those who abuse our democratic values, we learn that they cause the most harm to our culture and society at large. For years, The Western Intellectual Tradition's smartest and brightest Ivy League MBAs, physicists, mathematicians, and lawyers have been flocking to Wall Street to join those who are rich by doing whatever it takes to enrich themselves. Rigid left-brainers have insatiable appetites for money, status, power, and material tings. To be so focused on self is an indicator they do not have access to their right-brain's virtues or ignore any pangs of a moral or social conscience.

The danger for our culture is the left-brain's atomized view of the world is not being modified by the right-brain's positive emotions and no attention is being paid to the greater good of all Americans and America. The danger is not only flawed thinking, but financial rewards are handed out: many players on Wall Streeters received bonuses for "bad" behavior while whistle blowers were fired for "good" behavior. It seems America is now a country where no good deed goes unpunished and bad deeds abound.

"For a society to function cooperatively, be it a hunter-gatherer tribe or a nation-state, its members or leaders must sanction those who break the rules...cheaters tend to be momentarily selfish, taking more of the pie, sharing less of the endowment."[139] If we're cheating Americans, America, and ourselves, is that smart? We know it isn't wise!

Power and Politics

The term *power* originated from the Latin posse and from the French infinitive pouvoir, both meaning to be able to. Max Weber's definition of power is the possibility of imposing one's will upon the behavior of other persons.[342] French and Raven provided five classifications of the bases of social power in institutions and organizations: 1. "Role or Legitimate" power is the authority vested in the role and the holder of the role. 2. "Reward" power supplies or controls resources. 3.

"Coercive" power applies sanctions or punishes. 4. "Expert" power controls knowledge or information. 5. "Referent" power is power by association through relationships with those in power in institutional and organizational roles [105] or wealthy.

Elizabeth Janeway's perspective that power is a relationship led her to question, "What do the powerful want?...it can't be the mere confirmation of their authority. They know they possess that...This, then, is where the legitimacy of authority enters the picture...What the powerful want is assurance that their power is held rightfully, within a relationship which sanctions its use and validates the right of these rulers to rule...the consent of the governed to their actions as proper, acceptable, free of blame; and this consent can be granted only by the governed."[170]

"Absolute intolerance is always a sign of uncertainty and panic. Why do you have to hunt down everyone unless you're weak?...if its members beliefs are based on faith or fear, conviction or coercion...what is the quality of a belief that exists simply because it's enforced?"[78]

However, people's unschooled right-brains are swayed by biased advertising, headlines without substance, and leaders' charisma, even toxic charisma. Therefore, the power of the other members of the power relationship, the weak, is compromised when language is used to conceal more than it reveals, setting up roadblocks to listening to other worldviews or willingness to disbelieve the powers-that-be. It usually takes a whole-brain practicing person to realize that there is power for the owning in every position or condition in the world.

With most institutional definitions of power based in hierarchy, Barry Oshry teaches that power is not static; it is the ability to recognize and realize the potential of whatever position we are in and to invoke the power of our minds.[250] Rollo May asserted that "power is essential for all living things"[223] and that humans cannot live well in the world without some sense of their significance. That's why so many poor children children need to be respected in a caring K-12 public school environment for them to succeed academically.

Carl Rogers' name is synonymous with personal power. His view of personal power is person-centered: power, control, and decision-making must be vested within individuals and away from institutions and organizations. He taught that when individuals discover their inner power, their outer world changes as they make conscious choices and decisions. Personal power is, therefore, "based on the premise that the human being is basically a trustworthy organism, capable of evaluating the outer and inner situation, understanding herself in its context, making constructive choices as to the next steps in life, and acting on those choices."[286]

Acting on choices became the position of Holocaust Survivor Dr. Edith Eva Eger whose mother whispered her last words to her, "If all is taken away from you, you still have what is in your head...they cannot touch the treasures in your mind," as her mother was directed to the left to the gas chambers by Auschwitz's prison guards and Edie was directed to the right to work at age 16. Dr. Edie, after experiencing much guilt, finally realized she was inspired by her mother's message to live and teach it: good can triumph over evil and the soul can endure all. War was not a solution to Adolf Hitler's inner demons and delusions of grandeur. He was defeated by the allied forces who were forced to defend themselves against him and his allies who had attacked them.

Senator J. William Fulbright, who served from 1959 to 1974 as Chairman of the Senate Foreign Relations Committee, wrote a book in 1966, *The Arrogance of Power*, to expose some well-intentioned Americans' tendency to lose touch with reality and to succumb to self-delusion that undermines our democratic culture of government of, by, and for the people. He believed it is "unnatural and unhealthy for a nation to be engaged in global crusades for some principle or ideal while neglecting the needs of its own people...an effective policy abroad depends upon a healthy society at home."[14]

During World War II, when America's military industrial complex got its first taste of global leadership and power, the U.S. Government's powerful agencies, such as the Pentagon, the Central Intelligence Agency (CIA), and Strategic Air Command (SAC) became permanent forces. With those agencies' powerful leaders, lobbies, and costly missions epitomizing left-brained-dominant people's aggressiveness and lack of compassion or respect for the American people's rights and welfare, they undertook covert interventions in other countries' affairs that did not concur with America's stated democratic ideals. War versus peace became our nation's forte.

America's readiness to be a warrior is not at issue here. Warrior as last resort is the issue. We are now a hawkish, not a peaceful, culture with a $700 billion annual outlay, in 2010, with 300,000 troops stationed at 761 sites in 39 foreign countries – permanently since World War II – and 90,000 sailors at sea plus SAC, now Strategic Command, ready to deliver cyberwarfare, known as CYBERCOM.[14] And, in 2012 the Pentagon's and the Federal education's budget were the same: $0.9 trillion, but cuts were made to the education budget.

Evidently, the bureaucrats did not learn from the Vietnam fiasco, President Reagan's "axis of evil," or the deceptive war against Iraq. We get a few media clips of the CIA's payoff-dollars to questionable "informants" in Afghanistan when American tax money ends up in the hands of the enemy or builds luxury projects. Nevertheless, the primary mission of the three agencies evolved to commit the U.S. to permanent international security crisis status, not U.S. national security. All render us more vulnerable to terrorism and to bankrupting our nation rather than rebuilding it. *The Ugly American* was not pretty overseas either. In a 1958 novel, said to be based on Vietnam, William Lederer and Eugene Burdick depicted Americans who lived overseas. Whether in Vietnam or other countries, Americans as tourists have demonstrated their arrogance, intercultural illiteracy, and their loud, ostentatious selves. Many nouveau riche people act that way at home in America too. Many isolate themselves from the natives by choosing the best hotels. In 1991, seven of us professionals traveled to Moscow, St. Petersburg, Novosibirsk, and Irkutz to give workshops to teachers and therapists. Three of our group transferred out of a comfortable ruble hotel to go to a fancier dollar hotel.

Our government's misdirected war responses to 9/11/2011's Saudi Arabian terrorists have hijacked America's opportunity to bask in the outpouring of the world's empathy and to spend our resources by creating jobs, caring for its own citizens, educating them well, and fully responding to natural catastrophes. America's internal problems are exacerbated by a parallel problem with smart, not wise war hawks whose devotion to global interventions has perpetuated a culture of "permanent war"[14] in the bowels of government's bureaucracy. The hawks' ideology favors addressing foreign affairs over America's domestic well-being. The bureaucrats, politicians, and their supporters are quick to label those who question their actions as Americans who are "not supporting our troops," "plain folks who get uppity and undermine the authority of institutions," "the educated," "provincial Americans," or "isolationists."

However, they are not so quick to acknowledge that "keeping America safe" has earned the U.S. more enemies and has depleted America's resources by also bailing out the smart bankers and insurance executives, capitalists, and industrialists whose access to politicians resulted in deregulations in the 1980s. Their ensuing and unconscionable get-rich practices brought America and Americans to their economic knees. They already have the U.S. Supreme Court's blessing/legitimacy to fund their alignment with the 1930's GE and DuPont CEOs' ultraconservative views through SuperPacs and Citizens United. Those 1930's robber barons feared all aspects of human kindness, such as health care or unemployment insurance, by labeling it "socialism". In their view socialism is the antithesis of capitalism, and that term is "the kiss of death" when applied to politicians or reformers, even today. "Socialism is the kiss of death" is double-speak for financial elites' wordsmiths to sway our emotions toward their desire to return to the unbridled capitalism of the 1920s through political action.

Actually, America's inherited and designed institutions and organizations follow the domination system, not the partnership system that existed in the early Minoan Crete culture and exists today in Norway, Sweden, and Finland,[91] for example. Labeling universal health insurance as "socialism" or "socialist" sways many people's emotions toward capitalism – greedy capitalists are not interested in sharing or partnering with America. Elite financiers don't want any restrictions, rules or tax obligations on their free enterprise system. Money is god so they are gods. Socialism and communism labels are scare tactics used to deny Americans our human rights and to steer us away from a true democratic republic as designed by our Founding Fathers' principles where one citizen equals one vote.

Politics (the art and science of government) is also about power and control. Politic (relating to a citizen) derives from politikos (Greek). The first meaning of politic is wise, prudent, and sagacious in devising and pursuing measures. American political and educational systems promote dualism not wisdom, and ideology not politics. Today, politics has been reduced to black or white, good or evil ideologies instead of being a venue for compromise. Politics makes visible the head versus heart hemispheric differences that get played out on our national and the world's stages. Conflicts require accommodation or compromise for the greater good of our country. Ideology is a fight between perceptions of good and evil, the way things and people should be in this world. Ideology is the enemy of politics.[237]

In fact, ideology is the enemy of politics, for ideology is founded upon a myopic view of the way things and people "should" be in this world. Ideology does not adjust to changing times, so what made sense in earlier centuries may not be in one's own or human beings' interests today. While some aspects of history's "tried and true" lessons are worth integrating with science and technology's findings, the two sides of partisan politics are conflicting ideologies: conservative versus liberal.

Ideologies may be perceived as rational, impersonal, and right hemispheric approaches to political issues. Ideology and politics are not good partners for a nation. Conservatives distrust change so they cling to what is familiar: the status quo. Conservatives respond emotionally from their narrow view of the world. Liberals are more adventuresome and envision the potential from trying something new; they, too, respond emotionally from their wider view of the world. Thus, individuals' emotional reactions to their world, and not necessarily ideology, are the underpinnings of individuals' political leanings. Ideology is responsible for the perpetuation of the past and ongoing atrocities against the world's population who are perceived as less than human.

The language of diplomacy between officials of different nations is usually organized around issues of power. Diplomatic language is narrow and breaks down easily. During such negotiations, war is more likely than peace.[222] However, the more diplomats, politicians, and leaders are at peace within themselves, the less need to play out their ego deficits on other people and nations. "A split within is illness, a split without is war...What we need to learn is to recognize and to solve our inner conflicts so we feel secure enough to move 'towards' another human being toward humanity."[163]

Change is a perceived threat to the status quo since disbelief and owning one's personal power signal what the powerful fear: a grassroots movement and usurpation of their status and power over others. By building grassroots organizations in communities and counties, we can press for reform of our half-brained-run institutions and organizations, from education and the medical field to the banking, insurance, food, chemical, oil, disease-care health care, and pharmaceutical industries. K-12 whole-brained public schools ensure the Four Freedoms and equality with the trickle-up-effect: "A little child shall lead them."

Only when we are confronted with experiencing the loss of our physical, psychological, and economic security do we find the motivation and courage to make a difference in our own and others' lives. We are at that stage in America when businesses are not creating new industries or jobs and are focusing on cutting costs and more jobs to save more money, and the financial elites are consolidating their power and influence to keep running America in their own self-interest.

The problem with people without a conscience, or heart consciousness, is they have huge egos to feed and don't appear to care about anything that doesn't make them look good, not be good, and they do not acknowledge they are successful because of our democratic form of government. Unfortunately for the rest of us, our democracy is, for them, all about money, not about loyalty, character, freedom, and the Golden Rule. By design or default, the rigid left-brainers' and right-brainers' actions are turning this democratic country into a totalitarian state.

The United States Supreme Court was conceived to keep in check the threat to democracy from excessive force by mobs, according to Susan Jacoby,[168] yet America is ailing from a combination of ignorance, anti-rationalism, and anti-intellectualism. Today's anti-intellectual forces label the Ivy League educated as elite or liberal, which are code words for *No one is better than we are.* In the 1960s, Richard Hofstadter suggested that there was a trend in American culture favoring the heart over the head, that intellect was correlated with cleverness, or smart, and that the purely theoretical mind was disesteemed.[157] The trend toward anti-intellectualism was evident during the confirmation of David Souter, to the Supreme Court in the 1990s, who was advised to tone down his smarts.

Judith Warner related that when Elena Kagan was nominated in 2010 for the U.S. Supreme Court – which is believed to be the bastion of the best-educated, elitest, and smartest – she was coached before undergoing a Senate hearing to use her right-brain to relate with humor, play down her left-brain, and demonstrate her "true intellect,"[341] which she did. Now we know that Justice Elena Kagan has access to her twin brains and her full intelligence.

Today, the word elite is used by those politicians and extremist TV personalities who hope to persuade citizens that a well-educated person is not one of them:[341] government of, by, and for the people. The fact that many elites are wealthy billionaires and many politicians will be or are multimillionaires is overlooked as "not one of them." "Any hint of an I'm better-than-you sentiment, especially if that sense of superiority is based on intellect or fancy speech or having attended an Ivy League school, can go over very badly in America today, where 'elite' has gone from being a word of admiration to one of insult,"[341] except if one is wealthy. Our nation is heading Right versus Rights?

The American Dream of upward mobility as the just reward for hard work, pride, equality, autonomy, education, and home ownership is primarily new immigrants' dream today. Americans perceive it as a vague and endangered slogan since the housing bubble burst after being the willing victims of home ownership with President George W. Bush's 2003 American Dream Downpayment Initiative.[43]

Meanwhile, The American Fantasy is Americans' New Dream: the wannabe-rich believe they could be lucky, hit the casino jackpot, win the lottery, or be the heir of a long lost relative, and be rich tomorrow so they vote according to their emotional, fantasized, and religious beliefs about their financial future. Some elites believe they are extraordinary and that they should be looked up to by ordinary Americans. Others believe that it's God's will that the "undeserving poor" be punished, so shrink government to make sure they get no welfare. Financiers believe in unshackling free enterprise from any government constraints. All are seductive beliefs for those who believe they, too, are extraordinary beings in God's eyes. They expect that Andrew Carnegie's "Gospel of Wealth" will prevail with God's blessing, but they do not realize they are breaking their unwritten contract as a citizen with America's democratic republic's principles.

America's cultural icon, The Western Intellectual Tradition, is not based upon democratic principles of equality. Nor do the K-12 public schools provide a whole-brain foundation for Americans to build personal and professional lives to withstand an assault on democracy by invisible hands: people who are "eager to 'squeeze the worker dry in his old age and cast him like an orange rind into the refuse pail.'"[281]

Kim Phillips-Fein's *Invisible Hands* traced mid-1930's American businessmen, GE's Lemuel Ricketts Boulware; Jasper Crane of DuPont, who opposed government reforms – as a result of the Great Depression – to rescue America from socialism, but primarily to ensure their profit margins.[268] Those two driven men formed think tanks, fought labor unions, and publicized their views through forming organizations long before the rise of the culture wars (have-mores against have-nots) and before the rise of conservative politics. During the 1980s, political conservative eroded 1930's government regulations on big businesses, resulting in the ongoing Great Recession. Today's conservatives are working on having the balance of political power swing right and to abolish the remaining safety nets for America's middle and poor classes: Social Security, Medicare, welfare, unemployment insurance, and any government regulatory agency that would inhibit business profit or increase taxes and hourly wages.[281] Corporate wealth and wealthy individuals are hell-bent on owning America as a cash cow for themselves: to pay minimum taxes, to pay minimum wages, and to subvert the U.S. Constitution through deception and double-speak.

Since the international terrorists' strikes against America on 9/11/01, our military's orange and red alerts have been used as a political tool to control public thinking. Those alerts caused fear so people were willing to trade some liberties for security, The Patriot Act, until the extent of the anti-democratic practices, from eavesdropping on citizens to the torture of prisoners, became public knowledge.

The "haves" do not acknowledge that we have two Americas operating simultaneously; one is about American families' sons who have died, are sent home damaged, or are dying in Iraq and Afghanistan, most of whom are from America's "have-not" culture. With 51 million Americans living and existing below or at poverty level and no health insurance, they are the loyal Americans who are not demonstrating in Washington. It's the "have-not" culture that is suffering the most from unemployment and politicians' budget cuts for the poor's services when the "haves" do not want to pay the bill for wars they supported. The majority of the "have-mores" are unaffected and are living the good life as if there is and were no wars. The "have nots" are deeply affected, not only economically but mentally, emotionally, and spiritually. Yet, only a fraction of our population is angry, frustrated, vocally blame the current administration's spending for the prior administration's spending. The political majority threatens to destroy any proposed universal health care programs as "socialism," abolish women's achieved rights, averse to create jobs or new businesses, or pay attention to our aged infrastructure. Our economic system is contaminated by the conflict between power politics, ideology, and self-interest.

"Before power corrupts it attracts and then seduces."[14] George Orwell's *Animal Farm*, where pigs considered themselves more equal than other animals and people.[249] His book is not about communism; it reminds us that some Americans consider themselves more equal than other hard-working Americans or are God's chosen or "saved" people in a democracy where people have equal rights. The divine nature of authority is a hierarchical holdover from medieval Europe that has no place in America's democracy.

Changes in politics, K-12 public education, health care, business practices, people's self- and worldviews, and parenting are not likely to happen without changing many people's enculturated beliefs, habits, and ways of thinking, doing, and being. Too many working-class people in our country feel disenfranchised.[282] Some people emotionally perceive themselves to be the "real, gun-toting Americans" who have been left behind in 21st century America. Or they choose not to be part of America that promotes racial and religious equality or an equally educated lower-, middle- and upper-class K-12 public school system.

Our roots in democracy mean that We the People can get our nation on a wiser and healthier course if we understand what we're up against and exercise our personal power, human rights, and wisdom for the common good of all. Americans who build "political will" may curtail corporate and financial power. The winds are changing: shareholder activism and the Sequoia Fund are resisting ludicrous compensation schemes for executives of America's industries, especially banks.[87] Since traditional power is concentrated in the uppermost part of a pyramid, the weight of people's power via word-of-mouth, cellphone, e-mail, BlackBerry, and the Internet can bear down on corrupt "authorities" and can turn the pyramid upside down.

In America, we could benefit from a citizens' organization such as in East Africa. On a trip to Africa in late 2009, Hilary Rodham Clinton, the U.S. Secretary of State, bypassed government officials and met, instead, with representative of independent organizations, such as "Twaweza, a citizen's organization... spreading across East Africa, helping people hold local officials accountable for managing budgets and delivering services."[26]

Pure politics, whether personal or interpersonal, local, national or international, is about competition between interests or about conflicting interests. It is not about ideology. Conflicts require compromise or accommodation, "depending upon the temper of the times, the political – or physical – strength of the contending sides, the willingness to compromise, the moral persuasiveness of one side or another on an issue, and the confluence of historical forces."[237]

The language of politics between the so-called liberals and the so-called conservatives has ushered in a period of incivility. Citizens' decisions that are left-brain-based only and are coldly logical and citizens' decisions that are right-brained only and anti-intellectual are not going to be whole-brained decisions. Politics, in theory, may work but, in practice, politics requires educated citizens who have access to and use both sides of their brains and have access to all sides of issues to make wise decisions for the greater good of our country.

Right-brain educated Americans are less vulnerable to the machinations of those who would seduce us by ideology and fear under the guise of partisan politics or of those who are self-invested. We elect politicians, expect stewards of democracy, but we get human beings whose egos are influenced by power and money. The quality of our elected leaders or politicians used to depend upon the quality of the voters until recent years when alleged manipulation of voting machines and negative, misleading advertisements have undermined the authenticity of the democratic voting process in an emotionally illiterate and vitriolic society.

Apparently, Americans are so divided that politicians politicize the schism when they don't rise above ideology toward stewardship. Representing Americans and America is a politician's job priority, not just his or her constituents, corporations, the elites, or ideology. As the dispensers of governmental largess and as willing targets for lobbyists to finance their ongoing campaigns for re-election, many career politicians cater to moneyed interests and lose touch with Main Street Americans and what it means to make a living in America, yet Main Streeters are the nation's primary revenue source and backbone. We the People would benefit from limiting politicians terms. Despite their claims of their longevity and self-importance to America's governance, many of them don't remember what it's like to earn a living in the workplace jungle. Blue and white collar Americans are expected to eke out a living, pay federal, state, city, real estate, and excise/sales taxes; and buy, buy, buy imported and sometimes inferior goods on credit to enrich more elites, not grow America's economy.

Over the past forty years or so we have gone from a culture that reminds people of their limitations and the greater good to a culture that encourages people to think highly of themselves and to be selfish. Our nation's Founding Fathers had a realistic view of themselves, the voters, and an unrealistic view of people's elected representatives. They devised institutional and social restraints to protect Americans from themselves, not from their politicians. Over the past few decades, voters have lost a sense of their responsibility for self and to others. They raise their children amid a chorus of applause to expect entitlements, which is narcissism not self- and other-esteem.

Pundits believe that "Politics has become less about institutional restraint and more about giving voters whatever they want at that second... So, of course, you get narcissists who believe they or members of their party possess direct access to the truth...They feel no need for balance and connection."[35] Giving voters what they want appears to be about those who have the power of money or the power of beliefs. Thus, we are a nation divided over right and wrong where each side believes it is right and the other side is wrong with considerable invective and stand-offs accompanying the sound bites.

Our K-12 public educational systems have created our class system by failing those who do not measure up to the sanctioned left-brain's logic-mathematical-information-timed-tests model. That model is white culture-based and elitist; it neglects and fails those who have other intelligences that are experience-based and practical. By disregarding the right-brain's role in learning and preparation for life, not only human minds are divided within themselves but human beings are divided against each other's worldviews. However, with treasures in our minds instead of deficits, anger, revenge, ideology, or apathy, we can withstand the Hell on Earth that others create for us or we create for ourselves and enjoy the Heaven on Earth that is within our power and is our birthright to live. America needs inspiring leaders right now. In Judith Warner's article, "Egghead Alert," she noted that Americans prefer politicians who relate to people and inspire them.[341]

"The American political system was, as the saying goes, 'designed by geniuses so it could be run by idiots.' But a cocktail of political and technological trends have converged in the last decade that are making it possible for the idiots of all political stripes to overwhelm and paralyze the genius of our system."[108] "Politics is a major part of life beginning in the home and becoming more visible as power is manifest in the larger institutions and the local, national, and international level"[138] and in all relationships. As American citizens, only we – not our elected politicians or our moneyed industrialists and financiers – can save America from becoming another of the many failed empires by resolving our differences and voting to save democracy's Four Freedoms for all Americans, not just the few: Freedom from Fear and Want, Freedom of Speech and Religion.

In America, although America is a democratic republic, our elected politicians have made themselves more equal that the rest of Americans; their partisan actions have reached a tipping point. A republic form of government was chosen by our Founding Fathers; they felt "a chosen body of citizens [elected politicians] whose wisdom may best discern the true interest of their country and whose patriotism and love of justice will be least likely to sacrifice it."[97] Current and past politicians have set a bad example by pandering to the wealthy financiers and corporate entities' priorities. Politicians are giving us a frightening future view of America's democracy when their personal benefits are primary, from health care and pensions to dependency upon wealthy donors for re-election after re-election.

The symptoms of Americans' divisiveness and differences are visible, from the Occupy Wall Street Movement's citizens' anger, resentments, grievances, and joblessness to religious-oriented Tea party politicians who ensure that the Party of No does not underwrite any programs to save Americans from poverty during the years 2008-2012. Lobbyists are paid by the financial elites at the top of the pyramid; therefore, it is no accident that Lobbyist Grover Norquist's "Taxpayer Protection Pledge," a euphemism for "Read my lips," may be translated as American workers' protection means they won't earn enough money to pay taxes if capitalists have their way. The Pledge was signed by 95 percent of the Republican Congressmen, to protect the 2 percent elites from fair taxation primarily. So, now we have politicians whose minds are controlled by lobbyists and their souls by money.

Democracy's cultural, educational, economic, and political forces need an infusion of human and humane development and common sense. The widening gap between the rich, the middle class, and the poor; the gap between the partially educated versus the undereducated; and the gap between feelings of entitlement versus humility or modesty have created divisiveness and cancers in America's society that are profoundly unhealthy for America's soul.

American voters would have more control over how their tax money is spent and their economic futures if they limited politicians (U.S. Senators and U.S. House of Representatives) to eight or twelve years of service, eliminated their royalty benefits: free medical insurance and free lifetime retirement benefits at full salary that are totally unrelated to Social Security. If politicians had the privilege of paying into the same Social Security program with the same benefits as the rest of us, including Medicare, there would be less incentive to tamper with our human rights every time there is a change in political party power. Career politicians gain more experience and power, but they are more accessible by lobbyists and are more out of touch with ordinary Americans' lives. As politicians, they have the visibility and networking capabilities to earn a comfortable living in any of America's states. And we get politicians whose priority is not campaigning for re-election after re-election.

We do not have to accept "what is *is*" when we have the political will to change the status quo to enjoy the fruits of our Founding Fathers' wisdom that requires an upgrade to include our lived experiences and our new knowledge so we may enjoy the full development of being human in Heaven in America on planet Earth.

To begin the process, consider this e-mail that was circulating the Internet in 2011:

> Subject: Politicians are more equal than tax-paying Americans!
> We need to get a Senator to introduce an8-point Bill in the U.S. Senate and a Representative to introduce a similar Bill to the U.S. House to repeal the largest that past politicos have granted to themselves in perpetuity without the public's voice. Whether or not politicians will come forward and sponsor such a Bill remains to be seem. If they do not, there are still grassroot alternatives.
>
> SERVING IN CONGRESS IS AN HONOR, NOT A CAREER. THE FOUNDING FATHERS ENVISIONED CITIZEN LEGISLATORS: SERVE YOUR TERM, THEN GO HOME AND BACK TO WORK.
>
> I. Term limits: 12 years only with one of the possible options below
>   One of the possible:
>   A. Two six-year Senate terms
>   B. Six two-year House terms
> II. No Tenure / No Pension
>   Congresspeople collect salary while in office and receive no pay when out of office.
> III. Congresspeople (past, present, and future) participate in Social Security. All funds in the Congressional retirement fund move to the Social Security system immediately. Retirement funds flow into the Social Security system, and politicians participate with the American people.
> IV. Congresspeople may purchase their own retirement plan, and pay for it, just as Americans do.
> V. Congress people will no longer vote themselves a pay raise. Congressional pay will rise by the lower Bureau of Labor Statistics' Consumer Price Index (CPI) or 3%.
> VI. Congress people lose their current health care system and participate in the same universal health care system as the American people.
> VII. Congress persons must equally abide by all laws they impose on the American people.
>
> All contracts contrary to the above, past and present, are void, effective..."

***

American citizens have witnessed considerable political grandstanding over the past four years by veteran congressmen and new representatives who have served themselves, not We the People. It is a wake-up call to fix the governing process that is not working for America or Americans. Twelve year maximum terms for Senators and Representatives are generous and ensure that our 1776 legacy will endure when the foregoing Bill is enacted.

The Politics of Economics

When Christopher Columbus landed in, invaded, America in 1492, Native American tribes inhabited the land. Illegal immigration is not new; it has been a problem in America ever since: ask any Native American Indian! Spanish and other nationalities settled in the south, then, in 1620, the Pilgrims, Puritans/Calvinists, and others seeking religious and economic freedom settled primarily in the northeast. America never was an all-white country, despite being officially founded in 1776 and ruled by White Anglo-Saxon Protestants (WASPs). The nation's wealth was made and sustained by the sweat of imported black slaves from Africa, other non-whites, hard-working immigrants, and women.

Left-brained whites may have made it possible to create our Western civilization and Corporate America, but left-brainers' self-interest has run amok, so they and the anti-intellectuals are ruining our future and our nation. Now is the time for the right-brain to be made a full partner of the left-brain, so wisdom may prevail, money may be dethroned as god as we revert back to "In God We Trust," and equality, prosperity, democracy, and multicultural Americans may thrive.

We learn that the source of satisfaction with life and happiness is "not wealth but the reciprocal relationship between ourselves and one another, ourselves and the world."[225] Iain McGilchrist reminds us that the pursuit of self-interest and wealth has not made people happier. In fact, America's prosperity over the past twenty-five years has contributed to many Americans' dissatisfaction with their lives and reliance upon material things, food, drink, illicit sex and drugs to temporarily quell such feelings.

Economically, America's "politics and economics don't mix well. Politicians have all sorts of reasons to pass all sorts of laws that, as well-meaning as they may be, fail to account for the way real people respond to real-world incentives."[207] For example, "wages are determined in large part by the laws of supply and demand, which are often more powerful than laws made by legislators."[207] Employers can drive wages down, as we have seen with the exporting of jobs overseas, and employers can drive wages up for its top managers only (as we have seen with excessive CEO salaries and perks and their use of bonuses to reward and perpetuate business). Also, the U.S. Government policy of punishing those who supply goods and services, instead of those who consume them, drives prices higher and leads to more suppliers, such as more powerful drug dealers and more creative brothels.

"But if a government really wanted to crack down on illicit goods and services, it would go after the people who demand them."[207] The arrest of "johns" who seek prostitutes' services and the illicit drug users, especially the role models at the top of society, would constrain both markets in the U.S. However, left-brain, short-run thinking declares "wars" on the suppliers of illicit drugs and services, whereas whole-brain, long-run thinking would focus on the healing the demanders' addictions sooner rather than later. Of interest, the drug cartels and brothel establishments, including pimps, have the money to "buy" protective services from politicians, police, and the army

In Washington, D.C., professional lobbyists representing America's profitable industries have deep pockets to make sure that money buys politicians' votes in our democracy in their favor. It is interesting that the mindset that imposes excess taxes on alcohol and cigarettes is not extended to include such taxes on the purchase of guns. Similarly, the rhetoric that people kill people, not guns, is irrelevant when weapons of war and ammunition are freely available to all over people 21 with clean records. Gun control is an emotional issue for some Americans. Owning a rifle used to be about hunting and protecting oneself; today is about high-powered assault weapons in the hands of young men to kill scores of innocent people.

It is evident that our corporate leaders, politicians, financiers, and industrialists are slow to change their mindsets. They did not learn from the economic waters in which we swam before and during the

Depression of 1929-1939. In the 1980s when President Roosevelt's safety nets were dismantled during the Ronald Reagan years our economy began flattening as the rich got richer and the poor got poorer. For "when the distribution of income gets too far out of whack, the economy needs to be reorganized so the broad middle class has enough buying power to rejuvenate the economy over the longer term."[148]

America's prosperity era has eluded most of the middle and poor classes in the recent past. Dissatisfaction with life may be measured by the dollars spent annually by all Americans to purchase self-esteem (beauty products, cosmetic surgeries, fashion, luxury cars, homes and furnishings) and legal and illegal drugs to get high to numb their psychic pain or forget their problems, to feel better about themselves, or to belong. The conscious desire to belong, for union with others, may be an unconscious desire for union of the two hemispheres within the self, to be whole. Similarly, an unconscious bodily need for Vitamin C, an apple, may be interpreted as a conscious desire for a candy bar: another example of the alienation of the head from the body's needs.

In addition, our left-brained society is wedded to the left-brain and the Newtonian model of order and control of everything that influences and shapes our lives. Many American industries' left-brain leaders are fixated on "If it ain't broke, making money, don't fix it," so they are slow to acknowledge or invest in new businesses and new technologies to keep up with other nations' innovations and to create new jobs that will upgrade America's antiquated infrastructure, transportation, and energy systems. Since "Big is Better" or the "Gospel of Growth" has been the prevailing economic theory since World War II, local economies have been devoured by corporations.

Capitalism's free market idea – make cheap, sell high, and chase low wages – "is freest to those who have the most money and is not free at all to those with little or no money."[22] In fact, "If the government does not propose to protect the lives, livelihood, and freedom of its people, then the people must think about protecting themselves...one way...develop and put into practice the idea of a local economy...beginning with...a local food economy."[22] Instead, our government's war hawk mindset that is still in the Cold War syndrome has spent billions of dollars on war technology and on building unfinished or unworkable fiascoes in other countries, rather than upon peaceful technology and programs to rebuild our nation's local economies and public educational and health care systems that would ensure mental and physical health for most Americans and would foster healthy relationships.

It's capitalists' revulsion and fear of democracy's equality of income and education rights that keep universal health care at bay, for profit disease-care to be in charge of American's health and for K-12 public education to maintain class distinctions. Generally, capitalists vote Republican but want democratic liberalism for themselves so their financial undertaking have no government constraints or fair tax obligations, but they want Republican conservatism to rule us in an attempt to eliminate two of our Four Freedoms: freedom from fear and want. from no health care, minimum wages, unequal educational, and no job opportunities. However, they would retain the freedom of speech and religion to police the flock and keep us quiet and preoccupied. That has been capitalists' ongoing contract on America. There is absolutely nothing wrong with capitalism in our democracy, it's the few greedy capitalists who ruin it for everyone but themselves. In today's restrictive economy, there is little opportunity for closing the gap between the upper, middle, and lower classes in a democracy that used to level human development differences through education and economic opportunities. If the moneyed elites have their way, ordinary Americans will be serfs and they will be gods who rule for themselves.

Corporate money runs the majority of our country's politicians and stifles innovation. Each CEO is more interested in how much money is made or saved each three-month period "on his watch" than in America's future or employees' welfare. General Electric's former CEO Jack Welch is an example of allowing the lawyers to advise him, before he became CEO, to delay cleaning up their Hudson River PCB problem when it was in the double-digit millions. The Environmental Protection Agency (EPA) had to sue GE and eventually won. CEOs came and went and were the winners of golden parachutes, but the Hudson River and its fish were the long-term losers.

Since 1953, many politicians have concurred with General Motors' CEO, Charles E. Wilson, who was convinced that "what was good for the country was good for General Motors and vice versa."[14] It is our taxpayer money that bails them all out. If corporations are people as 2012 Presidential candidate Mitt Romney informs us, and the U.S. Supreme Court agreed by giving corporations some people rights, who will bail out We the People from the ongoing Great Recession? Not the corporations so far. Corporate CEOs and managers perceived the Recession as an opportunity to layoff workers and exploit employees to take pay cuts, and produce more, so Alcoa's CFO reported "a turnaround in profits and a 22 percent increase in revenue... The staggering job losses and stagnant recovery are central reasons why any real recovery has been so difficult."[149]

It seems that nonfinancial corporations have been sitting on cash to the tune of $1.84 trillion. Alcoa's CFO "assured investors that his company was in no hurry to bring back 37,000 workers who were let go since 2008,"[149] and more restructuring was planned. Corporate CEOs, managers, and investors are making out like bandits in this recession. The nation could have emerged from the recession in 2009 if the smart capitalists had any morals and ethics, respect for human beings' rights, or any loyalty to our country. Instead, it seems like Americans were being punished for voting in Barack Obama in 2008.

Data about a compensation gap between Federal government employees and private workers[51] indicates that the U.S. government treats its employees much better than corporations or the private sector. For the past nine years, Federal employees' salaries and benefits surpassed state and local government levels – except for Bell, California's officials – in the private sector to the point that, in 2009, Federal employees' salaries were double those in the American workplace: averaged $123,059 versus $61,051 in the private sector with fewer benefits.

A libertarian Cato Institute analyst thinks the Federal employees are being overpaid[51] instead of Americans in the private sector being underpaid. Those average salaries for employees in the Federal and private sector show that democracy works best at the top and in government but democracy is not working for employees in the free enterprise system or private industry when corporations' elite employees (yes, employees!) are paid to make money for themselves and the investors at the expense of its workers.

With corporate America's devaluation of workers and its short-run, profit motive, our government cannot leave it up to individual Americans to solve problems of joblessness caused by a confluence of financiers' greed and the lack of proper K-12 public education for the mind and body: from anti-intellectualism and anti-emotionalism to addictions. Behavioral economics works when people learn the facts and care about their own and others' lives, so they upgrade job skills, stop taking illegal drugs, smoking, and/or lose weight when informed of advertised unhealthy food and drugs, and learn how to be fully functioning human beings. But, finding a job when there are no jobs is beyond most individuals' capacities. Some creative unemployed may *Unlock the Hidden Job Market*, according to Mathison & Finney,[220] if they have access to their right-brain's creativity and they have the capital or a financial support system.

When corporations run America for short-term profit, it's just a matter of time before America becomes a country where there are rich people and poor people and dependent middle class serfs who do their masters' bidding. China, despite its 1.3 billion population versus America's 300 million and the world's nearly 7 billion, is spending its resources on transportation, infrastructure, and innovative energy devices to keep supplying the world with its goods and to keep lending money from its profits to enable the U.S.A. to squander its resources beyond American shores for so-called security reasons since 9/11/01. Of course, the politicos and connected industrialists are making billions and the taxpayers are stuck with the budget deficit.

In recent decades, with bottom-line economics as their guiding force, many young college graduates, especially with MBAs, physicists, and mathematicians from Ivy League schools, gravitate to Wall Street. They and their bosses succeeded in capturing 41 percent of U.S. corporate profits since 2000 with their phantom paper-generating deals, from derivative products to credit default swaps. "What's in it for me?" drove those traders' and CEOs' Ponzi-type schemes, believing that more business, more deals, more profit, that more was growth, great for them, not for borrowers who were urged to buy homes they couldn't afford, not for the American economy.

Not only did those greedy financiers contribute to the creation of a financial bubble but also to an economic tsunami around the world when their debt pools exceeded capital and mortgages defaulted. Some of those so-called experts got exorbitant bonuses for blindsiding the economy; then the American taxpayers had to collude in rewarding them for failing by bailing them out of their stupidity and greed. Of course, moneyed interests and beliefs in free markets influenced the government's deregulation of the financial industry, without oversight, also led to our current economic debacle.

It seems that permission to be greedy was sanctioned by the Economist Adam Smith in his 1776 *The Wealth of Nations* or in his *An Inquiry into the Nature and Causes of the Wealth of Nations*. According to Roy Porter, Smith proposed that an economy would "work best...when each individual (homo economicus) was left free to follow his own business or to deploy his labor as he pleased. Let the laws of supply and demand operate freely, without privileges, monopolies or government busybodying, and everything would find its own level, rather as in Newtonian physics... Efficiency would be optimal, and thirst for profit would ensure that demand – that is, the consumer's interests – was best met, indeed, it would spur technological and business innovation (the division of labour). Self-interest would optimize the system thanks to the operation... of an 'invisible hand,' or what Christian followers sometimes called Providence."[272] Note that Adam Smith said, "Let the laws of supply and demand operate freely, without privileges, monopolies or government busybodying," but American capitalists interpret "without privileges, monopolies" as "Government busybodying," not their busybodying by employing lobbyists or cozying up to politicians to change government laws.

Adam Smith presumed that human beings had innate faculties and capacities for pity and sympathy, for he wrote "How selfish soever man may be supposed, there are evidently some principles in his nature, which interest him in the fortune of others, and render their happiness necessary to him, though he derives nothing from it, except the pleasure of seeing it."[272] Smith argued that "Even among 'ruffians'... 'fellow-feelings' for others are present; there is honour among thieves."[272] Like most postscripts and retractions, they are not read or heeded when passions override common and uncommon sense.

"Economics has long objectified the human being, reduced to an idealized homo economicus, a hypothetical rational actor who...always acts rationally and in his or her own self-interest. In this model, emotions, altruism, fairness, community, and so on have no real place in the economic calculations."[272] Nor are the health and environmental costs caused by manufacturers' pollution borne by them but by people's health and the Earth's resources. Economics has long taken advantage of "the commons:" the air, water, fish in the sea, the forests, and tillable soil. Without a sense of responsibility for the commons and society, especially when government's environmental policies are deregulated by moneyed interests, traditional economics works in favor of industry. not citizens.

In Beijing, China, where businesses override human health, industries were temporarily shut down to improve Beijing's air quality before the 2008 Summer Olympics. In the U.S., the billionaire Koch brothers are reported to be Tea Party funders; they own Koch Industries, whose many oil refineries may pollute the commons. They hold secret meetings with hundreds of fellow industrialists, prominent conservative politicians, and former bureaucrats to influence political appointees and government deregulations in their favor. The brothers have been holding conferences since 2006; the latest conference, held in California, January 30 – February 1, 2011, attracted hundreds of business and politically-connected leaders as well as citizens opposed to their tactics.[131] Business practices are about free economic climates and free enterprise. And the freedom to use the Earth's resources and to spend money on posturing lawyers to delay or obfuscate any environmental laws.

"Without someone acting on behalf of everyone, without a selfless sense for the whole, the tragedy of the commons will take place...The significance of this failure was recently underscored by the Nobel Prize committee when they awarded the 2009 Nobel Prize in Economics to Elinor Ostrom for her work on the tragedy of the commons."[254]

How convenient it is for industrialists and political leaders to love Adam Smith's "An economy would work best...when each individual (homo economicus) was left free to follow his own business or to deploy his labor as he pleased" and to overlook Smith's assumption that "there are evidently some principles in his nature, which interest him in the fortune of others, and render their happiness necessary to him."[272] Goldman Sachs' amazing financial recovery from the ongoing financial bust, after having "benefited hugely from the government's provision of a financial backstop,"[191] reverted to business as usual. Goldman's huge 2009 bonuses indicated the "financial-industry highfliers are still operating under a system of heads they win, tails other people lose...financial superstars in general, whose paychecks are rapidly climbing back to precrisis levels...[is] bad news for almost everyone else"[191] and America.

How inconvenient it must be for Goldman Sachs to have an insider, Greg Smith a former executive, publicly resign his position in an Op-Ed article in *The New York Times* about a corporate culture that "values only one thing: making as much money as possible, by whatever means necessary."[240]

It's centuries later, but many human beings in the executive branches of the workplace have not evolved beyond the thinking that led to "the medieval feudal principle that everyone had a preordained position in the divine Chain of Being, in the hierarchical order of lord and serf, master and man, husband and wife, parent and child; the whole was greater than the part."[272] It is said that Western and Christian societies inherited the Ten Commandments from the Jewish faith. Thus, an obedient mentality was ripe to be formed into a workforce during the Industrial Revolution, 1750-1850, in England, led by their "intellectual superiors"[272] who held rational views of future progress and their own enrichment. The Industrial Revolution reduced men to machines, to robots who responded mechanically to sticks and carrots and, later, to the assembly line.[272]

From the foregoing, we learn that the divine Chain of Being and the yokes around men's and women's necks were religious-conditioned beliefs and the ensuing divine rights of kings were intended to control the masses. Daily life, even in the 18th century, "remained a grind for the great majority... Most power was still muscle power; long child-bearing careers were the curse women bore (many could not take the strain and died prematurely); cold, damp, overwork and poor diet were ubiquitous."[272]

In his poetry, William Blake attributed humankind's condition at the time in England to be due to "mind-forg'd manacles,"[272] which was a precursor of perpetuating the status quo and the politicalization and specialization of work, based upon economic theories.

Economic history repeats itself in left-brained dominated Western society. For America and all Americans to thrive, history is a teacher. Former U.S. President Franklin Delano Roosevelt chose Adolph Augustus Berle's 1932 *The Modern Corporation and Private Property* as the basis of his New Deal program which rescued America from the Great Depression. Adolph Berle argued that the Great Depression indicated that America's corporations had failed the public as well as its stockholders and would do so again if they were not regulated. In the 1930s, Berle's burning questions were, "Will democracy rule the corporations? Or, will the corporations rule democracy?"[256] Those questions are applicable today.

From an economic perspective, formal education has evolved over the centuries from educating the elite to educating all, including those who fail themselves or are failed by the K-12 public education system in our left-brain dominant society. As a result, the field of economics emerged as an unrealistic science by "amputating most of human nature... The moral and social yearnings of fully realized human beings are not reducible [and]... cannot be studied like physics."[37]

Voodoo economics exist when some politicians are obsessed with the nation's trillions of deficit dollars, not with acknowledging their financial collusion when they voted to wage costly wars in Afghanistan and Iraq. Now they are opposed to any social programs that help the middle and lower classes survive in jobless times ($30 billion), but they are also obsessed with renewing tax cuts for the rich ($739 billion) and keeping the military industrial complex fully funded. Didn't any of those politicians take a basic Economics class in college? Paul Samuelson taught economic hindsight and foresight: Austerity in the midst of recession is a bad idea.[296] A hard copy of his original text sells for $92.00 on amazon.com.

Some politicians' rationale is the tax cuts will jump-start the economy. From Economist Krugman, we learn that "voodoo economics... [is] a cover story for the real doctrine... 'starve the beast;' slash revenue with tax cuts, then demand spending cuts to close the resulting budget gap... deliberately creating a fiscal crisis, in the belief that the crisis can be used to push through unpopular policies, like dismantling Social Security."[196] In an anti-intellectual America, voodoo economics could dismantle democracy too.

It is beyond voodoo economics when the super rich in America decided to cash in their stocks, in early 2008, before the stock market really plummeted, and hoard the money – estimated to be about $3 trillion by an insider – to have the cash on hand to tide them over comfortably for a few years until the market recovered. The rationale for continuing the $739+ billion in tax cuts for the rich, in 2012, is the fallacy that their spending will stimulate the economy and provide jobs.

Many super rich people are notorious for not paying their bills or making vendors wait, or waiting to be sued. In *This Time Is Different: Eight Centuries of Financial Folly*, Carmen Reinhart and Kenneth Rogoff disclosed that "Kings, emperors, and other sovereigns have found inventive ways to avoid paying debts throughout recorded history."[280] The rich are no exception. For sure, the millions the government spends in unemployment benefits will get back into the economy. And the millions of dollars it spends on Grades K-12 education will result in future billions in taxes for the U.S. Economy. The millions that the super rich save will probably end up in off-shore trusts.

While *This Time Is Different* is a huge analysis of the economic crises and guises to cause them that occurred in the past 800 years, well before America was founded, the authors found that money was and is the engine that drives not only economies but people. Today's economic crisis is not different because most people are not different. People have entrenched, unexamined beliefs, which reinforce their poverty mentality, so people's lives don't change because they rarely upgrade their belief systems, except in crises.

Economics is influenced by both moral and amoral people who work the system for their own gain, so Economics is an art, not a science. Hope for our individual and national economic future lies in whole-brain education and practices. Problematic for America's democracy is "The United States is getting accustomed to a completely crazy level of inequality," according to two French economists: Emmanuel Saez and Thomas Piketty.[210] They argue that historical facts are on their side: "the United States is becoming like Old Europe... [America] used to be very egalitarian, not just in spirit but in actuality. Inequality of wealth and income used to be much larger in France... Absent drastic policy changes [in the U.S.]. I [Dr. Saez] doubt that income inequality will decline on its own."[210]

"Piketty-Saez," as they are known in the economics profession, "have been denounced on the editorial page of *The Wall Street Journal*[210] for their calls for higher tax rates on the rich. The two economists spent 10 years in tracking the incomes of the poor, middle class, and the rich throughout the world, but what they found in the United States "startled them... inequality is greater than in the time of Roosevelt... income inequality... fell after World War II... and remained stabilized through much of the 1970s. But then inequality started increasing again, with the top 1 percent of earners drawing a bigger and bigger share of overall income"[210] when the Ronald Reagan presidency held the power to deregulate in favor of Big Businesses.

The Picketty-Saez data released in March 2012 "showed that the top 1 percent of earners got nearly every dollar of the income gains eked out in the first full year of the recovery. In 2010, the top 10 percent of earners took about half of overall income."[210] "Mr. Saez has estimated the 'optimal' top tax rate for the wealthy – getting the most revenue from those most able to surrender it – to be between 45 and 70 percent."[210] But those who have the gold in this country break the rules and love their status and wealth.

Massachusetts Institute of Technology (MIT) economist Daron Acemoglu, who is Turkish; educated in London, and Harvard political scientist James A. Robinson have written *Why Nations Fail: Origins of Power, Poverty, and Prosperity*. They inform us why some nations are rich and some nations are poor and what it takes for a nation to thrive. They divided institutions (for-profit businesses and politics/governance) into two categories: Inclusive or Extractive. Inclusive institutions honor property rights, create level playing fields, encourage investments in new technologies, and teach new skills which are conducive to economic growth. Extractive institutions are designed to extract resources from the many by the few.[1]

The authors' research and their economist mentors' thinking, Adam Smith and Henry George, resulted in their concepts: inclusive versus extractive institutions and political processes. Global history is rife with extractive economic institutions supported by extractive political institutions where the concentration of power is in the hands of a few to extract resources from the many by the few. It began with monarchies and clergy to rule the masses by asserting their divine right/nature of authority; it emerged in America as plantation owners with slave labor. Such extractive political and extractive institutions and organizations exist today throughout the world.

In America, though, there had been a preponderance of inclusive economic institutions supported by inclusive political institutions. But America's economic inequality is not only undermining the inclusiveness of its institutions but may also lead to political inequality due to extractive processes. The authors, Acemoglu and Robinson, found that "countries thrive when they build political and economic institutions that 'unleash,' empower and protect the full potential of each citizen to innovate, invest and develop."[107]

With our economic institutions on a path toward enriching the few and our K-12 public educational institutions on a path toward failing its students, "Who's in charge?" What will it take to underwrite innovative environments in our public schools to grow smart and wise students? Money and change. "Who's in charge of our nation when economic institutions have the power to make-or-break our democracy?" The American citizens. The President of the United States of America has little power to change America's current course toward extractive institutions when, it seems, the majority of the U.S. Congress and the House of Representatives hold adamant positions for whatever reason. I wonder, "Are their hard-line positions in their own Party's or America's best interests?" As a long-term, registered Republican, who votes for the best individuals for the country, in my opinion, the Party has definitely changed since I licked many envelopes to mail in support of Republican candidates.

It was ever thus that he who has the gold makes the rules, but today's morphing of corporations into people with deep pockets to sway voters' emotions and common sense means financiers and capitalists and their SuperPacs, in effect, have direct access to more voting rights by proxy, or, by appealing to voters' emotions through a barrage of advertising. In addition, the millionaires and billionaires' extractive market economies now benefit themselves. A change toward an extractive political process, instead of an inclusive one, would leave the rest of America's citizens politically disenfranchised: Why bother voting?

Our Founding Fathers' worst fear – pure democracy's unruliness – was misplaced. They feared the common people's passion more than the elites' greed and shortsightedness. They, too, failed to learn from history and the excesses of the divine right/nature of authority. Their beliefs and faith were based on their good intentions for America to be a nation of "We the People" with a "wall of separation" between church and state. Only We the People, the voters, can save America from those who abuse their freedoms and the gold gained in our democratic republic to impoverish and imprison us. What is happening to us in America today is not a Nietzche fable, I referred to in Chapter Two. Iain McGilchrist used the fable as the basis of his 2009 book's title, *The Master and His Emissary: The Divided Brain and the Making of the Western World*. Americans and America are being betrayed by many emissaries, not just one, but we still have time to save our own and our nation's soul.

Chapter Six

Your beliefs become your thoughts
Your thoughts become your words
Your words become your actions
Your actions become your habits
Your habits become your values
Your values become your destiny
—Mahatma Gandhi

The Politics of Beliefs

All living beings are about survival and reproducing. The human brain is wired for beliefs to help the human species survive. Beliefs are thoughts embedded in the mind. Some beliefs are in our conscious minds and other beliefs are stored in our unconscious minds. Conflicting beliefs and those beyond conscious awareness underlie our behaviors. We have beliefs that feed off each other, so we have belief systems. Placebos and nocebos have demonstrated the power of belief systems in human beings' healing and nonhealing.

Some beliefs are not about reality, for we have "a belief in place of knowledge about reality...The function of belief has to do with the activation of capabilities and behaviors."[71] Thus, beliefs are powerful forces that impact our thinking, behavior, and run our lives without input from the conscious mind's left- and right-brains. But, the left-brain makes up stories to justify behaviors that originate in the unconscious mind.

Beliefs are insidious in that imprinting occurs around ages two and three when we assimilate beliefs from our families. At that time we may hear expressed beliefs, such as, "Heart disease runs in our family" or "We are better than..." or "You have to be 'saved' to go to Heaven!" At an age when we are learning, impressionable, vulnerable, and innocent, family commentaries are suggestive programming. Similarly, things we hear on TV, a babysitter's or a teacher's remark, a scolding, lecture, and a word or a behavior may grab our attention and get stored in the unconscious mind.

A child who does not feel loved by his parents or caregivers is at risk for not loving self and others. In the 1960s, a visualization exercise demonstrated how negativity impacts human development. Visualize a child starting out each day with a blank sheet of paper, 8 ½ x 11, strung around the neck. He awakens to criticism instead of loving messages: "If you don't get out of bed, you'll miss the bus!" "Fix your own breakfast!" He tears a piece off the sheet. On the bus, the kids make fun of him for looking "hung over." He tears off another piece. In class, the teacher asks for his forgotten homework; he tears off another piece. Another teacher compliments him on answering her question. He tacks on a piece of paper to his tattered sheet. You get the picture! He rarely leaves or arrives home with an intact sheet of paper around his neck. Without nurturance at home, to offset the daily grind of negative experiences, the accumulated tattered sheets add up to negative self-esteem, powerlessness, and resentments. Those feelings may escalate into lack of motivation, concentration, passive-aggressiveness, bullying, or violence against self or others. The underlying belief becomes: "I'm not lovable or capable."

Thus, most of our beliefs are inculcated in us as children, intentionally and unintentionally, by our parents, caretakers, peers, media, teachers, culture, religious and political figures, and our environment. A belief may be perceived as an imprint or an identity-forming experience that happened in our early personal history. Konrad Lorenz coined the term imprint when he studied hatched ducklings who looked for a "mother-figure" in anything that moved during their first days. The ducklings that followed Lorenz around, curled up around his boots at night, and when they grew up they wouldn't court a mate of their own species. From this, Lorenz concluded, "This shows that when the ducklings grew up, the imprint of the mother also transferred to the imprint for a mate."[71]

To a degree, the same imprinting process occurs in human beings. Our early experiences impact our feelings, sense of self, and create core beliefs that are models for relationships with ourselves and others. For example, a young girl who is abused by her father may find herself in abusive relationships, despite what her logical left-brain knows about relationships, for that is her model of a relationship with a man. On the other hand, if a young girl is abused by her mother, she may abuse her own children and not know why.[71]

In addition, we have developmental stages that are biological, emotional, intellectual, social, aesthetic, and spiritual. During such stages, significant others may tamper with our sense of self, but those experiences may be relegated to the unconscious to physically survive. Later on, we may experience conflicting beliefs that put us in a double bind. A person with a serious illness may say, "I believe I'll get well again," but the person may have no model of what it would be like visually, auditorily, and kinesthetically to live without the illness.[71] There is only empty hope without access to the unconscious to achieve congruency and a higher level of consciousness.

From the foregoing, we learn that beliefs do not always function at a reality level. Our beliefs interpret our perceptions of reality and guide our behavior based upon the data stored in the conscious and unconscious minds about our lovability, identity, capability, and environment. People hold hundreds of beliefs. While some are core beliefs held in the unconscious mind that are out of conscious awareness, they run our behavior. Such beliefs may be about self's worth, intelligence, capabilities, health (psychological, emotional, physical, and spiritual), worldviews about different others' worth, intelligence, capabilities, and behavior, for example.

Our beliefs about others are located in the right hemisphere. If we are disgusted by others' beliefs, we may dehumanize them. "This is what occurs during war: the enemy group elicits disgust and is dehumanized and pejoratively labeled."[116] Such beliefs motivate war hawks to drum up weapons of mass destruction/deception (WMDs) to promote war to topple perceived enemies. When pro-life believers vigorously disagree with pro-abortion advocates, they may kill them to save a fetus's life: one they do not have to support financially, physically, psychologically, emotionally, or educationally.

If some people are consumed by beliefs that denigrate women, children, and their human rights, such as the violence of rapists and pedophiles to satisfy their power, desires, or entitlement needs, they may justify learned habits and actions. Such beliefs are difficult to change without right-brain education and higher levels of consciousness. Change begins with acknowledging we don't see things or people as they are, but as we are. Our disowned self emerges with a negative response that is symptomatic of what needs integrating within ourselves to be fully functioning human beings. Just as when we see lightning and count 1-2-3-4-5-6-7 until we hear thunder, then we know how close the storm is to us, our automatic negative beliefs about people are similar personal stormy reactions that tell us more about ourselves than about our "victim."

Historical consciousness enhances human consciousness. Both provide the capacity for nations and individuals to self-correct and to utilize past data as future guides. History is a way to understand that the status quo, or the accepted way things are believed and done today, are not necessarily the way things could be. To learn lessons from history, though, history must contain truths, not propaganda. But truths are not as interesting as fairy tales or as coercive to the right-brain if they are not tinged with fear or shame. Secrets hide truths. Evidently, "for everyday operational purposes, truth is whatever is subjectively convincing at one's current level of perception. At the lower levels of consciousness, propositions are accepted as true even when they're illogical, unfounded, and express tenets neither intellectually provable nor practically demonstrable.[147]

It is said there is only one constant, and that is change. Resistance to change belief systems and the status quo in America is threatening our democracy and Americans' survival: physically, cognitively, emotionally, socially, spiritually, educationally, and economically. The evolution of our awareness and consciousness is dependent upon revisiting our own and our nation's roots and the ancient mindsets we continue to perpetuate: the belief that white men have dominion over the Earth, women, children, other minorities, its creatures, and resources.

Despite our good intentions to change, beliefs are difficult to change through logical or rational thinking on a conscious level. The baser emotions – fear, anger, shame, or guilt – and unconscious belief systems often keep us from creating a future of health, happiness, and success. Our beliefs feed our assumptions. Assumptions may be likened to puppet strings which control the puppets; tenets control us. Tenets are beliefs held as truths which are the underpinnings of The Western Intellectual Tradition's diverse fields of study, from philosophy to medicine. We continue to clone, via culture, the past curricula without paying attention to emerging data that refute current and past beliefs and assumptions that sabotage our best intentions.

In Western civilization, central to diverse cultures' inherited beliefs is religion. In early civilizations, religious and political power was in the hands of the gods until the divine right/nature of authority evolved to empower and perpetuate monarchies who reigned for their gods. An uneasy alliance existed between kings/emperors and leaders of diverse religious and pagan sects until Rome's Emperor Constantine became a Christian in 313 AD, consolidated his divine power from the Christian God in 314 AD, and sanctioned the power of Christianity's bishops and clergy by apostolic succession through Jesus Christ's Apostle Peter.

The evolution of Christian religious concepts was aided by how hard it was for masses of people to survive at the bottom of society, the cruelty they experienced, and the short lives they lived. Jesus Christ showed them loving kindness and healed their bodies and gave them hope that a better life existed, primarily in Heaven. For centuries, the perpetuation of religious beliefs to illiterates was transmitted by fear, parables, music, hymns, and stained glass windows. The perpetuation of the Roman Church's hierarchical legitimacy with its Nicene Creed and canons – The Hebrew Bible's Old Testament and the revised New Testament – and the powers of the church and the state appear to have been a holy alliance sanctioned by Emperor Constantine.

There is a tendency for people not to question the way things are that are understood to be God-given. "The Evangelical Rejection of Reason"[118] informs us that "The rejection of science seems to be part of a political monolithic red-state fundamentalism, textbook evidence of an unyielding ignorance on the part of the religious."[118] As one fundamentalist slogan puts it, "The Bible says it. I believe it, that settles it," so they "know" that the earth is 10,000 years old, that humans and dinosaurs lived together, and that women are subordinate to men."[118]

"But when the faith of so many Americans becomes an occasion to embrace discredited, ridiculous and even dangerous ideas, we must not be afraid to speak out, even if it means criticizing fellow Christians."[118] At whole-brain levels of consciousness, history's truths, untruths, and injustices are data to be integrated with today's new knowledge, scientific findings, and realities to meet the myriad challenges of the 21st century.

Either we learn from the history of human beings' prejudice, intolerance, distrust, and incivility or we are doomed to repeat it. Or, as Voltaire, 1694-1778, said, "History never repeats itself, man always does." Ponder Arthur Schlesinger, Jr.'s words:

> History is the best antidote to delusions of omnipotence and omniscience. Self-knowledge is the indispensable prelude to self-control, for the nation as well as for the individual, and history should forever remind us of the limits of our passing perspectives. It should strengthen us to resist the pressure to convert momentary impulses into moral absolutes. It should lead us to acknowledge our profound and chastening frailty as human beings – to a recognition of the fact...that the future outwits all our certitudes and that the possibilities of the future are more various than the human intellect is designed to conceive."[300]

The Birth of Religion

Our worldviews govern how we understand the world which, in turn, influence how we behave. Worldviews are deeply entrenched assumptions in human psyches and appear to be passively accepted without critically reflecting on them to see where and how they may be changed to incorporate new ideas, newfound historical records, and up-to-date scientific research about the heart-brain-mind-body-spirit connection.

Religion is a learned human belief system that began somewhere in human evolution and is credited by some scholars to helping the human race to survive.[338] One of religion's tasks is "to help people find ways to be at peace within themselves, to be content. Another task is to motivate people to have compassion for others, to love others even as we love ourselves."[264]

Religion impacts most of our lives, for better and for worse. In theory, religion is a blessing in God's hands, but in practice, in many religious authorities' hands, it has become not a moral compass but a curse. Religion has divided families, cultures, and nations. The Holy Bible has endowed man with dominion over other men, women, children, all life forms, and the Earth itself.

Religious beliefs promote a group's survival by the willingness to deal ruthlessly with other religious groups, outsiders, or perceived heretics or enemies. Nevertheless, religions have endured throughout the ages, for they are built into the world's major civilizations. In *The Faith Instinct*, Nicholas Wade informs us that, "The existence of an instinct to believe explains both the enduring power of religion and the reason why many who reject organized faiths still look for spiritual transcendence."[338]

Human beings are believed to be the only religious primate. The presence of gods is recorded as art and later as "writings" (hieroglyphics, hierative, and cuneiform) in ancient records. The unearthing of "Java Man" and other specimens by scientists and archaeologists led to historians' proposing that Africa is the cradle of humanity and originated some 150,000 BC to 15,000 BC years ago. However, by latest estimates, the human species is more than 500,000 years old on Earth. Did primitive, splay-toed Ar, ramidus undergo some accelerated change in those 200,000 years and emerge as the ancestor of all later hominids?"[309] In the 1990s, we learned of 4.4 million year-old Ardi's incipient bipedality. In the 1950s, we learned that 3 million year-old Lucy, Australopithecus genus, appeared in the same African region; she was fully bipedal, as were the hominoids that followed. William Kimbel of Arizona State University led the team that found a 2.3 million year-old jawbone, in Ethiopa, Africa. It is linked to Homo, humankind's ancestor. Using Google Earth, Lee Berger's recently discovered fossils of families near Johannesburg, South Africa, that appear to be 1.977 million years old. Another find by Dr. Berger, a paleoanthropologist at the University of the Witwatersrand, would be "another unexpected emissary from the dawn of humankind that will rewrite the story of our origins once again."[349]

Until the rest of our human story is rewritten, we accept that early human species, known as *Homo erectus*, migrated from Africa to Eurasia, and *Homo sapiens* is said to have evolved from *Homo erectus*. Migration is alleged to be possible due to the masses of dry land and the glaciers on

Earth. We are told that global warming around 10,000 BC melted the glaciers that had covered most of the Earth, creating continents separated by seas, which became ideal habitats for animals and for growing food. By 8,000 BC agriculture and the domestication of animals led to a settled lifestyle. "Anthropologists have assumed that organized religion began as a way of solving the tensions that inevitably rose when hunter-gatherers settled own, became farmers, and developed large societies."[216]

Western archaeologists use the initials BC, Before Christ, and AD, After Death, to refer to the Christian/Gregorian Calendar beginning with Year One AD. With sketchy evidence, the 6th century scholar Dionysius Exiguus could not establish an accurate date for the birth of Jesus Christ; however, it is believed he was born years before One AD. St. Bede, the 8th century English theologian/historian initiated the practice of counting backward the years prior to One AD; thus One AD is preceded by One BC or today's One BCE, which acknowledges that not all archaeologists are Christians. BCE = Before the Common Era; CE = Common Era are preferred. Also, Chinese, Hebrew, and other calendars are different from our Western calendar. The Western calendar year 2012 is year 5772 by the Hebrew calendar.

We learned from inscribed clay tablets' "writings" that gods, goddesses, and religions were linked to Nature, the seasons, agriculture, the issues of life and death, and to the struggle for existence.[169] For at least 350,000 years, ancient civilizations with gods and goddesses existed on Earth, according to mythology, but knowledge of archaeological excavations in the Middle East show a Neolithic site in 1,750 BC. It appears that "the life-producing mother...was the dominant figure in ancient Near Eastern religions."[169] Recovered clay figures indicate the worship of gods and goddesses. "With the establishment of husbandry and domestication, however, the function of the male in the process of generation became more apparent and vital, and the Mother-goddess then was assigned a spouse to play his role as the begetter."[169]

We appear to accept myths as myths rather than asking relevant questions for factual information, such as: "How did life begin? Why did life begin?" Those are biology's most daunting but unanswered questions. There are other philosophical questions: Who are we? Where did we come from? Why are we here? Did we evolve from other life forms? Was the Earth populated from other planets? Is there intelligent life in the Universe beyond Earth? Is there one God, many Gods, or no Gods? Are the creation stories oral legacies, truths, facts, myths, metaphors, or fables? Are males the dominant gender in the world's cultures today the result of Nature, Human Nature, God's Will, or Male's Will? The controversy between evolution and creationism continues. What if both theories are valid? "We did not come from nowhere. We are embedded in a very deep but biological and cosmological history."[19]

The discovery of the world's oldest temple in Turkey suggests that the urge to worship sparked the birth of religion. Scientists have excavated a religious sanctuary that may have been built 7,000 years before Stonehenge in England. The Göbekli Tepe temple in southern Turkey may have been built some 11,600 years ago, circa 9,600 BC, by hunter-gatherers, a band of Nomadic foragers. The discovery overturns previous hypotheses about human beings' religious past: that temples were built after they became settled farmers. "What it suggests, at least to the archaeologists working there, is that the human sense of the sacred – and the human love of a good spectacle – may have given rise to civilization itself."[216]

Now archaeologists hypothesize that "the human impulse to gather for sacred rituals arose as humans shifted from seeing themselves as part of the natural world to seeking mastery over it,"[216] or there was "a conceptual shift [change in consciousness] that allowed humans to imagine gods – supernatural beings resembling humans – that existed in a universe beyond the physical world... The animals were guardians to the spirit world."[216] "Animals carved on pillars at the site are native to the area and may represent guardian spirits: Boer, Crane, Fox, Scorpion, Snakes."[216] "The reliefs on the T-shaped pillars [stylized human beings] illustrate that other world."[216] Although "less than a tenth of the 22-acre site is open to the sky... what we are learning is that civilization is a product of the human mind."[216]

From archeology and mythology, we begin to know more about our past, but what is true and untrue remains to be proved. While *Homo erectus* appeared on Earth around 1.8 million years ago and our own species *Homo sapiens* emerged around 200,000 to 300,000 years ago, our distant past is "shrouded in uncertainty, although we have reason to believe that modern rapid language is at least 150,000 years old."[19]

In *Religion in Human Evolution*, Sociologist Robert N. Bellah asserted that "in all early civilizations, the religious and the political are not different spheres, but aspects of a total understanding of cosmos and society."[19] "Archeology reveals...After 4000 BCE, in the alluvial plain of Southern Mesopotamia, only very sparsely settled before, a large number of fairly large settlements appeared rather suddenly, and by about 3200 BCE the first true cities in the world had emerged. These cities focused on monumental temple compounds but also had palaces, markets, and extensive residential quarters."[19]

Dr. Bellah informs us that in early Sumerian mythology, "kingship came down from heaven."[19] "In Babylonia from the time of Sargon of Akkad [ca. 2350 BCE] until the time of Hammurabi [1792-1750 BCE], the name of the king was often written... DINGIR ('god'), used normally for gods and objects intended for worship."[19] "The sanctity of the royal person is often, especially in Assyrian texts, said to be revealed by a supernatural and awe-inspiring radiance or aura which, according to the literature, is characteristic of deities and of all things divine."[19] "And the claim by a number of Assyrian kings to be 'king of the universe' would seem to imply a power more than human."[19] However, a king was often characterized as the servant or slave of his god, but his closeness to divinity was emphasized by his building temples, lavishing offerings, holding festivals, and attributing prosperity and military victories to his god.

According to mythology about Mesopotamia, a few gods were important to them. Dr. Bellah writes that "Anu, the father of the gods; Enlil, his son and actual ruler of the gods; Ninhursaga, the goddess of birth; Enki, the god of fresh water, but above all the god of intellect and cunning, and of all the productive arts. Each city had its own patron god: Uruk was devoted to Anu."[19] Mythology and metaphors have provided us with "knowledge that has allowed human beings to understand and transform the natural world – though... it has not yet similarly transformed, and is unlikely to transform, our knowledge of the human world."[19]

In academia, the dawn of civilization is said to have occurred between the years 3,000 and 1,500 BC with the Mesopotamia-Sumerian, now Iraq, culture. That culture gave rise to writing, cuneiform written with a stylus on tablets of soft clay; a calendar; and wheels. The Babylonian King Hammurabi conquered Mesopotamia, around 1,750 BC, and established the first Code of Laws. He was defeated by northern invaders with new weapons: the horse-drawn chariots. From then on, history is peppered with tribal and nation state wars. "A large part of mankind's ingenuity had gone into inventing new ways of killing and torturing other human beings, and the threat of pain or death has been found to be the best, and often the only, means of ruling large numbers of people."[335]

During Greece's Golden Age, circa 1,000 BC to 350 BC, Greek philosophers and mathematicians made strong arguments that the Earth was a sphere and honored the god Zeus, 776 BC, by establishing the Olympic Games. Yet, the stirrings of individual consciousness asserted itself – in defiance of the decrees of the gods and traditional values – toward Socrates' "Ideals of inner goodness, truth, and sacred conscience"[272] with "emergent conflicts between the individual and divine."[272] Athenians forced Socrates to drink hemlock as a result. Centuries later, Stoic philosopher Seneca "valued suicide as the only permitted expression of freedom and autonomy."[272] The Roman Church promoted self-denial. "If the cause of individuality was advanced under medieval Christianity it was largely by those heretics who defied it."[272]

Separate states led to warring states, headed by kings or pharaohs, expanding into Syria. Queen Hatshepsut ruled Egypt for twenty years until her death in 1,468 BC. From 500 BC to 500 AD, the great Empire Eras began in China, Rome, Persia, and India, and so did political wars with the killing or enslavement of people. From 4 BC to 314 and 325 AD, sectarian conflicts in Europe were accommodated to spread Christianity by the Roman Church with Jesus Christ as the Son of God. Christianity was built upon Jewish traditions: The Holy Bible, the Commandments, but the Jews maintained their own religion. The Buddhist missionaries and Hindu and Buddhist merchants influenced India, the Himalayas, Afghanistan as well as Burma, China, and Indonesia, until Islam came into being.

A second age of empires existed from 500 to 1000 AD with the emergence of a new religion in the 7th century: Islam. Islam's emphasis was on militarily attaining submission of all people to Allah. That mission became the catalyst for dividing the world into Western and Eastern realms. An overview follows of the stories of how males developed patriarchal societies and used their warring masculine skills or brute force to rule the masses. They devised religious "laws" that empowered men and relegated women and races other than white to second-class citizenship. Some of us may realize that "the way things were and are" are not "the way things could be today" in our society.

Religions and the Bible have been created by man in the name of their beliefs in Gods, God, Allah, Buddha, Creator, Divinity, or whomever or whatever we call our Higher Power. Men as priests, kings, or rulers empowered themselves and their institutions and organizations in the process by writing the Gospels or holy tracts that excluded women. Prophets, from Jesus to Muhammad, are teachers of God's "Word." Great teachers have vision, called Grace. They lift the levels of consciousness of humanity, and the gift they bring is Peace.[144] Peace eludes us as people whose left-brain dominance and low levels of consciousness prevail over humans' higher virtues. War will be inevitable until we attain whole-brain-heart-mind-body-spiritual consciousness.

Andrew Newberg reported in *Scientific American* that many studies have demonstrated that religion has beneficial effects on human brain function, reducing depression, and as a coping mechanism for stress. Neurotheology is a new field of scholarship about the complexity of the relationship between religion and the human brain. A March 30, 2011 research article, "Religious factors and hippocampal atrophy in late life" by Amy Owens and colleagues at Duke University, had a surprising outcome. Her study of 268 religious and non-religious men and women, age 58 and older, who answered questions with respect to their religious beliefs and affiliation, was separated into two categories: those individuals who were born-again Christians and those who had life-changing religious experiences. "The results showed significantly greater hippocampal atrophy in individuals reporting a life-changing religious experience. In addition, they found significantly greater hippocampal atrophy among born-again Protestants, Catholics, and those with non-religious affiliation, compared with Protestants not identifying as born-again."[236]

The hippocampus is a central structure of the brain's limbic system; it is involved in emotions but primarily with memory formation. Stress is known to depress the volume of the hippocampus over time. Whether or not people who have religious experiences have less hippocampus volume to begin with or their stress levels lead them to life-changing religious experiences is not clear. Men and women alike showed hippocampal atrophy in the study. More studies of the the acute and chronic effects of religion on the brain are warranted.

Religious beliefs have been central to humanity's history. "Religion is a system of beliefs and practices relative to the sacred [something set apart or forbidden or the realm of non-ordinary reality] that unite those who adhere to them in a moral community."[19] Why we follow a particular religion is usually inherited through family participation or is an individual's choice that is separate from science, politics, or philosophy. Although some nation states' religions are synonymous with Israel and Islamic countries, for example, there are huge differences in beliefs and practices among moderate, orthodox, ultra-orthodox, extremists, or fundamentalists in Israel, Muslim, and Western countries. The separation of church and State was central to the Founding Fathers of the United States of America, and there are huge differences in Christian religions as well. The Vatican's Roman Catholicism expects total obedience to its tenets established during Emperor Constantine's reign and Christian fundamentalists want to make America a Christian nation. A brief outline of four of the world's religions follows and a more in-depth outline of the fifth, Christianity, due to its its ongoing influence upon Western society's institutions and organizations and human beings' minds.

Five of the World's Religions

Worldviews were constructed by men in ancient times who had the power and the passion to impose their order on the masses. Those ancients developed and perpetuated their beliefs about gods, God, Jesus Christ, Indra, Buddha, Muhammad, Allah, other deities, or themselves. Their worldviews evolved to make sense out of the world, to solve their problems, to attract and control people's lives, or to attain control, status, wealth and power. Their beliefs were passed down to us through the ages. Their worldviews have been interpreted and adapted by succeeding generations, so divisiveness, political wars, the historical West versus East Crusades, and ongoing religious wars are our legacy. In effect, our 21st century institutions and organizations are peopled by many authoritarians whose minds are run by 17th century and earlier inherited beliefs and mindsets.

Below are summaries of five of the world's religions that are popular today. They represent the religions that have contributed to men's higher status and to women's lowered status, to the mind-body problem, and to the perpetuation and validation of the left-brain's attributes of logic and rationality only. "Most religious traditions that stress individual salvation or care and cure of individual souls have not provided much help in thinking about the common good,"[265] especially those who are not members of a particular religious sect.

Religious beliefs are the source of conflicts and solace for many human beings on Earth. Ancient records indicate that religions appear to have Jewish roots, but each of the four ensuing religions – Christianity, Islam, Hinduism, Buddhism – expressed the passion of its originators. Religions' Bible, Torah, Koran, Veda. and other texts are also a source of our inherited myths and diverse attitudes and practices. Judaism is purported to be the oldest recorded religion.

Judaism

Judaism is alleged to be the oldest recorded religion based upon oral traditions from around 10 BC to 1 BC "In one small corner of the world, a race of men grew up calling themselves Jews and affirming a novel story of the creation... these people said, the one God had made a paradise from which man, through his own fault (or rather the fault of woman), was exiled. Henceforth, God told man, he would have to work for a living. But since God loved man, he gave him the earth and all it contained for his sustenance and survival."[335]

Dr. Bellah says, "From the point of view of a modern historical approach, the data concerning ancient Israel, and the scholarly interpretations of the data, are very nearly baffling."[19] Essentially, what scholars have to work with as their primary source is the Hebrew Bible: Christians' Old Testament. "Much of the Bible presents itself as history

– not, of course, in the modern sense of critical historiography but as a more or less continuous narrative extending from the creation to the fifth century BCE. But every page of that narrative serves some religious purpose and can only be of use for the reconstruction of 'what really happened' by the most painstaking scholarly analysis... we must deal, with the Bible as it is, namely a collection of stories, some of which may have some connection with actual individuals who lived in ancient Israel, but we don't know what."[19]

He continued, "Some scholars believe that the entire history of Israel was created out of whole cloth in the Persian period (538 BCE to 333 BCE) or even in the Hellenistic period (333 BCE to 165 BCE)."[19] "This means that the five books of Moses – the Pentateuch or the Torah – is folklore, legend, and epic, created or, at best, elaborated from the sketchiest of fragments... To one raised on the idea that what made Israel different from its predecessors was that it was based on history, not myth, it has come as a shock that the single most central figure in the Hebrew Bible, Moses, has no more historicity than Agamemnon or Aeneas. But that the epic – the story of Moses, the Exodus, and the revelation at Sinai – was given its present form in the monarchy, perhaps in the seventh century, many centuries after the supposed events to be sure...that it was the product of an even much later date."[19]

Jim Marrs writes, "According to the Bible, it was Moses and his exodus from Egypt with the Hebrews that set world history on the course that we all know...Moses gained the oral tradition of knowledge from the Egyptian Mystery Schools, which he handed down through subsequent Hebrew leaders."[218] "The famous Egyptian Book of the Dead, in a passage containing a confession to the 'Lord of Righteousness,' reveals a remarkable correlation to the Ten Commandments of the Old Testament"[215] of the Bible. The Egyptians' knowledge and beliefs could have been handed down from the older cultures of Babylon and Sumer.

Dr. Bellah writes that "the Israelite monarchy was a latecomer – monarchy in Mesopotamia and Egypt were thousands of years old by the time of Saul, David, and Solomon."[19] "If there were a people called Israel in the hill country of northern Palestine in the late thirteenth century, as the victory stele of Pharaoh Merneptah indicates, it was of marginal importance, as it never appeared again in Egyptian (or any other) records in the premonarchical period. In all likelihood it was only one of several groups of inhabitants, of various origins, among whom a collective identity formed only gradually – Judah, for example, not being part of Israel until the time of David. Although the power of New Kingdom Egypt in Palestine was in steep decline after 1200 BCE, sporadic efforts to defend trade routes from highland raiders led to Egyptian incursions involving occasional deportations of Palestinians to Egypt. Memories of such deportees who managed to return may have provided the nucleus of the Exodus/Moses narrative, though beyond the fact that Moses is an Egyptian name, there is little evidence to go on."[19] "Evidence for Israel and Judah as independent states dates only from the ninth century. According to the Bible, they splintered from the 'united monarchy' of Saul, David, and Solomon in the late tenth century."[19] Evidently, scholars today question the origins of the laws delivered by Moses and contained in Exodus, Leviticus, Numbers, and Deuteronomy, "Yet the Torah, the first five books of the Bible, has been at the heart of Jewish worship for over 2,000 years."[19]

Dr. David Hawkins, a psychiatrist who is an expert in using kinesiology, writes that "the level of truth of Christianity which occurred at the time of the Council of Nicea... had been in the 900s, dropped over 400 points due to the inclusion of the Old Testament with the New Testament as 'the Bible,' plus the inclusion of the Book of Revelation... This was a very devastating error inasmuch as all the books of the Old Testament, with the exception of Genesis, Psalms and Proverbs make one go weak with kinesiology, thus indicating that their level of truth is below 200 and therefore untrue"[146]

Dr. Bellah concluded from his exhaustive research that "Israel was characterized by a distinct religion, long before the monarchy – think of Abraham, Isaac, and Jacob, much less Moses... Yahweh, it seems, is not the original God of Israel, but a latecomer, arriving from, of all places, Edom and generally identified with the south... The original God of Israel was El, not Yahweh, as is evident in the patriarchal narratives: the name Isra-el means 'El rules,' not 'Yahweh rules... Or maybe not El, the personal name of the old urban Canaanite high god, but el, the generic West Semitic term for god, spirit, or ancestor."[19]

Nevertheless, Judaism is the forerunner of Christianity and Islam and other religions. Judaism's roots stem from the ancient religion of the Hebrews whose culture, religion, laws, and practices were influenced by the ancient Mesopotamian and Babylonian cultures. Jews believe in one all-powerful God, YHWH (Yahweh), of the Hebrew Bible. The Hebrew Bible (24 books) was composed primarily from oral traditions. They include the creation story, history of the Jewish people, and prophecies about the fate of God's chosen people.

The Jewish faith is based upon Jews' exodus from Egypt and the transmission of the Ten Commandments from God through Moses, who lived around 1450-1290 BC. The Jews conquered and settled in Canaan: the Promised Land. They were ruled by judges and were conquered by the Babylonians in 722 BC, which marked the beginning of their dispersal or exile until 538 BC. Jews and Judaism survived under Roman rule, but they lost their land and temple. Judaism's body of law is an extensive guidance and regulation system of religious practice and daily conduct. The affirm three things: "First, they are a people of the law as given in the body of books of Moses. Second, they are the chosen people of God, having an eternal covenant with him. Third, they are a witness that God is and will be forevermore."[335]

The Jewish Sabbath is from sunset on Fridays to sunset on Saturdays. Devout Jews observe dietary rules and restrictions. Bar mitzvahs for boys and the recent bat mitzvahs for girls are coming-of-age rituals for teenagers. Reform Judaism, originated in the 18th century, advocated integrating Judaism with mainstream European culture. Men and women may worship together, and women may become rabbis. Orthodox Judaism is the most rigorous branch; services are conducted in Hebrew; there are strict dress codes, and men and women are required to pray separately. They maintain their separate communities and do not integrate into larger multicultural societies.

Bible records indicate that Jesus Christ cleared the temple of Jews dealing in money lending and changing, although Jews were the designated, legitimate financial dealers. The Talmudic tradition (200 AD) flourished in the early Middle Ages until the Jews' expulsions from France in 1306, from Spain in 1492, and the attempt to eradicate them during the Nazi Holocaust in the 1930s and 1940s. Israel, as a Jewish homeland, was established after World War II when Great Britain arranged for them to reoccupy the Promised Land by removing the natives, the Palestinians. The Middle East has been at war ever since.

Today, an ultra-Orthodox sect, the Haredim, make up approximately 9 percent of the Jewish population in Israel, but collect about 50 percent of the country's welfare payments since only 35 percent are in the workforce, but they are so astronomically fertile that it is estimated by 2030, they will represent 25 percent of Israel's population. Back in 1949, Prime Minister David Ben-Gurion was persuaded by Rabbi Isaac Herzog to exempt 400 ultra-Orthodox men from the draft so they could study [the Torah] full time in yeshivas."[292] In 1998, the draft-exemption law was reauthorized. Today the number of draft-age men benefiting from the 1949 covenant is 58,000. However, some male Haredi are serving in specialized army units catering to their needs and in secular universities, so more are entering the workforce. Resistance to change is voiced by a Torah Institute of Contemporary Issues Haredi rabbi: "This is national service no less than anything else...In our minds, it's more so."[292] In February, 2012, the Israeli Supreme Court invalidated the draft exemption for the Haredim which had been a Tal Law since 2002, but expires July 2012.

Judging the Law to be unconstitutional reflects the government's decision that the burden of citizenship must be shared by all Israelis.[29] Instead of disappearing into modernity, the Haredi males will not abandon the yeshivas and join the army; they continue to defend and renegotiate their religious studies that do not include math and science or marketable skills.

Jewish immigrants to the United States in the 1900s were from cities – since they had been forbidden to own land – unlike the Irish and Italian immigrants who were farmers and peasants, or country people. "Seventy percent of the Eastern European Jews who came though Ellis Island in the thirty years or so before the First World War [1914-1918] had some kind of occupational skill."[120] With a history of valuing education, Jews became doctors, lawyers, and entrepreneurs. Malcolm Gladwell tracked the careers of several New York lawyers and quoted Louis Auchincloss, member of an old WASPy, white-shoe legal establishment, as saying "I am running a firm of shysters... It is simply war and you know the quality that applies to that and love"[120] [All's fair in love and war!] Old-line legal firms were more genteel; they did not do hostile takeovers, enmesh clients in hopeless tangles of red tape, or sue for accidents and dubious liabilities.

If there are lessons to be learned from expulsions, holocausts, and warring religious factions, no one appears to be learning from them. History seems to be repeating the Old Testament's rivalry between the gods; their wars, punishments, revenge, gluttony, greed, and Thou Shalt Nots for ordinary humans to keep them in line.

In a kinesiology test by Dr. David Hawkins for truth of Judaism's teachings, he found that Judaism, as expounded by Abraham, calibrated at 985.[147] Modern Judaism calibrates at 499. The Kaballah is 720; the Zohar is 730."[147]

Christianity

America's original inhabitants, the Native Americans, have their own ancient religious belief systems and practices. America is not a Christian nation although its early invaders/discoverers were Spanish Roman Catholic Christians and America's later immigrants were Northern European, primarily Protestant Christians. America's Founding Fathers were of Christian heritage. Due to their exposure to, knowledge of, and experience with Christianity, "They were appalled by the fusion of religious and political power, epitomized by the divine right of kings"[88] in Europe, so they made sure the U.S. Constitution included religious freedom and the separation of Church and State.

From its beginning, America was not a Christian nation; it was and is a nation of diverse nationalities, races, cultures, and religions. Most Americans believe in a Creator, God, Yahweh, Buddha, Allah, or a Divine or Higher Power. Christianity is given more space in these summaries of five of the world's religions because Christianity appears to have had the most impact upon Western civilization's institutions and organizations, such as, The Western Intellectual Tradition, the American K-12 public school system, and human beings' divisiveness.

Western society has inherited thousands of years of Christianity's religious beliefs and practices about women that many women continue to believe. As a result, some human psyches are embedded with beliefs that negatively affect women's equality, education, economics, and potential as well as the male-female relationship, creating misogyny and patriarchy. There is no dearth of negatives about women by misogynists in history. Western literature is rife with the tomes of "Isaiah,

Jeremiah, Plato, Aristotle, Paul, Pliny, Jerome, Augustine, Aquinas, Bacon, Luther, Calvin, Nietzsche, Schopenhauer, Marx, Hegel, and Freud [who] ranged from outright woman-haters to those who weren't quite so blatant but nevertheless strongly promoted the patriarchal agenda."[306]

Christianity's legacy of Thou Shalt Nots permeates our Western society's Christian religions, families, K-12 public schools, and laws, creating an aura of negativity, fear, and suspicion around people, not love, security, and compassion. Churches are perceived as welcome wagons for the like-minded while Heaven is welcomed as a loving and safe haven. Although, as the saying goes, "Everybody wants to go to Heaven, but nobody wants to die."

In the 15th century, the power and corruption of the Roman Church's hierarchy led to the Reformation and to the formation of many Protestant sects within Christianity. Each Christian sect reflects the charisma of its originator, and the field is open to self-proclaimed preachers who attract followers. The fact that no one knows for sure which of Jesus Christ's teachings are genuinely authentic and which are not may mean that only one true Christian exists, and he died on the cross.

No one knows for sure what happens when we die. Ministerial parents have published credible stories of their children's "near death experiences." I question the inclusion of the postscript: "But you must be saved to go to Heaven!" Children learn what they live and hear at home. Believing in a Heaven and a Hell placates those who seek revenge on their transgressors or those who do good only to rack up heavenly points. As an Episcopalian, I think it is smart, wise, intuitive, and spiritual to believe than not to believe that God exists and that our lives have a purpose here on Earth and meaning in the hereafter.

The separation of Church and State is mandated by the United States Constitution. George Washington, Thomas Jefferson and all America's Founding Fathers believed in religious freedom. In fact, "the victory for religious liberty, first in Virginia and then in the American republic, was so decisive that no venerator of the founders could plausibly challenge it."[88]

Nevertheless, David Barton, a founder of Wallbuilders, is a Baptist, and an activist who was hired by the George W. Bush campaign as a

Republican National Committee consultant, is making a living attacking the separation of church and state in America. He interprets Jefferson's phrase "the wall of separation" between church and state to mean that the wall was meant by the Founders to be a one-directional wall, that is, "the 'wall' works only one way, as does the constitution's ban on a state religion. This principle, does not, he says, exclude governance by Christian principles; all it bars is state interference in church life or theology. This argument has been adopted by many other Christian conservatives since he first made it 20 years ago."[88]

David Barton links the 1962 and 1963 Supreme Court rulings banning public school-sponsored religious exercises to God's anger at America, which led to the lowering of students' SAT scores nationally, raising crime rates, and increasing alcohol consumption. Believing he is on a mission for God, he and the Religious Righters are trying to rewrite America's foundational history to suit their political agenda that America is a Christian nation and restore their "divine right" to spend their years "saving" heathens, punishing heretics, and regaining dominion over the Earth, as promised in Genesis. We already have a Pentagon empowered and enriched by a culture of "permanent war"[14] that could repeat The Crusades of 1095-1291 all over again; they began in 2003.

Christianity was one of many religious sects founded by the disciples of a Jew, Jesus Christ. It is estimated he was born around 4 BC. "Jesus said he would not change his inherited Jewish law, but he added to it a kind of supernumerary law, based on love...and not only on justice."[335] However, "Jesus almost always spoke in parables, which required interpretation in those days and still do today."[335] While Christianity as we know it is ostensibly based on Jesus Christ's teachings, today's scholars trace Christianity's evolution back to the philosophies of ancient Greece, Egypt, and Babylon and to the older Sumer culture. Christianity's antecedents are traceable to stories in the Old and New Testaments of the Bible and to translations of cuneiform-enscribed tablets of events that occurred hundreds of thousands of years ago. There is no mention of Jesus Christ or of his coming in the Old Testament of the Bible.

"The Bible – without question the most influential book ever produced – was written by men with secrets to conceal both from the

Roman and Jewish authorities and from other competing [religious] sects... a hodgepodge of myths, legends, and parables from various cultures cobbled together with bits of history and philosophy."[218] Many Biblical passages are written as metaphors or in code words whose meanings have been lost through time or translations. Other passages are deliberate tampering to advance religious and/or political agendas.

Tampering's primary purpose was "to support the aims of those who sought to make Christianity more attractive to potential Jewish converts by proving that the events of Jesus' life fulfill prophecy from the Old Testament."[218] Other tampering by scribes may be at the behest of their benefactors who perpetuated their beliefs and biases. Subsequent Biblical translations have led to erroneous editing, misunderstandings, suppressed secrets, and deleted texts, especially those that were at odds with prevailing church dogma.

Biblical scholar Patricia Eddy wrote, in 1933, "'In order to completely understand the dynamic of tampering with Jesus' pronouncements, the reader must understand how the minds of the first-century religious protagonists worked."[89] Jesus Christ's parables are presented in the New Testament, not his ancient secrets for his followers vied with each other over control of them.

Recorded history informs us that before and after the crucifixion of Jesus, there was rivalry between the followers of Jesus and those of John the Baptist, as well as with the Essenes and the Gnostics. "'Jesus Christ rose from the grave.' With this proclamation, the Christian church began...Christianity insists that in one unique historical moment, the cycle reversed [Other religions celebrate cycles of birth and death], and a dead man came back to life!"[253] "Orthodox Christians since then have confessed in the creed that Jesus of Nazareth, 'crucified, dead, and buried,' was raised 'on the third day.' Many today recite that [Nicene] creed without thinking about what they are saying, much less actually believing it."[253]

After the crucifixion, according to the Gospel of Mary, one of the Gnostic gospels discovered by a peasant at Nag Hammadi, Egypt, in 1945, presents another view of Jesus' resurrection: historical event or symbolic vision. The Gospel of Mary opens with "disciples are mourning Jesus' death and terrified for their lives. Then Mary Magdalene stands up to encourage them...Peter invites Mary to 'tell us the words of the Savior which you remember.' But to Peter's surprise, Mary does not tell anecdotes from the past; instead, she explains that she has just seen the Lord in a vision received through the mind and she goes on to tell what he revealed to her."[253] Peter and Andrew disbelieve her, but Levi said to Peter, "If the Savior made her worthy, who are you to reject her?"[253]

Evidently, Peter had been jealous of Mary Magdalene's relationshp with Jesus Christ, that he appeared to her first, and, later, to the apostles, and he disliked women. "Luke says that Peter excluded metaphorical interpretation of the event he said he witnessed: '[We] ate and drank with him after he rose from the dead.'"[253] Nevertheless, the gospels of Mark and John, in the New Testament, "both name Mary Magdalene, not Peter, as the first witness of the resurrection."[253] "Peter, apparently representing the orthodox position, looks to past events, suspicious of those who 'see the Lord' in visions. Mary, representing the gnostic, claims to experience his continuing presence."[253]

The New Testament's account of Jesus' bodily resurrection as an actual happening served, for the Christian movement, "an essential political function: it legitimizes the authority of certain men who claim to exercise exclusive leadership over the churches as the successors of the apostle Peter."[253] Elaine Pagels writes, "Whatever we think of the historicity of the orthodox account, we can admire its ingenuity. For this theory – that all authority derives from a certain apostle's experience [not Mary Magdalene's] of the resurrected Christ, an experience now closed forever – bears enormous implications for the political structure of the community."[253]

Christianity's orthodox church deemed all rivals to be heretics, especially the Gnostics. During the early years of Christianity, the rivalry continued, diverse sects flourished, including the Essenes, and each claimed to be the true doctrine of Christ, but the Roman Church encompassed them all, except for the "Gnostics, who claimed to have an intuitive understanding of the mysteries of God and Earth...The church found Gnostics particularly dangerous, for they disdained the need for a hierarchy of priestly officials to interpret the word of God."[218]

The correlation between religious theory and social practice was evident in the Valentinian sect of the Gnostics. Elaine Pagels found that "women were considered equal to men; some were revered as prophets; others acted as teachers, traveling evangelists, healers, priests, perhaps even bishops...But from the year 200, we have no evidence for women taking prophetic, priestly, and episcopal roles among orthodox churches. This is an extraordinary development, considering that in its earliest years the Christian movement showed a remarkable openness toward women."[253] "Gnostic Christians often take the principle of equality between men and women into the social and political structures. of their communities. The orthodox pattern is strikingly different: it describes God in exclusively masculine terms, and typically refers to Genesis 2 to describe how Eve was created from Adam and for his fulfillment... by the late second century, the orthodox community came to accept the domination of men over women as the divinely ordained order, not only for family and social life, but also for the Christian churches."[253]

What made the Gnostics more dangerous to the Roman Church was their claim to have papyrus books of secret knowledge. Their secret is said to be man's regeneration of his human spirit or energy that involves elevated consciousness. Initiation takes place by degrees through thirty-three steps, involving the thirty-three vertebra of the human spinal column. Gnosticism influenced European men's minds and other secret societies up to and after the Middle Ages.

Gnosticism also played a role in the Essenes, a Jewish ascetic sect that conflicted with Christian and Jewish sects. The Essenes moved out of Jerusalem to Qumran, at the Dead Sea's northern end. The Essenes were considered the better educated class of Jews, the custodians of esoteric knowledge, and the protectors of Mystic Christianity: the earliest form of Christianity based on Ancient Mysteries, including ancient Hebrew writings of secret and sacred mysteries known as the Cabala. Researchers state that Jesus was an Essene as well as his parents, Mary and Joseph, and his brother James. Both Gnosticism and the Essenes may be forerunners of Freemasonry. Gnosticism flourished but was declared a heresy by the Roman Church's council of bishops in 325AD.

Conflicts continued between Christian sects, including the Gnostics, and pagan or cultist beliefs in gods, such as Jupiter and Neptune, but the Roman church concentrated on missionary work in Europe and in the Christianization of heathens or barbarians. "The Jewish historian Josephus mentions Jesus of Nazareth in a list of troubles that disturbed Jewish relations with Rome when Pilate was governor, roughly 26-36AD. A comment attributed to Josephus reports that 'Pilate, having heard him accused by men of the highest standing among us... condemned him to be crucified.'"[253] In any event, according to Mark, "the chief priests and leaders in Jerusalem planned to have Jesus arrested and executed because of his teaching against them."[253]

Jesus Christ's popularity had attracted followers to his Christian movement, especially among the uneducated masses who called him the Messiah who would liberate them from oppression. Persecuting the Christians was a way of keeping the peace between the Jewish population in Jerusalem and the occupying Romans. After Jesus' crucifixion, especially when the most prominent disciples, "Peter and James, were arrested and executed, every Christian recognized that affiliation with the movement placed him in danger."[253]

Historians of the Roman court, 115 AD, were contemptuous of Christians; they recorded that one of the great things Nero did was the punishment he inflicted on Christians. Marcus Aurelius, who succeeded his father as Emperor, despised Christians as "morbid and misguided exhibitionists"[253] and continued persecuting them. Some Christians considered themselves martyrs, including Ignatius, Bishop of Antioch, a great opponent of heresy, was condemned and sent from Syria to Rome to be killed by wild beasts in the amphitheater, which he welcomed as a martyr.

Martyrdom's suffering was questioned by the Gnostic Christians who considered Jesus Christ to be a spiritual being who did not suffer and orthodox Christians insisted that he was a human being who suffered. Opponents of martyrdom were called heretics and those who encouraged martyrdom by acknowledging, "I am a Christian!" were called foolish and cruel. Nevertheless, Christians became the least expensive entertainment for the Roman holidays to celebrate the greatness of Rome and the Emperor.

"Why did the orthodox view of martyrdom – and of Christ's death as its model – prevail? I [Elaine Pagels] suggest that persecution gave impetus to the formation of the organized church structure that developed by the end of the second century... dissidents who are scientists, writers, Jews, or Christian missionaries may arouse the concern of an international community of those who identify with the victims by professional or religious affiliation."[253] Not only the martyrs, but all Christians who have suffered for 2,000 years, who have feared and faced death, have found their experience validated in the story of the human Jesus."[253]

Christianity emerged from the ruins of the Roman Empire inflicted by barbarian invaders from the north, but they spared the Roman Church. Jesus' teachings about the Kingdom of God and his healing and performing miracles attracted the negative attention of Roman civil and religious authorities in Jerusalem who tried and crucified him. While the Apostle St. Peter is said to be the first Bishop of Rome, he is assumed to be the first Pope, 33-64/67 AD, but other sources make a case for Roman Emperor Constantine being the first pope (306-307 AD) because he exchanged the eagle for the cross: the mark of the Papal Roman Empire. Constantine, 272-337 AD, was the first Emperor to convert to Christianity in 313 AD.

Sectarian conflicts were settled at the Council of Arles in A.D. 314, when Emperor Constantine, who built his palace in Constantinople, "retained his own divine status by introducing the omnipotent God of the Christians as his personal sponsor. He then dealt with diverse doctrines by replacing certain aspects of Christian ritual with the familiar pagan traditions of sun worship, together with teachings of Syrian and Persian origins. In short, the new religion of the Roman church was constructed as a 'hybrid' to appease all influential factions. By this means, Constantine looked towards a common and unified 'world' religion – Catholic meaning universal – with himself at the head."[218]

Any attempt "to co-opt Christianity was sealed at the Council of Nicea in AD 325... which formally defined God as a deity of three equal and coexisting parts – the Father, Son, and Holy Spirit or Ghost"[218] with the accompanying Nicene Creed (I believe in one God... in one Lord Jesus Christ...in the Holy Ghost...) and canons/laws, thereby establishing what the followers should believe to show their obedience as true believers. One year later, the New Testament underwent serious alterations and "Jesus assumed the unique status he has enjoyed ever since."[218] Christianity was sanctioned as the Christian Church in 380

AD; it adopted the Ten Commandments from the Jewish faith. which may have been adapted from The Egyptian Book of the Dead – and the Church's mission became to teach the masses they were sinners: that Adam and Eve, humankind's first parents, were punished for disobeying God in the Garden of Eden and that God's son, Jesus Christ, was crucified for their disobedience. The Church forbade women any roles in the Church's leadership due to Eve's Original Sin, so all Christians became sinners.

Basically, most Christians believe Jesus is the Son of God, that he died on the cross but physically rose from the dead, and that he appeared to his waiting disciples and was said to be sacrificed by God for the salvation of humankind. The Church's hierarchy required Christians' strict adherence to the Holy Bible and the Roman Catholic Church's beliefs, and rituals. Those who disagreed or dissented were heretics. The Roman Church's mission was not only to inculcate Original Sin for disobeying God, but instituted "All such Christian ideals of self-distrust, of trampling down pride and vanity through submission and selflessly serving in the Corpus Christ, the community of the faithful, [which] squared with the medieval feudal principle that everyone had a preordained position in the divine great Chain of Being in the hierarchical order of lord and serf, master and man, husband and wife, parent and child."[272]

While a woman may have been the first of Jesus' disciples to learn of his resurrection in a vision of him, Peter said he appeared in the flesh, the attitude of the male hierarchy of the early Christian Church toward women became: "Woman was the Church's rival, the temptress, the distraction, the obstacle to holiness, the Devil's decoy...Theology being the work of males, original sin was traced to [Eve] the female."[49] As the cult of celibacy grew in the early Christian Church, women were perceived as sexual temptresses and were blamed for Eve's sin of eating the apple in the Garden of Eden. St Augustine taught that all women – wives and mothers – must be avoided for they were all associated with Eve who was responsible for the fall of humanity into sin. St. Paul taught that in Christ there was neither male nor female. However, in the New Testament – Titus and Timothy – women's equal status was taken away.

Who was Mary Magdalene? From the New Testament, we learn that she was one of the women who stayed with Jesus through the Crucifixion and the first person to whom Jesus appeared after his resurrection. She has been confused, in the Gospels' 8th chapter of Luke, with other Marys. Mary Magdalene has emerged from a composite of female figures to one particular repentant prostitute, as portrayed in the New York City Broadway play *Jesus Christ Superstar*.

So, "Mary was transformed, from a confidante of Jesus to a former prostitute noted for her stricken conscience."[49] Whether through suppression or neglect, over a period of years of Christianity in the 4th century when the New Testament was established, "the Gospel of Mary was lost in the early period – just as the real Mary Magdalene was beginning to disappear into the writhing misery of a penitent whore."[49]

At the same time, women were disappearing from the church's inner circle. Despite Jesus' rejection of male dominance, male dominance became the overriding feature of Christianity. Pope Gregory I, 540-604, sealed Mary Magdalene's historical fate when he recast her as "The redeemed whore and Christianity's model of repentance, a manageable, controllable figure, and effective weapon and instrument of propaganda against her own sex."[49]

The politics of the female body may hark back to those ancient times when women were feared because of their power: when women bled menstrually, they didn't die, as most men did when they bled.[306] It is written in the Bible that God admonished Eve for eating a forbidden apple in the Garden of Eden by making her subservient to her husband, Adam. Eve's fall from grace was perceived by the early Roman Christian Church as "a badge of infamy, borne conspicuously by all womankind"[278] and of the origin of original sin.

"Until the fall of Constantinople [to the Muslims] in 1453, the Roman church stood as the ultimate authority in the Western world. Through the lending of both its money and blessings, the Vatican dominated kings and queens and controlled the lives of ordinary citizens through fear of excommunication and its infamous Inquisition."[218]

In the 15th century, Catholic Church leaders called for the reform of clergy who led lives of scandal and wealth. In 1537, Augustinian monk Martin Luther began the Reformation by calling for a cleansing of the German churches of priestly abuses and dogma, such as purgatory, and an end to the sovereignty of the Pope by establishing the Lutheran religion. He "felt impelled by his own religious experience and his transformed understanding of God to challenge practices endorsed by his superiors in the Catholic Church."[253] In Roman Catholic England, King Henry VIII, 1509-1547, was anti-Lutheran but severed England from Rome and Catholicism by establishing The Church of England to solve his marriage-divorce problem.

The Reformation split Christianity's base into two entities: Catholicism and Protestantism – The Roman Catholic Church and the Church of England/Anglican/Episcopalian religions and diverse Protestant religions: Methodists with African counterparts, Presbyterians, Lutherans, Baptists, Salvation Army, Jehovah's Witnesses, Quakers, Mormons, and Pentecostals, and many other Protestant sects. The founders and practitioners of the Reformation transitioned from right hemispheric reactions to abuse within the Catholic Church to sliding into left hemisphere Christianity: "the preference for what is clear and certain over what is ambiguous or undecided; the preference for what is single, fixed, static and systematized over what is multiple, fluid, moving and contingent; the emphasis on the word over the image, on literal meaning in language over metaphorical meaning."[225]

John Calvin, 1509-1564, consolidated the Reformation by establishing his religion, Calvinism, which spread from Geneva to France, Holland, and England. As a follower of St. Augustine, 354-430 AD, he was convinced that the Bible is the Word of God, that humanity is totally depraved, that Eve destroyed Adam's original relationship with God, and that Jesus Christ died as atonement for humanity's sins, not all humanity, only Christians. Calvinism's 5 points of Salvation – known as TULIP in Holland – are through Faith alone, Scriptures alone, Jesus Christ alone, Grace alone, and all to God's glory. John Calvin's teachings reinvent Christianity, adopted Western capitalism, democracy, religious liberty, and mentored Puritan values.

With similar beliefs to the Calvinists, the Puritans became known as activists within the Church of England because they believed the break with the Roman Church had not gone far enough. Puritans were English speaking Protestants in the 16th and 17th centuries. The political civil war-religious struggle between the Church of England/Anglicans and Puritans led to a harsh military dictatorship under Oliver Cromwell, 1649-1658. After the English Restoration of 1660, almost all Puritan clergy left the church or became nonconformist ministers. Puritan congregations emigrated to Holland and later to America's New England where the movement retained its character much longer than in Europe.

There is a neurological condition, hypergraphia, which affects men more than women. Hypergraphia is a lesion in the left-brain that causes people to be compulsive diarists to detail all aspects of their lives. "They often endow their tedious writings with great religious significance... These men [Augustine, Jerome, Luther, and Calvin] were 'obsessed' with the importance of their written words. Using fear and threats to carry out their aims, they were all misogynists whose writings turned people away from the goddess, nature, and the feminine."[307]

George Fox, 1624-1691, "moved by an encounter with the 'inner light'[253] rebelled against the religious and political authorities in England by establishing an alternative to the Christian faith: Society of Friends known as the Quakers or Friends. His ministry expanded to the Low Countries: Belgium, the Netherlands, and Luxembourg, and to North America.

The Puritans who set sail for America sought political, religious, and economic freedom when they arrived as immigrants. They brought their religious beliefs with them, specifically Puritanism/Calvinism. "Puritans became noted for their breast-beating spiritual diaries. Guilt, sin and submission remained central. Calvin taught predestination and burned heretics."[272] Puritanical elements included attacks on music and on replacing implicit wisdom with explicit orders. Puritan belief confined women's authority to head of family; husbands had power over wives, parent over children, and masters over servants. Eve's corruption extended to all women, in Puritan eyes; they were marginalized as helpers. Material success, wealth, was perceived as God's rewards to his deserving faithful. The Gospel of Wealth was christened before being coined by Andrew Carnegie.

Many Protestant sects emphasize the importance of making, having, and tithing money. Some of America's immigrants from England and Holland had Puritan and Calvinist roots and sought freedom for their religion as well as material freedom as their goals. The Puritan Work Ethic, The Devil finds work for idle hands, is embedded in our culture's consciousness, along with material success, so the unemployed and unemployable are perceived as undeserving of God's bounty or of any "socialistic" sharing. "Protestantism being a manifestation of left hemisphere cognition is – even though its self-description would deny this – itself inevitably linked to the will to power"[225] and capitalism.

Over time, Protestantism divided into numerous sects with charismatic founders, from Dwight Moody, Russell Cornwall and Billy Sunday to Billy Graham. Some of America's Protestant sects with charismatic preachers emphasize the gospel of wealth. When Jesus said, as in Matthew 19:24, "It is easier for a camel to go through the eye of a needle than for a rich man to enter the kingdom of God," he was referring to the gate, in ancient Jerusalem, known as "the needle." It was so narrow that camels' baggage had to be off-loaded before they could pass through the gate. Jesus' parable appears not to be a conflict for preachers or parishioners who believe God rewards those who are industrious and successful in business and punishes those who are not.

Religion in America is about faith, primarily, and religion was important to and had been a haven for black slaves. The black Protestant churches are life affirming with gospel songs and the energy of movement and expressiveness. Their churches were and are a source of freedom and hope. A large percentage of Americans are Roman Catholic. In the 21st century, Roman Catholicism's medieval practice of not ordaining women as priests has been reclaimed when "new Vatican documents also links raping children with ordaining women as priests, deeming both 'greviora delicta,' or grave offences. Clerics who attempt to ordain women can now be defrocked"[80] whereas predatory priests have been transferred to another diocese.

"'It cannot be justified, no matter how hard we priests and church leaders, beginning with the pope, might try to justify the exclusion of women as equals. It is not the way of God. It is the way of men...I see this very clearly as an issue of sexism, and like racism, it's a sin' said Father Bourgeois, a member of the Maryknoll religious order."[123] While "157 American priests support Father Bourgeois's 'right to speak his conscience'"...Pope John Paul's 1994 apostolic letter reigns: "the church 'has no authority whatsoever' to ordain women. Among the reasons...the apostles of Jesus Christ were all men."[123] Other priests, from Austria to Australia, have been informed by the pope that "the teaching barring women's ordination was 'infallible.'"[123]

The Roman Church's "branding of sex as a primal sin was a primal sin itself and a direct attack against Eve... Noble vows, statements of belief, and creeds have failed, as has the patriarchy that invented them. Picking up the cross shifts us out of hindbrain survival instincts and opens us to the higher frequencies of love, forgiveness, and trust."[260]

"Worlds Without Women" where wealthy or ascetic men disdain modernity and are cloistered behind walls and in religious institutions – where women and modernity are also disdained – are places where little children suffer as well as women and men. For thousands of years, the Roman Catholic Church has required its priests to not marry women or to be intimate with them, but the Church's fathers are slow to protect young children, especially young males, from its own sexual predators.[81] Some Roman Catholic bishops have turned a blind eye to the plight of sexually abused children within the Church and of poor women who are abused, raped, and saddled with children they cannot financially support, just to perpetuate centuries-old man-made religious beliefs.

"Negating women is at the heart of the church's hideous – and criminal – indifference to the welfare of boys and girls in its priests' care."[81] Columnist Maureen Dowd avers, "The Vatican must realize that the church's belligerent, resentful and response to the global scandal is not working."[81] "To circumscribe women, Saudi Arabia took Islam's moral code and orthodoxy to extremes not outlined by Mohammad; the Catholic Church took its moral codes and orthodoxy to extremes not outlined by Jesus."[81]

Has God been redefined through the ages so now the Church rules not for God but for itself? From the ancient Sumerian civilization's recorded historical process, we learn it consisted of three ages. "The first age was definitely the age of the gods; men insisted that they did not build the great cities, that gods from the sky built them and brought to man all the arts of civilization... The gods departed.... said they would return... left a steward... stewardship evolved into kingship... For a while the kings ruled with respect for the old cosmic mythology, but... the cosmic myths that held the civilization together and rooted it in the universe were torn apart... The military state... is the last desperate collectivization of a disintegrating society. But states organized for conquest inevitably organize their enemies to conquer them... Thus the three ages of Sumerian civilization can be summarized in the following beliefs of the rulers: 1) 'The gods rule through me'; 2) 'I rule for the gods'; and 3) 'I rule'!"[331]

The Roman Catholic Church is in crisis mode. As in ancient times, when "states organized for conquest inevitably organize their enemies to conquer them,"[331] the Roman Church appears to be repeating a similar pattern when entrenched beliefs collide with changing times. A May 2012 scandal called the "Vatileaks" has emerged with the Vatican police arresting Pope Benedict's butler for possession of Vatican correspondence and/or leaking Vatican letters alleging corruption, tax evasion, the Vatican bank, money laundering, and internal power struggles for who gets on the list to be the next pope. The Vatican had been looking for whistleblowers who may have provided documents to Gianluigi Nuzzi, an investigative reporter, who wrote a book, *Your Highness: The Secret Papers of Benedict XVI*,[75] which details the infighting for high-stakes power and other internal intriguing dramas.

In April 2012, the Vatican harshly condemned American nuns for "failing to uphold Catholic doctrine... promoting 'radical feminist themes.'"[122] The nuns serve the poor and disenfranchised, and those who work in hospitals had supported universal health care overhaul, but they had remained silent about their concerns over the ongoing resistance to allowing women a place in the church's hierarchy. The Catholic bishops worked with Congress "to forestall the bill's [universal health care] passage because of their concerns about abortion."[122]

While the American nuns plan to confront the Vatican's criticism, Cleveland's laypeople, other nuns, and a handful of priests met in a Catholic church for a prayer service to honor the nuns. Sister Christine Schenk, executive director of FutureChurch, a liberal church reform group that helped to organize support for the sisters in Cleveland [Ohio], said that "laypeople she knew were outraged that the Vatican had barely consulted with the sisters before issuing its assessment. 'Here you see women, very competent, highly educated, doctorates in theology, masters in ministry, C.E.O.'s of hospitals, heads of school systems, being treated as if they were children.'"[122] Some bishops' responses to the nuns in the media are, in effect, follow the Vatican rules or leave the nunnery.

Essentially, educated women, beyond the Bible's teachings, are a problem for Christian churches that are Vatican-driven or fundamentalist-designed. All women may not follow the male-sanctioned dogma and rules that give religions the power over women's bodies and lives. To save a fetus of rape or incest over the mother when only one can live is beyond belief in an institution that hides or transfers pedophile priests instead of removing or arresting them. Any institution or organization that destroys, hides, or denigrates any historical records that disagree with their teachings or practices is also short on moral principles. From Christianity's recorded history and its treatment of women, we learn the early Roman Church suppressed all knowledge and documents that did not concur with man-created Church doctrine and traditions. Church leaders eradicated all challenge to its divine authority by violence.

With the discovery of the Dead Sea Scrolls in 1947 and, two years earlier, of the Gnostic library of scrolls hidden in earthen jars and buried in caves near Nag Hammadi, more is now known about the ancient religious rivalries by scholars, not by the general public, and the reason for their burial: anti-orthodoxy. Translations of the Dead Sea scrolls are largely unpublished. Israel captured the scrolls in its 1967 Six Day War from the Rockefeller Archaeological Museum in Palestine.

It appears that religions are not the only ones not open to any historical findings that do not affirm current beliefs. Politics and religion have a history of being aligned, so do the elite powerholders. "All We Like Sheep" (Isaiah 54:6) is basically about followership and leadership; we Christians are supposed to be content to follow our Earthly shepherds or God or else suffer the consequences. The Roman Church's hierarchy included the Book of Revelation in the New Testament to instill fear in those who question their divine right/nature of authority.

Some Christian sects have concentrated on the New Testament's Book of Revelation. They believe that all Christians are sinners and must be saved because Armageddon is nigh and that the Christian God will "save" the true believers of Jesus Christ only and will let the rest of the Earth's billions of so-called heretics go to Hell. That belief system is not representative of a loving or a compassionate God. Despite Jesus Christ's caring parables for all humanity and his healing miracles to save the physically afflicted, his crucifixion became a Church-made cross for Christians to bear: Original Sin. The doctrine of original sin is a weapon to control human beings. That doctrine is not found in any of the writings of the Old Testament. Elie Wiesel said, "The concept of original sin is alien to Jewish tradition."[343] Nevertheless, entrenched beliefs propel Christians who believe they are "right" to also believe that the disbelievers, sinners, and enemies are "wrong," so today's self-proclaimed Christian preachers have to bring the unsaved into the fold to be "saved."

My grandfather was the lay preacher of our Christian church. Between three and eight years old, I attended church three times on Sundays (morning service, Sunday school, and Evensong). I resisted judgment by tugging on my mother's dress, and insisting, "I am not a sinner!" I invented counting and recounting the railings around the altar and the number of glass panes in the church windows so I would not have to listen to sermons and Bible readings that scared me. While I learned from my British child-rearing to be seen and not heard, I could quietly think what I liked to think and disbelieve adults who could destroy my inner knowings or break my spirit "for my own good."

My mother's first cousin, with a high school education, "the gift of the gab" including glossolalia – speaking in unknown tongues; perceived by some as manifestations of deep religious experiences – and Hollywood looks, became a preacher. He founded a prosperous Pentecostal church with many loyal followers. My friend Alma, his piano-playing, hymn-singing daughter, told me I had to be "saved" or I'd go to Hell. My father's common and uncommon sense assured me we worshiped a loving God of all religions, not just one.

Bible Study in Sunday School taught me that the Bible was the epitome of violence, greed, revenge, and man's inhumanity to all. Hardly the behavior of a loving, compassionate God when people in the Bible behaved like immature human beings. I questioned why Adam lived 930 years (Genesis 5:5), Seth lived 912 years (Genesis 5:8), Methuselah lived 969 years (Genesis 5:27), and Noah lived 950 years (Genesis 9:29) when ordinary people I knew then rarely lived to be 90. Later I learned that those Biblical ages were calculated by a different calendar than the Western one where an individual's age is the time it takes for the Earth to travel around the Sun (365 days, except 366 every fourth year). Could those long-lived men in the Bible have inherited genes from life on another planet with a longer orbit? In any event, the Western civilization's Christian calendar is roughly centered around before and after Jesus Christ's crucifixion and death.

College level courses did not satisfy my need to know more about human and church origins other than "approved" recorded histories of Western Civilization, mythology, and Biblical texts and their foundational impact upon Western civilization and The Western Intellectual Tradition. It took a long time for old manuscripts and Sumerian tablets to be translated. Elaine Pagels published her research of *The Gnostic Gospels* in 1979, which is excluded from the New Testament and would have been destroyed by the Church's powers-that-be if unearthed much earlier than 1945, when they were discovered in Nag Hammadi, Egypt. Then Zecharia Sitchin published *The Stairway to Heaven*, in 1980, based upon his translations of Sumerian tablets. Not all the Dead Sea Scrolls have been translated or published. Both added pieces to the big puzzle of human origins and history, except the findings do not conform to the status quo's "approved" knowledge. However, there is no lack of interest in the topic as entertainment when Dan Brown has become a bestselling author of novels, *The Da Vinci Code* and *Angels & Demons*, for example, and James Redfield's *The Celestine Prophecy* about an ancient manuscript with insights into life itself.

"The level of truth originally expounded by Jesus Christ," according to Dr. Hawkins, "calibrates at 1,000 – the highest level attainable on this plane."[147] He estimates that the level of truth of the practice of Jesus Christ's teachings in the 2nd century was 930, by the 4th century his teachings had dropped to 540, and by the 11th century Crusades, his teachings fell to 498, which is today's calibration.[147] Although there are variations between the levels of truth of different Christian practices, "Most major persuasions – Roman Catholicism, Anglicanism, Christian Science... Quakers – calibrate in the high 500s... Course in Miracles, or the 14th century mysticism of Meister Eckhart, calibrate at 600... however, extreme fundamentalist groups with explicit reactionary political agendas can calibrate as low as 125."[147]

Of interest, Dr. Hawkins writes that the inclusion of the Old Testament, except for Genesis, Psalms and Proverbs, with the New Testament as 'the Bible' at the Council of Nicea was unfortunate with long-term consequences since "their level of truth is below 200 and therefore untrue."[146]

Christianity's Apocalyptic Belief

There have been and will continue to be institutions and individuals who tell us what to think, to believe that we are sinners, to think that we are heretics because we espouse diversity, gender- and race-equality, are integrative thinkers, ask questions, and think "orthodox understandings of the faith must yield to contemporary insights."[15] In Russ Douthat's *Bad Religion: How We Became Heretics*, he traced recent heretical beliefs to the revisionist Jesus Seminar, Elaine Pagels, and Dan Brown,[77] not to theology "literacy" and anti-women, anti-gay, and educational illiteracy and not to the prosperity gospel, Original Sin, priests' sexual abuse of children, or the abuse of power and money, and the use of fear to control human lives. The first Roman Catholic mother in St. John's, Newfoundland, who reported a priest's sexual abuse of her son was excommunicated and called "the scum of the earth." The foregoing are some of the reasons why, since the 1950s and 1960s, many people, especially Americans, prefer nontraditional spirituality over traditional institutional religions.

The controversy, fear, and hope surrounding the New Testament of the Bible's Book of Revelation's "end time" prophecies and the Mayan Calendar's ending on December 21, 2012 require an integration of left-brain and right-brain intelligences gleaned from historical records that often concealed more than they revealed until hidden records were found that tell the rest of the story. While John of Patmos' Book of Revelation is apocalyptic (revealing rather than moralizing), it has been used for nearly two thousand years as a rationale for human beings' actions, sins, and wickedness, from earthquakes, famine, world wars, we-they conflicts, cultural decadence, and justification for Adolf Hitler and Charles Manson's madness to victimized and downtrodden human beings' hope that Judgment Day will punish their perpetrators.

It is the Holy Bible that told us all that we knew about our human history until 20th century technological advances introduced the carbon dating of historic sites and artifacts, and hidden scrolls and Sumerian tablets were found and translated. What if interpretations of the Bible's Book of Revelation's "end-time" and the Mayan Calendar's Great Cycle ending on December 21, 2012 are just a repeat of the hoax about Millennium in the year 2000? What if the alleged "coming" or Jesus Christ's "return" is not about catastrophe but about humans' awakening to higher levels of consciousness? Apparently, the Bible reveals less than it conceals to literal minds and more than it conceals to metaphorical minds. There is opposition to human awakening to higher levels of knowledge, of consciousness, when apocalyptic beliefs guide people's religions, politics, and lives in America.

The source of apocalyptic beliefs in the Bible was not confined to John of Patmos' Book of Revelation, but his was chosen by the Church's hierarchy in the "authorized" scriptures of the New Testament. Elaine Pagels' *Revelations: Visions, Prophecy, & Politics in the Book of Revelation* [252] is based on sound scholarship with profound insights. An Episcopalian, Dr. Pagels' timely book addresses how and why John's Book of Revelation, written three hundred years earlier, became the capstone of the New Testament due to Bishop Athanasius' ploy, with Roman Emperor Constantine, as "divinely inspired prophecy."[252] There was resistance to including The Book of Revelation in the New Testament by other bishops and monks. They disputed its origin: It was not written by Apostle John but by John of Patmos, a Jewish, pro-celibacy orthodox Christian who experienced, in 70 AD, the Roman's persecution of Christians, burning of the Great Temple to the ground, leaving the inner city of Jerusalem in ruins. Roman Church's monks and other bishops considered his book to be "'unintelligible, irrational, and the title false...not a revelation at all,'"[252] but of John of Patmos' reality.

Exiled, John of Patmos had traveled throughout Asia Minor, according to Dr. Pagels' research; "he could see evidence everywhere that the kingdom that actually had 'come to power' was not God's – it was Rome's:[252] "There were pagan temples, theaters, huge municipal buildings with statues of pagan gods, statue of Titus who led the Roman forces against Jerusalem, godlike emperors dominating female slaves:

Claudius raising his sword to cut the throat of a female slave held by her hair; Nero forcing a naked female to the ground; Augustus being honored among the gods by Venus. All the degrading displays could have been seen by John as tribute to "a demonic parody of God's truth, picturing rulers... under whom Jesus was crucified, as divinely ordained – by gods whom John loathed as demonic powers."[252] Elaine Pagels writes that John not only created "anti-Roman propaganda that drew its imagery from Israel's prophetic traditions – above all, the writings of Isaiah, Jeremiah, Ezekiel, and Daniel."[252] But "Revelation reads as if John had wrapped up all our worst fears – fears of violence, plague, wild animals, unimaginable horrors emerging from the abyss below the earth, lightning, thunder, hail, earthquakes, erupting volcanoes, and the atrocities of torture and war – into one gigantic nightmare... John's visions of dragons, monsters, mothers, and whores speak less to our head than to our heart: like nightmares and dreams, they speak to what we fear and what we hope."[252]

Bishop Athanasius' view of an ideal monk was "an illiterate and simple man."[252] He "denounced 'spiritual teachers,' especially those respected for their education."[252] He "ordered Christians to reject all 'illegitimate secret books' as 'invention[s] of heretics,' full of 'evil teachings they have clearly created'"[252] and warned Christians "not to alter any of 'God's words'."[252] "Athanasius interprets Revelation's cosmic war as a vivid picture of his own crusade against heretics and reads John's visions as sharp warnings to Christian dissidents: God is about to divide the saved from the damned – which now means dividing the 'orthodox' from 'heretics.'"[252] He died in 373AD, forty years after Emperor Constantine's death, but he "succeeded in his triple-pronged agenda mandating [Nicene] creed, [orthodox] clergy, and [authorized scriptures of the New Testament] canon."[252]

Censorship of secret books led to the burial of The Gnostic Gospels and other banned books which were discovered at Nag Hammadi, Egypt, in 1945. Those secret writings tell us the rest of the story surrounding the confluence of politics and religion to perpetuate the Roman Church's influence. From the latter part of the second century to the fourth century AD, the Church developed institutionally as "some Christian leaders began to divide 'the saved' from 'the damned' less in terms of how they act than whether they accept a certain set of doctrines and participate – or don't – in specific religious communities."[252]

"Ever since, Christians have adapted his [John of Patmos] visions to changing times, reading their own social, political, and religious conflict into the cosmic war he so powerfully evokes."[252] John's vision of "fighting for God's truth against evil... see [ing] themselves living in the end-time, and... strive [ing] to live as 'holy ones'... hoping to enter God's kingdom"[252] was repeated in 19th century America. "Christians in America calling themselves by such names as Jehovah's Witnesses, Seventh-day Adventists, and members of the Church of Jesus Christ of Latter-day Saints (whom outsiders call Mormons) began to proclaim Christ's immediate return, as many of them still do."[252] Other Christian sects emphasize being "saved" in order to be raptured up to Heaven when the end time on Earth, or Armageddon, arrives.

Harold Camping of Family Radio Stations, Inc. is 90 years old and has worldwide followers and financial supporters, at least until he apologized for his "False Teachings."[228] He had averred, for years, from his calculations from data in the Bible, that the world would end on October 21, 2011, that the "saved" would be raptured up to Heaven on May 21, 2011, and that no more people would be saved after May 21, 2011.

In Mr. Camping's 2008 booklet "We Are Almost There!" he predicted: "With no apologies, it is the intent of this book to warn as many people as possible about the abundant Biblical evidence that the end of the world is almost here. The end of the world is that awesome and terrible moment when Jesus Christ, The Supreme Ruler of Mankind, will complete the Judgment Process that began in the Garden of Eden when Adam and Eve disobeyed God."[46] By carefully studying the Bible, he said, "we discover that the world was created about 13,000 years ago... we know that the year of creation was 11,013BC."[46] He stated, "About A.D. 95, God completed the writing of the Bible."[46] Then he stated that the "Bible is altogether a spiritual book. It is the Word of God, and Christ is the very essence of the Word of God, John 1:14. Because it is written by God, all of the historical information, the conversations that are recorded, and the anecdotes that are noted, are absolutely true and trustworthy."[46] "And of course, the commandments of God are the Bible. We must understand, of course, that if we never become saved, the law of God will cause the damnation of His anger to fall upon us. However, if we are one of God's elect (and we can know we are, if we have received our new resurrected soul), then we are not under the penalty of eternal damnation for our sins... we are eternally secure in Christ."[46]

Mr. Camping used the King James Bible to make his end-of-time calculations. The Bible has undergone many revisions, interpretations, deletions, and additions. Whatever, the data he used did not fit his methodology. "Muslim fundamentalists – like Protestant fundamentalists with their Bible – condemn any reading of the Koran that is not purely literal."[247] Forbidden by the fundamentalists is reading the Koran or Bible from a metaphoric perspective. It is sad when Mr. Camping or people with good intentions expend so much time, energy, and passion on one source, whether it be the Bible, Torah, or Koran, seeking literal truth in metaphors or words that may be coded, like the hidden communications within black slaves' Underground Railroad spiritual songs of freedom. In early Jewish history, some rabbis taught no one under 40 should study the kaballah. In L. Ron Hubbard's "Scientology," only people who have spent years in study, and paid thousands of dollars for the necessary coursework, are eligible for the highest levels of knowledge."[247]

Instead of worrying about the hereafter, for eons, philosophers and heretics concerned themselves with such unanswered questions as, "Where does humanity come from, and how?" "Where does evil come from, and why?" For Tertullian, 160-225AD, a heretic-bashing, anti-women Christian author, "the catholic church prevails because it offered 'truer' answers to these questions."[253] "What can never be proven or verified in the present, Tertullian says, 'must be believed, because it is absurd.'"[253] A dictionary definition of *absurd is laughably inconsistent with what is judged as true or reasonable*. Either a statement is true or not true, not truer, just as a woman cannot be a little bit pregnant. What if answers to the age-old questions can be proven or verified in the present by heretofore unknown scientific techniques that are available to us today? Ancient data, though, are considered mythology, just the ancients' fantastical thinking. Nevertheless, scientists have discovered evidence of 100,000 BC mining in South Africa.[218] Monuments and temples scattered throughout the Earth are evidence that they were constructed by more advanced than today's technology. "History turns into myth as soon as it is remembered, narrated, and used, that is, woven into the fabric of the present. The mythical qualities of history have nothing to do with its truth values."[13]

"To the extent that we are also creatures of myth in that 'we are what we remember,' we are in the same boat as the ancient Egyptians"[19] or the Sumerians. What if the gods of mythology and of those written on Sumerian tablets are oral histories people's reality? – "not invented by human beings but experienced by them"?[159] Would that knowledge make a difference in our society? Would the knowledge unify our nation? What if "the divine right of authority," "apostolic succession" and "divine lineage," which have served as the bases to construct Western civilization, Christianity's religions, and The Western Intellectual Tradition have no divine basis, just the man-made means to fuel power-hungry male egos? Unanswered questions have a way of inviting more questions. Until then, we can answer questions that have answers for ourselves.

For thousands of years, men have destroyed evidence of human beings' origins to assert their power, status, and control. Who is in charge of data that "treats ancient tales... not as allegories, utopias, or fantasies, but rather as actual journeys to actual places on Earth"[310] Despite Christianity's rocky beginnings of rivalry between the sects, controversies, and choices that created and organized the Roman Church, its legacy, with God as its ultimate figurehead, is embedded in the hearts, minds, and souls of many Westerners and in an overall membership estimated to be about a billion people. Today's controversies, schisms, and contentiousness over entrenched beliefs and practices are similar to Lord Alfred Tennyson who immortalized King Arthur's death on the battlefield with his poem "Morte D'Arthur." An excerpt is apropos: The old order changeth, yielding place to new, And God fulfills himself in many ways.[328] People's passion and cognitive selves will prevail as we and our institutions evolve. Religion, as Karl Peters writes, helps people "to find ways to be at peace within themselves, to be content...to motive people to have compassion for others, to love others even as we love ourselves."[264]

Since the 1960s, research of evangelical literature indicates a phenomenon has arisen: "Psychological Christocentrism."[20] Evidently, the need for personal intimacy in American religions has led to the thinning of "biblical language of sin and redemption to an idea of Jesus as the friend who helps us find happiness and self-fulfillment. The emphasis on love, so evident within the [Church] community, is not shared with the world, except through missionary outreach."[20] With a drawing together of those "who have found a personal relationship to Christ into a special loving community... it separates its members off from attachment to the wider society. Morality becomes personal, not social; private, not public."[20]

The truth of our human condition is its poverty. The poverty of meaningful relationships, with ourselves and with others, and the aloneness of the heart when it is not educated, formally or informally, are visible in our culture and in people's embrace of emotionally expressive religions. Since our K-12 educational systems are numbers-oriented, "it cannot provide either personal meaning or civic culture."[20] Each of us has the power to reform and inform our minds to follow what feels right within our hearts, souls, and innermost being.

An aesthetically pleasing book, about 4 x 6 inches with 382 pages, that physically feels good in my hands is Sarah Young's *Jesus Calling: Devotions for Every Day of the Year – Enjoying Peace in His Presence*. We've all learned not to evaluate books or people by their covers or appearance. A birthday gift from a loving cousin when my husband was very ill, the book was meant to comfort me as it has continued to comfort her. Since the book's purpose is to read a daily devotion – identified with its source in the Books or Psalms of the Bible – I read it with an open mind for about a month. The theme – co-dependence – kept recurring over and over. I continued reading *Jesus Calling*. It reminded me of a beloved neighbor – a New York City police captain in the Narcotics Squad whose job required dangerous "buy-sell" missions – who died of cancer after he told me on one of our morning walks along the Hudson River that he had "given it to God." The "it" was his cancer, the treatments he was undergoing, and his take-charge, can-do attitude. I accepted his decision, and reminded him that my Protestant faith included, "God helps those who help themselves."

Some excerpts of the devotions in *Jesus Calling* were not comforting; they felt coercive to me: "Keep your focus on me." "I want you to be all MINE, filled with the Light of My Presence." "Worship me only.

Whatever occupies your mind the most becomes your god." "Who is in charge of your life? If it is you, then you have good reason to worry." "When some basic need is lacking – time, energy, money – consider yourself blessed. Your lack is an opportunity to latch onto Me in unashamed dependence"[352] Some of the statements reminded me of a girlfriend who wanted to be my only friend; I couldn't. Her insecurity felt claustrophobic to me. Evidently, *Jesus Calling* is reaching and helping people all over the world and is uplifting human spirits. That makes *Jesus Calling* a wonderful alternative to the Bible's Book of Revelation and, probably, to my book too. Many people prefer our Western society's status quo over their examining comfortable belief systems toward effortful change.

"Christian leaders have understood the uses of fear and hope from the time that Justin 'the philosopher' threatened Roman emperors with hellfire... Thus John's visions speak to what one historian calls the Christian movement's most powerful catalyst – the conviction that death is not simply annihilation."[252] The belief that life is eternal justified murdering those they considered heretics: they'd suffer once, not forever in Hell.

"Throughout the ages, John of Patmos' visions, in the Book of Revelation, have fortified religious anger like his own, the anger of those who suffer oppression and long for retaliation against those who torture and kill their people. Yet those who torture and kill in God's name often cast themselves into the same drama, seeing themselves not as the 'murderers' John denounces but as God's servant delivering divine judgment."[252] The human needs that are satisfied by religions' promises may be satisfied by compassion, not intolerance, as manifested by Jesus Christ's parable of divine judgment: "Whenever you did it [hungry and you gave me food... a stranger and you welcomed me... sick and you took care of me] to the least of these members of my [human] family, you did it to me. Shut out from God's kingdom are those who withhold care and compassion for those in need."[252]

We are part of a culture and world that is increasingly chaotic and schizophrenic. Apocalyptic beliefs originate in the right-brain and are usually written with metaphors and vivid imagery and not to be taken literally. Iain McGilchrist, a psychiatrist, suggested that abnormally functioning right-brain exhibit traits similar to schizophrenia.[225] The

Greek etymology of schizophrenia means broken soul or broken heart which is manifested by ideological actions and apocalyptic beliefs that lead them to make decisions to benefit the chosen few. Such rigidity, when confronted with truth and wisdom, could lead to healing through an "inner apocalypse," versus an outer apocalypse, where the word apocalypse means a revealing.[321]

As intelligent as we think we are in this 21st century, we are products of The Western Intellectual Tradition, especially the K-12 public school system, with its boundaries and limitations without the right-brain's intelligence. If we allow our right-brain to open up our whole minds, we may understand "More things are wrought by prayer Than this world dreams of,"[328] to evolve faster, and join the universal community of human beings instead of today's us-versus-them version of America. We discover truth by using our whole brain intelligence to seek knowledge and uncover truths. We do not discover wisdom by seeking it, but by acknowledging the wholeness within ourselves, our holiness or our divinity, then uncovering the wisdom hidden within each human being and sharing our knowings. Wisdom will become manifest when we accept that Judaism, Christianity, Buddhism, Hinduism, Islam, and other religions, not mentioned herein, are part of multicultural America, and we are all Americans.

Islam

The word Islam means surrender or submission or total obedience to the will of Allah. Islam's prophet Muhammad was born in Mecca around 570 AD. Muhammad's father died before he was born and his grandfather died when he was eight years old. Muhammad, raised by an uncle, was a trader and through his travels was exposed to diverse religions. At age 25, he married his older widowed employer, a Jewish woman. and later married another Jewish woman. At age 40, he claimed to have had a visitation from the angel Gabriel who ordered him to bring the word of God or Allah to others.

In 622 AD, Prophet Muhammad and his followers were forced to leave Mecca. Their journey (Hegira) marks Year One in the Muslim calendar. Muhammad "founded not only a state, but also a religion that would eventually be adopted by nearly a billion persons. His moral sternness and seriousness are almost unique in his time. He is one of the most remarkable and charismatic men in history."[335]

The 7th century Koran endowed women with rights of inheritance and divorce, and the Koran made it clear that men and women had equal rights. The first Muslims promoted compassion, kindness, honesty, and charity. There seems to be nothing in the Koran to the effect that all women should be placed behind a curtain or veiled and secluded from society. The Prophet Muhammad's wives were covered and secluded from society as a security measure and possibly due to his third wife (of eleven wives in his harem), A'isha. She was accused of adultery at age fourteen. The Prophet died at age sixty-two. Later Muslims promoted monotheism, prohibited statues and images, railed against usury, and promoted the veiling of all women.

Islam's religious imperative is to convert the world to Islam. Its mission is underway. Women have the fewest rights (they rule their households and the females) in Muslim dominated countries, the least education beyond religion training, and the highest rates of childbirth. For centuries, birthing many children has been religion's and uneducated poor families' way of enhancing their familial and religions' survival power. Not all Arab or Muslim countries are alike; therefore, women have more liberties and opportunities in some Middle East countries than in others.

Pure patriarchy reigns in the Muslim world, despite women's liberties and opportunities in some Muslim countries. Muslim women agree that their challenge is theological. Women's repression comes not from the Koran but from Muslim men's interpretation of it that has led to Islamic laws and mandated dress code for women. Women believe that the Koran must be read in a historical context, and that laws derived from it can change with the times. "Muslim societies are trapped in a battle between two visions of Islam: one legalistic and absolutist that emphasizes the past; the other pluralistic and more inclined toward democracy."[324] However, scholars say that reform would have to "ignore more than a thousand years of Islamic legal scholarship and practice."[324] Religious authorities are the only ones with the power to interpret laws, and circumventing that well-entrenched system would require replacing it altogether."[324] Women from 47 countries have a project called Musawah, the Arabic for the word equality.³²⁴ Members of the Taliban in Afghanistan do not want women to be educated, so many young school girls have been disfigured by acid being thrown into their faces, which is not deterring them from seeking an education. Women activists for women's rights in Malaysia, Egypt, Iran, and Morocco agree that "It's important for us to show positive experiences from within Muslim societies that are not from the U.S. or Europe."³²⁴ Muslim women believe that change is coming.

The nine Pakistani Muslim terrorists who went on a killing rampage on November 26, 2011, in Mumbai, India, have evoked Indian Muslim's criticism: "'Terrorism has no place in Islamic doctrine. The Koranic term for the killing of innocents is 'fasad.' Terrorists are fasadis, not jihadis."¹⁰⁹

Thomas Friedman, an author, world traveler, and writer for *The New York Times* quoted a Saudi author's (Wajeha al-Huwaider) poem, "When." Four of the ten stanzas are:

> When religion has control over science – you can be sure
>   that you are in an Arab country
> When clerics are referred to as 'scholars' – you can be sure
>   that you are in an Arab country.
> When you discover that a woman is worth half of what a
>   man is worth, or less – do not be surprised,
>   you are in an Arab country.
> When fear constantly lives in the eyes of the people – you
>   can be certain you are in an Arab country.¹¹⁰

Not all Arabs agree with Tom Friedman's article in *The New York Times*, "The Silence That Kills," including the translation of the above poem by MEMRI and his interview with Mamoun Fandy, director of the Middle East program at the International Institute for Strategic Studies.¹¹⁰ Some Arabs resent reading Fandy's assessment that "Muslims, the very people whose future is being killed, are also mute... the real danger is highly enriched Islam... that is 'highly enriched Sunnism' and 'highly enriched Shiism' that eats away at the Muslim state... The battleground in the Arab world today is not in Palestine or Lebanon, but in the classrooms and newsrooms."¹¹⁰ Tom Friedman concluded his article with an introduction to the poem: "Occasionally an honest voice rises, giving you a glimmer of hope that others will stand up."¹¹⁰

According to David Hawkins, the "level of consciousness of Muhammad was 740, and the Koran calibrates at 720."[147] He asserted that by the end of the Crusades, wars between Christians and Muslims, the truth of Islamic teachings had evolved from loving acceptance to encompassing religious warfare, or jihad. Further, "the ascendancy of fanatic nationalistic religious movements, characterized by paranoia and xenophobia, has rapidly eroded the spiritual essence of this faith. At the present time, the level of truth of the teachings of militant Islamic fundamentalism is 130."[147]

Hinduism

Hinduism evolved during the second millennium BC, although the term Hinduism was introduced by British writers. The Vedas, from 1500 BC are the source of Hindu's religious truth. The Upshanishads are a collection of about 100 works of prose and poetry that were written over hundreds of years. While there are regional differences, the articulated concepts in the Upshanishads are basic to most Hindu schools and sects. Hinduism is noted for its belief in karma.

Karma is the moral consequences of every human act during his or her lifetime. Karma is not good or bad, except for the person who inherits it from other lifetimes or experiences it. Best known to the West is Yoga. Yoga is one of the active paths to spiritual perfection through stretching, breathing, and exercising.

According to Suriah Mukerjee, Ph.D., who calls herself a progressive Brahmin, "Hinduism as a religion is dead; as a way of life it is very much alive. The basic ideas of Hinduism have become part of the thought and behavior patterns of our people... there has never been a Hindu church, no ecclesiastical organization, no structures or administration. Our people have prayed, built temples... [with a] belief in the existence of a Supreme Being at once immanent and transcendent in the universe, an unborn, eternal, universal Spirit, guarantee and justification of the moral character of the universe."[104]

The Indian solution to establishing political and social order in a nation of many people was to establish a caste system. "Basically, this meant widespread agreement that a person's birth both explained and justified his social position.[335]

"The [Hinduism] teachings of Lord Krishna calibrated at 1,000 and have weakened over time, but the truth of the current practice still calibrates at 850."[147]

Buddhism

Buddhism's central tenets were developed by a Hindu, Siddhartha Gautama, born in 563 BC in India. Ordinary people's suffering led him to leave his royal family home to travel, study, and meditate. After a long period he experienced enlightenment and earned the title Buddha, which means awakened one. He died in 483 BC after founding an order of monks and teaching them his philosophy of nonviolence, compassion, and moderate living.

Buddhism in America is primarily Tibetan Buddhism, associated with the Dalai Lama. The Dalai Lama and the Panchen Lama existed in harmony in Tibet until the Chinese created a rift in 1950; then the Chinese persecutions of the Tibetans led to the exile of the Dalai Lama to Dharamsala, India. While science may seem at odds with Tibetan religious rituals, the Dalai Lama "views science and Buddhism as complementary 'investigative approaches with the same greater goal, of seeking the truth.'"[350] Emory University sponsors Science for Monks, Science Leadership, and Science Meets Dharma programs.

The Buddha's teachings are known as Dharma, which means the truth – similar to the Judeo-Christian teachings of the truth. However, a proper definition of Dharma is the way things are. Senior yogis or psychonauts are "explorers of inner space, the interior of our mind and experience."[293] Psychonauts tell fellow explorers: "when their minds have doubts about what is taught, is to have faith – but not in any blind sense of the word. Rather they are asked to suspend drawing conclusions based on their current knowledge and level of judgment until rigorously applying the 'skillful means' (the male principle in the development of awakening or Enlightenment)... [and] there needs to be wisdom (the female principle in the development of awakening or Enlightenment)."[293] Essentially, Buddhist methods are designed to "help to develop and hone our critical thinking skills."[293]

The Dalai Lama avers, "if scientific analysis were conclusively to demonstrate certain claims in Buddhism to be false, then we must accept the findings of science and abandon those claims."[350] The Emory University programs broaden the views of its science teachers because they "think about science through the lens of ethics and human values as emphasized in Buddhism."[350] Science may be advanced in the West, but environmental engineer Bryce Johnson who teaches Science for Monks believes something is missing in Western science. He acknowledged that "The meeting of science and Buddhism is 'a healthy exchange that is as much for the scientists'"[350] as the Buddhist monks and nuns.

The morality of the Buddhist Dharma is based upon the observation: "'If one does this, then this will follow.' This law of cause and effect, also known as karma is a central pillar of the Buddha's teachings. It lays out in clear and explicitly observable terms what the Bible states generally in the adage, 'What you sow, so shall you reap'... But if the Buddha is correct and we all possess awakening potential, then deep down we 'know' when we are cutting corners; we 'know' when we are taking advantage of a situation or someone else; we 'know' when our actions are based on our own self-interest."[293]

David Hawkins asserts that the level of truth of the teaching of the Buddha was also originally at 1,000.[147] By the 6th century, its truth had fallen to about 900. He proposed that, "These teachings [Buddhism] have deteriorated less than any other religion; Hinyana Buddhism (the lesser vehicle) still calibrate at 890; Mahayana Buddhism (the greater vehicle) calibrates at 960; Zen Buddhism is 890."[147]

Religions' Common Denominators

Throughout the ages, men have dedicated themselves to creating cultures and religions and to conquering and using the Earth's resources with their man-made tools and technology to overcome the forces of Nature to fulfill the Bible's promises. The Bible endowed man with dominion over the Earth, its creatures and resources. Our ancestors wanted to understand their place in the world and to control the forces that hindered their lives and livelihood, power, and status. The left-brain makes sense out of the world by creating rational not necessarily factual stories. Many stories have been handed down to us as "truth." Males and females been indoctrinated with the belief that women are not worthy of equal rights. Men need women to pass on their genes. They also need women until they integrate their right- and left-brains within themselves to civilize and humanize those men whose rigid left-brainism tampers with their wisdom. With K-12 whole brain perspectives, men and women relationships could be equalized and mutually enhanced.

We've been taught that men's way of thinking and being are legitimate, whereas, women's are not. The reviewed five religions are human's creations; most do not include women in their view of humankind. Women, though, perpetuate religion by their devotion to their religious indoctrination, especially when in many countries of the world, women are not educated to have identities or careers other than as men's mothers, children's mothers, companions, wives, housekeepers, slaves, or prostitutes.

Women appeared to be equal with men when gods and goddesses were recorded and artifacts were abundant in earlier times. For nearly two thousand years, few of the world's religions have been good for women after diverse religions' inheritances were revised from their initial beginnings by emperors, popes, and bishops. In effect, men hijacked their religions from their original egalitarian positions and created patriarchy. It appears that each upgrade of the Bible's Old and New Testaments and other religious texts are revised to suit prevailing beliefs. Even Darwin's evolutionary theory attributes human survival to the fittest, which affirms physical strength, not psychological, mental, emotional, spirituality, or the fitness/strength that most women enjoy. The devaluation and stereotyping of anything feminine in our society – whether in a woman or man – are assigned derogatory terms such as effeminate or sissy.[91] Such thinking sets the stage for abuse and violence by those who feel entitled to be dominant or king of their homes, not partners.

Human beings' instinct to believe, when reinforced by religions' advocates, has led to the enduring power of religion. Faith is said to have helped human beings survive by promoting moral rules and putting the interests of others/society above their own.[338] Religions are not just cognitive and emotional but also about social and cultural programs and politics. The function of programs is to enhance human survival and to provide the illusion of control in an otherwise man-created hostile world. Since one diet does not fit all people, we take from philosophy and psychology what fits our experience; therefore, religion is an example of choosing the tenets, the music, or the love of community that we can cognitively and passionately support and basically ignore the rest or give voice issues. Spirituality is an option; its origin is the Latin verb for the act of breathing, spirare. Spirit is the life, breath, and spirit within us – our invisible but vital essence of mind. "Spirituality fosters engagement with the world, not escape from it. It is this-worldly, not other-worldly."[56]

Human beings appear to have an innate predisposition to learn music, language, and religion. Music is the means by which religious narratives or stories are optimally transmitted from generation to generation. Even today, religious institutions prefer stories as the basic tool for perpetuating their traditions because they impact our right-brain, but religions also incur in-groups versus out-groups, divisiveness, and encourage active proselytizing. Hungry egos are attracted to religious leadership positions; they capitalize on people's instinct to believe and their faith. Religions provide an outlet for right-brain expressiveness. Dogma, rituals, music, and history remain after truth has been massaged to perpetuate powerful, institutional, and man-made, patriarchal religious texts as God's Word.

Few of the world's religions, only Buddhism and Islam, have not had human sacrifice as part of their religious rituals. In South America, the Aztecs and the Incas were steeped in fear, force, and human sacrifice. It is reported that the Jews were the first people who decided that human sacrifice was wrong, probably after Abraham was prepared to sacrifice his son Isaac when God ordered him to do so, but God spared Isaac, so Abraham sacrificed a ram instead.

For past centuries, traditional science and technology have serviced human beings' reason – left-brains – while theology and religion have serviced human beings' passion – right-brains. Science and theology's missing pieces have brought us to the brink of combustion. Revelation alone is not a viable solution, for religion, war, and politics are less about logic and more about emotions and feelings. Neither is traditional science alone a viable solution, for the scientific methods lacks humanness. Indirectly, human sacrifice still exists when current social and individual chaos and uncertainty derive from the overuse of technology and scientific knowledge. We have environmental degradation and individuals' diseases due to industrial pollution and pharmaceutical consumers' pollution. We have genetic re-engineering of plant foods, animals, and humans. We have governments' and terrorists' use of explosives and munitions as well as rogues' access to nuclear and biological devices.

As Kevin Sharpe wrote, "All these contribute to the plague of moral dilemmas... Society lacks a convincing morality. People need wisdom to help guide them. Wisdom used to come through immersion in religion, but religion has become either irrelevant to secular modernity or it has tried to recreate backward-looking worlds in parallel to it. Religion can even make the world a worse place with terrorist and military clashes between ardently held religious (militant fundamentalist Islam versus militant fundamentalist Christianity)."[305]

World wars, after the Crusades, were more political-oriented than religious-oriented until 9/11/01 when Extremist Islamists attacked the United States' World Trade Towers in New York City and the Pentagon in Washington, D.C. Today's ongoing war and terrorism are primarily religious from the East's perspective and business (oil) from the West's, except for the Religious Right's perspective. While each side has diametrically opposed, politicized religious and economic agendas, neither East nor West is operating from whole-brain perspectives.

Today, the Western world is confronted with a potent combination of ancient and modern ideologies. According to Conservative Mark Steyn, "Islamism is a twenty-first century political project driven by seventh-century ideology,"[318] minus women's rights. It appears that Islam's Extremist (Wahhabism) practitioners are determined to deliver the world's people to Allah, to indoctrinate them into an extremely biased interpretation of Allah's word as developed by Prophet Muhammad. Conservative Steyn does not mention the correlation between the political agenda of Islam and the political agenda of America's ultraconservative politicians and some capitalists.

The Western world is under the delusion that its own modus operandi is the way the world should be, according to God: the war gods not the peace gods. The East-West confrontation is, though, another opportunity not only to focus upon a formidable foe but to educate ourselves about how the West's emotional illiteracy is undermining its own democracy and its self-righteousness that God is on our side or that our God is better than their God, as voiced by a U.S. military officer, which is widening the rift between the East and the West. Evidently,"The higher the level of consciousness, the lower the fear of God"[145] or of religious "rules." Hence, extremist religionists do not value education; they fear it instead.

Passionate religious Extremists in Western Christian and Muslim Islamic societies have been programmed to believe that only their views of God, Allah, and the world are true and correct. Both confront the "life of reason." When the emotions are conditioned to be fear- and hate-oriented, instead of acceptance, love- and trust-oriented, then fear short-circuits access to the left-brain's attributes of logic and reason. A low level of consciousness – negative-emotion-based convictions – fuels people with Extremist passions and plans to dominate the world.

Not only are both Extremist Christian and Muslim sects not motivated by "affection and optimism," they are anti-women's rights when women comprise half the world's population. Both Extremists sects are challenging education, science, our secularism, and our social mores. Our social mores could benefit from upgraded behavioral and ethical standards. However, the East and West Extremists' solutions are not remedial. They hold ideological, emotion and belief based worldviews; their religious and political agendas would obliterate art and culture, science and medicine, innovation, energy sources, basic liberties, and push the negative level of consciousness below 200[147] in the world's population. Shades of the Dark Ages all over again!

Today's male and female Islamic suicide bombers are made, not born, so the challenge is to educate women, the children's mothers, so they are not prey for Extremist religious hatemongers. Religionists count on women to obey. Extremist Muslims' right-brains have been indoctrinated at an early age by those clerics who hate or fear Western nations. The West is the antithesis of what they preach and teach: women are nobodies in their eyes and under their laws, the Muslim God is the only true God, and the Muslim way is the only true way. Muslims believe and practice there is no God but Allah; Muhammad is his messenger. When we are secure within ourselves and in our beliefs, we do not fear others' beliefs.

Muslim women also submit to Allah and to men. Even though Muslim women, in most of their own countries cannot drive vehicles, vote, or be in charge of their destinies, including wearing apparel, they may be in charge of running their households. Many Muslim women have insisted on adhering to the Islamic dress code in Western countries, including when they drive vehicles. Due to their religious enculturation and their religious dress code, they may not assimilate as well as other immigrants into Western countries. Recall that "To circumscribe women, Saudi Arabia took Islam's moral code and orthodoxy to extremes not outlined by Muhammad; the Catholic Church took its moral codes and orthodoxy to extremes not outlined by Jesus."[81]

Women's lives in the church are beginning to improve, but their status may not. Women are becoming priests in most of the Christian denominations, except the Orthodox and Roman Catholic churches where women as priests are not options today. Jewish women are becoming rabbis. Muslim feminists are establishing Islamic Feminism based upon the Koran, the Prophet, and Muhammad's emancipation of women. Originally, the Buddha was opposed to allowing women to become mendicant nuns; they did, though, which was unprecedented in earlier times. Even Buddhist nuns are demanding that men acknowledge their status in the Sangha.

At a December 2009 conference – the Parliament of the World's Religions, in Australia, former U.S. President Jimmy Carter said in a speech there, "The belief that women are inferior human beings in the eyes of God gives excuses to the brutal husband who beats his wife, the soldier who rapes a woman, the employer who has a lower pay scale for women employees, or partners who decide to abort a female embryo."[190]

While religions are part of the problem of discrimination against women, religions and individual women may take steps toward being part of the solution. "The Dalai Lama has taken that step and calls himself a feminist."[190] Some religious sects allow women to be priests, ministers, deacons, and rabbis; however, some of these sects also deny women's rights over their own bodies, from physical, emotional, and mental abuse to abortion.

A German theologian, Jurgen Moltmann, includes ecological and feminist concerns in his Christian theology. He promotes alternatives to a wrathful or vengeful God. Professor Moltmann, is convinced that "eschatology [beliefs about the ultimate future] is central to understanding God, humanity, all the basic teachings of his faith."[315]

The Worldwide Laws of Life, funded and edited by Sir John Templeton, a former Wall Street titan and founder of the John Templeton Foundation and Laws of Life Essay Contests, is a compilation of 200 spiritual principles on which the world's five major religions seem to agree. "One law that surprised some people is the spiritual principle that those who do good, do well."[262]

Through his foundation, Sir John Templeton teaches that "Human beings have a natural tendency to think they've found the answer, the truth. And they stop thinking. Or if they attend religious services, they're told what the answers are, so they don't do much thinking... We're trying to encourage people everywhere to become enthusiastic about the discovery of spiritual information."[262] People who are free of fear, and are confident of their manhood, womanhood, and faith are not threatened but enlightened by others' different faiths.

Since it is practically impossible to predict the future course of diverse, established religions and cultures, some scholars are expecting that in the future it will be "humanists, following humanist principles, who will lead humanity, not Christians or Muslims or Jews or Hindus or Buddhists."[58] Carl Coon states, "most people may continue to stick with their old religions, they will increasingly view humanism as a kind of second language, a useful bridge to the larger global community."[58]

Believing in democracy and in Jesus Christ's truthful teachings begins with humanely raising whole-brained children in a humane society where money is dethroned as god and excess materialism is hubris. Since happiness cannot be bought, those who do good, do well – especially when we evoke and nurture human beings' talents as part of caring for our natural resources, share our resources with the less fortunate, and have compassion for all.

Compassion is a common denominator of all religions. Compassion could be a meeting ground for transcending differences of the diverse religious sects by extending compassion to religions other than our own. Compassion and gender equality are women's human rights, despite the inequities placed upon them through the ages.

Chapter Seven

*A little boy begins life loving his mother.
Why, then, are virtually all societies
steeped in misogyny and patriarchy?*
Shlain, 2003, p. 334

The Politics of Gender

The founders of institutional Christianity with their beliefs about women's inferiority to men have negatively affected most females' destinies and male-female relationships for centuries. The adage, "The hand that rocks the cradle rules the world," is a myth, if the hand is a woman's. Instead, it is men's hands that reinvent religions, write the history books, make the laws, and control knowledge, communications, banking, women's sexuality, people's perceptions, and their beliefs and behavior. After all, history is about his story of left-brained teachings, writings, achievements, and wars and about the unquestioned assumptions and religious beliefs about women that, for nearly two thousand years, have been the foundations of familial, cultural, religious, educational, relational, social, economic, and political systems in Western civilization.

What's wrong with our society is a reflection of what's wrong with not educating the right-brain, either informally or formally, in The Western Intellectual Tradition's K-12 public school system. The right-brain has been mistakenly or purposefully branded as female. Unconscious beliefs, values, and gender conditioning – inculcated from birth on – by genetic, familial, cultural, religious, educational, and other institutional practices are powerfully ingrained into the human psyche and are destructive of all human beings' innate wholeness and behavior. Without access to our right hemisphere's data, our heart consciousness, we lose touch with our humanity, so "Greed is good; sharing is bad" becomes the mantra of America's nouveau riche young and old men and some of our old moneyed dynasties, if they value money more than people. The aura of wealth and power is most seductive to beautiful young women who are brainwashed by our society to be beautiful, to develop their feminine wiles, not to develop their own minds or acknowledge their personal power or, as some men call it, pussy power.

To become whole, humane human beings, male and female babies must be loved and cared for so they can, in turn, love and care for themselves and others. When both of our human brains are educated, formally and/or informally, to be whole, loving, compassionate, and wise, then we do not have to focus on outside-self substitutes, such as money, status, power, power-over people, sex, food, drink, drugs, material possessions, physical appearance, or worship media-manufactured idols to feel loved and loving. All promise to make us special and happier. Instead, as a group, we are a nation that is undernurtured, born and living in toxic soup, and so immersed in our own little world of beliefs, values, and images that we become unaware of the larger world that will determine our individual destinies. When we rely upon only one brain, either the left or the right, to do our thinking for us, we neglect another worldview waiting in the wings to be acknowledged. For whatever reason, if we turn our thinking over to others to do our thinking for us, or neglect our civic responsibilities to help keep our country as democratic as possible for the greater good of all Americans, we diminish the value of hard earned human rights in the world's eyes.

Our democracy was founded by white men who were products of their inherited beliefs and values that perceived women as unequal under their inherited men-made laws. Many women, in the past, have proven their worth as equal human beings, not as subservient to men. They paved the way for women's rights, under new Amendments to our Constitution, but legislation does not change human minds. Many men in colonial times believed that women's brains were inferior to theirs and uneducable, that women are the cause of Christianity's original sin, and that their sexuality must be regulated by men. Those inherited beliefs, voiced and unvoiced in our culture, may be ongoing obstacles to women valuing their minds and self-worth. Many concentrate on building up men's self-esteem instead, or, unlike Narcissus, who wanted to see himself reflected in his mother's eyes; many women want to see themselves reflected in men's eyes. With a power-over mentality that women are physically and mentally weak, men have used women not only as the source of their sexual and ego gratification but also as their toxic waste dump for resentments against society and their families for not giving them what they wanted or for giving them what they didn't want.

Responsibility for self and to others used to be a given, part of human's contractual arrangements in our Founders' lives, so it was not included with human rights in promulgating the U.S. Constitution. Responsibility for self and to others is not taught in K-12 public schools, nor are any topics perceived to be "women's right-brain domain." It is the right-brain, heart, and gut that include human virtues (honesty, respect, morals, ethics, empathy compassion, altruism, creativity, intuition) and humans' negative emotions (fear, anger, pride, desire, guilt, shame) that often override their positive emotions (peace, joy, love, reason, justice, courage).

However, many women obey their religious and cultural beliefs because they were conditioned to accept their roles as subservient to men in much of the world, where it is more difficult for women to become financially independent. Few women are willing to disbelieve what they have been conditioned to believe from the cradle. "It isn't well-planned conspiracy that keeps us down but our own agreement to our unimportance, the acceptance of insignificance."[170] Women who are dependent upon men for their identity, support, and beliefs perpetuate women's lower status and religions' anti-women rights when they do not develop their own minds or talents.

Unfortunately, in our Western culture, many men's and women's beliefs lead them to be obsessed with money and with their own and others' exterior selves; the material dimension of being: appearance, youth, money, status, power, and material things. Since men are cognitively trained, socially accepted, and historically expected to win at the material game, dependent women are the primary losers in the material dimension because many of them concentrate so hard on getting and keeping their good looks that they neglect their minds. With marriage in mind, young women expect Prince Charming to rescue and complete them, so they may live happily ever after. Of course, not all women are so enculturated. Many are independent or interdependent with nurtured minds.

Many women compete with each other for available resources, primarily men who have status, money, and system power. Whether that competitive aspect is a holdover from evolution is debatable. Women's pay for their services in the workforce is certainly due to the devaluation of women in favor of higher pay for men, usually for similar or lower jobs. Since few women are able to support themselves in the style to which they were accustomed in their families or they'd love to become accustomed to, marrying "up" has been a solution. Until women age, then their men may prefer a younger, more malleable woman, for our culture focuses on women's bodies, not their minds.

The laws may have changed, but biased mindsets have not. While the 19th Amendment to the U. S. Constitution, allowing women to vote, was ratified in 1920 by 36 of the 48 U.S. States, the remaining states tried to invalidate the Amendment. The other states joined the rest of the country: Delaware in 1923; Maryland in 1941; Virginia in 1952; Alabama in 1953; Florida, Georgia, Louisiana, North Carolina and South Carolina between 1969 and 1971; and Mississippi in 1984. Despite the gender and race conflict that divided Americans for years, memories are short and many young women assume their right to vote is a given. If you think women's rights are a given, why hasn't the Equal Rights Amendment been ratified?

As Christine Stansell wrote in *A Forgotten Fight for [Women's] Suffrage*, "Today the country is again divided... How remarkable, then, that a parallel conflict – one that similarly exposes the fears and anxieties that the expansion of democracy unleashes – now largely lost to memory."[314] Some differences rarely heal: many southern states turned red, Republican, as payback to the Democrats for the 1965 Civil Rights Act. Now the Muslims are the recipient of some Americans' fear and anxiety. Women's rights, abortion, racism, and same-sex marriage are at the center of much of the ongoing divisiveness and political discord in America, instead of the dearth of job opportunities in new industries, the widening gap between the rich and the poor, and the sorry state of the nation's K-12 public education systems. Those priorities negatively impact girls and women's destinies as well as boys and men's destinies.

Traditionally, women's career options used to be limited to sex-defined roles. Since World War II, women have entered all fields, and most careers have become professionalized, requiring higher education and credentialing. While more educated women are marrying educated men, many educated women in the workforce, today, prefer partnering with men who may not be academically educated or hold elite jobs to balance their lives. Many women, though, are behaving like the traditional left-brained, ego-driven, competitive male, or political animal, in the work world.

The Sexual Revolution since the 1960s has not liberated women from sexual dominance, rape, or physical, psychological, emotional, and sexual abuse. Women as sexual predators may be rare, but cougars are said to be circulating. Female teachers who seduce students are not as common as male teachers who seduce females and young boys. Women's promiscuity may be more of an expectation since the 1960s than a reality. Evidently, women's turn-on is a "love" connection for sex to be meaningful. More women and men live as partners, rarely get married, enjoy satisfying long-term relationships, and avoid the traditional wife/husband cultural stereotypes associated with "marriage." Of course, commitment has also become an issue for many males and females. Nevertheless, youth and good looks are still society's preference for women over their brains, common sense, and health. Some books and newspaper articles include statistics indicating that the marriage rate has declined over the past forty-five years. Some women are opting not to have children. Other professional women are adopting or bearing and raising children as single mothers or in same-sex partnerships. Males, too, are adopting and raising children in same-sex partnerships. The old order is changing and is slowly yielding toward Sexual Resolution of heretofore ancient men-made rules about gender, sex, and sin.

Mating instincts have changed little over the centuries. Primitive women (*Gyna sapiens*) selected men (*Homo sapiens*) for their genes and hunting skills to birth healthy babies and ensure their physical survival.[306] Even today, men perceive male offspring as the survival of their name and genes beyond their own mortality: their ego survival.

When ancient males figured out their roles in sex with women and childbirth, and realized that they fathered specific children, they became interested in the fates of their offspring, hoping for immortality through their genes, unlike other species' males.

"Men eventually concluded that the only way they could be confident that a man's 'begats' were his and his alone was to plot together [with other men] to restructure societies' sexual relationships...men set out to achieve the impossible – control women's sexuality and reproductive abilities."[305] Here began the first left-brain rationale for subjugating women: women are baby-making machines, so own the machines and put a lock on them so other men do not have access. In medieval times, when men went to battle, they put an actual "lock," known as a chastity belt, on women's genitals, and they took the keys with them. Today, under the guise of right-to-life, many men and women seek control of women's rights to their bodies, health, and lives.

Ancient men's fear of women's power was common. It probably began when women bled monthly, menstruated, and didn't get weak or die, as men did when they bled, so mystical powers were attributed to women. Men who attributed malevolence to the menses indicated they were fearful of or mystified by menstrual blood. Add the fact that women nurture and bear children within their wombs made her an object of fear and envy. "The first century, A.D. Roman pseudoscientist Pliny warns men that a menstruating women, by her touch, can 'blast the fruits of the field, sour wine, cloud mirrors, rust iron, and blunt the edges of knives.'"[306] During the Middle Ages in Europe, women's menstruation became a pathological condition, something at odds with Nature and harmful to men: menstrual blood was judged to be the cause of gonorrhea in men. However, when a woman ceased to menstruate, she became a repository of evil humors for now she was not ridding her body of the poison every month, and she became a target of abuse. Women, in general, contended with prejudice: men were warned to "avoid 'flesshley' dealings with 'wymmen aged,' since they could prove both morally and physiologically harmful"[335] to them. Instead of realizing that human beings are harmonized with Nature's cycles of life, death, and the cosmos, especially the moon, age-old negative beliefs about women and their menstruation prevailed and forever labeled them as evil, inferior to men, and temptresses.

The Roman Church blamed women for Original Sin because, as the Biblical story goes, Eve disobeyed God in the Garden of Eden. Then Mary Magdalene said she had a vision of Jesus Christ after his resurrection, but later Apostle Peter said Jesus appeared to him in the flesh. The Church's founders had a historical rationale for excluding women from roles in their hierarchical plan. They probably feared women would not follow their rules and be obstacles, except as followers. Religious beliefs and prevailing beliefs about women were used to accuse women of being witches during the Renaissance in Europe and during America's Salem witch hunt era.

Those inherited beliefs about women impacted men's and the medical establishment's concept of women's bodies for centuries to come. Misogyny and patriarchy appear to be embedded in many men's psyches, but "Many men resist the pull of misogyny and remain favorably disposed to gender equality."[306] Ancient men's wisdom about women's equality is attributed to Socrates, 470-399 BC. He did not read or write, but his teachings have been recounted in Plato's Dialogues. Plato was born in Athens in 427 or 428 BC; he founded the Academy in Athens in 387 BC to conduct research in philosophy and mathematics. "Socrates and Plato...to their great credit, 'man' included all human beings, even women, even foreigners, even, perhaps, slaves."[335]

Aristotle, born in Macedonia in 384 BC, attended the Academy in Athens, invented the science of logic, divided science into fields of study, and believed that "the inferiority of slaves and women was innate. It could not be cured."[335] Aristotle never "questioned the idea that the most important being in the world is man...only men have rational souls."[335] Aristotle wrote and published many books which were popular and influenced Greeks' negative thinking about women, so his negative attitudes affirmed women's status, which have prevailed throughout the centuries.

About 5,000 years ago, writing was invented, and "a study of the origins of writing in less complex times...reveals how writing, first, and then the alphabet, altered the balance of power to women's detriment."[307] and favored one hemisphere of the brain, the left, over the other, the right, at wisdom's expense for thousands of years. Neurosurgeon Leonard Shlain asserted that "Writing of any form, but especially its alphabetic form, diminishes feminine values"[307] and empowers the left-brainers.

Thousands of years ago, wisdom was linked to the feminine, and "men began writing with passion about their desire for knowledge, using metaphors referring to male-female relationships...none of these writers seeks feminine wisdom. None aspires to intuition, prophecy, or woman-knowing; they all long for book learning!"[307] Thus, the introduction of writing and the ability of large numbers of people to read and write were the bases of our male-dominant, left-brained Western cultures.

Dr. Shlain proposed that "The most dangerous result of these all-male cultures bereft of the input from women is the loss of common sense. The phrase 'common sense' has several meanings. In one, it is the wisdom of all the senses, a holistic and simultaneous grasp of multiple converging determinants. In this meaning common sense is intuitive and is often the opposite of logic. In another meaning, it is the wisdom of more than one person. It is the result of give-and-take and of face-to-face conversations with another that allows one to 'hear oneself think.' In this second meaning, common sense is wisdom generated 'in common.'"[307] From Albert Einstein's quotation, we learn his definition: "Common sense is the collection of prejudices acquired by age eighteen."

Our sense of self implies that we have an understanding of our bodies. Yet, the fact remains that we cannot see into or even feel what is going on inside the largest organ of the body: our skin, except when a disease provides symptoms. The original meaning of the word autopsy was to look inside one's self. Another fact is, to take possession of our minds requires understanding the conscious and unconscious minds' role in our beliefs, behavior, and decisions today. Learning the history of the roles and status assigned to women and men throughout the ages is one reason for women to take full control of their minds, bodies, and health.

Television's daily negativity diverts our attention from the real issues confronting Americans: fear and love. Fear is depowering if we do not use it as a stimulus to look for the source of its power. Recall that Dr. Dorsey believed that all painful emotions stem from inhibited love; "fear is hurt (hindered) safety... Hate is hurt (hindered) love."[198] Respect from men or women cannot be mandated, but love and respect for oneself and one's mission to be respected as a woman means we have to be free enough to be our authentic selves.

Some women continue in the world's oldest profession for women. In 18th century England, one in five young women were prostitutes. When greater employment opportunities for women emerged, women became sex objects; they were "trained to adopt a femininity that was designed to gratify the male gaze – traditionally that had been the stigma, or prerogative, of actresses and whores."[272]

Make-up became popular with women when blushing was a sign of innocence. "The test of a lady's modesty proverbially lay in her capacity to blush: she who could not blush was the lady without shame."[272] Male's fixation upon the female body entailed and sustained the subjugation of women: "men sought women for their physical charms, and women colluded with flirtatious looks and demeanor so as to secure the most eligible males in the marriage market."[272] Women were "reduced to coveted sexual challenges and catches, pawns in a game of seduction, resistance and conquest."[272]

A 1790's feminist, Mary Wollstonecraft deplored the fact that women were treated as sex objects by men and that women were absorbed in their physicalness, preferring their bodies over their minds.[272] Her own life's dilemmas (by law, her father and brothers inherited her grandfather's estate) led to her becoming a wealthy lady's companion and a prolific writer about the female condition. Even in the 20th century, my grandfather's estate went to his two sons; my mother received a Singer sewing machine.

Ms. Wollstonecraft's solution was for women to cultivate their minds instead of being the "frivolous sex."[272] She wrote, "The perennial and unquestioned despotism of men – in scripting women's roles – must end."[272] For her, "Women could never control their bodies until they first took possession of their minds."[272] That advice holds true for women in the 21st century. However, being perceived as fragile and vulnerable is women's intergenerational inheritance which remains, centuries later, in the minds of men and women. Some young girls and women today, despite changed times and women's rights, collude in perpetuating the male social construct for women, just as fashion dictates their lives, thinness dictates their lifestyle, and traditional beliefs dictate their relationships with themselves and with other females and males.

Achieving the seemingly impossible goal of controlling women's sexuality and reproductive abilities was easy: create a division of labor between the sexes. Stay-at-home women, caring for their children, are often isolated and dependent upon the male for their own and their children's survival. It was an easy task during Agricultural times when both men, women, and children worked the fields. With the rise of Industrialism, though, families left the farm and their extended families for the cities. Women with children stayed at home and men went off to the factories and offices. Women who sought college educations were discouraged, yet many succeeded and carved out careers in the professions. Traditionally, only single women or spinsters worked in offices or as teachers and nurses.

In America, in 1848, the women and men who gathered in Seneca Falls, New York, called for the end to laws and customs that made women subordinate to men. Their demands were not met. Harriet Beecher Stowe's account of the brutality of slavery moved the minds and hearts of millions of Northerners. It sold a million copies. Writer Nathaniel Hawthorne, 1803-1882, author of *The Scarlet Letter*, called women writers – Susan Warner, Louisa May Alcott, and Harriet Beecher Stowe – "those damned scribbling women."

It was not until August 26, 1920, that the 19th Amendment would grant women the right to vote in the United States. After women received the right to vote, increased numbers of women graduated from college and entered the workplace. Women who studied in primarily male dominant fields, science and medicine, were not well treated in the universities or the workplace. During World War II, with necessity as the mother of invention operative, women worked in the factories and offices to make the goods and products necessary to run a war and men went off to battle. Women's roles in the workplace were expanded after World War II, but the glass ceiling was in place when I went to work in New York City.

After high school and a one-year business college course, I attended college at night and worked as a secretary in the insurance and mortgage banking fields. I studied general insurance, passed New York State exams, and parlayed my studies and skills into also working with insurance executives from diverse insurance companies. During a working session in a New York City hotel where insurance executives were promulgating insurance policy conditions, and I was taking shorthand notes of their progress and reading them back, a hand rested on my knee under the round table. I bent back a finger to see who it was, met his glance, mouthed "No!" and let go. I felt no need to report the incident to the executive in charge.

With licensed credentials in general insurance and the company's mouthpiece for agents in the field, I could promulgate insurance rates, accept insurance binders, authorize claims to be paid, do underwriting, and mentor my future bosses. As a woman, I could not be promoted into management. Management, though, was not that appealing. I knew bosses who acted like minigods, whose constant jockeying for more status, money, and power was augmented by expense accounts and the desire for entertaining women in spite of having wives and children.

Without a challenging future on the horizon in the insurance and banking fields, I expected academia to be more inclusive of women, so I went to school full-time. I may have been a better financial role model for my children to follow in the workworld, if I had accepted my lot as a woman then and had stayed in Corporate America until the tide rose for women. But, I would have ignored my passion at age three for learning and doing more and more about more and more.

Human Development was not offered in the mid 1950s. History was my favorite subject. Economics was a close second, Psychology was clinical and book-oriented toward what's wrong with people, so I settled on English Literature that nourished my need to know more about the human condition through the ages and to teach. In an essay for 18th Century English Literature, I referenced an antecedent from a previous century's literature class. The professor wrote in red pencil across it, "You did not learn that in this class!" His rigid thinking did not allow for an interdisciplinary perspective within his dog-eared lesson plan or in his field! From that smart professor I learned that expertise is achieved at the expense of narrowing one's concentration and repeating it over and over. When we learn more and more about less and less, we are conforming to society's preference for specialists, for experts, conformists. Society's disapproval is apparent in the adage, "Jack/Jill of all trades and master of none."

While I found academia to be more inclusive of women, academia is burdened by tenured professors and competing, insulated disciplines. To keep their students stimulated, colleges and universities' solution to bureaucratic problems is to hire qualified adjuncts. Thus, America's underemployed Ph.D.s are welcome as poorly paid adjuncts and rarely get a full-time position. Adjuncts may be an economic solution for academia's overhead costs, but not for those who are career-oriented or for those whose tuition costs led them to student loans. America's economic bubble bursts – Great Depression, 1929-1939 and the ongoing Great Recession – are economic disasters for ordinary Americans who have student loans to repay and for those who depend upon invested savings in the stock market for their retirement.

Despite the need for political issues to be relevant to today's economy, women's rights are still under siege, which encourages more violence against women in our society. The Supreme Court's decision in 1973, Roe v. Wade, legalized abortion, but that Court decision is still under attack by conservatives, Christian fundamentalists, the Roman Catholic Church, militant fundamentalists, and pro-lifers. Pro-lifers believe that the West's falling birth rate will be the downfall of traditional Western civilization.[318] Many fear that the rest of the world's rising birth rate means numbers will rule the world. Population-wise, China and India outnumber the world! Inherited perceptions, conscious and unconscious, of women and their abusive treatment do not change just because it's the 21st century. Even K-12 public education does not include a whole-brain approach that teaches that men and women are equal human beings who complement each other to survive and thrive. Violence against women ensues.

Rape is a fact of life for many young girls and women on Earth. Women are perceived to be easy targets of abuse by rapists, robbers, con artists, boyfriends, or husbands. In the Muslim world, women have few rights, are pawns in wars, and are lured by their mothers and other women to be killed by brothers or fathers when they "dishonor" their families. Poverty is a motive for women prostituting themselves, but passion/lust and/or power/control are men's motivation for sex with prostitutes and/or for enslaving prostitutes for profit.

Today's religious, secular, and tribal wars use rape as a way to perpetuate the victors' genes and to demoralize and destroy the countries and cultures that women preserve. Whenever a religious community feels threatened by the secular world or other religions, women's bodies become the focus of attention or targets, so pro-life and anti-abortion forces abound. Thus, male views of human sexuality, women, and other races are our society's unexamined inheritance. Sexuality is not one of the natural and sweet mysteries of love and life when it was masterminded to control women and children and to disdain homosexuals and lesbians.

There is a possibility, due to the power of the unconscious mind in our beliefs and behaviors, that pro-life positions advocated by some religions and individuals, may not be all about anti-abortion and the sanctity of life from inception when a fertilized egg is considered a human being. Historically, men have controlled women's sexuality and reproductive capabilities. Ego survival and reproducing oneself are paramount in human beings, especially in ego-centered, hypermasculine left-brained men. A pro-life stance may mean fetuses are perceived as ego extensions or as male egos' survival by insuring that one's genes are passed to the next generation. Pro-life may also be about perpetuating control over women's bodies and lives, as God-given, so women may continue to be dominated by men and their semen. The same right-to-life zeal is not exercised for abused, neglected, or poor children's rights after they are born; nor is the emphasis upon sex education to prevent unwanted pregnancies. Some right-to-lifers have bombed abortion clinics, maimed people, and killed doctors, so they kill people to save the unborn. Abortions are not the answer to unwanted pregnancies, except for rape and incest, but education of the right-brain would help adolescents and young men and women to manage their emotions and hormonal urges before their prefrontal lobes mature.

Women's achieved human rights in the 20th and 21st centuries have not been given to them; they have been earned by those women who fought for them and, with help from enlightened men, paved the way for women who take for granted their right to vote, own property, sign documents, and a college education. The social movements for women's rights and civil rights in the United States enfranchised millions of people. Now gay rights are one of the moral issues of the conservative Christian right. Fear perpetuated by religions, the military, and terrorists has only strengthened the power and resolve of the fearmongers to turn back the democratic clock. Historical ideologies of the past, primarily based on religions' dogma, require scrutiny when new data are available and in changing times and circumstances.

Biology is Destiny?

Sigmund Freud and other men may ponder, What do women want? Equality! Respect! Love! Safety! What many men really want to know is, "What must I do to convince her to let me have sex with her?"[306] Most Western women may choose to be impregnated, to refuse sex, or to take birth control pills. Many young girls do not have the self-esteem or confidence to say "No!" when pressured by young boys and men to have sex, especially those young women whose identities, emotional states, or financial status are dependent upon those men/boys.

Too many young women and children today are victims of male predators who perceive them as fair game or think access to their bodies is a natural right to physically satisfy their urges or rages. Many young women use their sexuality to attract men in power in the belief that the powerholders will provide for them materially or divorce their wives and marry them, such as some of the young women who gravitated to Tiger Woods. Some men have yet to learn the difference between love and lust. Many men wish to have sex with women all the time – indicating ego problems or addiction to sex – except when a woman is menstruating; then she may be less appealing.

So what do women want? Some women want affirmation of their whole selves as a special human being, which gets translated by some women into physical and emotional attraction and by men into sexual attraction only. Some men, who are emotionally illiterate or fear commitment, believe and practice: any women can do for me what you can do! The Sexual Revolution implied in the women's movement of the 1960s and the birth control pill have benefited more men than women in that many young women still pay more attention to how they look today than to educating their minds for a career to secure their own happiness.

Women "make" men: they birth and raise male babies to become men. Psychoanalytic theory informs us that boys have to reject their mothers' ways to become real men. Rejecting female attributes sounds innocuous, but by becoming venomous to include misogyny and disdain sounds more like Elizabeth Janeway's position on power and domination instead. "Domination and subordination are facts of life... What do the powerful want?... How do the weak threaten their masters?... What the powerful want is assurance that their power is held rightfully, within a relationship which sanctions its use and validates the right of these rulers to rule"[170] women, their families, and Western society's institutions and organizations. Men who are not empowered in the system by money and status, and live low levels of consciousness, still feel they have the male right to put any woman in her place and abuse her to make themselves feel superior.

The language we use, from labels to stereotypes, reinforces gender politics. While European languages divide all things and beings into masculine and feminine, in most languages the term masculine is used to describe the energy or attributes of the left-brain (logical quantitative, task-oriented) and feminine is used to describe the energy or attributes of the right-brain (emotional, qualitative, people-oriented). Our English language is more gender free, but it is not what is said but what is meant that subtly keeps women depowered, if they agree to it.

Thus, power corrupts, but it is not confined to the powerful: "the weak are not exempted from it by refusing authority over themselves"[170] and by refusing to accept the labels. If women learn to trust themselves and to think differently from becoming what they are taught, to express doubts, they learn to disbelieve. Disbelief "signals something that the powerful fear...the power to disbelieve...refusal to accept the definition of oneself that is put forward by the powerful"[170] and to stretch beyond the beliefs and attitudes that, traditionally, women have been raised to be dependent.

Dependent, Independent, Interdependent:
(Right-brained, Left-Brained, Whole-Brained)

Human development models are theories that attempt to make sense out of or to categorize segments of a human population from a left-brained perspective. What's makes them dangerous is they are diagnoses we accept as "That's me!" or "That's the way I am!" We become a label, a disease, a dis-ease, that empowers us, like "healthy" or depowers us, like "sick." Even when we are healthy or sick, there's so much more to know about us that the diagnosis missed in the rush to label us. Why are we healthy or sick? What is the source of our health or sickness? How do we use our health or sickness? Do we take our health for granted? Do we turn our sickness over to a third party? Since the diagnoses – healthy versus sickness – were made based upon the symptoms we expressed, what are the symptoms telling us? Usually, we are doing something right or we are doing something wrong to ourselves.

Being raised, consciously and unconsciously, by our parents – who were conditioned by our culture to behave as everybody else does – to be dependent, independent, or interdependent people does not emphasize a relationship with oneself. It does not emphasize we have two brains in our head that are labeled male, left, and female, right, so we are brainwashed to rely upon one and disown the other because of our gender. Nature is not that simple, we have two brains for a reason: to integrate them to accept the so-called masculine and feminine sides within ourselves so we have a fully functioning relationship with ourselves first before we can have fully functioning relationships with others. The brain is like any muscle, if we don't use it we lose it. When both sides are not integrated, there is conflict within that is played out in our relationships with others. We are unconsciously drawn to another human being who expresses the symptoms of our opposite brain to complete ourselves or to compete against when we resist or deny our opposite's intelligence and want to cure them of their symptoms. Hence, relationships can be rocky when we are not whole-brained or less rocky when one partner is and the other is not.

My interviews with at least fifty women of diverse backgrounds and occupations for a doctoral dissertation on Women and Power gave me a broad base from which to understand that women don't hate women across the board. Women may dislike or admire women who are not like themselves but may prefer women who are like themselves. Women do not support women or vote for women just because they are women, so there are variables at work in their decisions and biases. I was able to affirm psychologist Judith Bardwick's theory that how children are raised in our society affects their perception of themselves, their personal power, and of others.[18] But the early conditioning remains in our culture and in brainwashed minds.

Child-rearing has changed since the 1970s and 1980s. Diverse parenting styles exist in America because of our diverse multicultures and many parent their children as they were parented, whereas, some parent their children as they were not parented. Parenting runs the gamut from micro-managing their children's lives to be successful/wealthy or neglecting their parental duties so their children raise themselves and other siblings without much adult support. In between, there are parents whose unconditional love for their children gives their children the freedom, with limits, to unleash their curiosity and to learn and grow in any environment.

Girls used to be raised to be primarily dependent. Men are raised to be independent. Few girls and boys are consciously raised to be interdependent. Girls are generally raised to be dependent upon and associate their identity with others (family, husband, children), their physical attractiveness, family wealth, or material things. Their personal power is similarly outside self, in others or in their looks, their accomplishments, or things. Through crises, opportunity, or death, many dependent women transition to an independent status One of my master's students said, "My husband died, so I had to grow up." Traditionally, women have been followers; fewer women have been leaders. Thus, it may be difficult for dependent women to perceive women as equal to men as leaders instead of as followers. With maturity, though, women learn to trust themselves and to think differently from what they were taught and to express doubts.

Powerlessness may breed uncomfortableness within self in the presence of powerful women. Some powerful women may disdain women they perceive to be powerless. Dependent women, in particular, expend considerable "emotional labor"[155] being "nice" or "smiling" which estranges them from their whole selves. Emotional management is women's "currency" exchanged for economic support and family harmony.

More boys than girls are raised to be independent. Independent people attain and maintain their identities, self-esteem, and personal and system power through their careers, status, and money. Note that both dependent and independent human development models are dependent: one upon relationships, appearance, money, and material things; while the other is dependent upon the workplace or the system's status, power, money, and material things. In effect, dependent people are primarily dependent upon people and personal relationships, whereas, independent people are primarily dependent upon the workplace or their careers and professional relationships for their sense of self, identify, and power. Thus, their personal power is outside themselves, not within themselves.

Today, many women are raised to be and may be considered independent; some of them are called "near-men." Others may be careerists by design rather than default, and some may be harder on women at work than on men. The film starring Meryl Streep in *The Devil Wears Prada* was based on a real life career woman who was extra tough on women who worked for her. She cried when her husband divorced her; her disowned sensitive side awakened in her crisis. Since power and men are synonymous in many women's cultural experiences, women may be "startled by women's ambition and resentful of their power because of gender."[18] It seems that "The commonly seen hatred or resentment of or jealously of goodness, truth, beauty, health or intelligence is largely determined by threat of loss of self-esteem, as the liar is threatened by the honest man, the homely girl by the beautiful girl, or the coward by the hero. Every superior person confronts us with our own shortcomings."[219]

The dependent model is consistently lower in self-esteem since the locus of personal power is external: in others or material things. Dependent women may not like, vote for, support, or get along with other women. It's as if such women are mirrors for dependent women, invoking, "Who's the fairest of us all?" Although, dependent women may "see" in women unlike themselves what they didn't accomplish for themselves through their own talents, time, and effort. Dependent Western women are conditioned to be unfree in America and to be dependent upon men, just as Muslim women are. Western dependent women are not in charge of their destinies when dominated by left-brain practices and brainwashed by unexamined beliefs and attitudes. Many dependent women, housewives with children, develop wonderful organizational, people, and entertainment skills which are rewarded in the workplace. There is, as Barry Oshry taught, power in whatever position we are in,[250] if we recognize and actualize it.

When men view themselves as superior to women or as the breadwinner, they have disowned their right-brain, and the marriage may not survive unless their wives have a dependent personality disorder. Some left-brained men who have a gender-disorder may be attracted to whole-brained women, so they may spend their marriage days in competition with them, resent their achievements, or look for opportunities to belittle them as women, not their brains. Children raised in such adversarial atmospheres do not have healthy role models for orchestrating their own lives. A dependent woman's ingrained need to be cared for may be masked by learning how to make others feel good about caring for her. Dependent women come to marriage with different behavioral patterns.

Psychologists have found three distinct varieties of women. They appear to be dependent women: (1) submissiveness ("I am easily downed in an argument"); (2) exploitability ("I am afraid of hurting people's feelings"); and (3) love dependency ("Being isolated from others is bound to lead to unhappiness"). Many "submission" and "exploitation" marriages end in divorce. In the "love dependency" marriage, "studies now suggest that in severely troubled [marriages], the aggressor as well as the victim, often have a dependent fear of losing the relationship."[47] The institution of marriage works best when the partners complement each other: two whole-brained people make one whole relationship.

Independent men and women are at risk when they invest their whole lives, not their whole brains, in their work or career that is not nurture-oriented. They rarely become agents of societal change. They do not realize, until it may be too late, that their performance only is valued, not the self. When skills become obsolete or they retire or are fired, their self-esteem, bolstered by their roles in the workworld, is in jeopardy. The locus of their personal power is also outside self, just like the dependent's locus of personal power. Independents who do not have a social conscience and collude in the greedy aspects of capitalism are foes of capitalism and of democracy. Independent loners, both smart men and women, may lack a moral and social conscience.

"What's in it for me" is their mantra without loyalty to anyone, even their country.

Only the interdependent human development model is dynamically balanced with a sense of self, fulfilling relationships, and system power inherent in careers. The whole-brained model develops a keen sense of self-knowledge, intimate and harmonious personal relationships, meaningful, fulfilling work, financial autonomy, and a worldview that acknowledges we are all connected. To be connected to all, first we must be connected to ourselves. Thus, people who are interdependent can stand alone or together. A combination of personal and system power is a requisite for people to effectively and productively work with and relate to one another as equals and for adults to rear humane human beings. It is tougher on a woman to be interdependent, to have it all – a whole-brained sense of an esteemed self, a significant other, nurture children, rewarding career, and personal, social, and professional relationships, but it is doable as many such women are in the workforce by choice or life's circumstances.

Whatever human development model, or none of the above, we experienced, it is probable that we were not taught how to be comfortable with experiencing and managing a wide range of our emotions, especially love. Emotional literacy learned in K-12 public schools could balance young boys' brains that received a testosterone wash at eight weeks in utero to enlarges their sex and aggression area at the expense of their relationship center. Instead, our culture discourages emotional expressiveness in boys as sissy stuff; however, many of today's men are not afraid to cry. Neuroscientist Joseph LeDoux's 2002 research emphasized the role of emotions in developing children's lives, learning, and behavior:

> Because emotion systems coordinate learning, the broader the range of emotions that a child experiences the broader will be the emotional range of the self that develops. That is why childhood abuse is so devastating. If a significant portion of the early emotional experiences one has are due to activation of the fear system rather than positive systems, then the characteristic personality that begins to build up front from the parallel learning processes coordinated by the emotional state is one characterized by negativity and hopelessness rather than affection and optimism.[202]

Psychological explanations for beyond normal violence in boys and young men toward their peers, women, children, and animals may be rooted in child-rearing practices. For too long, "Spare the rod and Spoil the Child" at home and in boarding schools was the prevailing rationale for adults' passing on their own child-rearing experiences. Childhood abuse is devastating for themselves and for those whose lives they touch.

In our Western society, where boys are not encouraged to display emotions, except anger, unresolved childhood traumas of rape, humiliation, shame, and other right-brain negative emotions are bound to be played out against innocent victims who are perceived to be physically weak: young boys and girls and women. Lust is not the primary drive of sex predators, power over women is their motive for violently attacking their victims. Blaming the female victims of rape – "She asked for it!" – has been the rationale for our society's past denial of criminal intent by sex predators.

Denial: A Memoir of Terror is a 2010 book by Jessica Stern, a world expert on violence and evil. Ms. Stern and her sister, aged 15 and 14, were raped by a stranger who cut the telephone lines and entered their home in Concord, Massachusetts. The local police didn't believe them or take their story seriously; their plight was not publicized, and she believes that the whole community was in denial. Their mother had died earlier and their father was away, which exacerbated their trauma. Their rapist was not caught until after he had raped a total of 44 girls. Her research of the rapist – who committed suicide – and the people who knew him uncovered the fact that his life had been blighted by unresolved child abuse.[316]

"A little boy begins life loving his mother. Why, then, are virtually all societies steeped in misogyny and patriarchy?"[306] Improper attachment or non-bonding of a boy with his mother may be due to her abuse, neglect, death, war, illness, or catastrophe, which will impact his ability to love himself and other women. However, surrogate caretakers or significant others may be substituted for their missing nurturance. On the other hand, most mothers dote on their sons and do everything possible to ease their lives to make them happy. As a result, many young males expect to be treated accordingly by all females – and for free. Fathers' ill treatment of their children's mothers means that male children may learn to mistreat women and female children may learn to expect abuse from men. Children learn what they live and live what they learn.[242] Adolescence is a particularly tough time for boys and girls as their hormones kick in. Boys, with larger sex and aggression areas in their brains appear to perceive love as pleasurable but dangerous and to dread feeling embarrassed by positive emotions, especially love, when aggression is more natural to them,[198] so they'll hit or tease a girl they like. Girls, though, become more relationship-oriented and start dumbing themselves down to please boys who don't prefer smart girls. Culture plays a role in how boys and girls perceive and act out their adolescence.

During the 1960s and 1970s, American society underwent changes from intact, nuclear families to blended, single, and foster parent families. In the early 1970s, I became aware of the pressure many children were under to gain approval by succeeding in academia at all costs, so they cheated. Children's basic human needs for love, respect, trust, security, and belonging have not changed. Things, from toys to electronics, are not substitutes for parents' or caretakers' face-to-face time.

In transitional times when parents are focused on their own needs, many children do not get their needs met, if they suffer from abandonment, neglect, or abuse. The next logical moral misstep of many of those cheating and emotionally, physically, and psychologically deprived youths is to pass on what they learned and experienced, so they torture people and/or animals.

No child escapes unscathed from divorce, the limited resources of a single parent, or the burden of early childhood emotional trauma. Children's emotional, moral and ethical development suffers when the traditional sources of educating the right brain are missing. The media serve up not only violent movies and video games, but male role models for young men in our culture are "Neanderthal professional wrestlers; hockey 'goons,' ready at the slightest provocation to drop their sticks and pummel an opponent; multi-millionaire professional athletes in trouble with the law, demanding 'respect' from fans and the press; and angry, drug-using misogynist rock stars."[177] Tough guys seek positions of power to dominate others, so do some cowardly guys.

According to Money and Lamacz's *Vandalized Lovemaps*, many sexually abused men are predisposed to aberrant sexual behavior, including pedophilia. "The idea that certain individuals or segments of society were predestined by hereditary inferiority to be degenerates of one sort or another had as its converse the idea of hereditary superiority."[231] That doctrine – the basis of the social eugenics movement – led to Hitler's Nazi Germany's Holocaust, genocide in Africa, and sterilization of "mental defectives" in America.

Biology may be a contributing factor to men's inherited sense of superiority. Males have ten times as much testosterone circulating in their bodies than women do, which may account for their domineering and often cruel treatment of women. Testosterone may affect attitudes: weaken attachment and love. Men with higher than normal testosterone levels, without access to their right-brains – not femininity – are said to be more likely to be abusive and marry less frequently, as they desire to bed every available and unavailable woman.

Generally, as human beings age, men's testosterone levels fall and women's testosterone levels rise as their estrogen falls. With aging, women's chemical transition may account for their newfound wisdom with maturity. Many decide, "Now, it's my turn!" Is it a hormonal coincidence that many men divorce their wives, preferring younger women who are more malleable? Although, some left-brained men never forgive their wives for the expectation of monogamy, they may have residual resentment, competitiveness, and adversarial tendencies that will emerge, in ensuing new relationships, until resolved by integrating their disowned right-brain.

"Misogyny is a disdain for women and denigration of the values commonly associated with the feminine."[309] Physiological explanations for rampant misogyny throughout diverse cultures are suspect since other male and female animals have similar hormonal differences, yet those males do not treat their females as human males do. More likely, when male hormones rage, they need a willing female. Lust versus love emerges. If the male is strong and the female is weaker, consensual sex or rape ensues. If the male is rich, handsome, and articulate, economic negotiations may ensue. If females resist male' advances, there are many scenarios from acts of violence to feelings of rejection, and hate, for

"Her veto over sex is the primary source of her power and becomes the root of his anger."[309]

Other men who hate women become serial rapists and killers. There actions against women are violence- not sex-related. Sexual proclivities beyond normal may be found in unresolved, unacknowledged, or not remembered early experiences that reside in the unconscious mind and run their lives.

Patriarchy, Misogyny, Prostitution, Pornography, and Torture

"The two most pervasive [sexist biases] that affect relations between men and women are misogyny and patriarchy... Misogyny is a disdain for women and denigration of the values associated with the feminine [including the right-brain's attributes]... Patriarchy is... social rules put in place by men to control the sexual and reproductive rights of women."[306] While psychoanalytic theory proposes that boys' renounce their mothers "to make the transition to men, they must reject the ways of their mothers."[306] Such theories appear to support inherited religious and cultural beliefs to perpetuate hypermasculinity promoted by ancient men who projected their lack of self-love onto women. "The hindrance of a positive emotion brings out its negative (unconscious) aspect... Inhibited love takes on its negative aspect of hate,"[198] symbolized by women. Thus, in our society, boys and men learn not to be sissies by disowning their right-brain's positive emotions of love and respect for girls and women and to disown their intimate selves. That's an example of original sin.

Although young girls, in general, passionately love their fathers, they do not seem to have to reject them in order to make the transition to being women. Our homophobic society is obsessed with ball games where men have rough body contact with each other and are often rough with woman, while those with distorted love maps may be pedophiles or are obsessed with prostitutes, pornography, physical and mental torture. The rationale for female circumcision, condoned in Africa, was presented by a male medical worker: "women, otherwise were overly sexual and 'prone to prostitution.'" An American doctor suggested instead, "Isn't it just possible... that women are prone to poverty, and men are prone to prostitution?"[42]

Patriarchy

Patriarchy may have been useful in earlier times – to grow civilization's institutions and organizations – but it has led to history's documentation of humankind's inhumanity to men, women, and children. Patriarchy, as an evolutionary role, is no longer necessary in the 21st century. We are at an evolutionary point where both men and women can transcend their biological, familial, racial, and cultural levels of human consciousness, or traditional roles, and learn to incorporate the opposite side of their dominant brain. When we balance and harmonize our lives through self-education and experience to counter entrenched beliefs, we transform ourselves and eventually our society and nations for the greater good of all. Educating the right-brain's emotions and virtues will ameliorate unresolved traumatic issues from early childhood, inherited cultural beliefs, attitudes, and behaviors, and servicepeople's war injuries and experiences that are currently played out on innocent others or on themselves.

Patriarchal lineage is millennial old, but "those raped women singled out for their gender to receive the hate and rage bottled up in young soldiers incited or driven to the ultimate murder of war and its atrocities"[260] has been and is being replayed in Iraq, Afghanistan, and other war-torn countries. Patriarchy has failed women. From "The Women's War," in Iraq, we learn that "Many female soldiers have lived through the terrible violence of the war in Iraq. Others have experienced sexual assault or worse, a combination of the two. They have found themselves struggling to cope with their lives."[60]

In addition to being harassed and propositioned for sex by squad leaders, one female solder asked where to report for duty and was told by her superior officer, "On my bed, naked."[60] Journalist Corbett interviewed women who'd spent time in Iraq and had returned with post-traumatic stress disorder (PTSD). She heard stories, over and over, of "sexual trauma, often denied or dismissed by superiors; ensuing demotions or court-martials; and lingering questions about what actually occurred."[60] Female soldiers come home from Iraq demoralized and depressed; one went AWOL.

As in secular life, "Women who have suffered abuse in childhood are more likely to lose their self-protective instincts. Men who have experienced abuse are more likely to act aggressively and angrily. When these men and women are placed together in the military, 'what do you think will happen?' one Veterans Administration psychiatrist says, 'The men do the damage, and the women get damaged.'"[60] One female soldier said, "I kind of liked the Army before all that stuff happened. I was good at my job. I did what I was supposed to do. And then in Iraq, I got disillusioned. All of a sudden this Army you care so much about is like, well, all you're good for is to have sex with, and that's it."[60]

A formal Sexual Assault Prevention and Response program trains advocates for victims on military bases. From 2004 to 2005, "the number of reported assaults across the military jumped 40 percent... While victims may be feeling more empowered to report sexual assault, it appears that the number of assaults are not diminishing."[60] Nor may they be reported more since there is a pervasive sense among women soldiers of "Why bother?" Only one-tenth of those cases reported result in court-martials; more than half are dismissed for lack of evidence; others result in transfers or slaps on the wrists. A hypermasculine military culture is a sexually vulnerable one for women where some women are willing, many are coerced, and others fear of reprisals by superiors."[60] Where there's no respect of women, there is no love of self or others. There is only the lust of uneducated right- and left-brainers who perceive wars to be opportune times for acting on their own unresolved emotional issues, which also makes them more susceptible to PTSD.

New research indicates that PTSD may have a physical and a psychological basis. Just as there's a degenerative brain condition known as chronic traumatic encephalopathy (CTE) that affects boxers, football players and other athletes who have had repeated blows to the head, now Iraq and Afghanistan veterans are being diagnosed with CTE. CTE means abnormal proteins accumulate from not only blows to the head, but from blasts from bombs or grenades that cause the brain to crash against the skull, even when encased in a helmet. The protein destroys cells throughout the brain as well as in the frontal and temporal lobes, which regulate judgment, impulse control, multitasking, memory, and emotions – all similar to PTSD.[184]

The CTE findings are "likely to fuel a debate that has raged for decades over whether veterans who struggle emotionally and psychologically after returning from war suffer from psychiatric problems or brain injuries."[64]

Brain injuries are more acceptable in our society than psychiatric problems, which continue to carry a stigma. Many afflicted soldiers have committed suicide. The cost of the Iraq and Afghanistan wars will continue for years since 2.3 million troops have served there and hundreds of thousands of them have been injured and require disability benefits for the rest of their lives. For whatever reason, PTSD or CTE, soldiers' suffering is real and may be factored into the cost of war and of not educating the right-brains of those left-brainers (generals and politicians) who act out their personal and uneducated ego issues on the world's stage.

Misogyny

Misogyny is usually defined as the hatred of women by men. Is it hatred of women only or violence against women because of power issues? Women are perceived to be weak and, therefore, easy targets for what males experienced at the hands of men, women, peers, and/or other authoritarian figures in their early and ongoing lives. Or is the hatred the result of disowning their right-brain's emotion, love, which evokes its opposite emotion, hate, which is projected onto women who symbolize love?

Jessica Stern learned from her experience that humiliation and shame are risk factors for savagery. Even the male psychiatrist who evaluated her rapist considered him not to be a sexually dangerous person. It's OK to rape but not to kill victims? Carl Jung believed that where your wound is, that's where your genius will be. The price Ms. Stern continues to pay for her reputation as an expert on terrorists is, as an adult, she feels little pain but also little joy. Numbing the emotions is what people do to manage what cannot be extinguished. Her ongoing anger at being robbed of her innocence, not taken seriously by the authorities who are supposed to protect citizens, and her father not cutting short his trip abroad to be with her and her sister – their mother died when she was 3 – is justified. Their trauma is an addition to the list of reasons for educating the right-brain along with the left-brain in all grades in public school and identifying those childhood traumatic demons that lead to revenge and bullying.

Prostitution

Prostitution is the oldest wage-earning profession open to women throughout the ages; it has become a globalized business. Too many women and children are lured or kidnapped, drugged, raped, addicted, and forced to be prostitutes until they outlive their usefulness, then many are summarily killed! A few may be allowed to purchase their freedom, if they have access to money.

Prostitution rings are in every major city of the world; some of the pimps and owners buy protection from the authorities, the mobsters, the drug cartels, or are located in countries that condone the prostitution of children and women. Prostitution will continue to be a big business while there are men who do not have healthy sexual outlets, including preferring children or young girls, to satisfy their lust or uneducated, negative right-brains. Until our international society takes action, women and girls and boys are at risk of becoming sex slaves of the rich and infamous and of enriching their owners or "pimps."

In the impoverished world, young girls and women are pawns for families to sell, marry off, or put to work to support them; for husbands and their families to use, abuse or kill; or for pimps to purchase or kidnap for money-making prostitution or pornography. Throughout the world, prostitution continues to be girls'/women's oldest profession to physically survive at the street level or to financially thrive at the escort level. Prostitutes are criminals in most societies, not their male clients or pimps. In war, soldiers rape girls/women to destroy families, cultures, ethnicity, and to emasculate men. Respect for women's equality is a moral, global issue.

The politics of gender is rampant and nowhere is it more evident than in forced prostitution and abuse of women. For the past two thousand years or more, all religions have denigrated women and so have monarchy and secular states. The fact that women and children are treated as second-class citizens, abused, raped, and murdered by their so-called "loved ones," or strangers, serial killers, drug dealers, and religions or tribal wars, is unconscionable in the 21st century.

Dr. James Gilligan, a prison psychiatrist in Massachusetts and a professor at Harvard and New York University stated, "What I've concluded from decades of working with murderers and rapists and every kind of violent criminal is that an underlying factor that is virtually always present to one degree or another is a feeling that one has to prove one's manhood, and that the way to do that, to gain the respect that has been lost, is to commit a violent act."[151] And women, children, and the elderly are easier targets!

In the United States, a woman or girl is sexually assaulted every couple of minutes. It is beyond the ability of any government agency to assess the number of seriously battered wives and girlfriends that occur all the time. "Life in the United States is mind-bogglingly violent. But we should take particular notice of the staggering amounts of violence brought down on the nation's women and girls each and every day for no other reason than who they are. They are attacked because they are female."[151]

The world of pimps and hos is the ghetto. While pimp and ho are street names and ho is a put-down of women, they are also archetypes. They're the financial roles people play in the underworld of prostitution, but, as archetypes, they are the power roles people play in real life. The power dynamic between a pimp and his or her ho in the 'Hood, the ghetto, is eerily similar to the players on Wall Street, the corporate executives (pimps) and the (hos) workers, women and men, in our professional world.[38] *Ghetto Physics: Will the Real Pimps and Ho's Please Stand Up!* was written by E. Raymond Brown and co-directed, written, and produced as a film by William Arntz who directed *What the Bleep Do We Know?* in 2004, which has been seen by 100 million viewers. Director Arntz examined and portrayed the provocative interplay of power and money in our work world where the oldest financial profession in the world is replayed every day.[12] A pimp garners most of the money through others' work or resources, realizing their dream through the hos, but what about the ho's dream, authentic self, and raison d'être?

Arntz believes a transformation of society is needed where dreams are not only outer-oriented (money, status, power) but also inner-oriented (enlightened self-fulfillment, compassion for others, sharing the dream). The unsustainable way is to learn to play the established game or the game plays us. The sustainable way is to design and play our own game and to wield our own power for the greater good of all. K-12 whole-brain education is the beginning of transforming our workworld and our lives.

Pornography

America's inability to rein in the perpetrators who sexually abuse children, take videos of their exploits, and flagrantly sell them on the Internet is a shameful example of the ongoing abuse of boys and girls. Child molesters know during their adolescence that they are sexually interested in young children. Sexuality researcher, Dr. John Money stated that the derailed sexuality of child molesters has roots in their early childhood. In fact, he concluded that the brain connections that are linked to perversion are established around ages 5 to 8.[231]

For whatever reason, child molesters are among us, from strict antisexual upbringing to a warped lust-love connection. The fact that boys and girls as young as four are being sold or kidnapped, bound, continuously raped by adults in the presence of other children, and videotaped for other paraphiliacs is a heinous crime. Evidently thousands of Americans, male teenagers and adults, are "turned on" by watching child and women pornographic films.

Pornography is not just an American problem; it is an international problem. Adult pornography is lucrative and popular. Many unsuspecting young women from all over the world have been lured by respectable-sounding job offers that, instead, ensnare them by drugging, beating, repeatedly raping, and selling them to pimps and hard core film makers. It takes a vast number of sex perverts to support such nefarious and thriving sex industries. Those who purchase or watch sex or films are just as guilty of misogyny as the makers and sellers.

"The mainstream culture is filled with the most gruesome forms of misogyny, and pornography is now a multibillion dollar industry – much of it controlled by mainstream U.S. corporations."[151]

Another underground and lucrative industry, similar to child pornography, is the use and abuse of animals that are forced to fight each other for gamblers and those who run such "games." Michael Vick, a National Football League player, was convicted of his involvement in animal abuse gambling and spent time at a Federal prison in Leavenworth, Kansas. His remorse and admitted terrible mistakes are factors in his being reinstated by the NFL Commissioner, Roger Goodell. Only his future actions will determine if his sensitivity training has "cured" him of his ugly gambling habit. By becoming a proactive sponsor of People for the Ethical Treatment of Animals (PETA), he may participate in his transformation, if PETA wants or trusts him.

The Dominance of Violence:
Entertainment, Torture, and Educational/Economic Inequality

Violence beyond verbal abuse and hate speech was elevated to "violence as entertainment" in the Roman Empire's "Gladiator games" from 264 BC to 483 AD.[299] Western society's addiction to violence as pleasure and source of money is fulfilled by today's games: soccer, football, wrestling, ice hockey, and video. "Clearly the phenomenon is driven by the male members of our society, especially those who already possess aggressive behavioral tendencies,"[299] unmodified by right-brain education.

America surrendered its moral character and compass to the forces of evil when the U.S. government authorized the military to covert use of torture on suspected terrorists after 9/11/01. The normalization of torture since 9/11/01 was a return to primitive warrior states. "We are in the middle of a process of moral corruption: those in power are literally trying to break a part of our ethical backbone, to dampen and undo what is arguably our civilization's greatest achievement, the growth of our spontaneous moral sensitivity."[353]

Those men and women without emotional literacy, respect for human life, or compassion are ripe pickings for roles that make them feel potent, otherwise they would not collude in torture or terrorism. Their inability to differentiate between right and wrong is similar to pathological liars' and psychopaths' actions. At the extreme, they have no compassion and no conscience. Others are mindless followers who do the bidding of their so-called superiors or handlers.

Whatever the reason for participating in torture, it is an evil act that begets more evil on planet Earth. Despite our government's edict to stop its various agencies from torturing its terrorist-related prisoners, torture continues to be practiced in America by those who condone or practice torture, prostitution, child molestation, and animal abuse.

What is the best way to get information out of terrorists? "The most effective strategies for relationship building... Interrogators who were familiar with the detainees' language and culture, and who exhaustively studied each prisoner's case, used charisma and empathy to patiently elicit vital intelligence."[180] "Interrogation is both art and science, like any profession... Learning to be really good at handling and questioning detainees is prelude to becoming truly great as a nation."[180] What is the best way to get people skills? K-12 public education!

As a result of the government's war in Iraq and Afghanistan, more Americans are suffering tortured minds and souls, leading to post-traumatic stress disorder (PTSD) or suicide. PTSD is a fact of life in the military, especially after returning home. Traumas often alter brain chemistry. If the negative experiences are not processed and resolved, they tend to persist as emotional or unconscious memories in the amygdala, the center for fear in the brain. Unresolved conscious and unconscious past experiences may be triggered in the present by sensory stimuli that bypasses the cerebral cortex – the center for rational thought – so fear of survival rules and even ordinary tasks are overwhelming.

Treatment consists of visiting and revisiting traumatic memories to organize and defragment the stories to lessen their power over the mind. The recent V.A. Health care cuts and revelations of poor care at Walter Reed Army Medical Center in Virginia bodes ill for returning physically and mentally wounded veterans.[60]

A woman soldier with PTSD asks, "What's wrong with me?" Based upon the successful experiences of those professionals who have deprogrammed people who have been inducted into cults, the plasticity of the human brain means terrorists, sex abusers (of men, women and children), and those who take pleasure in frightening, raping, and killing people may benefit from intensive brain work, including computer technology that treats brain dysfunction designed by Stephanie Reese of BrainAdvantage.[279]

"Don't ask, don't tell!" was operative for years but has been outlawed. Don't ask, don't tell encouraged secrecy by victims of incest or sexual abuse and by those whose life experiences, genetic predispositions, or testosterone wash in utero, directed them to same-sex partners in a society that does not formally educate the right-brain or examine beliefs that limit optimum human development. We know that human beings' early experiences, including those buried in the right-brain and the unconscious mind, play major roles in their beliefs and behaviors. We know that males are ranked higher in our society than females. Our inherited institutions and organizations follow the domination system, not the partnership system that existed in the early Minoan Crete culture and exists today in Norway, Sweden, and Finland,[91] for example. The devaluation of anything effeminate – in a woman or man – is stereotyped. Even the right-brain is deemed to be the domain of women and not worth formally educating in our K-12 educational system. As a result, our democratic society has become violent, insensitive, divisive, narcissistic, and homophobic.

Humans' genes are blamed for our experiencing increased violence. Males with high levels of the hormone testosterone and a version of a gene monoamine oxidase (MAO) do not commit violence, unless they were mistreated as children, such as rejected by their parents; physically, psychologically, or sexually abused; foster children who were subjected to turnovers in their primary caretaking; or mistreated in our environment beyond family: culture, public schools, and religions. Therefore, people without the benefit of an educated right-brain have ego deficits that are often nurture-caused not nature-caused, but they are discharged against women and children or society. It makes sense to integrate basic Human Development studies with the current curricula in K-12 public education.

Left-brained domination systems are run by people who are hierarchically ranked and rigidly top-down controlled. They are not confined to the work world but also to the familial, educational, and religious worlds. Insensitivity and objectivity trickle down the hierarchical tiers so that their negative actions are experienced more by women and those at the bottom of our society. The domination system works for the left-brain dominant men and women, but, in a rigid system, the right-brain dominant women and men may unconsciously suppress their caring, empathy, intuition, and creativity to survive or go along to get along.

"When people are socialized to accept top-down control and injustice in their gender and parent-child relations [and in public educational systems], many will find nothing wrong with being told that they should content themselves with the droppings or scraps from the opulent tables of those on top."[91]

"Since male-dominance and violence to control women and children are integral to this social configuration... Is it coincidental that extreme Christian activists in the United States who wish to impose theocratic rule and launch 'holy wars' make it a priority to place women in subservient roles and support a highly punitive family structure?"[91] The holy wars against women began in ancient religious institutions by denigrating and denying them leadership in the church. Unholy wars are practiced today in war zones and in America when women and children are victims of male predators.

Thus, the real question is "What has been going wrong, for years, in our American society?" The Western Intellectual Tradition's "mind-forg'd manacles" have separated human beings from their humanity and have validated the left-brain's domination system. With half-brained perspectives, they are locked into their own point of view, rules and deregulations, and pursue wealth to use to take over America for the few.

Men and women with access to truthful knowledge about the domination principles upon which our institutions and organizations were built and beliefs were born, may engage their wisdom to defend our Founding Founders' Dream in 1776. Some women do not abide by man-made rules, so they may use their personal power to vote for a more caring economic and equal partnership system to sustain America's democracy for themselves, their children, and grandchildren.

Chapter Eight

> *We are not afraid to entrust the American people
> with unpleasant facts, foreign ideas, alien
> philosophies and competitive values.
> For a nation that is afraid to let its people judge
> the truth and falsehood in an open market
> is a nation afraid of its people.*
> –President John F. Kennedy

The Politics of Hidden History and Secret Knowledge

America has not changed for the greater good of all Americans since the 1960s, but the world has become more technology-oriented, opaque, and violent since President John F. Kennedy made the above statement. It is possible that – given the fact that American presidents have little power to gain access to or have knowledge of the workings of the bowels of government bureaucracy or to change our nation for the better – the President didn't even know he didn't know that the American people are not privy to secrets or the truths of events, communications, and policies. Even the official "truths" of his assassination and of his brother Robert have left huge question marks for many Americans.

Politicians with "permanent war" agendas, government agencies, corporations affiliated with the military-industrial complex, and in-the-loop financiers – the "they" – are not committed to trusting Americans with truths. We understand why the Manhattan Project was secret: to develop a weapon to end World War II. However, President Reagan obsessed with communism, like Republican Joseph McCarthy in the 1950s, established a precedent when he operated secretly and outside the domain of our elected politicians when he and his administration officials supplied financial support to the Nicaragua Contras whom Reagan considered to be "the moral equivalent of our Founding Fathers." President Regan or his followers sent 1,500 missiles to Iran to release three hostages, but three more were taken instead. The scandal came to light in 1986 and those officials who were indicted or convicted were pardoned by George H. W. Bush when he succeeded Ronald Reagan as president.

Politicians' secret acts are fused with philosophies, beliefs, and prejudices, and some believe they are above the law. After 9/11/2001, the military's red/orange alert system of possible terrorist acts kept the American people fearful and willing to surrender some freedoms, known as the Patriot Act, for homeland security. Even after the American public learned that President George W. Bush, Vice President Cheney, and their war hawks had trumped-up a weapon of mass destruction/deception (WMD) story to justify a costly 2003 war against Iraq's dictator Saddam Hussein, their loyalty to the United States of America was not questioned. But the loyalty of CIA officer Valerie Plame and her husband, Joseph C. Wilson, for example, who disputed the reality of WMDs was punished; both were punished and pushed through a CIAgate. And those who voted against the war were labeled unAmerican.

In our society, WikiLeaks' public disclosures of political secrets, from whistleblower sources, are pale in comparison to our leaders' ruses, but such disclosures are deemed to be treasonous. Politicians with hidden agendas who make costly wars and decisions are exempt from prosecution while the whistleblowers are demonized and those who publicize the lies and collusions that compromise Americans' access to truthful knowledge are hunted down.

"For a nation that is afraid to let its people judge the truth and falsehood in an open market is a nation afraid of its people," said President Kennedy. Are "the they" afraid of us, the voters? No. wordsmiths project their fears onto us. Those with silver tongues are paid to manage malleable voters' voices by making sure that truthful words are fused with half-truths fused with passion, concealing more than they reveal, so the real truth is perceived as unAmerican. The powermongers and goldsmiths know that most people vote with their emotions so untruths or half-truths are hidden within ideology. emotions, and semantics.

Ironically, the K-12 public education of the right-brain means people would not be so morally gullible, fearful, or make mindless decisions. It is no accident that the right-brain is left out of the curriculum in public education. Instead of an open market to judge truths from falsehoods, we have closed doors, and it has ever been thus, as borne out by the importance of men who empowered themselves throughout history, not necessarily in factually recorded history, who were motivated by passion and ideology to make themselves the center of the universe.

The elites of societies' institutions, organizations, governments, and "royal" families are organized. They form secret societies and networks to perpetuate their power, status, and control of financial, media, political, educational, energy, food, health care, and national resources. Out-of-the-loop members of such societies are so diverted by their membership status, "pomp and circumstance" rituals, and rewards for "good public works" that they rarely learn of the rationale for secret societies' founding or of their real mission. Hierarchical structures ensure that each layer only knows what is needed in each tier to do his or her job. Many people believe that the powerful status quo is God-given. They have learned to be dependent upon the establishment that keeps them indebted to the bank or credit cards, for food on the table, a roof over their heads, and transportation. The rest of us are not organized, so the status quo reigns with its tools, power, money, and control to deceive Americans and to undermine our democratic republic for the few.

Knowledge is power and secrets mask truth; so those in-the-know or have secrets not only control knowledge and communications, they have a stranglehold on power. When knowledge is closely guarded by secrecy, what we don't know can harm us, for absolute power corrupts absolutely. The dictators in the Middle East may kill and torture their dissident citizens to punish them or to obtain their knowledge of other dissidents, just as the President George W. Bush era (2000-2008) war hawks tortured prisoners to gain knowledge of terrorist activities. The Roman Church burned historical records and monk/philosopher Giordano Bruno on February 17, 1600. He had refused to reveal his "magic" or esoteric knowledge to a Venetian prince who had him arrested by Church authorities for heresy. Bruno did not recant his belief that the Earth was round and revolved around the Sun; whereas, Church authorities believed and taught that the Earth was flat and was the center of the universe.

Knowledge is still the currency of power; both power and money reign supreme in America. The dollar value of knowledge is apparent in the medical field where pharmaceutical companies charge obscene prices for their drugs to "cure" cancer and heart disease, which drugs work for the short-term, but not without severe side effects that impair the human immune system and mind. Even health-minded doctors charge money for their "come-on" newsletters to purchase books that reveal what supplements to purchase for every ailment. A friend was proud of herself for how much money she saved at the grocery store with coupons, until she was diagnosed with pre-diabetes and then found that most coupons are for manufactured foods – usually made from cheap products subsidized by government welfare – that are now off her dietary list. Money can't buy health, but it buys media advertising and fancy packaging which also seduces our uneducated right-brain's desires and overrides our left-brain's reason toward health. Money, though, can buy the best disease-care insurance, the best medical services, and 24/7/365 home or hospital care. Without adequate health insurance or money, we get Death Sentences.

Politics attracts dominant left-brain people who are money- and power- and ego- and ideology-driven. Corporate lobbyists have deep pockets to "buy" legislative action favorable to the products or services they represent, from Big Pharma and Oil to manufactured foods and agribusiness. If money cannot buy what the deep pockets want, they spend money to destroy the careers of "dissidents" or to launch TV advertising campaigns that influence a gullible public's emotions, thinking, and actions. Wall Street's Bernie Madoff was very successful with his Ponzi-type, get rich scheme because he and his clients were greedy for more money than the market would provide. However, the stock market is not only ego/emotion/greed-driven, it is subject to volatile flash trading by large investors: computers that run wild without built-in governors.

Since the 1980s, some corporate CEOs command salaries thousands of percent higher than their workers at the bottom because their knowledge, networks, and reputation are perceived to be corporate assets. Yet, too often they are just numbers-oriented hatchet-men who lay off employees, destroy company morale, sell off unprofitable divisions, ship jobs overseas, look good on paper for the short-run, and destroy America's industries for the long-run. Political deficit hawks are similar to CEOs who cut off the company's/country's nose to save their own financial/ ideological face. Dr. Kahneman's extensive research of financial traders indicates they their "luck" is similar to gamblers with no better odds, but they are endowed with extra confidence so the "halo effect" ensues.[173] They are smart but not wise.

Smart versus Wise people result when the proven science and experience of education are at odds with the politics of K-12 public education. Truthful knowledge and wisdom are the losers. The K-12 public education system in America is left hemisphere dominant. It devalues the right hemisphere's feelings and emotions – attributed to women – and the larger view of humanity and human virtues, including heart consciousness. In the K-12 educative process, what makes us human and humane is eliminated at the expense of logic, ABCs and 123s. The system rewards those students and adults who excel at the manipulation of by-the-book knowledge, acing tests, and making money. Smart, narrow-minded people ensue: the kind of mind programmable by cognitive science, such as Watson (IBM's smart robot), because it is not plagued by right hemisphere virtues (love, anger, fear, deceit, guilt, shame, compassion, or empathy) when it responds. Michio Kaku reminds us that "there are at least two stumbling blocks to [robots'] artificial intelligence: pattern recognition and common sense,"[174] which are similar stumbling blocks for those human beings whose right-brains have not been informally or formally exercised to function normally.

A psychiatrist informs us that when the "right hemisphere is not functioning normally...an imbalance in favour of the left hemisphere occurs in schizophrenia"[225] in individuals, so schizophrenic behaviors are played out in our culture. Figuring out where truth and knowledge are intertwined in an insane society is epistemology's realm (the study or theory of the origin, nature, methods, and limits of knowledge).

Epistemology's access to the origin, nature, and methods of knowledge is limited if knowledge is suppressed or destroyed, so beliefs and dogma are substituted for understandable and verifiable knowledge. We learn that dynasty-driven foundations' may not authorize grants or support for books or authors who think "outside the box." "Woe betide any book or author that falls outside the official guidelines. Foundation support is not there. Publishers get cold feet. Distribution is hit and miss, or nonexistent."[218] Self-publishing and word-of-mouth get attention by publishers who do not abide by society's status quo "norms." An insane society is historically perpetuated by the inextricable intertwining of religion and politics to maintain the status quo.

In our official Western history and in the Holy Bible, beliefs and knowledge are thrust upon us to blindly accept as truth and conventional wisdom without understanding. Understanding should preclude belief. Truth has no place in corrupt financiers' decisions and ideological stands when truth would undermine their status, money, and power. Ideology is based upon beliefs in the way things and people should be in this world instead of belief in self and loyalty to profession or country. Inner personal power results from a keen sense of an esteemed whole self. When positive self-esteem is missing, things become people's ego extensions as they seek status, money, and power outside themselves to feel potent, powerful, and important to compensate for a lack of inside self personal power and positive esteem for self and others.

Money- and power-dominated people now consider corporations to be "people" as Presidential candidate Mitt Romney said on August 11, 2011, in Des Moines, Iowa. Corporations are extensions of people for political, economic, and power and control purposes. Attributing personhood to a thing, a man-made entity, such as a corporation, is anthropomorphism: the attribution of human shape or characteristics to a god, animal, or inanimate thing.

Justice Antonin Scalia of the United States Supreme Court wrote his 2010 opinion that the association of individuals in a business corporation "cannot be denied the right to speak [or donate money!] on the simplistic ground that it is not 'an individual American.'"[79] That unprecedented power to the corporations ruling paved the way for organized associations of elites within corporations and societies to collude with secret donor money to vote via advertising by Super PACs and Citizens United – actually financial elites' united – to seduce voters' emotions and to influence politicians. Individuals' political voices and contributions are disorganized and limited. When people vote, they have to be identified and their signatures verified; however, now when corporations and wealthy individuals "vote with their money," their identities are hidden.

Corporations are man-made entities, not human beings. They are composed of employees and run by elites/managers/CFOs/CEOs for their own and investors' profits. Calling corporations "people" is a vanity attempt to superfeed individuals' hungry egos by making corporate insiders/deciders more equal than ordinary workers/voters. Corporate wealth influences domestic and international policies, welfare, resources, and public communications. The wealth that has created interlocking corporations or financial elites has spawned America's "royalty," from the Rockefellers and the Morgans to their Rothschild and royalty counterparts in Europe.

A host of secret societies in America are powerhouses for America's elites to consolidate their power and networks to influence political, economic, K-12 public educational, energy, and social decisions. So, who really controls the United States? "Elites, not masses, govern America"[86] was the conclusion of *The Irony of Democracy* by Thomas R. Dye and L. Harmon Zeigler.[86] Washington's real rulers may be invisible minorities, unknown names to the public, for they exercise their financial power behind the scenes.

It is a fact of life in America that power accompanies vast wealth and those who embody both power and wealth are "the real masters in the United States and the world."[218] Their invisibility allows them to exercise power behind the visible but controlled media show. Secrecy is power's political, economic, and social tool. A handful of men and some women and their families, about 2 percent of America's population, control America's resources, are the richest, pay the least amount of taxes, belong to secret societies where they have interlocking relationships that cement their financial power, and control the media's knowledge to the public.

Throughout human history, the invisible powerholders have influenced the news media, the world's governments, and academia's history books to the point that we are brainwashed to learn and reinforce the status quo's "approved" knowledge only. We, the colonized by our culture's established "norms," collude in ridiculing or destroying the reputations of those who gain wisdom by studying materials that are deemed to be politically incorrect, such as myths, fables, science-fiction, or ancient records. We are the enforcers of politically correctness, the loud voice of the status quo, when we act on unexamined beliefs, values, and accepted "facts."

A Federal Reserve Board Survey indicated that 2 percent of U.S. families controlled 54 percent of U.S. financial wealth.[96] The 2004 Federal Reserve Board's figures indicated the wealthiest 1 percent of American families owned about 34.3 percent of our nation's net worth.[96] In 2011, America's wealth disparity is widening when its top 400 families control as much wealth as America's bottom 60 percent. Thus, it is estimated that the wealthiest 5 percent control 72 percent of America's financial wealth. The cycle of the rich getting richer is apparent when 80 percent of all economic gains of the past 30 years have gone to the nation's richest one percent.

The rich getting richer and the poor getting poorer accelerated since the 1970s when top corporate elites made 30 times what hourly workers made. Today's elites make thousands of percent more than hourly workers who have jobs. Interlocked banks, corporations, insurance, pharmaceutical companies, and even the military-industrial complex shape Americans' destinies and control knowledge, events, and finances that are not in the general public's best or moneyed interests.

The quality and truth of the knowledge of both hemispheres is intrinsic to making wise decisions for the highest good of America and Americans. If left-brained knowledge is based upon false knowledge and right-brained knowledge is based upon false selves – unexamined selves and beliefs – then intelligence and wisdom are flawed. Smart and Wise is the result when people's right hemisphere authentic knowledge – experience, intuition, emotionally sensitive data, and altruism – are combined to temper, synergize, and elevate authentic knowledge from the left hemisphere with that of the right hemisphere for the greater good of all Americans. If we take care of ourselves and our families only, our larger family, our democratic nation, will not survive.

What happens when knowledge is flawed, based upon false premises or foundations, or new knowledge is suppressed? In science, new knowledge that makes old knowledge obsolete is common, but it may take years before new knowledge replaces old knowledge and is accepted and disseminated, especially in academia. In faith-based institutions, knowledge that conflicts with church dogma, teachings and practices, may be suppressed, hidden, or destroyed by the shepherds and never reach the flock.

Secrets may be benign, but some secrets, from suppressing cancer cures and energy sources to fostering wars, are not acceptable to people with a conscience. Secrets that cost and ruin lives for profit (like our hospitals, medical field, health insurance companies, and pharmaceuticals) or for control of the winners and losers (like our K-12 educational system) are unacceptable to most people, except to those without a conscience or to those who value the status quo more than people or our democratic republic. Families, institutions, organizations, corporations, and governments have secrets under the guise of not sharing them "for your own good" that are for their own good. Sometimes false knowledge is handed down from generation to generation and is so common and accepted that it is considered true knowledge, but unexamined selves and beliefs are not the basis of authentic human beings or wisdom.

Truthful historical knowledge may be known to a few power elites, for history informs us that religion and politics have been inextricably intertwined in the past. Insider trading is a no-no; Martha Stewart went to jail for it, but for years our elected politicians took advantage of insider trading to get wealthy, until recently. When we have some people in our society who are more equal than others, by being above the laws and policies for everyone else, guarded secrets and our blind faith means those in charge of knowledge shape our destinies for their own good, not for the greater good of Americans.

Bill Moyers defined secrecy as "the freedom zealots dream of: no watchmen to check the door, no accountant to check the books, no judge to check the law."[218] We have to exercise our uneducated right-brains to lift the curtain of secrecy that perpetuates ignorance, fear, and divisiveness that conquers us in order to release our human spirit from bondage.

Foster Gamble's DVD, *Thrive: What on Earth Will It Take?* is not a welcome documentary for those who are involved in the global consolidation of power in most aspects of human lives, from political economics to knowledge. This timely documentary was made from authenticated data by Foster Gamble of the founders of Procter & Gamble, Cincinnati, Ohio. He researched why today's America is working for the wealthy elites only, the top one or two percent, and not for the rest of us.[112]

When financial elites use their insider trading and their access to secret knowledge to network and manipulate nations' governments, finances, and world events, our lives are being ruled by money, ignorance, and the power of fear. They are in charge of us! And we don't even know their names. "There are many forces at work in U.S. society, but the most powerful by far are the interlocking directorates of the major banks, corporations, and insurance companies, with the backing of the leaders of the military: In the words of former President Dwight Eisenhower, 'the military-industrial complex.'"[340]

Europe's Historic Secret Societies

Secular secret societies are natural outcomes of suppressed knowledge by reigning authorities. Throughout the ages, ancient knowledge has been preserved by men who established secret societies to avoid control by the Roman Church or reigning despots. Some of their knowledge contradicted the teachings and traditions of the Church. Historical records of secret societies are more opaque today, even on the Internet. Jim Marrs' *Rule by Secrecy* [218] was one of my research sources of secret societies.

Knights Templar

Diverse historical sources inform us that The Crusades were a number of Pope-sanctioned military wars with the goal of restoring Christian control of the Holy Land. A series of Crusades occurred between the years 1095 and 1291. The Crusades was an opportunity to take back the

Holy Land from the Muslims and for some Crusaders to search for confirmation of traditions that contradicted the teachings of the powerful Roman Church and to seek hidden, mystical knowledge.

In the Holy Land, some Crusaders found affirmation of heretical ideas which conflicted with Church dogma. One group of Crusaders created a secret society, the Knights Templar, to preserve their knowledge and artifacts they had excavated from vaults under Mount Moriah, beneath King Solomon's Temple, and in Languedoc, France, where Mary Magdalene was said to have fled after Jesus Christ's crucifixion. Languedoc became the home-base of the Knights Templars. Their findings there may have included the legendary Ark of the Covenant, which could undermine the Roman Church's authority. Since the Church had banned the Gnostics' mysticism, the Templars believed a true church would teach mysticism and follow Jesus Christ's teachings, so they rejected the Roman Church for its dark power and for not being a true faith.

While fighting in the Crusades, the Knights Templar gained much esoteric, astronomy, and construction knowledge from their contacts with the Assassins. The Knights Templar Order flourished, becoming extraordinarily wealthy and powerful. During 1208 and 1244, thousands of people were murdered by the Vatican's papal and Knights Templar armies. In 1307, a power-envious French king and a protective-of-its-secrets Roman Church crushed the Knights Templar, but they may exist today within Freemasonry. Lore presumes that Knights Templar Grand Master, Jacques de Molay, had the Order's treasures transported to safety to Scotland. But, legends persist that the Templars buried treasure on an island in eastern Canada, nearly 200 years before John Cabot discovered Newfoundland and Christopher Columbus discovered America.

History informs us that the members of the Knights Templar and the Islamic Assassins were similar in that members were brutish, ignorant, and bloodthirsty men who did what they were told and carried out the orders of their intelligent leaders who knew the truths of their Orders.

Knights Templar Bankers as Multinational Corporation

The development of modern banking is attributed to Jewish and Italian lenders; however, the Knights Templar predated the Rothschilds and de Medicis of Europe. While Christians were not permitted to practice usury, the Templars emphasized its military not the religious aspects of their Order. With people's fear of traveling with sums of money and being robbed by highwaymen and by papal authorities demanding alms, the Knights Templars saw an opportunity to become bankers. They began issuing letters of credit, probably the forerunner of credit cards. that set the modern stage for bankers.

The Knights Templar brought back from the Middle East to Europe many trophies and new knowledge, especially of astronomy, mathematics, architecture, and medical techniques. In their time, the Knights Templar served the purpose of today's multinational corporations that are also power- and money-based.

The Assassins

The Assassins, a fearless and feared Islamic sect, had a top-down commanded pyramid structure, probably copied from monarchies and the Roman Church. The Assassins had a reputation for terror and sudden death. Hierarchical leadership became the organizational structure of secret societies and of today's institutions and organizations. The Assassins were spawned from Islamic sects around 872 AD. Their roots are linked to the prophet Muhammad. By the 12th century, the Assassins' power had increased; their ruthless leader claimed knowledge dating back to Noah and beyond. The Assassins' murderous reputation was their downfall. By 1250, they were attacked by Mongol hordes who captured their last stronghold. The official order of the Assassins ended, although pockets of Assassins may still exist in the Middle East.

Freemasonry

Freemasonry has ancient roots in religious sects' secrets, the Essenes and Gnosticism, and knowledge from the Middle East's Assassins via the Knights. Freemasonry created a system of apprentices, fellows of the Masonic Temple's (Freemasonry) degrees. Initiation into Freemasonry's secret organization utilizes Gnosticism's 33 degrees (related to the 33 vertebra of the human spinal column), the letter "G" is a prominent Masonic symbol and may represent Gnosticism or "G for geometry. The mason's trowel is an Essene's symbol. Gnosticism was outlawed by the early Roman Church.

While the term Freemason is traced to the 1450s, it is presumed that Freemasonry began with the construction of Rosslyn Chapel, near Edinburgh, Scotland. It was built by the Saint-Clair family who were associated with the Knights Templar. Freemasonry developed an aura of mystique, not on the divine right/nature of authority but upon the power of knowledge. Its early members had knowledge passed down from generation to generation based on mystery schools' knowledge of stone cutting, geometry, and architecture from Egypt, Greece, and the Middle East. That knowledge was crucial for constructing Europe's churches and cathedrals. Masons of the Middle Ages learned about construction from the Architects of Lombardy, Italy, who called themselves "Freemasons" which was shortened from the Fraternal Order of Free and Accepted Masons.

The possession of esoteric or secret knowledge made Freemasonry a source of underground anti-Roman Church thought. Opposition to the Roman Church was forced underground, but the guild of stone masons, whose meeting halls were called lodges, were free to move throughout Europe. The rift between the Roman Catholic church in Italy and the breakaway Protestant Church of England led to many Masonic records being lost as wars and revolutions decimated Masonic libraries. In 1723, Freemasons in England – under the auspices of the Church of England – granted membership to all religions. While there are an estimated six million Freemasons active in the world in nearly one hundred thousand lodges, Freemasonry used to be the largest worldwide secret society due to the British Empires' colonialism in the 19th century. Offshoots in America are: Ancient Arabic Order of the Nobles of the Mystic Shrine (Shriners) and the Order of the Eastern Star (women), DeMolay, Builders, and Rainbow. My father was a Mason; my mother belonged to the Eastern Star. Both were protective of their initiation and membership. Other relatives advanced to be

Shriners. The Shriners are known for their support of hospitals for children and other good public works.

Most members perceive their affiliation with Freemasonry to be similar to joining the Lion's Club or the Chamber of Commerce. Those who progress beyond the thirty-third degree status are educated in some of the Order's secrets and goals. Freemasonry is an hierarchical order with a fraternity within a fraternity so that its outer organization conceals an inner brotherhood of elite members. A pyramid organization allows the elite at the top to control those at the bottom by keeping them in the dark. However, the visible Freemasonry society is devoted to ethical, educational, patriotic, and humanitarian interests.

Freemasonry is also said to have roots in an earlier mystical tradition, the Rosicrucian.

Rosicrucians

The Rosicrucians is a secret brotherhood of knowledge with ancient bases. Documents show that the Order of the Rosy Cross was founded in 1188. Other researchers aver that Rosicrucianism and Freemasonry were separate entities and philosophies but were consolidated in the 18th century under the influence of the Illuminati.

Rosicrucians were perceived by the Roman Church as Satanists while others saw them as the forerunners of today's scientific inquiry. Dante Aligheri, who wrote *The Divine Comedy*, and Sir Francis Bacon, whose writings inspired America's colonization, were Rosicrucians. Some researchers find pre-Rosicrucian ideals in Leonardo da Vinci.

The Protestant church also forced the Rosicrucians underground by labeling them pagans, occultists, and heretics. Rosicrucians are active in America and claim to hold secrets handed down from ancient Egypt, the philosophers of Greece, and the first Cabala of the Jews. Religious fundamentalists are fearful of Rosicrucians and dismiss them with ridicule.

Illuminati

The Illumaniti was a mysterious and infamous German secret society. Its crest – skull and bones – is also the official crest of Yale University's

Skull and Bones, a secret fraternal order founded in 1832. There appear to be links between the order and the Bavarian Illuminists and Freemasonry: all claim esoteric knowledge. The Illuminati was publicly identified in 1776 on May 1st, a day to honor communists. The Bavarian Illuminati was formed by Adam Weishaupt, a Canon Law professor at Ingolstadt University. One of his co-founders was royalty's William of Hesse, the employer of Mayer Rothschild.

The Rothschilds and German royalty were connected through Freemasonry. Weishaupt had deep knowledge of the Jesuits and may have created the name "Illuminati" from the Spanish Alumbrados, meaning enlightened or illuminated, which was created by Jesuit founder, Ignatius Loyola. The Alumbrados believed the human spirit could attain direct knowledge of God, so formal, hierarchical religion was not needed for the enlightened. Those beliefs are similar to those of Gnosticism.

The Spanish Inquisition issued edicts against the Illuminati. Weishaupt's connections to the Muslim Assassins is also believed to have influenced his opposition to the tyranny of the Roman Church and the national governments it supported. He wrote, "Man is not bad, except as he is made so by arbitrary morality. He is bad because religion, the state, and bad examples pervert him. When at last reason becomes the religion of men, then will the problem be solved."[218] Who knew that reason would be co-opted by rationale and that passion would submerge rationale as well as reason? With the additional belief that the end justifies the means, Weishaupt set the precedent for Adolf Hitler's atrocities and today's despots and emissaries. All ignore the right-brain's virtues that defy man's inhumanity to men, women, children, and animals.

Secrecy was the Illumanti's greatest strength. Illuminism expressed the tension between the institutional religions' dogma and the humanism based on ancient esoteric, theological, and secular knowledge. Many researchers believe that the Illuminati still exists, that its goal is the abolition of all government, private property, inheritance, nationalism, the family unit, and organized religion. The underlying Weishaupt goal may be to have absolute power in the hands of a few who have the reason/logical knowledge of how to rule people "for their own good," despite their followers' passions, which may be controlled by fear and force. The existence of the name Illuminati is irrelevant when its modus operandi still exists when some elites are in favor of a new world order with power in the hands of a few.

Bilderbergers

The Bilderbergers are a group composed of rich and powerful men and women, some of European nobility including the British royal family. Members meet secretly each year. It was created in the early 1950s after frequent meetings of Europe's elites during the 1940s. A Polish socialist Dr. Joseph Hieronim Retinger is said to be the official father of the Bilderbergers. He was persuaded by Britain's Lord Victor Rothschild to have Dutch Prince Bernhard conduct regular Bilderberger meetings.

Prince Bernhard had been a former member of the Nazi Schutzstaffel (SS) and a German I.G. Farben employee in Paris until he married Princess Juliana of the Netherlands in 1937 and became a major shareholder in Dutch Shell Oil along with Rothschild. Dr. Retinger was brought to America by U.S. Ambassador to England Averell Harriman, a Council on Foreign Relations (CFR) member.

The connecting link between the Bilderbergers, the Council on Foreign Relations (CFR) and the Trilateral Commission is the Rockefeller family, specifically, John D. Rockefeller. Jr.'s youngest son, David.

America's Secret Societies

America's "royalty" used to be composed of wealthy, well-known businessmen, from steel magnate Andrew Carnegie, banker Andrew Mellon, transportation moguls Cornelius Vanderbilt and Edward Harriman to the Rockefellers and the Morgans. The staying power of America's "royalty" is attributed to their moneyed additions, from the Fords to the Bushes, their secret societies, and their intermarriages.

The Rockefellers were already in business before the Civil War. William "Big Bill" Rockefeller sold cancer "cures" from a wagon. His son John Davison Rockefeller, an agricultural commodities broker in Cleveland, Ohio, saw the potential of the oil industry. In 1863, he and investors built an oil refinery, which was incorporated in 1870 as the Standard Oil Company of Ohio.

Rockefeller practiced, Competition is a sin, as he forced oil competitors to sell by merging with them, buying them out, or cutting his prices to force them out of business. He secured rights with railroads which insured his near-monopoly on the transportation of oil. In 1880 Rockefeller owned/controlled 95 percent of all oil produced in the United States. It was not until 1902, with Ida Tarbell's exposé of her father's Pennsylvania oil business being ruined by Rockefeller, that the Ohio Supreme Court ordered Rockefeller's trust to be dissolved, but he avoided penalties by moving his headquarters to New York City. In 1899, a new creation, Standard Oil Company of New Jersey, contained all their assets and interests.

The Rockefeller family amassed wealth, power, influence, had close ties to England, and were interlocked via directorships and commercial banking with other oil industries. They founded the Rockefeller Foundation, the University of Chicago, and Rockefeller University in New York City.

The Rockefellers had great interest in eugenics, which was Sir Francis Galton's brainchild to genetically maintain and improve the gene pool through "ideal" human characteristics. America's Eugenics Record Office (ERO) was founded, in 1910, by Charles Benedict Davenport, directed by Henry H. Laughlin, and financed by Mary Harriman of the railroad family, the Rockefellers, and the Carnegie Institute. They provided $11 million to create a eugenics research laboratory at Cold Spring Harbor, New York, and research studies at Harvard, Columbia, and Cornell universities. The ERO advocated for laws which led to the forced sterilization of those who were labeled genetically defective and socially inadequate. Dr. Ernst Rudin, of the Kaiser Wilhelm Institute for Genealogy and Demography in Berlin, was brought to the 1932 "blood-lines" congress in New York, paid for by the Hamburg-Amerika Shipping Line, allegedly "controlled" by Harriman associates, Prescott Bush and his son, George H. W. Bush.[218] While the Bushes' link to the Hamburg-Amerika Shipping Line is obscure, Senator Prescott Bush was an associate of E. Roland Harriman, younger brother of W. Averell Harriman, and Fritz Thyssen, a German industrialist. They allegedly continued their dealings with

Nazi Germany, where eugenics was practiced openly, until 1942 when the U.S. Congress took action against its enemies, including the Bushes who eluded prosecution, according to documents in the National Archives.

The U.S. joined 14 other nations in passing eugenics legislation which led, in 30 U.S. states, to at least 60,000 legal sterilizations of mental patients and imbeciles labeled "defectives." A forerunner of Hitler's racial institutes was Dr. Rudin's work on race eugenics, primarily funded by the Rockefellers. Eugenics work continues under more politically correct names such as population control activities at the United Nations.

Since the Rockefellers had the money, power, and access to those with ancient, secret knowledge of Biblical, Gnostic, and secret societies' sources, they and their ilk may have considered themselves to be descendants of a specie of humans called Aryans. It is theorized that ensuing Aryans lived separately from the rest of human beings on Earth, influenced future civilizations, and, despite the lack of DNA evidence at the time, provided the background for some elites' specialness. Since translations of the Dead Sea Scrolls, found in 1947, are largely unpublished, it makes one wonder why Dead Sea Scrolls were sequestered at the Rockefeller Archaeological Museum in Palestine, until they were captured by the Israelis in its 1967 Six Day War.

Elitist blood-lines and nepotism linked America's "royalty" figures for, like their British and German counterparts, they considered themselves to be racially superior and sought to protect their superiority and their power positions similar to the Bilderbergers of Europe. Whether or not their annual meetings are aimed at creating and managing world events is not known because the American media do not report on the group's activities, including its 1957 meeting on Saint Simons Island near Jekyll Island, Georgia. However, rare but public talk of the need for creating a new world order has been voiced by others and by President George H. W. Bush, a Council on Foreign Relations member, a Trilateralist, and a brother in Yale's Skull and Bones.[112]

Council on Foreign Relations (CFR)

The American secret society, the Council on Foreign Relations (CFR) was an outgrowth of meetings of 100 prominent men during World War I to discuss the postwar world. The end of WWI was negotiated on President Woodrow Wilson's peace terms. The 1919 Treaty of Versailles was so economically harsh on Germany that it paved the way for Adolf Hitler and his Nazi Party to rise to power. President Wilson's plan for peace included forming a League of Nations, which failed ratification by the U.S. Senate, so two organizations were formed instead: The Royal Institute of International Affairs in England and, in 1921, the Council on Foreign Relations (CFR). It is a secret society because Article II of the new CFR's bylaws stated that anyone revealing details of CFR meetings in violation of the CFR's rules could be dropped from membership. CFR headquarters, since 1945, is the Harold Pratt House in New York City, which was donated by the Pratt family of Rockefeller's Standard Oil.

In 2000, CFR membership was more than 3,300 of leaders in finance, banking, commerce, communications, politics, and academia. A common objective of the CFR is said to have the elites of world banking monopolizing and in control of global governments' finances. While every CIA director since Allen Dulles has been a CFR member, so was Henry Kissinger, an unknown academic in 1955, until he met Nelson Rockefeller, was given a $50,000 outright gift, was introduced to David Rockefeller and other prominent CFR members, and became Secretary of State. The administrations of Richard Nixon, Jimmy Carter, Ronald Reagan, George H. W. Bush, Bill Clinton, and George W. Bush have been top-heavy with CFR or Trilateral Commission members.

The Trilateral Commission

Due to more opaque, technology-oriented communications in the 1970s, the public's awareness of the secretive activities of the CFR motivated David Rockefeller to deflect public attention away from the CFR by creating a more public adjunct: the Trilateral Commission. It was formed in 1973 through the diplomatic machinations of David Rockefeller and Zbigniew Brzezinski who was President Jimmy Carter's national security adviser, and by private citizens of North America, Western Europe, and Japan. Its public mission, with headquarters in New York, Paris, and Tokyo, is to foster closer cooperation among these three regions on common problems. It's real mission may be becoming more visible with the talk of A New World Order, as voiced by George H. W. Bush, Henry Kissinger, England's Gordon Brown, an European Union official, and Pope Benedict XVI.[112]

As head of Russian Studies at Columbia University, Brzezinski, envisioned a society composed of nations without national sovereignty but with a world government funded by a global taxation system, which he had presented to the Bilderberg group in 1972. With members in positions of power, the Trilateral Commission is reputed to be a shadow government. Indeed, its goal appears to be to control the world, create a supernational community dominated by multinational corporations which are now perceived to be "people" by some wealthy men. The hands that "rock" the corporations, rule the world?

David Rockefeller's tentacles led to the appointment of Paul Volcker as head of the Federal Reserve Bank during President Jimmy Carter's tenure. Alan Greenspan, appointed by President Ronald Reagan as chairman of the Federal Reserve was also a member of the Trilateral Commission, the CFR, the Bilderbergers, and a follower of Ayn Rand's *Atlas Shrugged* with anti-democratic leanings. The closeness between Rockefeller-dominated organizations and U.S. government employees, politicians, and policies is problematic for the American public.

Since the mission of the Council on Foreign Relations (CFR) is reported to garner acceptance for one-world idealism, the Trilateral Commission's (David Rockefeller's adopted brainchild) mission is reported to be the means for multinational consolidation of the commercial and banking interests by controlling – thanks to members in top U.S. political posts in the government of the United States – and the independent Federal Reserve System controlled by financial elites.

Tea Party

A more recent tool by individual and corporate financiers to influence or take control of the U.S. and State governments is the Tea Party.[128] The Tea Party is a Christian fundamentalist-oriented group that is anti-big government, anti-women's rights, and probably anti-all forms of social safety nets, from Medicare and universal health care to unemployment insurance and food stamp for the "undeserving poor." It appears to be an example of the religious right's ideology masquerading as politics. Members are indoctrinated by ideology and economic voodoo to seek political power without understanding they are being used as weapons by financiers, industrialists, and corporations to undermine our nation's democratic principles, American workers, and citizens. The thrust began with the rhetoric and manipulation of voters to elect anti-government, Tea Party governors as a subversive way to break down gains by America's working class – resulting from abuses that led to the 1929-1939 Great Depression – from collective wage bargaining to pensions and social services.

Ultraconservative members of the U.S. Senate and House of Representatives fiddle, so partisan politics addresses budget cuts and abortion, not infrastructure and new energy needs, unemployment, or home foreclosures by banks, often illegally. All delays chew up the assets and retirement savings of middle America and plunge the unemployed, hourly wage cash workers and paycheck-to-paycheck people into poverty.

The financiers' true mission and dynamics remains hidden from public view as they continue their divide-and-conquer quest to diminish America's democratic government and its middle and poorer class citizens' sovereignty and economic freedom.

Banking

Western culture's system of banking operates whereby currency was and is issued as debt as a means to control the financial market and ensure a steady income. Fractional reserve banking means a $10,000 customer's deposit in a bank, with the legal authority to retain only 10% or $1,000.00 in reserve, which becomes $9,000 to lend, which ends up as a deposit in another bank with the same central bank: the Federal Reserve system. Following the money means banks can create an extra $90,000 to lend based on ten customers' original deposits of $10,000 each, or a total of $100,000 with only $10,000 held in reserve. The overseer, known as the Federal Reserve System, is an independent agency, disguised as a government system, that cannot be overruled by U.S. Laws.[112]

Institutional models that are based upon consumers' debt produce consumers' debt-slavery. Thus, past and current international financiers in banking and corporations with positions of wealth and control have a structured banking system to expand their sphere of influence and perpetuate their wealth. Known as a fractional reserve banking system, it is not fixable; it is a long-term scheme for building and maintaining power for the few.[128]

"True reform of government on national, state, and local levels requires a model of economy and currency that is not based on debt, but upon opportunity"[128] for all, not just the insiders. Instead, we have been brainwashed by the financial system that winners and losers are the outcome of playing high stakes financial games: the stock market. The financial elites can manipulate the stock market to their advantage too.

Alternatives to the win-lose financial/banking system, based upon altruism – improving community and ordinary people's financial security and the environment for example – are an anathema to our left-brained, authoritarian personalities who use money as a weapon to inculcate their ideologies without caring or understanding how they damage our nation.

Home ownership is as American as apple pie. Thanks to bank loans with favorable interest, after World War II, many Americans were able to buy affordable homes and build up equity in them. Over the years, the housing market soared, so, at the urging of a barrage of mortgage company telemarketing enterprises, some people remortgaged their homes to the hilt and spent the money. People's credit/affordability was not a problem for mortgagors who lent money to purchase new homes because they bundled the mortgages and sold them at huge profits to investors without even bothering to complete the transfer of Deeds, etc.

The signs of an economic recession began in 2007, but it took hold in 2008. AIG was bailed out by President Bush; housing prices dropped, people lost their jobs, and they defaulted on their mortgages. It was a natural outcome. Many banks foreclosed without having the proper documentation or the legal right to do so, but new businesses cropped up to furnish banks with fraudulent ownership documentation, as reported on one in Georgia on national TV. The story of banks and investors holding worthless derivative products (bundled and bungled paper that sold the same mortgages over and over) became apparent as America reels from its worst greed-caused Great Recession since the the Great Depression of 1929-1930s.

Small business owners rely upon bank credit to begin and maintain their businesses, especially when accounts receivable are slow, such as from U.S. government agencies. Government bailouts of banks, specifically, resulted in banks' hoarding the money. Bankers overreacted by putting a hold on credit for businesses and refinancing mortgages. That act exacerbated employers' layoffs, more home foreclosures, and a downward economic spiral.

"What is killing the economy is lack of credit... This was true during the Great Depression, and it's been true during the Great Recession. And until normal credit standards return, economic growth will continue to be stunted."[241] Journalist Joe Nocera reported that Northern Trust's Chief Economist, Paul Kasriel's paper is entitled, "If Some Dare Call It Treason, Was Milton Friedman a Traitor?" The title is a play on 2012 Presidential candidate Rick Perry's comment that more quantitative easing by the Federal Reserve (Ben Bernanke) "would amount to borderline treason."[241] Ben Bernanke, a student of the Great Depression, learned from Milton Friedman that the tight money policy of that era compounded the lack of bank credit, so he acted to ease credit. Mr. Kasriel admits that "Quantitative easing is not nearly as efficient at expanding credit as having the banks involved, but it does work."[241]

America's banking system and interlocking memberships in secret societies allowed financiers to collude in destroying government regulations that curtailed their power; yet, when they got into financial trouble they were bailed out by the U.S. government as "too big to fail." Those bankers took no risks with their own or the company's money, they risked Americans' financial security so ordinary people lost their savings, retirement, homes, and jobs. The culprits go unpunished; they are financially secure while their victims are financially ruined. The American Dream is still operative for the elites, but it is a nightmare for most of us. It seems that the elite powerholders' dream of democracy is one where there are "no watchmen to check the door, no accountant to check the books, no judge to check the law" which is Bill Moyer's definition of "secrecy," and perpetrated by the Tea Party.

The motivation to shrink government is to destroy workers' earned rights to unions, equal pay for equal work, health and unemployment insurance, and retirees earned rights to Social Security and Medicare. Under the guise of reducing State government spending and deficits, Tea Party governors in some states pushed through legislation outlawing unions, collective bargaining, and pensions.

America's political, banking, financial, and corporate systems have demonstrated in the 1930s, and during our ongoing Great Recession, that corruption exists throughout our country. We are experiencing a divide-and-conquer mentality in politics, big businesses, and by the wealthy Koch brothers. Escalation of the conflict perpetuated by the ideologues has already "eaten" people's assets, jobs, and quality of life. Do we have to wait until we are unable to buy food, have a roof over our heads, or die early with no job and no health insurance before compromise and true reform are achieved for all Americans?

Evidently, reform is not going to come from above, with the power elites, it will have to be a grassroots effort by a collaboration of individuals who feel they have nothing left to lose by confronting the status quo to reform government, social institutions, and major corporations or to develop new ones that are not based on financial slavery or wealth. Until 1971, America was on the gold standard. Gold bullion at Fort Knox determined whether or not paper money could be run off on a printing press.

The gold standard was the basis of the world's financial exchanges, until paper money was easier to manufacture and manipulate. Economic measures taken by President Richard Nixon on August 15, 1971 canceled the direct convertibility of the U.S. dollar to gold, ending the Bretton Woods system of international financial exchange. The costs of the war in Vietnam, the U.S. balance-of-payments deficit and a trade deficit, and excess printed dollars led to holders of the U.S. dollar losing faith in the U.S. government's ability to cut its budget and trade deficits. "In the first six months of 1971, $22 billion in assets left the U.S... nations began demanding fulfillment of America's 'promise to pay' – that is, the redemption of their dollars for gold. Switzerland redeemed

$50 million of paper for gold in July [1971] France...acquired $191 million in gold, further depleting the gold reserves of the U.S."²³⁸

As Nobel-prize winning Economist Paul Krugman wrote on "The Unofficial Paul Krugman Web Page" about the post-Nixon Shock, "The current world monetary system assigns no special value to gold; indeed, the Federal Reserve is not obliged to tie the dollar to anything... a system that leaves money managers free to do good also leaves them free to be irresponsible—and, in some countries, they have been quick to take the opportunity."¹⁹⁷

Microfinance is the gospel of antipoverty programs that lend small sums to people, usually women, to develop and promote a profit-making approach to work. Microfinance is at work in 23 countries. Critics of the program say it does borrowers some good while others say it does borrowers some harm. Diana Taylor, former New York Superintendent of Banking, and longtime companion of New York Mayor Michael R. Bloomberg, is associated with Acción, the Boston-based largest micro-lender.⁴ Diana Taylor contends, "There is not a silver bullet for poverty alleviation... There are ways to abuse the micro-finance system, just like there are ways to abuse the mortgage system."⁴ Nevertheless, Taylor believes the solution is strong regulation, not the abandonment of micro-finance or mortgages.⁴

Wealth versus Income

The distribution of wealth in America, as indicated by the Federal Reserve Board surveys, which are the bases of G. William Domhoff's "Wealth, Income, and Power," and Fairfield University faculty's "The Distribution of Wealth in America,"⁹⁶ is about the value of everything an individual or family owns less debts. Such marketable assets are real estate, stocks, and bonds, not nonmarketable assets such as cars and household furnishings or even jewelry and art. Thus financial wealth is liquid or readily convertible to cash. Evidently, wealth rather than income represents a measure of the ability of households to consume, according to Alan Greenspan, former Chairman of the Federal Reserve. However, those with great wealth usually pay state property taxes but no federal taxes on their wealth, except for taxes on income from dividends, stocks and bond sale, and rentals. The wealthy may or may not have high incomes, but the government taxes income more than wealth. Income is more readily discernible for tax purposes. Income is what people earn from work, from hourly wages to monthly salaries. Income includes dividends, interest, and rents or royalties that are paid on properties they own. Incomes are subject to all kinds of taxes – federal, state, city, county taxes and innumerable sales taxes.

In 2004, for example, the top 20 percent of Americans held 84.7 percent of the nation's wealth and 50.1 percent of Americans' income. Whereas 20 percent of Americans held 11.3 percent of wealth and made 23.2 percent of the income; while the remaining 20 percent of Americans held 3.8 percent of the wealth while making 14.7 percent of the income. But the bottom 40 percent of Americans had only 0.2 percent wealth and made 12.1 percent of America's income.

From this, we see that America's bottom 60% possess only 4 percent of the wealth while earning 26.8% of all income on which they pay taxes. The wealthy not only earn 50.1 percent of America's income but also have 84.7 percent of the nation's wealth which may be used to protect income and minimize taxes through tax loopholes, depreciation, and real estate tax deductions.

Too many Americans are seduced by our buy, buy, buy materialistic culture. What did President George W. Bush tell us to do the day after the 9/11/2001 terrorist attacks in America? "Go shopping!" Too many Americans live from paycheck-to-paycheck and necessarily so when the costs of housing, food, health insurance, education, and entertainment are very high, even in these recessive times. Nevertheless, TV advertising is seductive, urging viewers to keep up with the rich Americans' lifestyle as portrayed on TV by buying material things with no money down and two years or more before paying interest. The Great Recession has pushed heretofore middle class Americans into poverty and into the poorer class. The gap between the rich and the poor is so wide that America is fast becoming a third world nation: rich versus poor with few middle class.

Corporations are posting huge profits as they lay off workers, require existing workers to take up the slack, and sit on trillions of dollars in the bank. Their tax attorneys find tax loopholes so they pay little or no government taxes, and their lobbyists continue to seek subsidies – corporate welfare – such as handed to the corn/agribusiness and oil industries who poison our land, air, water, food, health, and human brains. The big corporations resist new energies not based on oil; label organic food as fads and genetically altered foods, GMOs, as the future with no studies of their long-term impact, just like cigarettes. The politicians resist universal health care so death sentences ensue and settle for a K-12 public system that is failing half our students, not the other way around.

Yet, the insurer AIG received an $85 billion bailout in 2008 before the election whereby Barack Obama succeeded George W. Bush. The precedent was set, so ensuring bailouts went to corporations, Fannie Mae, Fannie Mac, and banks: Chase, Citibank, Bank of America – controlled by the Rothschilds, the Rockefellers, and the Morgans, for starters. Big Businesses are too big to fail and have to be bailed out by the taxpayers? How about a big nation, like America? Those corporations or megamillionaires and billionaires are not bailing out America! In fact they appear to be colluding in paying less taxes and in the dismantling of democracy in their own cash cow self-interest. But, there seems to be more at work here than just accumulating wealth. Power is an aphrodisiac. Absolute power is the ultimate aphrodisiac.

American Businessmen's Belief in the Gospel of Growth

Businessmen and women, academics, economists, politicians, and heads of corporations driven by the erroneous concept that "all economic growth benefits humankind and that the greater the growth, the more widespread the benefits [also believe] that those people who excel at stoking the fires of economic growth should be exalted and rewarded, while those born at the fringes are available for exploitation."[261] America has learned and now many countries have experienced that economic growth benefits the few at the top of the hierarchy and the majority of the small nations' population exists under more desperate conditions as the result of debt to the World Bank or the IMF for infrastructure projects.

"Ecuador is in far worse shape today than she was before we [Economic Hit Men] introduced her to the miracles of modern economics, banking, and engineering. Since 1970... during the Oil Boom... the official poverty level grew from 50 to 70 percent, under- or unemployment increased from 15 to 70 percent, and public debt increased from $240 million to $16 billion."[261] John Perkins avows that "Ecuador is not the exception. Nearly every country we EHMs have brought under the global empire's umbrella has suffered a similar fate,"[261] and "the share of natural resources allocated to the poorest segments of the population declined from 20 to 6 percent, and public debt increased...the share of national resources allocated to the poorest segments of the population declined from 20 to 6 percent."[261]

In John Perkins 2004 book, *Confessions of an Economic Hit Man*, he related that he was an employee of a consulting group whose job was "to encourage world leaders to become part of a vast network that promotes U.S. commercial interests. In the end, those leaders become ensnared in a web of debt that ensures their loyalty. We can draw on them whenever we desire – to satisfy our political, economic, or military needs. In turn, they bolster their political positions by bringing industrial parks, power plants, and airports to their people. The owners of U.S. engineering and construction companies become fabulously wealthy."[261] Such U.S. firms are GE, Bechtel, and Dick Cheney's Halliburton, for example. The Gospel of Growth appears to be aligned with the Gospel of Wealth.

Perkins' clients had been Jaime Roldós, president of Ecuador, and Omar Torrijos [Herrera], de facto leader of Panama. On May 24, 1981, Roldós died at age 37 in a fiery plane crash. On July 31, 1981, Torrijos Herrera died at age 52 when a Panamanian Air Force plane crashed during bad weather. Perkins stated, "Their deaths were not accidental. They were assassinated because they opposed that fraternity of corporate, government, and banking heads whose goal is global empire. We EHMs failed to bring Roldós and Torrijos around, and the other type of hit men, the CIA-sanctioned jackals who were always right behind us, stepped in."[261]

Although Perkins had been told by MAIN's original interviewer, "Once you're in, you're in for life,"[261] before the deaths of his clients, he resigned on April 1, 1980, but was persuaded to remain "as a highly paid expert witness – primarily for U.S. electric-utility companies seeking to have new power plants approved for construction by public utilities commissions."[261] He kept track of Jaime Roldós who was resisting the oil companies, but "the deeper issues pointed to the fact that we [U.S.] were entering a new era of world politics.

The political climate in our nation changed in November 1980 when Jimmy Carter lost to Ronald Reagan in the presidential election, primarily due to Carter's Panama Canal Treaty and the failed rescue attempt of American hostages in Iran. However, something subtler was also happening. A president whose greatest goal was world peace and who was dedicated to reducing U.S. dependence on oil was replaced by a man who believed that the United States' rightful place was at the top of a world pyramid held up by military muscle, and that controlling oil fields wherever they existed was part of our Manifest Destiny."[261] President Reagan fit the needs of a corporatocracy: an actor who followed moguls' orders and knew how to take directions.[261] Under Regan's presidency and George H. W. Bush, as vice president, the deregulation of safety nets for businesses, instituted after the 1929-1939 Great Depression, set the stage for the ongoing Great Recession.

The vice president's son, president-to-be George W. Bush, had failed in his first energy company, Arbusto, but was rescued by a merger in 1984 with Spectrum 7; then Spectrum 7, on the brink of bankruptcy, was purchased in 1986 by Harken Energy Corporation with George W. Bush retained as consultant and board member at $120,000 a year. In 1989, with George H. W. Bush as President of the U.S., Amoco was negotiating with Bahrain for oil drilling rights, but State Department consultant Michael Ameen was assigned to brief the new U.S. Ambassador to Bahrain and also arranged a Bahrain and Harken meeting. Harken got the rights in Bahrain, not Amoco.[261] Follow the money time!

After President George H. W. Bush, President Bill Clinton's legacy was a balanced U.S. budget for our next President George W. Bush, his war hawks, and their economic hit men to do to our country what has been done to other countries, like Ecuador. With President Reagan as model, President George W. Bush's wars in the Middle East were not about Saddam Hussein or terrorists on 9/11/01 or human rights or democracy; they appear to have been all about preserving the oil industries at home, the military-industrial-complex, the status quo, and possibly finish the job his father, George H. W. Bush, began. George W. Bush's legacy is his commitment to costly, no-win wars, and to a huge national debt that would give the financiers – Think Harken! – the leverage to make all the calls about America's future direction.

Enter President Barack Obama, the people's choice, who has demonstrated that he is whole-brain-oriented. The rigid left-brainers' have resisted his leadership and maligned his character and questioned his birthplace origin. America's "royalty" and financiers had other plans for America's future that did not include hope or change in the status quo. They were aided by the U.S. Supreme Court's ruling that led to SuperPacs and by the ongoing visions of the megamillionaires, like Mitt Romney, and the megabillionaires, like Sheldon Adelson and the Koch brothers. Their view of America's future became so visible that it's not their secret any more. It's also ours to collude in or to confront with our votes. Public knowledge is power. Do we have to wait for the hit men to do their job? President Kennedy and his brother Robert were assassinated and the leaders of Ecuador and Panama, who resisted the subjugation of their countries and people to debt slavery died in plane crashes? Can we see that, like Ecuador, we are in worse shape politically, economically, morally, and educationally today than we were before 2001? Americans did not get new infrastructure for the huge U.S. budget incurred after November 2000, just the military-industrial-complex expenditures for wars in Iraq and Afghanistan that enriched the few and mortgaged the rest of us. Like communication-incompetent cancer cells, control freaks have glommed onto us and our nation. Will we wake up and insist on preserving America as a democratic republic for all Americans, not just for the capitalistic few with delusions of absolute power in A New World Order?

A New World Order:
(A Left-brained Concept)

We are supposed to believe that all those secret societies were organized for like-minded elites' just for fraternal or social purposes. The agenda of the financial elite appears to be to create A New World Order. The European Union is a reality and a beginning that consolidates the financial power of the few at the top. Financial power is based on fractional reserve banking. Fractional reserve banking ensures that the elites will have the gold and the consumers/nations will have the debt.

We already have a World Bank (WB) and the International Monetary Fund (IMF) that lend money to poor countries rich in Earthly resources for their leaders to spend money on projects that do not improve the country's financial condition, especially when outside North American (Bechtel, Halliburton/Dick Cheney, General Electric) and European contractors. are awarded the contracts, and collect all the money. When the indebted countries cannot repay the loans with their natural resources as collateral, the WB and IMF and/or Big Businesses may gain access to their natural resources.

We already have a central bank, the Federal Reserve System, that is independent of the U.S. government. In 1907, depositors feared unwise investments and misuse of their money by their bankers and closed their accounts. The Knickerbocker Trust Company of New York collapsed. With runs on the Trust Company of America and the Lincoln Trust Company to the point the U.S. was in a recession, banking leaders like Jekyll Island Club members George F. Baker of First National Bank and James Stillman of National City Bank met with financier J. Pierpont Morgan to arrange loans to the ailing banks. J. Pierpont Morgan decided which firms would fail and which would survive, averted a shutdown of the New York Stock Exchange, and bailed out New York City. Republican Senator Nelson W. Aldrich, the grandfather of Nelson Aldrich Rockefeller and great grandfather of John Davison Rockefeller, was party to the re-structuring of America's financial system, while becoming wealthy with his investments in railroads, sugar, rubber, and banking. His granddaughter Abby married John D. Rockefeller, Jr., the only son of John D. Rockefeller, Sr. Her son, Nelson Aldrich Rockefeller was U.S. Vice President under Gerald Ford.

The U. S. Congress formed the National Monetary Commission, but Senator Aldrich led a secret party to Jekyll Island in 1910 to restructure the financial system. His party included executives of the major banks, including Paul W. Warburg and J. P. Morgan, to discuss the restructuring of the banking system with a central bank, without the knowledge of the American people. The U.S. Congress did not pass the original bill but a similar bill to create the Federal Reserve System as an independent group of elite financiers in 1913. Today's Federal Reserve System is run by an insider group of financial elites whose decisions cannot be overruled by the United States Government's laws, according to former

Chairman Alan Greenspan who is an advocate of Ayn Rand who has become a mentor to Wall Streeters. Ayn Rand was no friend of democracy; she was an advocate of selfishness and a sexual predator as well. Nathaniel Branden, a psychologist, is one of her followers and victims? Who's in charge of our democracy and our future financial well-being? Ayn Rand's books are popular reading today among the young and old who have sights on becoming megamillionaires in America.

It seems that all those secret societies of the world's elites have been working behind the scenes on consolidating their financial power since before World Wars I and II. As we read from John Perkins' confessions, our country's Big Businesses have used and abused, to their advantage, the World Bank and International Monetary Fund, the World Health Organization, and the World Trade Organization. Now they want an international taxation system under the guise of saving the Earth. Our financial elites protect Big Businesses' investments in oil but not in new sources of energy, in agribusiness but not organic farming, in disease-care insurance not health care insurance (in fact no disease- or health care at all), and limit K-12 education and knowledge for the public, especially the poor. Their ongoing secrecy means they do not appear to be interested in sharing knowledge or money with America or in Americans' thriving. Suddenly, the threat of world domination at the hands of other power-driven human beings is more dangerous than any sightings of UFOs alleged to be scientific experiments or what we don't know about our origins. Science fiction may be stranger than reality, but it is a welcome diversion while some of us lean toward America's future transformation.

Unexplained Source of Huge Stone Structures on Earth and other artifacts

Roughly 25,000 years ago, in caves in southwestern France, human beings drew painted images of animals on the cave walls and ceilings with materials such as sticks, charcoal, and iron oxides. They painted images of lions, mammoths, and spotted horses as they walked, grazed, and congregated in herds. Their cave paintings demonstrate human creativity. For years, archaeologists have been divided: cave art representing real animals or representing mystical creatures, specifically the spotted horses. Thanks to science, by comparing modern horses' DNA with those that lived during the Stone Age, DNA has validated that the 25,000 year-old spotted horses are real spotted horses, not mythology.[289] Scientific methods for working with ancient DNA have matured to the point scientists are working on other questions about the past.

The Russians have revived an Arctic plant in northeastern Siberia that had been dead for 32,000 years. A squirrel had buried the plant's fruit which was permanently frozen until excavated by scientists. The narrow-leafed campion is the oldest plant to be resurrected from ancient tissue's DNA.[337]

The existence of a super-intelligent race of beings who spent some time on Earth, thousands of years ago, is evidenced by the stone structures they left behind that are star- or heaven-centered and allegedly visible from space as directional landing sites.[311] No tools were left behind to account for the construction that rivals our technology today. Today's scientific research and technology appear to be light years behind. Yet, our scientific research and scientific knowledge are ahead of our Western society's public educational, medical, political, and socio-cultural realities. Science is providing us with knowledge and stories that are verifiable with DNA sequencing and with carbon dating technology. Both the Hebrew Bible and the New Testament inform us that "the secrets of the Future are embedded in the Past, that the destiny of Earth is connected to the Heavens, that the affairs and fate of Mankind are linked to those of God and gods."[310]

Zecharia Sitchin's *The Stairway to Heaven* contextualizes the Biblical tales of Enoch and Elijah within his translations of Sumerian cuneiform tablets relating cosmological tales of "the Righteous Ones of the Rocketship,"[310] and of his search for understanding humans' past. The creation story uncovered by Sitchin's translations involves "Those who from heaven to Earth came" or the Anunnaki from Nibiru, whose planet was described in the *Epic of Creation* on seven tablets. Nibiru and the Annunaki King Anu and his sons, stepbrothers Enlil and Enki [310] are considered to be primitive minds' allegorical myths. Dr. Robert Bellah, in his *Religion in Human Evolution*, discussed the nature of the relationship between gods and men, as epitomized in a mythical "Story of Atrahasis." The heavens were allotted to Anu, his sons Enlil and Enki were allotted the earth and the waters under the earth, respectively.[19]

Sitchin considers the *Epic of Creation* to be a sophisticated cosmology about "a stray planet, passing by Earth's solar system, that collided with a planet called Tiamat; the collision resulted in the creation of Earth and its Moon, of the Asteroid Belt and comets, and in the capture of the invader itself in a great elliptical orbit that takes about 3,600 Earth years to complete... It was, Sumerian, texts tell, 120 such orbits – 431,000 Earth years – prior to the Deluge (the "Great Flood – which appears to have occurred over 13,000 years ago) that the Anunnaki came to Earth,"[310] represented by King Anu, his sons, Enlil and Enki. and daughter, Ninhursaga.

We may disbelieve the foregoing creation story, but the fact remains we have ancient and huge structures on Earth that defy our construction capabilities today. Without extra intelligent and technological assistance, Earthlings were not able to replicate the 11,600 year-old construction of temples in Göbekli Tepe, Turkey. "Bewilderingly, the people at Göbekli Tepe got steadily worse at temple building... As time went by, the pillars became smaller, simpler, and were mounted with less and less care. Finally the effort seems to have petered out altogether by 8200 BC."[216]

The ensuing Sumerian, Iraq and the Middle East, civilizations recorded on tablets their inherited or lived experiences of the impact of Earth's visitation from their so-called gods. DNA of the gods may have been more evolved than Earth's human beings, for they were purported to be immortal, free of diseases, and to have knowledge of cloning, but their sibling rivalries, power struggles, and violent tendencies demonstrated emotional illiteracy and huge egos to feed with monuments, temples, services, gifts, and gold. However, the Sumerian translations are considered fables, as figments of human imaginations. It appears that the ancients' recordings of intelligent space beings who visited Earth were assumed to be gods. If, in fact, there were visitations by super-intelligent beings, it does not deny the existence of a real God.

What if ancient architectural wonders of the world were constructed by intelligent life from the cosmos? A couple of unexplained anomalies on Earth are the Great Pyramids in Egypt and Stonehenge in England, both of which have astronomical significance. There is evidence of ancient gold mining in Peru and Africa, and there are the Mayan and Aztec civilizations with sophisticated calendars based upon the stars with the sun as the center of Earth's solar system. There are many examples of architectural wonders throughout the world that today's technology would not be able to replicate.

Traditional wisdom informs us that the Great Pyramids and Sphinx were built by Egyptians 4500 years ago. But, now we know they were built more than 10,000 years ago, thousands of years before the Egyptian civilization. Edgar Cayce, the famous psychic, reported a Hall of Records beneath the Sphinx's paws, but excavations have not been authorized to date.

Now we know that a 1977 archaeological dig at Monte Verde, Chile, revealed the area was inhabited until at least 12,500 years ago, which is 1,000 years earlier than original Americans were said to have crossed the ice over the Bering Strait. The physical signs of an advanced prehistoric civilization are evident throughout the world, and bits and pieces of prehistoric knowledge have survived, but they do not fit our inherited view of humans' "approved" origins and history provided by Biblical teachings.

The Biblical stories of Earth's creation a few thousand years ago by God in six days, his resting on the seventh, the creation of Adam and then Eve from Adam's rib, and the Flood and Noah's Ark had been written centuries before in Hebrew, Egyptian, and Sumerian texts before the Bible was composed. Other stories or legends in the Bible have been considered myths or confused translations, especially those dealing with gods' visitations from the heavens, their "creating the first man and woman," Jesus Christ's immaculate conception, human beings' punishment by God with a flood except for Noah, his family, and two-by-two "saved" creatures.

We have had the science since 1969 to travel in space, to put men on the moon. We can now clone animals and grow human beings via in vitro fertilization. We build submarines with crews that can survive for months under the ocean's surface. Scientists are amassing the DNA of Earth's species and extinct species to preserve them for future generations. Is that what Noah did? It certainly makes more common sense to store DNA than gather thousands of male-female animals, house them in an ark to be fed for five or six months until the flood waters receded. Are we, in the 21st century, just catching up to our ancestors' knowledge thousands of years ago?

According to the records of the ancient Sumerians and Egyptians, civilized humankind has been on Earth for more than 500,000 years. Through the ages, to defend long-cherished theories, the Roman Church and despots have destroyed artifacts, monuments, and libraries. The Greek tyrant Peisistratus destroyed Homer's poems; the Romans burned a library in Carthage said to contain 500,000 volumes; Julius Caesar leveled Egypt's great library at Alexandria as well as another 700,000 volumes of accumulated knowledge in its two branches. The Crusaders sacked Constantinople, Turkey, and destroyed Muslim libraries. The Catholic Inquisition burned an untold number of ancient works. Even Chinese emperor Tsin Shiu Hwant-ti ordered a book burning in 213 BC.[218]

As a result of powerful men who destroyed human beings' origins in order to preserve their status, power, and control, scholars have had to rely upon fragmented tablets, parchments, statues, paintings, diverse artifacts, and gigantic stone shrines throughout the world to contest conventional wisdom, conventional science, and theories that underlie "the divine nature of authority" that affirm approved knowledge and the status quo. Today's scholars know that they won't be burned at the stake like Giordano Bruno in 1600, but their writings may not see the light of day because The Western Intellectual Tradition prevails. Only knowledge that is "consistent with what is already known"[48] will be published. In addition, character assassination is a cultural weapon to make sure scholars and scientists are kept on a straight and narrow path. The status quo "colonized" take care of the rest of us.

In *Religion in Human Evolution*, Sociologist Robert N. Bellah explored the origins of religion in antiquity. One of the tribal religions he studied was Hawai'i, which focused on kings. Dr. Bellah, now age eighty-four, found that "Some form of divine kingship can be found in Old Kingdom Egypt, the Aztecs, Mayas, Inkas and Yorubas, and in Zhou China the king was the 'Son of Heaven'... In Mesopotamia, the earliest period of what was probably priest-kingship is obscure, but there were sporadic claims to divine status by kings in the Akkadian and Ur III dynasties in the third millennium BCE, and perhaps even in the Old Babylonian dynasty in the first half of the second millennium."[19]

Dr. Bellah's well-researched book avers that "in quite early Sumerian mythology it is said that 'kingship came down from heaven,' even though the king himself did not claim to be a god."[19] He wrote that "the claim by a number of Assyrian kings to be 'king of the universe' would seem to imply a power more than human... But... the king was characterized as the 'servant' or 'slave' of the god (a usage that, in an entirely different context, will reappear in Christianity and even more extensively, in Islam) rather than as divine himself... a few gods were particularly important: Anu, the father of the gods: Enlil, his son and actual ruler of the gods; Ninhursaga, the goddess of birth; Enki, the god of fresh water, but above all the god of intellect and cunning, and of all the productive arts."[19] Dr. Bellah made no reference to the alleged origin of the gods, Anu, his daughter, and two sons, as recorded on Sumerian tablets. He quoted from many scholars' writings, including their mythic views of power, including "we must inquire after their [Egyptians] gods and employ all conceptual armory in order to seek out the reality of these gods – a reality that was not invented by human beings but experienced by them."[159]

The gods as the source of benevolence and paralyzing fear is epitomized in the Old Testament of the Holy Bible. Dr. Bellah relates that "Enki... always the clever one, had a suggestion: why not create men to do the work the lesser gods found so tiresome?... men took over the work of the gods but greatly prospered in doing so... the noise level rose... Enlil sent a drought... [Enki intervened]... Enlil sent a great flood to kill every human being. Enki, however... had Atrahasis construct an unsinkable boat, load it with every kind of animal, and last out the flood... Enlil finally realized that humans were indispensable to the gods."[19]

Dr. Bellah quotes Thorkild Jacobsen[167] regarding the ancients' reaction to Enlil's "fear, impulsiveness, and insensitivity. All the same it is clear that the myth views absolute power as selfish, ruthless, and unsubtle. But what is is. Man's existence is precarious. His usefulness to the gods will not protect him unless he takes care not to be a nuisance to them, however innocently. There are, he should know, limits set for his self-expression."[19]

Familiar biblical stories of creation, hierarchical dominance, gods' immortality, and man's lesser status were summarized by the Mesopotamian poem, the Epic of Gilgamesh – the Sumerian king of Uruk; Erech in the Bible – man has no alternative but to submit to death: "mere man—his days are numbered, whatever he may do, he is but wind."[19] The last found Mesopotamian text in cuneiform script dates from 75 CE: possibly the end of that civilization.

The Biblical story tells us that Adam and Eve ate from the Tree of Knowing: the Lord God became concerned: "Behold, the Adam has become as one of us [the gods] to know good and evil; And now might he not put forth his hand and partake also of the Tree of Life, and eat, and live forever?"[310] Immortality has been the goal of kings; most settle for gold. The Fountain of Eternal Youth, what makes old men young again, has motivated the explorers of new worlds. Ferdinand and Isabel, the King and Queen of Spain, were no exception as they sponsored Christopher Columbus' voyage to the Americas in 1492. While Columbus did not find Paradise and the Waters of Life or Eternal Youth, he did decimate the natives and confiscated the gold of the Aztecs and Incas who said the gold belonged "to the gods."

"Our entire human history is inextricably linked to the production [exhibiting and hoarding] of gold...the empowering effect it must have had on early humans, how it shaped their behaviour in times to come, and how it drove their own vanity, greed and desire to be like their gods... Not really knowing what to do with or, or what its true purpose was... They turned it into bracelets, necklaces, rings, ornaments, trinkets and an every growing list of items whose sole purpose was to show off its owner's elevated status."[19] Nevertheless, "He who has the gold makes the rules" is operative today just as it was some 500,000 years ago.

Intelligent Life beyond Human Beings in the Universe?

For two thousand years, since the 5th century A.D., the Roman Church has maintained that man is God's only supreme creation and the only intelligent life in the universe. It was a surprise when David Willey, BBC News, Rome, reported on May 13, 2008 that the Vatican's Chief Astronomer, Father Gabriel Funes, had announced the possibility that alien intelligent beings exist in the universe: "Just as there are multiple forms of life on earth, so there could exist intelligent beings in outer space created by God." And some aliens could even be free from original sin, he speculated. "The search for forms of extraterrestrial life," he said, "does not contradict belief in God."[344] Does the Vatican have knowledge that the general public does not? After all, the Church has ancient texts in its library. Or, is the Church preparing its one billion members for science's eventual contact with other intelligent life in the universe? Whatever, the motivation for the Vatican's announcement, it is a radical change in dogma and practice from its inception thousands of years ago. Father Funes said that mistakes were made, but it is time to turn the page and look towards the future.[344] How about beginning with the Roman Church's stance on original sin, its views on women, especially nuns' service to humanity, and women's leadership in the Roman Catholic Church?

Throughout human history, man has revered the stars and has used them for navigation, weather prediction, marked time by celestial-based calendars, attributed myths and legends to them, and constructed astronomical almanacs, an ephemeris or tables, that compute the positions of planets for every day of given periods. An ephemeris is the basis of the ancient art of astrology to construct horoscopes for individuals' exact birth dates, times, place, and planets' positions. Oral histories of American Indians, Mesoamericans, other South American and African populations, and the Sumerians in the Middle East tell us that intelligent space people or "gods" visited Earth hundreds of thousands of years ago and that they will return one day.

Extraterrestrials (ETs), flying saucers or unidentified flying objects (UFOs) are the source of media entertainment for people and any sightings are down-played by governments with normal explanations. In our left-brained Western society that is more schizophrenic than normal, it is not surprising that positive proof is needed in the here-and-now to change our society's status quo stance that the knowledge we have is irrefutable. Thus, authorities attribute the alleged sightings of UFOs to be figments of hysterical imaginations, myths, explainable as weather stations/balloons gone astray, or the testing of science-fiction-type aircraft. Scientists who do ET research are judged to be crackpots. There are penalties for scientists who appear to believe in UFOs: they face ridicule or dismissal. While there have been reported crashes of UFOs in the Black Forest, Germany, in 1936, and in Roswell, New Mexico in 1947. Roswell's event is said to be due to government experiments. Nevertheless, technology accelerated in Germany and in the United States after those alleged crashes, especially in Germany. German scientists were welcome in America during and after World War II; they were involved in the Manhattan Project that developed the atom bombs dropped on Japan to end the war in 1945.

With the Keppler telescope operated by NASA, five planets outside our solar system have been discovered. The Earth is about four and one-half billion years old; whereas the universe is estimated to be fourteen billion years old. There is strong evidence for life on planets in and outside our planetary system, but not necessarily intelligent life. Scientists follow a planet's signature for water and oxygen. If intelligent life in UFOs have been tracking us, as assumed by alleged visitations, they will be perceived as hostile since we may have no governmental or United Nations' official group to greet them. Any civilization that has mastered space travel will probably be more advanced than we are; however, superior knowledge alone is no indicator that they may be benevolent toward Earthlings, judging by Sumerian gods' behavior. The crop circles that have appeared in England and other countries appear to represent intricate geometric designs discernible from man-made hoaxes.[112] Are they giving us clues to the mysteries of the universe, like energy to travel in space or the energy technology that would make oil and gas obsolete? We still don't have answers to philosophers and scholars' fundamental questions.

Scholars' translations of Sumerian tablets and the Dead Sea Scrolls, American Indian Tribal Prophecies, and 5,000-year-old writings of Mesopotemia – The Mahabharata – with stories of flying chariots and atomic bomb-like star wars between the "gods" are science-fiction fodder for the entertainment industry. In life's journeys and travails, though, the most powerful weapons are knowledge, understanding, and wisdom for human beings to free themselves from those who would figuratively and literally enslave us for their own good.

Society's "approved" knowledge is upheld by the sociologist Harriet Zuckerman, author of *Scientific Elite: Nobel Laureates in the United States* (1977). As senior vice president of the Andrew W. Mellon Foundation, as reported by Journalist Benedict Carey, Dr. Zuckerman said, "We know people have ideas beyond the mainstream, but if they want funds for research they have to go through peer reviews, and the system is going to be very skeptical of ideas that are inconsistent with what is already known"[48] It's as if a left-brained long-range plan exists within the system to discourage "ideas that are inconsistent with what is already known," so those who benefit from obsolete knowledge will remain in power, especially in academia, big businesses, Rockefeller and others' oil, the financiers, and government's bureaucracies.

Wisdom is not wisdom if it is based upon left-brain logic that only approves of "already known" knowledge or is based upon age-old untruths. Wisdom is not practiced by our institutions and organizations where it pays to look and act smart, to get rich at others' expense, and to use money to figuratively bury versus burn at the stake those who disagree with their politics, policies, and practices.

Pseudo-blue-bloods in America have origins in inherited wealth and influence from lowly beginnings: wagon-dispensed cancer "cures," drug running, Prohibition alcohol, slavery, union-busting, monopoly practices, nepotism, and intermarriages between their families. Behind their quest for financial, political, and social dominance is their belief in eugenics, that their genetics are better than the average American's gene pool. They belong to organized secret societies and have tax-exempt foundations to perpetuate their elitism. Ancient rulers and kings believed in the divine right/nature of authority. Other elites' beliefs are based in early religious fundamentalists' teaching that wealth is God's gift to the deserving, not the undeserving poor, which means for the past thirty years or so, the rich got richer and the poor got poorer in America.

Human beings' origins and man's inhumanity to other men, women, children, and animals does does not deny "the existence of a universal creative force – God – the absolute All or Oneness of all energy and matter...of a Supreme Being."[218] Nor does the Vatican deny that there may be more to life than this one on Earth who do not have original sin, which beliefs have been nurtured by other religions, the secret societies, and the Mystery Schools. The knowledge and power of the elites – through possible access to ancient knowledge, bloodlines, history, and philosophy, have been used to perpetuate their wealth, power, hierarchical authority – have been used to usurp and control the majority of human beings' possibilities, overall security, and health.

When we integrate our left- and right-brains' knowledge, we may feel what's right within our minds, hearts, soul or innermost being, and we may seek alternatives to status quo knowledge: the Internet, documentaries, old library books, and unconventional book stores. A search for truth is the search for freedom from mind-forg'd manacles, which is an impossible quest when approved knowledge is based on incomplete or erroneous information manufactured to instill fear, divisiveness, and control. The control of seven billion people on Earth can only be accomplished through deceit, secrecy, and economics.

Just as the two forms of government, Republic and Democracy, need to cooperate for the greater good of America, our two brains, right and left, need to cooperate for our higher good. President Madison wrote in favor of our republican form of government: "As there is a degree of depravity in mankind which requires a certain degree of circumspection and distrust: So there are other qualities in human nature, which justify a certain portion of esteem and confidence."[97]

Truths enable us to flourish in America's constitutional republic of a democratic nature, if we have whole-brained leaders at the helm. In the blurred vision of our founders, they distrusted the masses and considered the people's elected representatives to be "more consonant to the public good than if pronounced by the people themselves."[97] Instead, it is We the People who have to regain "reason, justice and truth…[from being] misled by the artful misrepresentations of interested men."[97] Truth engages different philosophical discourses from diverse brain perspectives and intentions, so we have to be constantly alert to language's attempt to undermine our understanding and knowledge that help us recognize truth from falsehood.

There are questions herein with no answers that satisfy Western society's scientific methods, so all the questions without answers are offered as food for thought. Just as the Earth was round and orbited around the sun, despite the Roman Church's teachings to the contrary, it was not an issue of belief but of eventual proven fact. Similarly, we may choose to believe or disbelieve the Sumerian tablets' record of "gods from heaven" and their impact on Earth's human beings. Again disbelief or belief, but no facts to date, except carbon dating technology that indicates that constructed archaeological findings throughout the world are older than assumed and beyond today's technology. Ancient structures, such as the Egyptian pyramids and Stonehenge, are real reminders that knowledge and practices superior to ours today probably existed many thousands of years ago.

Since there is global awareness in 2012 – the Mayan calendar ends in December which has been the source of much "end of times" speculation – humanity is at a tipping point. Will we destroy ourselves with modern technology's warfare or transform ourselves toward an enlightened level of consciousness and a narrative that unites us all? Joseph Campbell's immersion in mythology had taught him that our human stories, our narratives, are not ideology. It is not something projected from the brain, but something experienced from the heart.

A unifying story of humanity with a vision of collaborating rather than colluding in a man-made global disaster is preferable to messianic, prophetic expectations fueled by religious' fantasies of more wars, atrocities, and slaughter. Whole-brained thinking and new knowledge as sources to redefine our identities as human beings on Earth may unite us globally, not just culturally and nationally.

Chapter Nine

> *Oh what a tangled web we weave*
> *When first we practice to deceive.*
> –Sir Walter Scott, Marmion, 1808

Who's in Charge?

"You have cancer, and it's not curable!" said the blue-eyed, white-haired doctor as he entered the room where I awaited the results of my routine blood work in 2002. Stunned, "What do I do now?" I asked. "Nothing!" he said," until multiple myeloma symptoms appear." I was so put off by his lack of people skills and his "I'm in charge!" behavior that I said, "Thank you!" and left to go to a library to look up a disease I knew by name only. I did not like myself in his presence, and I did not see him again.

My experience with that doctor was a teachable moment for me. I had tolerated such doctors and imperious adults before but this time was different, I was in a vulnerable condition and had flashed back to visiting my friend Joan at a famous New York City hospital. She was dying of breast cancer and worrying, not about herself, but about her two very young children's future. She told me her oncologist had told her "You're a hysterical woman!" My doctor's factual approach and his demeanor had dismissed me as a person, just as Joan's doctor had treated her. We were diseases. Professionalism has a way of distancing adults from their whole selves, their humanity, and of recreating the divine nature of hierarchical authority. I decided I was going to be in charge of my destiny.

Do Nothing!? Wrong! I had saved my own life years before when I needed three blood transfusions after an accident. The first transfusion was my blood type O-negative; the second was not, which I checked after the nurse had left the room in the hospital where I was born, in Brooklyn, New York. It was minutes before the transfusion was interrupted; I went into shock, had to be wrapped in an ice blanket, and wanted to scream, "The Russians are coming!" but couldn't. Basically, I had a reaction to the antibodies in the small amount of not-my-blood type. I survived, thanks also to my doctor, a general practitioner, who had told me about blood types.

Back in 2002, the blood was the primary indicator of the transformation from MGus to full-blown multiple myeloma: cancer of plasma cells, a type of white blood cell in bone marrow; plasma cells make proteins called antibodies. After nearly five years and no sign of MGus transforming and physically and mentally involved in completing a book (2003) on self- and other-esteem, I had relaxed, especially after an acquaintance, a hematologist, told us that in 80 percent of people with MGus, it did not transform. Every six-months, blood work showed the M-spike was within "normal" range, even in August 2007. In my case, my blood did not indicate that MGus had transformed to Multiple Myeloma. Instead, it caused osteoporosis before the M-spike met the medical parameters.

A month later, the spinal compressions began in September, and the sternum fracture in October, 2007, led to hospitalization for a blood clot. I was diagnosed with osteoporosis. In the age of doctors' specialization, it took two more months before I was diagnosed with multiple myeloma, thanks to the intervention of another GP. I agreed to chemotherapy treatment. One of the four drugs, Thalidomid, left me with neuropathy in both legs, knees to feet. My mother's first cousin's son's wife had a Thalidomide Baby – legless and armless – and my memory of him was often present when taking that medication every day for a year. It's possible that my negative thinking conjured up my neuropathy.

Since January 2009, with blood checks every three months, the multiple myeloma had been "in remission." Until blood work in July, 2012, indicated I am out of remission with an up-and-down IgG protein factor and an M-spike for the first time in three and one-half years.

In January 2009, I redoubled my efforts toward rebuilding my immune system after a year of chemotherapy. Son Malcolm built an infrared electric sauna for me; we bought a treadmill since my gait was unsteady, and I involved myself in mind-body physical therapies and, during two critical periods, I used and am using a photon/electrical generator[312] designed in 2009.

In 2010, my IgG immune factor/protein was high but still within normal range, so I undertook 20 half-hour, twice weekly sessions in the photon machine, in a doctor's office, which led to a decrease of 350 IgG points. A May, 2012, check-up six months ago indicated the IgG was above normal. In two months, I had fourteen more sessions before the July 5th blood work. It showed the IgG had decreased by 170 points but also showed an M-spike, so I will undertake more sessions over the next three months. Cancer has been a fact of my life for so long that I continue to learn lessons from it and to "sing my own song," at least on paper. I am not finished yet! I have a book in my head about disease care, health care, and prevention.

Cancer has been one of the topics of my research since 1962 when my father died of colon cancer that had metastasized to his liver. His doctor had said the liver could be regenerated through "proper" nutrition. I studied nutrition and completed a thesis on it for my 1975 master's degree in Human Development since nutrition that fuels the brain and body was not addressed in the Physical Processes course in the program. In the early 1980s, I attended a conference on alternatives to treating cancer held at the Grand Hyatt Hotel on 42nd Street in New York City. One of the famous presenters was Nobel prize winner Albert Szent Gyorgyi, 1893-1986, who discovered vitamin C, ascorbic acid. His wife had died in 1963 of cancer. He theorized that there was a correlation between free radicals, vitamin C, and cancer. Free radicals are highly reactive molecules that are electrically unbalanced because they lost electrons. Free radicals occur in the human body all the time, but our intake of antioxidants found in fruits and vegetables – 5 to 8 servings per day – less meat, sugar, white flour products, and manufactured foods, and more beans appear to protect the body from free radical damage and from disease.

Very intriguing was Dr. Werner Loewenstein's presentation of his working hypothesis that a cancer cell is a normal cell that did not have or had lost its intracellular and intercellular communication system and that its communication incompetence played a key role in carcinogenesis.[209] He published *The Touchstone of Life: Molecular Information, Cell Communication, and the Foundations of Life* in 2000 and is now age 86. The human body is composed of some sixty trillion cells.[133] The cells in our bodies are constantly sending out and receiving signals. When cell communications go wrong, we learn that at least one breakdown in cell communication is responsible for most diseases. For example, the food we eat is metabolized into sugar, which enters the blood stream. Cells in the pancreas release an insulin signal for the liver, muscles, and fat cells to store the sugar for future use. If the pancreatic cells are lost, as in Type 1 diabetes, a cell's signal cannot reach its target.

Other examples of intercellular miscommunications beyond lost cells are when the targeted cell ignores the signal, the signal doesn't reach its target, or there's too much signaling, as in a stroke. Dying brain cells release large amounts of the signaling molecule glutamate; low concentrations control many cellular interactions, but huge concentrations are toxic to brain cells. Cancer involves multiple signaling breakdowns within a cell and between the cells in our bodies. Most alternative cancer treatments rely on reactivating intercellular communication processes and the body's immune system. Cancer appears in diverse forms from diverse causes, so there may not be one cure or treatment to fit all cancers.

Essentially, a cancer cell is a normal cell that has lost its connection to its genetic memory; it stops communicating with and becomes separate from the body's other cells. To thrive, a cancer cell consumes surrounding healthy cells and the human body that supports it. In multiple myeloma, plasma cells – which make proteins or antibodies – become cancerous; they multiply, raise the plasma cells beyond normal levels, and increase the level of abnormal proteins/antibodies in the blood, affecting bones, immune system, kidneys, and red blood cell count.

Scientific research continues to uncover the transformation process when a normal cell transitions into a cancer cell – possibly, in multiple myeloma, a cell's loss of its DNA molecule's genetic ability to decompress, unfold, and repair itself – so an otherwise normal cell becomes communication incompetent. Scientists will discover one day not only the how but the why of cancer: under what conditions in the human body does a normal cell transform into a cancer cell. Evidently, we have cancer cells floating around in our bodies much of the time; cancer ensues when our immune systems are impaired for whatever reason and/or human cells ongoing replication processes improperly duplicate themselves due to genetics, lifestyle, or aging.

Lawrence LeShan's presentation at the conference focused on the mind-body connection in cancer. He perceives cancer as an opportunity or turning point to view the relationship with self, not as "What's wrong with me? but as "What's right with me?" He emphasizes singing our own song – a commitment to our best and natural selves' ways of being and relating, thereby creating an environment within that maximizes the potential for healing.

When we perceive cancer as a metaphor representing the many roadblocks to communicating with our whole selves and others – the K-12 public education system educates the left-side of the brain only, creating duality within – we may perceive cancer as an opportunity to integrate our right- and left-brain's intelligences, heal, and/or find the meaning in or the lesson from it. With cancer cells present in the human body all the time that heal all the time too, something happens within human beings' inner and outer environments to finally trigger their transformation to communication incompetence. The body's immune system is our natural defense against bacteria, microbes, viruses, toxins. parasites, diseases, and abnormal cells; it detects, recognizes, and neutralizes pathogens. Pathogens, though, can evolve, adapt, and avoid detection, and live in the body a long time without causing problems, until the immune system's defenses are compromised.

We compromise our immune system when we are out of communication with our body-mind's needs that have not changed over thousands of years, but our lifestyle has and so has our food supply. For example, the body wants sugar, and the mind gives it a cookie or a soda instead of an apple. Thus, what we eat, what we drink, how we exercise, how we rest, what we breathe, what and how we think and feel, and how we relate to self and others are all factors that positively or negatively affect and enhance or compromise our immune system. It's possible that what and how we think may be twice as important as diet, exercise, and rest.[233]

Although we have two brains within our left and right hemispheres, when we rely upon one brain only, as we are taught in K-12 public school, our communication system becomes impaired, influencing what and how we think and feel and how we act, learn, communicate, and relate. Yet, adults and our peers use the right-brain to criticize, judge, and sometimes compliment us. We know that some people's passions override their reason and that other people are logical and insensitive to people's feelings and emotions. When two opposing right- and left-brain worldviews collide, anti-intellectualism or anti-emotionalism become conscious and unconscious knee-jerk human reactions that are not only personality or political differences but are rooted in hemispheric differences. Nature intended for us to be whole-brained, to use our heads and our hearts, not just be coldly logical like the doctor without empathy. But, that's The Western Intellectual Tradition's legacy by its half-brained approach to K-12 public education, producing students and adults who do not have access to their full intelligence or their potential to be effective communicators.

Since society's institutions, and organizations are entities made up of people, those entities are only as healthy as the individuals who people them as employees. Like cancer with uncontrolled cellular growth, people's uneducated and uncontrolled negative emotions, desires, and lifestyles overwhelm their immune system to the point cancer is the #2 killer. Similarly, financial growth empowers institutions and organizations and overpowers them, like the New York banks that were deemed too big to fail, bailed out, and continued to eat up America's and American's financial resources to the point that J. P. Morgan Chase has devoured its own resources due to communication incompetence. Cancer is a metaphor for incommunicado people and society's institutions and organizations.

How do we get to this cancerous stage in ourselves and in our society? Human beings' self-image as individuals, or group-image as members of a family, group, tribe, religion, or nation, governs their actions. Actions are conditioned by their heritage, experiences, education, self-education, and self- and/or group-knowledge. Elementary and high school public education is based upon ancient practices to pass on the habits of thought, knowledge, beliefs, and traditions held by older generations to new generations who have now lost their connections to their genetic wholeness.

The experiences that are impressed upon us in early childhood, when we are innocent and trusting, often blind us to becoming different, so we perpetuate what we learned without much attention to examining old beliefs, new ideas, changed circumstances, and changing times. To align young children's attitudes and behaviors with America's societal values, our K-12 public education system tends to alienate children from their genetic and intergenerational inheritances, in utero and lived experiences, and biological and psychological needs and to suppress their innate talents, aspirations, and spontaneous desires.

As a result, many students who succeed in the K-12 public education system leave their whole selves behind when they go to school and develop their cognitive minds to achieve society's recognition and affirmation for its definition of success: high IQs, high grades, and high-paying careers or wealth. In the left-brained educative process, students are conditioned to be competent in one brain only. They lose their humanity and ability to communicate from both brains when the corpus callosum – the communication network between the two brains – is not exercised. They can become robots without a heart, conscience, or loyalty to others and their country. Our K-12 public school system works better for left-brained students who are unencumbered by the disowned right-brain's emotions and virtues so they can concentrate on learning. Whereas, the right-brainers have learned to cross over and learn the left-brain's ABCs and 123s, but with ready access to their emotions. Negative emotions that are perceived as threats to their ego's survival may downshift into the fight or flight syndrome and diminish their access to learned data during tests. Grades are negatively affected.

Children's genius, creativity, and innovation are squelched by prolonged exposure to by-the-book learning toward academic excellence, as required and tested by our K-12 left-brain dominated educational system. Without access to their emotional, intuitive, and experiential intelligence, pattern recognition, both brains' worldviews, interdisciplinary perspectives, and "we" worldviews, children will not develop their full human intelligence, talents, and potential. But, as adults, they can make lots of money off other people's money and believe and behave as if they are very important people and also believe they are very important to their country's economy.

The right hemisphere is not only the seat of human emotions and virtues and the venue for the heart and gut's "knowings," it is also the data bank for humans' inherited, sensed, and lived experiences from in utero onward. Children are particularly vulnerable to physical and/or emotional traumas – incidents or events – due to their innocent, perceptive, and sensitive natures. Unresolved traumas interfere with their ability to learn and communicate. We have positive emotions (peace, love, acceptance) and negative emotions (anger, fear, guilt), and our uneducated negative emotions may be used by others to manipulate and control us. How to become emotionally literate is beyond the usual family's expertise, so people's emotions have been relegated to therapists and counselors, after encountering roadblocks to living, learning, and relating that can cripple children's lives for life, until resolved. Emotional literacy and human virtues are the underpinnings of human beings' access to their full human intelligence and humanity with a moral and social conscience.

Character building toward the traits of a good reputation and the right-brain's virtues (honesty, morals and ethics, intuition, compassion, altruism) are the human qualities that involve and require the integration of full human intelligence toward communicating in thought, word, wisdom, and deed with self and others. If character building is not learned or modeled at home, at school, in the environment, or is not formally or informally educated, then children and adults may disown their genetic connection to their authentic selves and to all human beings. Like a cancer cell that has lost its ability to communicate and consumes other healthy cells to survive and thrive, we have people behaving like that in America today.

Most of American leaders are products of The Western Intellectual Tradition; they may be smart, but not wise when their actions reveal to us their learned versus earned sense of entitlement. Without emotional intelligence, our unmet and unresolved conscious and unconscious psychological needs are usually satisfied by money and by using or abusing others when our esteem for and responsibility to them are missing.

We have been deceived by our leaders who, intentionally or unintentionally, don't even know they don't know that until we educate both human hemispheres of the brain, children and adults will be educated to be academically smart, but not fully intelligent or humane. Cosmologist Carl Sagan wrote: "The coordinated functioning of both cerebral hemispheres is the tool Nature has provided... We are unlikely to survive if we do not make full and creative use of our human intelligence."[294]

Evidently, our K-12 public education system is preparing many students to achieve high Grade Point Averages in Advance Placement courses and high-ranking SAT scores whose high school seniors compete for entrance to America's top colleges. Most of America's parents have swallowed society's definition of success – money – for themselves and for their children and do whatever it takes to succeed. "Parents will fight to the death for best high schools. Best teachers and best principals want to work in best high schools... Lists [of best high schools] are cash cows."[347] Of America's 26,000 public high schools, around 2,000+ submitted data to *Newsweek* for rating; 1,000 of them appear on the 2012 *Newsweek* List. New York's Scarsdale High School does not submit data to *Newsweek*; the school does not use Advanced Placement texts that "encourage students to go a mile wide and an inch deep."[347] Instead, Scarsdale High's students visit libraries, museums, and do field research. Two-thirds of its graduates are accepted by colleges listed in *Barron's Guide to the Most Competitive Colleges.*

Essentially, for public and charter high schools to be best, they must "accept only the highest performing eighth graders, who – if the school doesn't botch it – will become the highest performing 12th graders... Best in, best out, best school... Clearly, best schools would do best not to get bogged down serving students considered un-best."[347]

Michael Winerip critiqued the *Newsweek* Editors' List. He questioned, how is it possible "to quantify something as complex and nuanced as a high-quality education"?[347] *Newsweek's* science-sounding rating system quantitatively analyzes students' high school test scores by using six variables: 1) On-time graduation rate: 25%; 2) Percent of graduates accepted to college: 25%; 3) AP and International Baccalaureate tests per student: 25%; 4) Average SAT/ACT score:10%;

5) Average AP/ International Baccalaureate score: 10%; and 6) Average AP/International Baccalaureate courses per student: 5%.

According to *Newsweek*'s calculations, "Of the top 50, 37 have selective admissions or are magnet schools, meaning they screen students using a combination of entrance exam scores, grade-point average, state test results and assessments of their writing samples."[347] Eight of the top 50 are charter schools; the top two of the eight are Basis Scottsdale and Basis Tucson, Arizona. Basis Scottsdale, 3rd best high school on the List, has 701 students; 95 percent are Asians or white. Mandarin or Latin is a required language course of study. Unsurprisingly, "There are no children who qualify for subsidized lunches or who need special education."[347]

The top 5 schools on *Newsweek*'s list are "full of children from the nation's wealthiest families."[347] Fifteen of the top 100 high schools are in Texas and 10 are in Florida where George W. and Jeb Bush "have made standardized test results a true measure of academic excellence,"[347] which is not a true measure of humans' full intelligence or wisdom. Teaching to the test evolved, from No Child Left Behind, when results on standardized tests became the measure of K-12 public schools, teachers, and students.

From the foregoing, we learn that so-called academic excellence in K-12 public education does not equate with human intelligence. Academic excellence is confined to the book-smart and test-smart students whose parents' incomes and/or wealth give them direct access to tutors and to the wealthiest neighborhoods where more money is spent on real estate taxes to buy the best public schooling for their children. Other smart students have a sense of belonging and of their significance due to loving care and support. However, our American smart high school students with their high numbers do not reveal the rest of the story in today's global economy. In 2009, a test – Program for International Student Assessment, PISA – was held for 15-year-old students to compete from 34 developed countries. In the U.S., about 5,000 students were chosen from across America's best students. In China a similar number was chosen from Shanghai, a city of 20 million people. Chinese students scored 1st in all categories. America's students ranked 23rd in Science, 17th in Reading, and 32nd in Math.[69] Finland's

15-year-olds scored 2nd in Reading, 3rd in Science, and 6th in Math on PISA.[141]

PISA was organized by a Paris-based group and is administered by European and American officials. A Beijing, China, whole-brained educator stated, "Chinese schools emphasized testing too much, and produced students who lacked curiosity and the ability to think critically or independently. It creates very narrow-minded students...but what China needs now is entrepreneurs and innovators."[17] America? Ditto! Finland was commended for its comprehensive teacher recruitment and training program.[339] Wake-up calls to upgrade K-12 public education have been sounded in America since Russia's Sputnik was launched in 1957. But the data to find ways to strengthen teaching and learning are stuck in committees, without alarm clocks, committed to appeasing all America's high stakeholders in the K-12 public educative process.

The fact that U.S. best students are not even in the middle of the international pack gets more attention than the fact that 31 percent of American K-12 public school students dropout; they do not get a high school education or a diploma, which was not a problem in past years but is required in today's high-tech information society. Students drop out because those who do not conform to society's norms, or do not test smart, are judged, labeled, and sidetracked with lowered expectations. Thus, most of the dropouts are failed by the K-12 system; their potential for educational and social development ceases in adolescence.

Since each year in the U.S., about 1.3 million students leave public school, that means about 7,000 public school students, often beginning in the 6th grade, drop out every school day. Of the about 49 million students in 99,000 to 100,000 public schools, about 2,000 high schools are the nation's lowest performing schools, producing nearly 50 percent of America's dropouts. Those schools are blighted by lack of money, human resources, and cultural opportunities and are located in poverty neighborhoods in every state in the union, but predominantly in the southern states.

A worse picture of our K-12 public education system was painted when the U.S. Army released its test results of 350,000 young men and women aged 17 to 24 who applied for admission between 2004 and 2009. The Pentagon reported that 75 percent of the 350,000 didn't qualify to take the U.S. Army's exam, Armed Services Vocational Aptitude Battery (ASVAB) because they were physically unfit, obese, had criminal records, or didn't graduate from high school. About 25 percent of those high school graduates (25 percent) failed ASVAB, for they could not answer questions about basic math, science, and reading, even simple questions such as "If 2 plus x equals 4, what is the value of x?" according to a report compiled by Christina Theokas of The Education Trust[330] in a 2010 release by Associated Press.

About 50 percent of the high school graduates who applied and passed ASVAB joined the Army. The military is worried about its pool of young people qualified for military service. Maybe that fact will lead to upgrading the poor K-12 public schools since those poor students, unlike the richer and better educated students, often have no choice but to seek employment in the armed services. Test scores on standardized tests are not an individual's true potential or of his or her cognitive, emotional, moral, and psychological intelligences. Even the United States Army has acknowledged the importance of the right-brain's intuition to survive against the odds in enemy territory, and most poor youths from poor neighborhoods already have street smarts.

To grow its own pool of recruits, the military could accept ASVAB's failures and high school dropouts by spending a year or two educating them toward military careers, thereby rescuing them from passing on poverty to another generation or from prison. For years, Jay Leno has been highlighting, on his TV "The Tonight Show," the ignorance of America's teenagers and high school graduates. It is not amusing. Cancer, as a metaphor, for the lack of education, which is all about communication, is apropos.

A 2012 Associated Press release appears to based on the above AP 2010 data: "The nation's security and economic prosperity are at risk if schools do not improve."[8] Condoleezza Rice and Joel Klein concurred, "The dominant power of the 21st century will depend on human capital... The failure to produce that capital will undermine American security."[8] "According to the panel [a 30-member committee organized by the Council on Foreign Relations], 75 percent of young adults do not qualify to serve in the military because they are physically unfit or have criminal records or inadequate levels of education... 30 percent of high school graduates do not do well enough on an aptitude test to serve."[8]

With "security" on most politicians' and military minds and educators' blaming the undereducated students/victims, Tim Callahan with the Professional Association of Georgia Educators (PAGE) representing 80,000 educators, said, in 2010, "It's surprising and shocking that we are still having students who are walking across the stage who really don't deserve to be [there] and haven't earned that right."[10] What is more shocking, but not surprising, is knowing but not acknowledging that the unequal and undemocratic K-12 public school system is to blame when students' whole brains are ignored. What is more shocking is the fact that the PAGE group and all other professional groups across America have not addressed the K-12 dropout rate and the number of students who require remediation after being accepted into college. Don't they want to know why and how to fix the problems? We don't have to be Einsteins to learn from experience that basic human development deficits account for differences in smart and not-so-smart students, that students can't learn when they're not respected as people – just numbers, and that the rich neighborhood-poor neighborhood tradition that funds public schools is undemocratic. Instead, fix the blame not the problem appears to be the solution: flourish or perish or survival of the fittest.

Who's accountable? Hourly workers on an assembly line let supervisors know when there's a problem, but educators who are blind to the future consequences of their actions are as immoral as bishops who just reassign their pedophile priests to another parish. Public schools could be havens in impoverished children's lives, if the curriculum were more reality- and humane-based. Those students who couldn't pass the military's ASVAB test "graduated" from a poor K-12 public school that didn't offer them an education they rightfully deserve. Revamp the K-12 poor schools' curricula and send their teachers to Finland for retraining where they probably speak excellent English!

America's 2012 Defense budget is estimated to be $0.9 trillion and our Education budget is $0.9 trillion, which is being cut across the board. The Pentagon's budgets for "permanent wars" have eaten into education's budget for years, so Pentagon funds would be better spent at home if ASVAB's failures and dropouts were accepted and re-educated, which the U.S. Army does well. We are losing the wars in the Middle East that were begun with the same assumptions that led to the

Bay of Pigs fiasco: a lack of understanding of cultures, especially subcultures, other than the white dominant culture. We are losing the peace at home due to not properly educating the nation's poor youths and ignoring the importance of character and people skills in all students. If it is unacceptable to the Pentagon to educate the rejects in the basic 3Rs and citizenship, then the reallocation of much of its funding to the identified schools that are underfunded will refine its current wasteful operations.

Our military leaders, politicians, and professional educators think they have identified the problem but they do not think "outside the box" in order to fix the problems that ensue from entrenched K-12 public education. Our military's agenda has extended its reach to world "security." Our K-12 educators' agenda has unwittingly dumbed down, turned off, and turned human beings into inhumane numbers. Our war hawks and politicians do not appear to have working prefrontal lobes when the consequences of their actions override their humanity. Our wars are fought by America's lower and middle class young men and women and Americans' taxpayer money is lavished around the world, not on America's infrastructure, not on American' education or health care. Then some political leaders insist: "Don't tax the wealthy!" and "Cut the Budget!" for America's public schools; fire teachers, police, firemen, and eliminate their pensions; phase out retirees' Social Security, Medicare, and Medicaid; cut unemployment insurance for the unemployed; and a loud "No!" to universal health care and creating jobs by spending on our aged infrastructure. Although, on June 28, 2012, the U.S. Supreme Court's 5-4 decision upheld a version of the Affordable Health Care Law, thanks to Chief Justice John Roberts, Jr. who showed the nation that he has a social conscience. The final result will probably benefit the insurance companies, not the American people.

Americans' secure future is under siege at home by home-grown leaders who are sanctioned by The Western Intellectual Tradition. Such leaders are reinforced by the U.S. Supreme Court's legitimizing corporate and billionaires' SuperPacs to spend megabucks on videos, TV ads, and passionate speakers' fees to sway voters to their political positions. As a result, it's not just one citizen, one vote anymore. Corporations and the wealthy have advanced beyond their successful lobbyists' access to politicians for years and have finally found a way to go direct to voters and remake America in their image when emotions and beliefs sway citizens' decisions that may not be in their best interest. The powers-that-be have already begun with the K-12 public school system whose elite students become elite Ivy league students, and elite leaders of Corporate America, and many career politicians depend upon corporate and financiers' money for re-election after re-election.

While academic excellence is a competitive game of numbers, which guarantees access to the best colleges and universities, our democratic society's K-12 public schools are designed for the few's leadership and the majority's followership. Followership originated in ancient history when kings ruled for the gods by the divine nature/right of authority to rule the illiterate masses. Our K-12 public schools have already undermined our U.S. Constitution's laws when The Western Intellectual Tradition is the antithesis of equality and freedom. Thanks to its legacy, we have a surplus of smart not wise leaders who are self-invested and perceive America as their personal cash cow.

David Books, a journalist, author, and TV personality, has written that people and leaders who choose the service road – moral economy jobs: teaching, nursing, social work, some lawyers – tend to be more humane and less prosperous that people who take the financial superhighway of Wall Street: finance, big businesses, medicine, law.[36] He also wrote, "I don't know if America has a leadership problem; it certainly has a followership problem... we have to relearn the art of following... To have good leaders you have to have good followers – able to recognize just authority, admire it, be grateful for it and emulate it... Vanity has more to do with rising distrust [of leaders and institutions] than anything else."[30] He also castigated Americans for "fervent devotion to equality, to the notion that all people are equal and deserve equal recognition and respect. It's hard in this frame of mind to define and celebrate greatness, to hold up others who are immeasurably superior to ourselves."[30]

A leader's superiority is measured by the left-brain's numbers, from IQ and sales to wealth and hierarchical status. Therefore, a leader who is effective and exercises authority meaningfully requires more than wealth, intellectual abilities, an MBA or a law degree, or CEOs' money making abilities. The true measure of a person, a leader, is a right-brainer's specialty: from intuition to observed humane behaviors in the world of family, social, and work relationships. That's where virtues are tried: we show ourselves as having evolved, or not evolved, from childhood's narcissistic "I" to "We" as compassionate partners, leaders, stewards, parents, friends, and team players.

The statement, "To have good leaders you have to have good followers," is not relevant in America, today, when more SuperPac money is spent on advertising to illuminate issues with emotional content that do not address or obfuscate the larger issues facing our nation. Those tactics require reform, not better rubberstamp followers, and informed, integrative thinking voters. Good leaders get to be better leaders when they can learn from those citizens who behave like leaders, just as good teachers also learn from their students who behave like good teachers.

As a consequence of our K-12 half-brained public educational system, too many of our corporate and political leaders cannot manage their own passions, greed, and narcissism so they're not even management material. And we're supposed to look up to them? The media are controlled by financial elites, but good leaders are not, so we cannot expect unbiased news or commentary. When you read, hear, and experience how grateful ordinary Americans should be for having no leadership problems, just followers who are envious, vanity-driven, and/or too stupid to appreciate their leaders' superiority – then you know that we are on the brink of not living in a UNITED States of America any more or in a democratic republic either.

In a democracy, many people believe, as I do, that all people deserve recognition and respect just for being human beings, for the dignity of life, not for what they become in one aspect – the numbers game – of their whole selves. All people, though, are responsible for what they do with their talents and lives, to educate themselves, despite the odds and the residue of hierarchies' divine nature/right of authority, to be both leaders and followers, for there is still personal power for the owning in every position or condition in America.[250]

Otherwise we collude in our devolution by remaining fixed, unchanging selves in a world where change is the only constant. If you're inclined to place a so-called superior leader on a pedestal, climb up on the pedestal yourself and join him or her. It's dangerous and lonely at the top without another human being – not a "yes" man or woman – to hear oneself think and to reflect upon the man-made lines separating leadership from followership and followership from leadership. We experience that leadership or followership is situational under circumstances when the two roles reverse and followers become leaders and leaders become followers.

Leadership and followership are the yin and yang of leaders' power-over or power-with the people. Autocratic leaders have system power but they desire applause or the full consent of followers to rule or else. In a democracy, people have the personal power to grant or refuse their consent to be led. Revolutions, Civil Wars, uprisings in the Middle East, our current political divide, and the darkened "halo effect" of our financial leaders are primarily about the rigid positions of power-over people: "I lead for me and the like-minded who know what's best for America and for you: "Pull yourself up by your own bootstraps, as I did. Get a job!" versus power-with the people: "We lead America in America's interest and for the greater good of all people, not just the few, toward a common task."

Since the origins of the foundational principles upon which Western institutions and organizations were built are also based in the Old and New Testaments of the Holy Bible, it is intriguing to examine beliefs that hold sway over our minds and wills in the 21st century. In Biblical contexts, kings ruled for God and the masses were subservient. "All We Like Sheep..." – In Isaiah 53:6, in the King James version of the Bible, human beings were compared to sheep. The church's flock (congregation) were expected to be content with their lot on Earth and to look forward to Heaven: "Or what's a heaven for?"[40] "The Lord is my shepherd; I shall not want," in the 23rd Psalm, King James Bible, is another rationale that people/sheep need God for his everlasting fulfillment. Sheep/people who stray from their shepherd/king, evoke God's wrath. If anyone went his/her own way, then God's wrath had to be appeased by all, by more gifts, sacrifices, and services. Apparently, humans have a problem with other humans as leaders, so the divine nature/right of authority was designed to give exalted status to those who ruled: the kings, emperors, popes, and bishops. We learn from the Sumerian tablets that, in the physical absence of the gods or God, kings and emperors evolved to rule for themselves, not for God or for their followers. God's wrath was eventually interpreted as Nature's natural events, from floods to earthquakes, or man-caused catastrophes.

The Bible's metaphorical passage – "All we like sheep have gone astray; we have turned everyone to his own way; and the Lord hath laid on him the iniquity of us all," Isaiah 53:6, was interpreted by Margaret Rioch from a Tavistock-Washington School of Psychiatry perspective of studies of group relations, leaders-followers, and the nature of authority. While admitting that the Biblical simile, humans as sheep, is not complimentary when applied to human beings, she wrote, "the wish, and sometimes the need for a leader is so strong that it is almost always possible for one of the sheep to play the role of shepherd of the flock... who will guide them into green and safe pastures."[283] However, "underneath the cloak is one of the sheep, and not, alas, a member of a more intelligent and more far-seeing species."[283] She asserted that "there seems to be a tendency in human beings, which becomes aggravated when they are isolated or faced with unfamiliar situations, to find the exercise of their own powers of mind and will extremely burdensome...we are easy game for any teacher or leader who wants to take us over."[283] We need to understand that "Our followership consists of a kind of hypnosis, of giving over our will to the other and losing thereby that terrible burden we carry so reluctantly: responsibility for our own acts,"[283] but that helpless dependency generates resentment.

Despite Tavistock conferences being marketed as learning opportunities/situations in a nontraditional educational manner but in an educational setting, participants' prior experiences and assumptions associate learning with school and the military, so many participants behave like sheep. When they "get it," their freedom to remove their "mind-forg'd manacles," they assert their power to change. Then they realize "A group cannot function so long as each one insists upon her own autonomy"[283] and that "Human beings are never more fulfilled than when they are united to a whole...total union...that makes the experience in a working group committed to a common task so fulfilling."[283]

Dissatisfaction results when people do not find ways to use their talents or feel they are being misled by their leaders. Rioch writes, "Leader is a word that implies a relationship... The interrelationships of followers and leaders are among the most significant of human relationships... The teacher-student relationship is at the heart of the educational process... the word educate comes from the Latin *educere*, meaning to lead out, which suggests that this process has traditionally had something very important to do with leadership and followership,"[283] especially in Christianity. Essentially, "in the field of education... the teacher has as her function the training of future leaders... [if] only in their own families; or they may become leaders of nations. In either case the problem of putting one's power in the service of the group task remains essentially the same"[283] for leaders.

When a leader gets off task and into his or her own self-interests, the leadership-followership relationship contract is broken, so followers may behave as their leaders do, such as in communist countries, bureaucracies, corporations, and government agencies where petty power is exercised at the bottom tier of hierarchical institutions and organizations. We learn from history about the abuses of power and from Lord Acton, historian and moralist. He wrote in a letter to Bishop Mandel Creighton: "Power tends to corrupt, and absolute power corrupts absolutely. Great men are almost always bad men."[3] Examples are Roman emperors who succeeded Constantine; they lived like gods. When Constantine became a Christian, he invoked a divinely inspired right to rule for an omnipotent God.

What cannot be denied or proven today, by left-brain methodologies, is "the existence of a universal creative force – God – the absolute All or Oneness of all energy and matter."[218] "We did not come from nowhere. We are embedded in a very deep but biological and cosmological history."[19] A God exists in the minds, hearts, and souls of most of Americans, despite the 4th century AD redefinitions of God to suit ancient monarchies' claim of the divine nature/right of apostolic succession through Jesus Christ. Emperor Constantine and the Church officials created an everlasting Christian church – institution – with inalienable tenets, their exalted status, and the power to control men, women, and children's passions and souls.

Excommunicating women from Church leadership and eventually leadership in Western institutions and organizations appears to hark back to the ancients who learned that women do not always follow men's rules, so they were punished by depriving them of equality and leadership. Eve didn't abide by God's rules in the Garden of Eden, so

Adam was punished too, as original sinners, because he didn't control her actions. Mary Magdalene's vision of Jesus Christ after his crucifixion conflicted with Peter's proclaimed physical encounter with Christ. Thus, it seems that women and their passions, intuitions, and virtues had to be exorcised in order to create a hybrid of Jesus Christ's teachings as the path to Heaven with obey-or-else doctrines to inculcate fear of God's wrath and his everlasting hellfire. Christianity's founders knew that people's passion overrides their reason, so education was limited to the Bible, including today in extremist fundamentalist religions. If ordinary mortals could be intimidated, coerced, and threatened by the uneducated cognitive and emotional minds, then the use of sin, fear, shame, and anger would enhance the church's and clergy's power. From the foregoing my question becomes not Who's in Charge? but "Who's Taking Charge in God's Name in His Invisible Presence?

Recall that the three ages of Sumerian civilization is a progression of leadership: (1) "'The gods rule through me'; (2) 'I rule for the gods'; and (3) 'I rule'!"[331] Is God's physical absence the rationale for some ego-driven people to re-make themselves as Earthly gods, such as CEOs, megamillionaires and billionaires? Certainly many believe they are very important people and seek VIP perks. Redefining a corporation as people is not godly enough. If kings, emperors, dictators, popes, bishops, preachers, CEOs, or the super rich act like superior gods, talk like condescending gods, make rules like narcissistic gods, live like hedonistic gods, and behave as if the rest of us are followers or serfs, then they have transitioned to being self-centered gods who love only themselves and their power: "I rule!"

It appears that the Sumerian experience of rulers was repeated in the Roman Church and is being repeated today in the world, including the United States of America where our democracy's survival is in the hands of those dynasties and financiers who may not invoke the divine nature/right of authority, but they do have the financial authority to cripple and control our nation and its citizens. If you think secrets cannot be kept from the population, think of the Manhattan Project that developed the atom bomb in the 1940s. One hundred and thirty thousand people worked on the project but only the tip of the pyramid knew what the purpose of the project was. For example, in banking, we customers hand over our money to a teller who is subservient to a manager, who is responsible to a regional manager, who is accountable to a national managers on up the ladder to the CEO. Every hierarchical layer below the top has a job description and gets just enough information to do the job with a warm fuzzy mission that does not include the real agenda. Only the CEOs – unless they, too, have a layer above them! – know the real purpose or agenda of the bank.

Today's institutions and organizations are similarly run. When we think of the fact that financiers control the oil, food, health care, and education industries and the fact that economic hit men have plunged us into debt, we realize, with partisan politics, we have little financial clout left to lean forward into the future. We are not improving our dependence upon Mid East oil or improving our diet when subsidized oil and food are cheaper and keeping the money flowing into America's corporations. We cannot improve our health when prevention is an expensive alternative to disease-care Medicare and Medicaid. We do not improve our unequally financed K-12 public school systems when neighborhoods' real estate taxes determine the quality of their schools. The financial elites are ensuring that their K-12 public, charter, and private school students will be educated to be leaders without a heart, to follow the money, and to perpetuate the status quo's inequality across the board.

Wisdom, empathy, altruism (except as tax shelters), and compassion are missing in our Earthly gods, but wealth and power have not exorcised their felt ego and right-brain deficits that require followers' approval, applause, and appreciation of their superiority to assuage their egos. With disapproval of their actions, they project their sins onto us: vanity, envy. Without sin, guilt, shame, or fear to exercise, what would happen to such Earthly gods' power if our right-brain's intelligence and virtues were legitimized and formally educated as the left-brain's partner?

Currently, many leaders have the wealth or the backing of wealthy donors to run for political offices. Others in the corporate world have reputations earned in boom times, so many are overconfident of their financial acumen; their "halo effect" may be an illusion; often no better than luck at a casino.[172] A new American Dream could be that enlightened voters have the choice, within a moral context and in harmony with Mother Nature, to learn and figure out things for themselves – without all that expensive campaigning – and to choose a leader for stewardship. Then, we may conclude, like Robert Browning's Pippa, that God's in his Heaven – All's right with the world![41]

Our Founding Fathers were worried that the new United States of America would not survive if church and state were one, if one religion dominated other religions and the nation, if a powerful military rivaled civilian government, but they did not envision a nation of Earthly gods – aided and abetted by our military industrial complex, the U.S. Supreme Court, and our ideological-oriented, political representatives – to rival government's financial ability to sustain America's promise to "We the People." In 2012, we wonder whether our nation will survive if our country is run by so-called ultraconservatives: those wealthy corporations and individuals, who want liberalism for themselves, have the legal right to "buy" votes via the media by seducing voters' fears and beliefs to control America for their own self-interests.

Since the 1980s our nation has drifted off course as our U.S. Constitutional Four Freedoms: freedom from fear and want and freedom of speech and religion have been marginalized in favor of capitalism's free enterprise and big businesses, the military's use of fear of more terrorists' strikes, religious fundamentalists' fear of God's wrath and of women's human rights, and white supremacists' view that we are becoming a non-white nation. America's democratic system of elections used to be above reproach until we experienced the U.S. Supreme Court's 5-4 partisan decision in the 2000 presidential election for George W. Bush against Al Gore, but with the proviso that the decision was not a precedent. Then the Supreme Court's legitimized what morphed into SuperPacs. That ruling empowered wealthy individuals, unknown and known, to influence democratic elections toward their imperial causes: America in the hands of Earthly financial gods! A formally and informally educated citizenship will vote, in their own best interests, for an America for the majority, not the few.

With America's Earthly gods in charge, there would be an imperial Gordian Knot of corporate and financial power and religions' dogma that would diminish our middle class, increase our poorer class, and decrease women's rights. America is already experiencing the effects; it began with K-12 public education's budget cuts and teacher layoffs, then unemployment, phased out social programs, no universal health care like other civilized nations. Knots happen when some people value money more than people, except themselves and their families, not their country.

Even as a metaphor, the Gordian Knot is not a challenge. Challenges keep us happily working to solve problems, but the Gordian Knot is a metaphor for America's economic and moral knots when we are experiencing the results of an undeclared war on our democracy as we knew it, as manifested by the Earthly gods' capitalism and by anti-intellectualism. The Gordian Knot is about the Earthly financial gods, and their terrorist strikes against America's Constitutional Four Freedoms. The pen is mightier than Alexander the Great's sword that allegedly severed the Gordian Knot by cheating with one clean cut instead of finding and untying the Knot's ends. Evidently, the Earthly gods don't play by the Golden Rule or religions' Ten Commandments. The Earthly gods make their own Gold Rule, just as they have for thousands of years.

"The 'imperial presidency' malarkey that was invented to save Ronald Reagan's neck in Iran-Contra and that played as high art throughout the career of Richard Cheney is a radical departure from previous views of presidential power and should be taught and understood that way."[215] "The good news is we don't need a radical new vision... We just need a 'small c' conservative return to our constitutional roots, a course correction... And it's fixable."[215] Our political divisiveness is fixable; our K-12 public education problems are fixable. Our moral and ethical issues, rampant crime, violence, addictions, diseases, and the widening gap between the have-nots and the have-mores are fixable through K-12 whole-brained education for children and adults and so is cancer's communication incompetency problem. All are symptoms of deeper problems that need attention. But our financial problems are not fixable today because those who have the financial clout have been in charge of making the rules, so our Cancerian birthday nation is sick.

In these harsh ongoing Recession times, ordinary American families' net worth fell to 1990s levels, losing about 40 percent of their assets, while "the top 10 percent of households earned an average of $349,000 in 2010. The average net worth of the same families was $2.9 million."[9]

For the past thirty years or more, America has had a leadership problem, with intervening exceptions. Without a wisdom perspective, our nation's politicians, corporate leaders, and financial elites are responsible for America's 1929-1939 Great Depression. They are also responsible for business practices that occurred before 2007, when the economic crisis began and took hold in 2008, and are responsible for the ongoing Great Recession in 2012:

a) since the 1980s, corporate lobbyists' efforts succeeded in achieving deregulation of the safety nets instituted after the 1930's Great Depression, which set the stage for the economic bubble to rise; the real estate market grew and housing prices rose to new highs; people invested in houses to rent as investments or bought second homes;

b) after 9/11/01, our hawkish political leaders' ideology and deception, with an emphasis on "permanent war," led America to wars in the Middle East, earned us more enemies, and a huge budget deficit after their inheriting a balanced budget in 2000;

c) our financial and corporate leaders chased higher and higher profits, either by replacing American jobs with cheaper workers overseas or by inventing near worthless paper derivatives/products and by a mortgage frenzy: enticed homeowners to re-mortgage or buy homes they could not afford, fudging their incomes. Lost jobs meant banks foreclosed on people's homes without legal documents; new businesses arose to provide them with false documents. The economic had bubble burst, spiraling America into a Great Recession;

d) the majority of our U.S. Supreme Court justices gave corporations some people rights, or paved ways for SuperPacs to anonymously fund, then advertise to sway human emotions and beliefs toward views in the interests of America's corporations and the wealthy; and

e) some politicians' have intractable stances on balancing the budget – not by cutting corporate welfare or raising taxes on rich and wealthy Americans commensurate with hourly wage earners and salaried citizens' taxes: those hit the worst by the Recession – by cutting government budgets for State governments, education, and social services, no investments in infrastructure and the desire to eliminate the rest of the safety nets: Social Security, Medicare, Medicaid, pensions, unemployment insurance, and no universal health insurance, as in other modern nations.

Nevertheless, many Americans live active and rewarding lives behind the masked self-image that resulted from disowning their whole selves in the K-12 educative process. Since self-image is an imitation or a representation of an authentic self, it is the responsibility of each individual to earn a real self or positive self-esteem in the human development process. Since "no man is an island," there is no self-esteem without other-esteem. When adults stop and listen to their hearts, most can stifle the need for more and more money and material things and/or power-over people that hides the emptiness and loneliness of a false self-image. Some people, though, inflate their self-image by listening to their passions, ideologies, beliefs, or unresolved early childhood issues and play them out on the nation's population and the world's stage, reflecting their hungry egos. There appear to be more visible American institutional leaders and politicians with self-images and hungry egos today than leaders and politicians with integrated heads and hearts who esteem themselves and others and are working for America and Americans.

An inequality flaw in America's K-12 public education system, governed primarily by social conditions and economic resources, is society's emphasis upon and use of test scores – the numbers game – to separate "winners" from "losers." Since public education was designed to mold children's behavior, those labeled "losers" or "underachievers" or "misfits" receive minimal educational development in most public schools. Adults and peers who criticize our actions and reactions to our inner and outer environments influence our self-image-making. Stunting children's potential development creates a vicious cycle of negative self-image, anti-social behaviors, bullying, and passing on their learned negative experiences, helplessness, or hopelessness to those whose lives they touch.

Failing and labeling students in the K-12 public education system creates a horde of unproductive, uneducated citizens who exist by their wits or use/sell illegal drugs, which is the only cash cow available to them, thanks to our expensive War on Drugs. Instead of prevention, the bureaucratic response is more prisons to the point that America has more inmates, per capita, than the rest of the world and the need for more social services. Public education's obsession with daily or weekly tests indicates what has yet to be learned; it is not a cumulative, valid statistic of a student's human intelligence or potential. A final test at term's end would indicate the depth of a student's long-term learning and reasoning abilities. In effect, we are growing more leaders motivated to support capitalism's free enterprise system that fulfilled their personal economic goals while growing more and more followers with less access to an equal K-12 public education or to equal opportunities or to the safety nets necessitated by America's Great Depression of the 1930s.

America's future is in educating students' full intelligence to be citizens who desire to grow as persons and as stewards of democracy; otherwise "We the people" will forfeit the legacy of our Founding Fathers in 1776: the first country to deviate from being ruled by the divine nature/right of authority, except for those Scandinavian countries who have a partnership system versus the prevalent domination system of leadership.[9] Unfortunately, when our Founders designed America, they retained the old hierarchical institutional and organizational formats that reinforce power in the hands of the few, for that's what they knew.

Cancer is statistically the #2 killer of people in the U.S., and is nearly tied with heart disease, #1. Cancer as a metaphor is apropos today for Americans' lack of communication with each other as morals, ethics, and values have changed toward making more money, consuming more of our resources, and leaving too many uneducated people behind.

I became aware in the early 1990s of those who had to exist by their wits. I was parking my car in New Haven, Connecticut, near Yale University, when a boy about 14, during public school hours, started motioning to me to turn the wheels to get closer to the curb. When I got out of the car, I scooped up the change I had for paying road tolls and gave him a handful of coins. "That's not enough!" he said. "That's what I have for you!" I said. "I don't like to see people get hurt!" he said. "Can you tell me more about that?" I responded. He saw that I wasn't intimidated by his threat, so he just turned away and said, "I don't like to see people get hurt." I believed him. He was hurt by his life and by his lack of a good education. He's an example and one of the reasons why all students deserve an equal, whole-brained education.

Our Federal educators requested and received a state of education report in 1938. They were advised by Daniel Prescott's report and transmittal letter that attention must be paid to the educating the head and the heart or the freedom to teach and to learn would disappear. Attention was paid to building big public education complexes; no attention was paid to the curriculum or the students, especially poor schools and poor students. The Western Intellectual Tradition has continued to diminish children's and adults' communicative abilities and their natural intellectual and humane potential. Today, we have more Hell in America as Heaven on Earth eludes the majority of Americans. The antidote: K-12 Smart and Wise: equal, whole-brained public education for all.

"Know the difference!" is a theme that has propelled me since I taught 7th grade English in public school and was teaching literature (*Animal Farm, Diary of Anne Frank*, for example), basic theme writing, and grammar. "It's me!" everyone says in response to "Who's there?" "It is I!" is correct English grammar but deemed to be an affectation. "It's me!" is commonly used and accepted. But when Frank Luntz writes about *Words That Work*: it's not what you say but what you hear, we realize that the deliberate use of words and language to connect emotions and thought are being used to seduce our fears, beliefs and/or ideology, directing our decisions to buy, vote, or believe the advertised message. Luntz has helped clients to sell products and has turned public opinion for and against political candidates just by knowing what words trigger the emotions or memories. When Big Pharma advertised its drugs as prevention and wellness, not treatment, the public was snookered. Politicians who wanted to diminish Estate Taxes called them Death Taxes instead, and got their wish.[211] The financier-dominated health care debates were deflected by focusing upon death panels. That's just a few of the ways we have to be alert to being taken over, not by aliens, but by those who want us to be their followers.

The theme, know the difference, also motivated me to seek self- and higher-education degrees in human development (psychology, physiology, sociology, and some anthropology) and by teaching-learning, facilitating, and mentoring master's and doctoral students in their theses and dissertations. In addition, for fifty years I have had my own laboratory at home for experiencing my civil engineer husband's left-brain, my right-brain, and our two children's evolving brains. I have personally and professionally experienced left-brainers' worldviews, have felt the gamut of emotions, and have sought to integrate my left- and right-brains. I nurtured our children's brains by demonstrating to them the two measurable aspects of the left- and right-brains that are logically (bottom-line) and metaphorically (the big picture) differentiated in *Mindex*.[6] Knowing about brain difference allowed us to better communicate as a family. However, inherited beliefs about gender and the superiority of the left-brain and the inferiority of the right-brain are difficult to change. So were my early childhood experiences with an aunt-by-marriage who, I felt as a child, "picked on me" until I learned her story and became very fond of her. Society dictated in those days that a woman could not have a career she loved, be married to a man she loved, and have children too. That's why we used to have so many so-called New England spinsters as teachers.

Early childhood experiences are embedded in the right-brain; awareness of our inner demons may soften their impact. Just like vulnerable children in threatening testing environments whose left-brains downshift into the fight or flight syndrome, when I am criticized too much by a significant other, my right-brain's hurt feelings collide with my left-brain's words. Sometimes I respond automatically with "I believe you believe that" when I can't remember the words to frame a reasoned argument, so I count 1-2-3+ until my left-brain kicks in. Then I hear, "How come you can write, but can't talk?" Knowing the lasting impact of negative criticism, I cringe at adults' belittling of developing children. Their human potential is at risk of being undermined by a negative self-image and/or negative self-esteem. Similarly, teachers and adults who unconditionally accept and love children create an optimum learning environment. Children learn best from those they respect, admire, or love. Since we do not live in an ideal world where people have been treated and treat others with unconditional love or, at the least, with respect, we do have the personal power to weigh the pros and cons of our demons or relationships from our two sources: memory and experience.

Daniel Kahneman's distinction between the remembering self and the experiencing self is a whole-brained view of relationships and situations. Positive and negative memories are isolated episodes of the remembering self. "A memory that neglects duration will not serve our preference for long pleasure and short pains... A divorce is like a symphony with a screeching sound at the end – the fact that it ended badly does not mean it was all bad."[172] Breaking the habits within an unhealthy relationship takes effort since habits are neural shortcuts, so rewiring one's brain to be a more compassionate partner who is mindful of the other's inheritance, hurts, and desires is a way to renew a relationship and to create more positive experiences.

To change from "I" to "we" in a relationship requires the integration of the right-brain's attributes for the sake of the relationship as well as for the health of I-oriented people. The importance of others in our lives, of mutually rewarding relationships, is overlooked by America's "me-ism" people who are self-absorbed and neglect others. The conversations of nearly 600 men were taped by Dr. Larry Scherwitz of Baylor University in 1983. One-third of the men had heart problems. He counted the number of times the men used first-person pronouns – I, me, mine. He found that the highest users of those first-person pronouns were most likely to have heart disease.[284]

Relationship people are more "we" oriented. Dr. Ackerman's home schooling helped heal her 74 year old husband's left-brain stroke with caring gestures, pantomime, facial expressions, humor, play, empathy, and tons of affection to the point that he rewired his brain, through effort, and was able to talk and write books again. "The brain changes with experience throughout our lives; it's in loving relationships of all sorts – partners, children, close friends – that brain and body really thrive."[2] "Love is the best school, but the tuition is high and the homework can be painful."[2] Evidently, the areas of the brain that register physical pain – dorsal anterior cingulate cortex – are activated when a person feels rejected socially or is spurned or betrayed by a lover or family member. "But a loving touch is enough to change everything...If you're in a healthy relationship, holding your partner's hand is enough to subdue your blood pressure, ease your response to stress, improve your health and soften physical pain."[2] Loving human touch is magical and needed for babies to survive and for children to thrive.

Forgetfulness also helps us to survive. The loss of memory, the creation of new memories, and imperfect memory are evolutionary adaptations: to store critical information and to shed worthless data or information that impairs a fragile ego. Unfortunately, memory selectivity often works against us when we have memories we'd rather forget, but those memories are opportunities to learn to make a difference in our lives. Sometimes our memories are incorrect or incomplete, which means our own and others' lives may be affected by our distortions. However, there is enough data available about the hemispheres today so that we may, with effort, be in charge of who we are and want to be and how we want to remember and be remembered.

We can also create false memories. Neuroscientists' discovery of the plasticity of the human brain means our brains change throughout our lives. Its flexibility is essential to memory and learning. Most of us are familiar with the term, "Neurons that fire together wire together," which means the intensity of the activity between the brain's neurons due to an experienced event means the memory will be more robust. "That is one reason why emotionally charged memories frequently percolate to consciousness in vivid detail."[71] Where were you when you first heard of the 9/11/01 terrorist attacks in America? That was an emotional event accompanied by intense neural activity, but it may not be perfectly imprinted because memories may be easily altered. Deprogramming cult participants is one way memory may be changed or restored. An acquaintance is a psychic who works with a therapist not to erase but to restore clients' memories lost through physical or emotional traumas.

People's negative memories and experiences, especially those issues unresolved from early childhood, are bases of post-traumatic stress disorders, PTSD, when they are confronted with trauma in the present that triggers their past, unresolved negative experiences. Thousands of PTSD cases have been documented by the armed services in veterans, male and female, who served in Iraq and Afghanistan. In previous wars, those who suffered such mental breakdowns were deemed to have weak characters. The number of veterans afflicted with PTSD attests to the fact that there's something missing in our society's approach to raising and teaching children and adults.

A war is the inevitable outcome of people and nations using wars as an attempt to resolve, repair, or heal their own personal issues or achieve goals, often rooted in early childhood. The walking wounded, with awareness of their inner computer chip's software, have alternatives available to them other than feuds and wars when they have access to their two hemispheres' intelligences. The unaware seek targets to defuse their anger, seek refuge in careers or causes that fit their mindsets, or seek ways to prove "I'm better than you are!"

George Orwell's *Animal Farm* teaches us metaphorically that some people (he substituted pigs for people) believe and practice they are more equal [249] and entitled to a larger piece of the universal pie than others. Inequality is part of our democracy and of communist countries more blatantly. It is hearsay when we ban a book that we have not read or do not understand because someone says it does not affirm the Torah, Bible, Koran, or teaches communism, socialism, or is labeled by the status quo as pseudoscientific. Believing in hearsay, even from people we admire or agree with, is easier than the trouble of thinking for ourselves. We freely elect unthinking people to represent us without examining their hidden agendas or ideologies that are in plain sight, if we understand ourselves and take the time to understand others' motivations, assumptions, biases, and good or ill intentions We expect the near impossible or hope that their uncommon sense will override and take charge of their sense of humanity when they attain positions of power. However, many of us expect our politicians to make wise decisions by rubber-stamping ours. Thus, we don't see things are they are, but as we are.

Since 7th century BC, KNOW THYSELF has been etched into the walls of the Temple of Apollo, Delphi, Greece. Yet, we human beings prefer to live life instead of thinking about it. Many of us, especially the left-brainers who want black and white answers, believe we are in control of what we think, feel, say, and do. But, neuroscientists, including those who have worked with split-brain patients – men and women who had their two hemispheres divided by surgery on the corpus collosum – have unraveled the basics of how the hemispheres of the brain develop independently with opposite worldviews and processes. The left- and right-brains develop in harmony when equally relied upon. When they are not, a kind of battle goes on in our brains which the left-brain wins since Western culture educated the left- not the right-brain, and the right-brain may not be informally educated in many families since the 1960s.

"Education largely determines the direction of our self-education, which is the most active element in our development and in more frequent use socially than elements of biological [heritage] origin."[98] Self-education and self-knowledge are in our own and our parents' hands today or are rarely explored. With emotional intelligence, people are not so vulnerable to toxic charismatic leaders, whether they be corporate, educational, religious, or political. Whole-brained Americans are less consumer-driven – not inclined to buy outside-self trappings to bolster felt ego deficits and lack of self- and other-esteem – or to buy into society's definition of success: wealth. For the millions of do-it-yourselfers, self-education is usually relegated to Self-Help books and How-To Manuals. Learning from mentors' failures and successes on-the-job or in-the-field, is the experiential alternative to our inherited leadership-followership tradition from the ancient past that continues to infect democratic institutions and organizations.

Our ongoing warring, violent, and divisive American society is the visible impact of the K-12 public education system's not honoring and teaching the scientific brain research of past decades, not appreciating and evoking the innate talents hidden within each child, graduating them with less than the basics of math, science, and reading, not teaching how to think or integrate disparate data, and throwing its rejects into the streets. We have not addressed, in our K-12 public school system, what we know from psychology and history that people's self-image governs their actions until they graduate to self- and other-esteem: "A split within is illness, a split without is war... What we need to learn is to recognize and to solve our inner conflicts so we feel secure enough to move 'towards' another human being toward humanity"[163] in peace and love.

Recall that Konrad Lorenz studied hatched ducklings who followed him around and curled up around his boots as "mother figure" at night. When they grew up they wouldn't court a mate of their own species.

He concluded, the imprint of the mother also transferred to the imprint for a mate."[71] Similarly, an American who has not emancipated self from society's conditioning and numbers that are intentionally inculcated by K-12 public education systems – "does not strive to make himself any different from the patterns impressed upon him from the outset. In this way society comes to be made up of persons increasingly alike in their ways, behavior, and aims."[98] Thus, the K-12 public education system is in charge of our attitudes toward ourselves and our worth, our self-image, until we foster our own integrated educational redevelopment that is not confined to society's definition of success: the numbers!

Since most people feel unified and in charge of what they think, feel, say, and do, they are unaware of their brains' complexity and its options. "Harvard researchers... claim that the brain has specific knowledge systems (modules) for animate and inanimate categories that have distinct neural mechanisms."[116] Thus, "the brain is not an all-purpose computing device, but a device made up of an enormous number of serially wired specialty circuits, all running in parallel and distributed across the brain to make those better decisions... there is no hierarchy among the modules... it is a free-for-all, self-organizing system."[116] "Below our level of awareness is the very busy nonconscious [unconscious] brain hard at work."[116]

The brain modules that encompass all of one's inheritances, life experiences (personal, social, and professional) and beliefs are powerful forces that constrain the brain, "but also reveal that it is the interaction of the two layers of brain [left and right] and mind [conscious and unconscious or nonconscious] that provides our conscious reality...to yield the human condition."[116] As a result, "We no longer think of the brain as being organized into two conscious systems at all but into multiple dynamic mental systems."[116]

But, "why do we feel so unified and in control?"[116] We believe we have a seamless self so we think we are in charge of us. "We have discovered something in the left brain, another module that takes all the input into the brain and builds the narrative... the interpreter module."[116] "Once we understand that the left-brain interpreter process is driven to seek explanations or causes for events, we can see it at work in all sorts of situations."[116] However, the left-brainer's story is only as good as the interpretation of the input. The right-brain may signal its disagreement with the left-brain through its body language: a smile that doesn't fit the story's content, for example.

Now we know that our unconscious mind is often in charge of our communications. The left-brain confabulates and contorts the self to look and feel good to correlate with what the unconscious mind thinks, feels, says, and does on its own. If we examine our intentions, for example, we may learn that we are interested in being in charge of another human being, such as a child, spouse, partner, women's rights, or to have power over others rather than share power with them. The need to have power over or control others, to be in charge of them in a sense, reflects our low level of self- and other-esteem and low level of human consciousness, which includes heart consciousness.

Now we know that the left-brain-mind's interpreter can constrain the whole brain-mind's array of modules when it overemphasizes one module at the expense of moderation or balance.[116] The complexity of the human brain's hemispheres is mind boggling and there's more to know. A dangerous result of our K-12 left-brained educational system is innocent, developing children's inner worlds are not acknowledged, nor are their life circumstances, since they are treated as numbers ready to absorb the ABCs and 123s without attention to their uniqueness. "When we think about the influence of early [childhood] experience on adult life, we need to consider our human capacity for intervention."[124] How is it possible for human being to heal and to change?

The body and brain store old emotions, feelings, sadness and abuse from childhood, as emotions not words. We heal – the word derives from the Anglo-Saxon word healen or wholeness – when emotions are acknowledged and then released. Many children need more than squishy toys that self-soothe themselves to work off their anger and fears so they may be prepared for the threatening tests of their self-image. True educators do not teach the 3Rs only and impart knowledge. "They teach us to pull out hidden emotions, to develop a keener awareness of how our body and mind respond to the world."[290] That necessary educational process is missing in our K-12 public educational systems and in most home situations, so human beings' false self-images run their lives instead of authentic ones. "Wholeness is impossible, since the deeper reality of our life remains hidden,"[290] until brought into the light –

consciousness — and we combine our hemispheric lenses through which we view the world: purple! "The human capacity for change means that we can't figure out what it is to be human just by looking at the way we are now. We need instead to peer forward into the vast ramifying space of human possibilities."[124]

The foundations of Western civilization and The Western Intellectual Tradition rely excessively on the left hemisphere of the human brain. Now we learn from Iain McGilchrist that "If a culture were ever to rely excessively on one take alone [left hemisphere or right hemisphere], there would sooner or later need to be a correction."[224] Also, it's apparent that when a culture relies excessively on left-brained "approved" knowledge and practices only – when new knowledge and new ways of teaching-learning-being exist – a correction needs to occur for Americans to be smart and wise. Instead, Dr. McGilchrist says, "The left hemisphere ever optimistic, is like a sleepwalker whistling a happy tune as it ambles toward the abyss. Let's wake up before we free-fall into the void."[224]

Powerful political forces have thwarted any attempts to change K-12 public education in any meaningful way. It's as if America's public education elites refuse to lean forward into the 21st century and prefer to lean backwards toward the Dark Ages. Russian Count Leo Tolstoy, 1828-1910, author of *War and Peace* and *Anna Karenina*, who influenced Mahatma Gandhi and Martin Luther King with his non-violence and Christian morals and ethics, articulated the age-old human problem: Those in charge cannot admit that what is woven into the fabric of their lives and proudly taught to others is wrong. "I know that most (men and women), including those at ease with problems of the greatest complexity, can seldom accept even the simplest and most obvious truths if it be such as would oblige them to admit the falsity of conclusions which they have delighted in explaining to colleagues, which they have proudly taught to others, and which they have woven, thread by thread into the fabric of their lives."[319]

In addition, left-brainers constitute the powers-that-be in our nation, and rigid left-brainers are locked into their own point of view. With an attitude that students just have to learn the basics, No Child Left Behind, with an emphasis upon costly testing, made more sense to the policy-makers than upon how the test could be used: NCLB has spawned teaching to the test, shallow learning, decreased testing results, increased dropouts from high school, school shut-downs, and an increased prison population. It costs taxpayers nearly $64,000 a year to incarcerate a youth, it only costs roughly $8,500 a year to educate a child.[319] It may cost more to educate and prepare K-12 students to be fully intelligent, healthy, and loving human beings instead of labeling and ousting them onto the streets. Spending more on students now makes more sense than building more prisons and warehousing them later. Enlightened U.S. taxpayers' voices would be saner than those politicians and educators who are resisting changing bureaucracy's fiefdoms to upgrade our country to equal other modern countries who spend more money on its citizens' education, health, and well-being than on wars.

One of the committee's studying our nation's K-12 education issues has come up with its recommendations. The panel is led by former Secretary of State Condoleezza Rice and Joel I. Klein, a former chancellor of New York City's school systems. Of the three main recommendations, all are problematic: 1) "Common Core standards should be adopted and expanded to include science, technology, and foreign languages." 2) "Students, especially those in poor schools, should have more choices in where they go to school." 3) "Governors, working with the federal government, should develop a national security readiness audit, to judge whether schools are meeting targets."[8] Except in the best public schools, the real basics, the 3Rs, are needed to be emphasized before expanding the curriculum. For poor children to have more choices where they go to school is a good idea, if they are literate in the basics. Choices are meaningless for poor children in poor schools who need re-education to make up for their experience of their past educational and impoverished histories.

"Common core standards" implies that the status quo's curriculum will be unchanged. "A national security readiness audit" is reminiscent of color-coded terrorist threat days after 9/11/01. Governors' past decisions about public education have been a left-brained back to basics, more rigorous testing, and punishing students, teachers, and schools that did not measure up to standards. Asking governors and the Federal education bureaucracy "to develop a national security readiness audit, to judge whether schools are meeting targets" will rely upon more traditional costly standardized tests to separate the smart schools and students from the not-so-smart schools' students who do not perform well under threatening test conditions. A "national security readiness audit" may be politically correct but financially underfunded in the K-12 poor public schools: the source of recruits for our armed services. The thinking and unaccountability that got public schools/students into the current failure spiral, and our best students to be less than half as good as 33 other countries' students, will not get us out of the K-12 public education's bureaucratic mess. Current politically-motivated solutions on the table are panaceas and a waste of time, money, and students' brains.

Powerless teachers are the norm in K-12 public and some charter schools, it is also entrenched in some private schools. I am reminded of the old guard, The Board of Directors, in charge of our children's private elementary school in the 1970s in Montclair, New Jersey. The headmistress, Martha Johnson, knew the over 200 students by name and idiosyncrasy and their parents. She brought her Golden Retriever to school each day; he slept on a rug in her office. The children loved to go to the Principal's Office to pet the dog. It was not a place to be scolded. If children were advanced in reading, they could go on to the next grade in reading; if they were not doing well in math, they could go back a grade in math to get the basics all over again. There were no stigmas attached to the up-and-down movement into classes, for students helped each other. Martha Johnson and her team of teachers ran a school that our children loved, including the soccer games. Parents were totally involved. We held fund raising events and compiled the annual Year Book with children's art work, poetry, stories, and photos under the direction of a teacher.

Then, one evening, parents were summoned to a PTA meeting and learned that The Board planned to replace Martha Johnson with a former graduate, a male, who had achieved principal credentials. The Board's president attested to the wisdom of the Board's all-male decision by the hundreds of years they had cumulatively served the school and as individuals: fifteen years, eighteen years, twenty years, and so on. The Board President's final "selling point" to parents was the school had no tenure policy so there would be no financial repercussions. I couldn't resist standing up and asking him, "What about the tenure of the Board members"? The audience laughed; he got red in the face, but we knew it was a "done deal." Martha Johnson survived with grace. We helped her to self-publish her memoir about her Brookside years, *Sincerely yours*. She was hired by the local college as a professor. A year later, we moved to New York and more impersonal public schools. We have fond memories of Martha Johnson's leadership/stewardship.

The professionalization of K-12 public education means left-brained, by-the-book educators with proper credentials and licenses are subject to fads, such as the phonics and new math phases, which appeared to be more important than respect and love for children's innate intelligence with a gifted child within each waiting to be drawn out. Percy Bysshe Shelley, 1792-1822, captured, in his poem, children's potential when they come to public school bright-eyed and bushy-tailed:

> Know you what it is
> to be a child? . . .
> It is to believe in love,
> to believe in loveliness,
> to believe in belief . . .
> It is to turn
> pumpkins into coaches,
> and mice into horses,
> lowness into loftiness.

But something happens to children, to students, in the K-12 public education system: everything is transformed into nothing that means anything to them. The lowest common denominator prevails! Most public schools are more like factories than learning environments. Bells ring every 45 minutes or so; ready-or-not, the subject changes, and students are expected to adapt, conform, and learn another subject. Students are expected to mouth known answers to questions and to learn quietly, but learning can be exciting and noisy when students are engaged. Most principals, administrators, and some teachers perceive noisy classrooms to be out-of-control classrooms. Such schools are designed to create docile, obedient subjects who pivot around the teacher who, in turn, is structure- and hierarchically-controlled. Each student is assigned an individual desk, an island onto himself or herself, without the benefit of belonging to one of, say, four Houses, like Harry

Potter's Hogwarts School. Relating to and competing against a big school population by oneself is a huge undertaking with few winners and lots of losers. Random assignment to a "House" at public school provides a "home" away from home, creates relationships automatically, and provides a collaborative place or forum to celebrate individuals' and their small group's achievements: academic, the arts, sports, and awards.

With the full backing of New York City's Board of Education, an elementary school in Crown Heights, Brooklyn, is more like "an extended family compound."[31] The New American Academy, run by Shimon Waronker, has open rooms with 60 students, working and learning from each other in three groups with four teachers. The students sit around large tables or in areas for teacher-led discussions. The master teacher travels between the groups. "The students seem to do a lot more public speaking with teachers working hard to get them to use full sentences and proper diction. The subjects in the early grades... are interdisciplinary... The organizational structure of the school is flattened. Nearly everybody is pushed to the front lines, in the classroom, and salaries are higher."[31]

"The New American Academy has two big advantages as a reform model. First, instead of running against the education establishment, it grows out of it and is being embraced by the teachers' unions and the education schools... Second, it does a tremendous job of nurturing relationships. Since people learn from people they love, education is fundamentally about the relationship between a teacher and student... The New American Academy has the potential to create richer, mentorlike or even familylike relationships for students who are not rich in those things."[31]

> The secret of education is respecting the pupil.
> It is not for you to choose
> what he shall know, what he shall do.
> It is chosen and foreordained,
> and only he holds the key to his own secret.
> –Ralph Waldo Emerson (1803-1882)

If the designers of The Western Intellectual Tradition had known and understood how the human brain works, it is possible the K-12 public education systems would be more compatible with how human brains function. Human learning is suppressed by the way curriculum is fragmented and presented in a linear fashion. Instead of respecting the pupil, The Western Intellectual Tradition respects his or her performance on tests. Children intuit when they are disrespected or disvalued and are competent readers of adults' body language and voice tones. Educators have an obligation to keep up with the science of education and broadening their specialties, understanding how the human brain works and learns, just as medical doctors have an obligation to keep up with the science of medicine and their specialties. Real professionals never stop learning and wanting to learn, including from their students and patients. Students zero in on and try to avoid plateaued teachers and professors, for they feel disrespected and distrust such adults' behavior and demeanor. It is a truism that only dead fish swim with the stream.

Some aspects of the right-brain's humanity are being introduced and emphasized in some K-12 public and private schools, from relationships to respect. That is not enough for students to grasp the full scope of the right-brain's intelligence potential as complementary learning partner of the left-brain's logic, ABCs, and 123s. Nor is it enough for adults to cope with life's travails. Brain-based learning in public elementary and high schools transforms classrooms into environments where students feel safe and like themselves.

Sensory information from our six senses (kinesthetic-touch, intuition, visual, auditory, olfactory, and taste) streams in and is processed immediately in the limbic system, the right-brain's domain. Before messages reach the left-brain's cerebral cortex for higher thinking processing, our right-brain has already viewed the stimulation and assigned a feeling to it. "The limbic system functions by placing an affect, or emotion, on information streaming in through our senses... although our limbic system functions throughout our lifetime, it does not mature. As a result, when our emotional 'buttons' are pushed, we retain the ability to react to incoming stimulation as though we were a two year old, even when we are adults... Although many of us may think of ourselves as thinking creatures that feel, biologically we are feeling creatures that think."[325] Hence, objectivity is not primary, subjectivity is. Yet, The Western Intellectual Tradition ignores the facts and continues the fiction.

Since the right hemisphere is tainted by society's myths and misunderstandings, Jonah Lehrer understood that "Studying metaphors and holistic thinking seemed like a sure way to ruin a scientific career."[204] However, his research validated self-knowledge and the creative process. He writes, "We can learn from the creative secrets of the past, from those outlier societies that produced Shakespeare and Plato and Michelangelo. And then we should look in the mirror. What kind of culture have we created? Is it a world full of ideas than can be connected? Are we willing to invest in risk takers? Do our schools produce students ready to create?... We have to make it easy to become a genius,"[204] to release the genius within. If in *IMAGINE*, Lehrer put quotes in others' mouths, that's "a sure way to ruin a scientific career."

Our dominant white culture is habituated to perpetuating the status quo, even when our K-12 education system is broken for 31 percent of students and needs fixing for all Americans to be on a par with other modern nations' educational systems. Those nations have an education advantage when they are basically monocultures where everyone belongs to the same culture, although that is changing with new immigrants from other cultures and races. However, America's many races and cultures make America a multicultural nation with "barnyard pecking orders" that undermine "outsiders" belongingness and exacerbate their deficient human development issues. Hence, affirming and esteeming self and others are ongoing efforts, or non-efforts, for students to belong or not belong when confronted with our white culture's "norms." Non-white people, even those whites perceived to be different, may endure insensitive students' and adults' negative labels, put-downs, and ridicule which negatively impact their right-brain's emotions, feelings, and ability to learn. Thus, our K-12 public school system could level the learning field by including the right-brain in its curriculum to offset the inherent pecking order of our dominant white culture that infects our multicultural and racial citizens and our American society and thwarts their freedom to learn and divides us.

The Brazilian scholar, Paolo Freire wrote *Pedagogy of the Oppressed*; he documented his experience of teaching Brazilian adults to read and write. He also perceived that some were colonized or oppressed by their own people as colonizer/oppressor. He wrote, "Freedom is acquired by conquest, not by gift. It must be pursued constantly and responsibly.

Freedom is not an ideal located outside of man, nor is it an idea which becomes myth. It is rather the indispensable condition for the quest for human completion."[111] Freire advocated for a mutual approach to education, whereby students were informed of their incompleteness and to strive to be complete and more fully human.[111] Freire's ideas were considered by some to be Marxist. Arizona's former Superintendent of Schools, Tom Horne, banned Freire's book, so did totalitarian countries.

Our current public education system's 99,000-100,000 schools already have the intact infrastructure and the human resources, but not all the contents to humanize the educative process for its students. When the powers-that-be over the principals and teachers remove the bureaucratic constraints that get in the way of the freedom to teach and learn, then students won't be perceived as faceless numbers who have to perform or else the school and staff will be punished too.

Most teachers have empathy for their students; many students are round pegs that teachers have to fit into the curriculum's square holes. Teachers are expected to improve students' test scores without the power to change even a lesson plan or mandated text in some schools. Until we understand, from the decades of brain research, that young children have inner computer-like chips full of data embedded within them, from conception onward, and that attention must be paid to their inner data while teaching them with unconditional empathy and concern. I find it useful to visualize each student as a different size, color, and design of sets of Russian nested dolls. The smallest doll is the computer chip or embedded data bank upon which the many other dolls – selves – are built. The largest doll of each set is in front of me with all those selves' experiences below the surface. It's up to me to draw students out, learn from them, then their cognitive learning may begin in a less curriculum-fragmented, time-oriented manner and more organic way that is conducive to learning naturally in a welcoming atmosphere.

Not only are the right-brain's emotions and virtues missing from K-12 public education, it is also missing in college and university education, as was demonstrated by the doctor who originally told me I had cancer. "By now, even the most hard-core, old-school doctors recognize that emotions are present in medicine at every level, but the consideration of them rarely makes it into medical school curriculums. Let alone professional charters. Typically, feelings are lumped into the catch-all of stress or fatigue, with the unspoken assumption that with enough gumption these irritants can be corralled."[245]

Educators of the right-brain, in human development classes, could teach children about the workings of the two hemispheres, the quick responses from the amygdala to stimuli, and ensuing damage to memory stored in the hippocampus when they are chronically emotionally stressed. Children could learn that emotions are transient, so they have ninety seconds when they experience their own or someone else's anger or fear, for example, to not let the emotion rule them. Relaxation is just a positive thought away. They may take charge of their anger or fear by counting to ten or higher or by asking self if their own or another's anger/fear is a mask for feeling unloved, unworthy, or shamed. A delayed or detached response, rather than a reflexive one, could be mediated by knowing the source of the anger/fear, owning it, and considering the consequences, or by using the anger/fear as the motivation to change what provoked them. Hate and fear separate us from each other. Love unites our brains and people. "Love is the one emotion that expands intelligence because love connects us"[304] to ourselves and others.

Of course, it takes leaders, teachers, and administrators who feel safe within their own skins to give more than lip service to change toward whole brain-based learning that entails respect for differences, self-knowledge, authentic relationships, and commitment to ongoing, interdisciplinary learning and growing. Leaders will not be able to hide behind their superiority or under their halos. Teachers and professors will not be able to hide behind their subject's expertise in whole brain-based teaching-learning environments when self-knowledge and emotional intelligence are as important as cognitive intelligence to unleash the talent and potential of our nation's children. Today's top-down cultural and educational policies have to change so bottom-up, collaborative solutions may be found to foster geniuses instead of dropouts and to provide common spaces that foster the interaction of people from all walks of life since individuals and group interactions play a central role in innovation and collaboration.

So, who could be in charge of reconstructing the K-12 public school's fragmented, compartmentalized, and professionalized system toward correction in a whole-brained humane direction? Our public education's monolithic system is similar to the Titanic's iceberg fate. It runs full-speed ahead, fully aware of but ignores the dangerous waters ahead when the goal is the record, the numbers. Few survive. We've had a raft of fads to "improve" the K-12 public education system, but each has retarded the system's improvement for the inherited and inherent flaws are not addressed. Evidently, nobody's in charge when the K-12 public education is perceived to be bestowed upon us as though it were God-given. In the meantime, we are experiencing wholesale brain robberies in a dysfunctional society and culture with a dearth of self-awareness or the willpower to change the course of the public educative process for children and for the greater good of Americans.

First things first, though, and that is the moral fiber of America has eroded since World War II for a number of reasons. Our ongoing wars negatively affect both the winners and the losers who survive and our nation too. Soldiers on both sides have to numb their emotions, feelings, and love when they kill each other, even though they are conditioned to believe they are saving their countries from evil. Some lose their faith in themselves, in God, and their country for their collusion in carnage. A retired general we know is afraid he is going to Hell when he dies for his killing spree during World War II; he now has dementia. Many other veterans lose their socialized humanity and harm their families or commit suicide.

Wars' indirect impact on a nation's population has a way of shifting their priorities. Those with ego deficits may be addicted to a different god – success/money – have no time to be good enough parents; they put energy and their faith in capitalism – making "a killing in the market" or on the job – as they prioritize their goals and desensitize themselves to people. Others may succumb to the headiness of power over people's lives and destinies and seek positions of high visibility in the world. All may learn that money and power over people aren't the road to happiness either. The source of satisfaction with life and happiness is "not wealth but the reciprocal relationship between ourselves and one another, ourselves and the world,"[225] when we complete ourselves, not the American way of marrying our disowned self in a partner, then disowning the partner.

Wars' legacies remind us we are mortals, not immortal, so there's an urge to survive the competition, to do whatever it takes to satisfy a deficit need or hungry ego. In a left-brained, me-first environment, money and power are the symbols of being smart, successful, looked up to, admired, and recognized by the powerful media. Behavior at the top filters down to the next hierarchical level until there's only petty power left to use by not treating those at the very bottom of society with respect or making them "Hurry up and wait!" All power-over-driven people may be smart but they are not wise. They are in the minority, but their passions fuel them. They are permanent warmongers, like passionate ultraorthodox or fundamentalist/extremists religionists, whose unacknowledged evil intentions gradually turn democratic nations into theocracies. Cleansing their own blood of cancers means spilling "enemies" blood; they practice a form of eugenics when their soldiers and their enemies are of the same ilk: the unwanted, the despised, the undeserving poor. The trend away from democratic principles coincides with those whose black or white, rigid left-brained thinking conjures up the "axis of evil" or WMDs to rationalize wars that enrich the few and temporarily satisfies their egos. Now we understand why our Founding Fathers wanted wisdom and truth to be the underpinning of our democracy.

Truthful knowledge from the left and right hemispheres is the basis of wisdom: a knowledge- and experience-based process whereby intuitive, emotionally sensitive and altruistic processes of the right hemisphere are required to temper, synergize, and elevate knowledge that is gained from the logical, analytical processes of the left hemisphere. When the right hemisphere is missing from the educative process – and is not informally educated today as it used to be before the 1960s – and when truthful head and heart knowledge is missing from both the right and left hemispheres, is it wisdom, a belief, or ideology that emerges? Probably, what emerges is an individual's self-image bolstered by society's bottomless monetary values or a poor self-image diminished by negatively comparing self to society's values. With a scarcity or poverty mentality there is no desire to share resources with "undeserving" others when we don't experience, "I am enough!" or "I have enough to share." Smart and wise are missing.

Unfortunately, as knowledge increases and is not applied to the classroom, wisdom decreases. Throughout most of human history, knowledge has increased as wisdom has decreased. As wisdom decreased, self-knowledge and emotional resiliency have decreased. "Science is only a Latin word for knowledge... Knowledge is our destiny,"[294] but too little knowledge, especially if it has false foundations, makes us vulnerable to others being in charge of our destiny. Some parents or caregivers raise their children in loving, non-threatening environments to have whole-brain cognitive- and self-knowledge. Students whose knowledge is without a whole-brain conscience and are smart at acing tests, grow up to be adults who perpetuate decivilizing effects: family breakdowns versus children's welfare, wars versus negotiated peace, rampant poverty versus greedy wealth, and human torture and all forms of abuse versus respect for the dignity of life.

Never underestimate the power of a grassroots movement in America and the power of human passions and creativity to engage, sustain our democracy, and initiate our rights to quality whole-brain education, quality politicians, equality in the marketplace, and one person, one vote. In this age of knowledge explosion, we have the tools to learn some answers to our philosophers' and heretics' questions about human beings' origins and their religions. Would knowing make a difference to human beings, in general, in the short-term, in the long-term, or not at all? Truthful knowledge would not change history up to the present, but would most human beings be able to wrap their heads around "absurd" knowledge? World and national leaders and religions with vested interests in maintaining their power, wealth, and status would resist. Other leaders may emerge to help move us into higher states of consciousness.

Great leaders "ignite our passion and inspire the best in us...Great leadership works through the emotions."[121] Toxic charismatic leaders like Adolf Hitler and Idi Amin used negative emotions to inspire the worst in their followers and to eventually fail. Only emotionally intelligent leaders have the power to instill optimism, inspiration, and enthusiasm; whereas, the emotionally illiterate leader incurs antagonism, hostility, and dissonance. Which leader would the American people choose? We tend to choose people to be with and vote for those like ourselves. Would people own their power to be whole-brained intelligent? Would hierarchical, power-driven institutions and organizations be permitted to continue to consume the Earth's resources, the commons, enrich the rich, and diminish the human spirit? Would we create institutions and organizations that are chaordic?[156] The word chaordic encompasses chaos and order, competition and collaboration, a shared purpose, ethical principles, responsibility by all for themselves and to others, and the sustainability of the Earth. That's how America has been led at times by those with hungry hearts until after World War I ended in 1918 when capitalists' hungry egos emerged instead that had been smoldering since 1910.

Do we ever take the time to understand ourselves, our motivations, reflect upon the consequences of actions we took that led us to where we are today, our leadership abilities, so we may, in turn, understand others or, at the least, inspire them to lead? Do we have hungry hearts to learn, to know truth, to understand our world? "Not all students have hungry hearts, Some do, some don't, and having a hungry heart (or not) is what makes all the difference for a young person seeking an education."[90] Or for an adult who is interested in a better future than his or her present. How do we get hungry hearts? Evidently, it's the hungriest hearts that get the most out of their formal and informal education. They may not be the most intellectually gifted, but they come to school with curiosity and the motivation to learn. Their deficits are teachable. "What distinguishes them is that they take their lives seriously and they want to figure out how to live them better."[90]

A hungry heart is very different from a hungry ego. What hungry heart students have in common is they have had parents or significant others who loved them and didn't saddle them with spoken and unspoken unrealistic expectations. With confidence in their lived beliefs and values, they are secure enough within themselves to risk them in challenging situations, from travel and new ideas to society's new possibilities. "Hungry hearts – smart or slow, rich or poor – still deserve a place in the class"[90] and in a quality education institution that all students deserve.

Those with hungry egos have a different value system; they may consider themselves very independent, but they appear to be dependent upon or equate things and money with their esteem for self and/or others. They tend to "buy" status and relationships, because they do not have a keen sense of self within themselves, or love self, or feel, "I am enough!" without the culture's trappings of money and power. They may not feel or believe, "I am Somebody!" without society's highly regarded props and perks. The hungriest egos are more prone to ace tests, charm teachers, and be popular, but to use learning not for the love of it but for the love of how their learning, skills, and networks will reward them with money, status, power, and love. Those students and parents who fear that education will challenge their beliefs are not driven by a quest for truth, they are looking for affirmation: to feel good, look good, and be heard. And the more people they attract to their cause, beliefs, values, or ideology, the more they can believe in it. Those of little faith have fears: Matthew 8:26.

We may believe we are unbiased; however, our cultural conditioning and unconscious minds overrule our conscious minds. For example, for some Americans, racism may be easier to overcome than sexism.[192] However, racism has a long history in America and resides in many Americans' unconscious if not in their conscious minds. Sexism has a much longer recorded history and is the basis of hierarchical power in families. Sexism has been passed down from generation to generation for eons and has been accepted in human history as God's literal truth as writ in the Bible. Also, racism is passed down from generation to generation, and, in America's recent history, conscious and unconscious sexism and racism have determined political stances, government policies, and educational opportunities.

With their left-brains' good intentions, men created oral and written traditions to make sense out of their world and to perpetuate their beliefs, including the subjugation of women. "Many of the sexist biases and social institutions that persist in the world came into being as a result... Patriarchy is a set of institutionalized social rules put in place by men to control the sexual and reproductive rights of women... men's actions suggest that they believe in their superiority over women,"[306] even today. Women are perceived as the weaker sex, since they have been historically tainted, tamed and age-defined as maiden, mother, crone, prostitute.

Recall that Neurosurgeon Leonard Shlain proposed that "The most dangerous result of these all-male [run] cultures bereft of the input from women [or from men's own disowned right-brain considered unmasculine or effeminate!] is the loss of common sense.[307] Our current problem with many leaders' common sense is they usually emerge from having demonstrated their analytic, financial, or technical skills, which are the forte of the cognitive left-brain. They have been conditioned by The Western Intellectual Tradition to ignore the right-brain's positive attributes, emotions, and virtues, so by default, with easy access to anger, they are I-oriented and self-invested. I-oriented leaders who do not respect the poor, the undereducated, or even middle-class Americans may not have the heart or the faith to acknowledge that when we help others we help ourselves. The poor have a deep understanding of what it feels like to be poor, and as a class they have empathy and give to others what they can to enhance others' survival.

The human desire to survive appears to be an evolution-driven universal desire. For some, the desire to survive at all costs outweighs the Golden Rule. Religions fulfill the desire for everlasting life, a belief in God, and the belief that there is meaning beyond this life on Earth. Christianity and its diverse sects have not only impacted The Western Intellectual Tradition in America and Americans' potential, it has also positively and negatively impacted our institutions and organizations. Today's divisive politicians imply all citizens who do not follow them (the shepherd) like sheep are unAmerican.

With a know the difference or a whole-brained truth perspective, we can learn who's really in charge of our brain-mind when we think and believe we are making sound decisions and taking reasoned actions. America will be a paradise when the majority of us heal our genetic connections to our essence that connects us to all life and make the decisions that will secure our democracy and our future.

America's Founding Fathers did the best they could to untangle the web of beliefs and practices that had created Western civilization. Their vision for America, as set forth in the U.S. Constitution, was the antithesis of the divine rights of a ruling class or of one religion. The Four Freedoms and equality were for white males only, but later Amendments have added women, all races, and all cultures. They did not anticipate that financial elites would weave SuperPac gold chains around the heads of citizens, reminiscent of Mary Howitt's cautionary poem, "The Spider and the Fly": "Come into my parlor, said the spider to the fly." Through deceitful seduction and flattery, the naïve Fly succumbed and was eaten by the cunning Spider.[162] We have more options than the Fly, even though The Western Intellectual Tradition has already ensnared us by not teaching us how to separate emotionally-laden communications from reasonable ones for our own good. Our minds are barraged by political messages with hidden agendas that conceal more than they reveal. It is up to us to use our smarts, wisdom, our common and uncommon sense, to avoid becoming mindless sheep or clipping our own wings.

Who's responsible for becoming in charge of our nation's future? We are: the American voters! We cannot change anyone but ourselves To follow our unique path to emancipation, journaling and self-tracking are ways to be more involved in our whole lives, to find out from our own research what we and our nation are up against. In transitional and perturbation times, we need faith, love, hope, and a journal to record our stories and to sustain our souls. We could begin our empowerment process by journaling or by studying ourselves within the context of our relationships and the future we want for our nation that is more in line with Jesus Christ's original teachings and/or the Golden Rule. Since the purpose of life is to live it – not to be lived by life – "without stories there is no pattern, no understanding, no art, and no character – merely habits, events passing before our eyes of an aimless observer, a life unreviewed, a life lost in the living of it."[154]

"The future is not written. The future is made every day by the actions of people... Now you might argue that you alone cannot have any real or meaningful effect on the future. You are just one person... [But] you can do a lot."[73] Intel's Futurist Brian David Johnson asked Cory Doctorow, a bestselling science fiction author, "How can we change the future?" He replied: "I guess the way you change the future is to change people's narrative... just change the story we tell ourselves about the future and you change the future itself."[73]

We are narrative creatures. "Narrativity... is at the heart of our identity... We are forever telling stories to ourselves... Families, nations, religions (but also corporation, universities, governments) know who they are by the stories they tell."[19] "Narrative, with its capacity to reach into our bodies and reformulate our identities, individually and socially, also contains, in its womb so to speak, conceptual possibilities."¹⁹

In *Hope for the Flowers*, Trina Paulus wove a parable about what humans can conceptually learn from caterpillars: about life's ups and downs, love, instincts, choices, the unknown versus the status quo, dreams, and hope. Stripe's life began with eating the leaf he was born on, sensed there had to be more to life, struggled to climb to the top of a pillar made up of other caterpillars, met Yellow who also wanted to climb to the top, but she felt bad about stepping on and climbing over other caterpillars. So they went back down, but Stripe's curiosity won. He headed for the top again, while Yellow followed her instincts, continued eating leaves, and then spun a cocoon. Stripe reached the top, saw other caterpillar pillars, and was disillusioned: "Is this all there is?" Yellow had become a butterfly but waited for Stripe to climb back down, showed him her empty cocoon; he realized what he had to do; she waited until he emerged transformed into a butterfly and they were free to fly off to be nurtured by and nurture the flowers.²⁵⁸ The moral is simple: follow our instincts to discover our individual destiny and share our talents with others, for we are all interconnected. Sharing, to me and hopefully to you, means using our talents to make it possible for all children in our K-12 public schools to have access to their full intelligence in a caring atmosphere that becomes a haven away from home to draw out their talents and gifts and become humanly and humanely developed citizens of our democratic republic. What else is school for?

Homo sapiens' **Sustainability Manual**

Cancer is a powerful disease for human beings and a powerful metaphor for their society's condition. *Homo sapiens*, who are cut off from themselves, from their hemispheric wholeness, innate wisdom, and from their connected to all life, means their cancerous behavior, especially in institutions and organizations, trickles down to people, societies, and nations. The adage, The love of money is the root of all evil, is being played out in America and undermining the U.S. Constitution's equality and freedom tenets. Money determines the quality of a K-12 public school education, and our health care systems are run for profit, so money determines whether poor and even middle-class people get medical attention or not. The rigid left-brainers, who appear to love money more than people, collude in despoiling our human capital – our minds – capitalism – our businesses – and our resources – the air, water, and soil of our home, the Earth.

Michael Dowd, an Evolutionary Evangelist, wrote the last chapter of *Science, Wisdom, and the Future: Humanity's Quest for a Flourishing Earth*. He reasoned that changes in thoughts and perspectives take a long time to be assimilated because "humans do not live by truth alone. We require the sustenance of meaning – of beauty, goodness, relationships, and purpose. We require comfort in times of sorrow and suffering, We also require perspectives that encourage us to cooperate in ever-wider circles in order to solve ever-larger problems – problems that today encircle the globe."[82]

Cancer as a metaphor for our society's ills is becoming commonplace. Michael Dowd related an interaction he had several years ago, during one of his presentations' question and answer periods, with a medical doctor, an oncologist. The oncologist stated, "I work with cancer patients every day. From my vantage point, we are inadvertently destroying our larger body because we lack evolutionary guidance. We're acting like cancer cells, rather than immune cells. A cancer cell is a normal cell that, for one reason or another, loses its genetic memory. Cut off from the wisdom of millions of years of developmental guidance, it stops cooperating with the rest of the body. It experiences itself as separate from the body, overpopulates, and proceeds to consume the very organism that supports it. We call our society a consumer society, and to consume something is to eat it up... I believe we are consuming the planet because, like cancer cells, we've been trying to live without evolutionary wisdom."[82]

America is known as an overfed but undernourished nation with flourishing manufactured food marketing and pharmaceutical perspectives that defy the fact that all human bodies are unique with unique dietary inheritances and preferences, so one diet or treatment does not fit all, just as one standardized curriculum does not fit all unique children and standardized tests reduce human beings to numbers. Each of us is responsible for writing our own Sustainability Manual to sustain healthy selves with healthy immune systems and a sustainable home on

Earth. Russell Genet, Research Scholar, Astronomer, and a contributing Editor to *Science, Wisdom, and the Future*, reminds us that "Wisdom is often defined as understanding and aligning ourselves with reality. By consciously and actively altering our evolutionary trajectory from a fatal runaway success to a self-restrained species on a flourishing planet, we will, at last, have earned our species' name, sapiens."[117] However, many Americans are dominated by the left half of their two brains' logic and rules and are averse to new ideas or innovative ways of thinking, being, and doing that are housed in the right half of their brains. Could our nation's half-brained homo sapiens, who appear to be dominated by The Western Intellectual Tradition and by their left-brains' narrow world-views, be TWITs[334] and saps?

Homo sapiens is the scientific name for the only living species of the genus Homo (modern man, mankind, human being) and sapient is the Latin word for full of knowledge, wise, sagacious. Half-brained people cannot achieve full intelligence in today's society's institutions and organizations, which compromises wisdom's base: right- and left-brain data. Human beings lose their sense of wholeness, leadership over themselves, and responsibility for self and to others when they subscribe to the division of selves, either wittingly or unwittingly, the division of labor, specialization, and hierarchy in their personal lives and personal relationships, not just in their professional lives.

To be wise, we need a sense of our wholeness, our multiple intelligences, our possible range of archetypal human experiences, and a vision of the larger picture of humanity. With computers and the world-wide web, the challenge is to access and contribute our individual wisdom to the wisdom of the ages, and our unique stories, for the primary source of philosophy (love and pursuit of wisdom) is the life of the individual combined with other individuals. Recall that Margaret Rioch has learned from her experience that "Human beings are never more fulfilled than when they are united to a whole... total union... that makes the experience in a working group committed to a common task so fulfilling."[283]

Hope

"What is is." That was Thorkild Jacobsen's conclusion regarding ancients' beliefs about the gods and their power.[167] It is not a position of hope, but it is an acceptance of what is when we have no access to history of our origins and no power to change our circumstances. Acceptance, though, does not necessarily mean agreement with what is. But acceptance is a necessary process before we initiate changes toward hope's possibilities for our future. We do have the power-over and can prioritize the issues that confront us.

Hope is defined as a feeling that what is wanted will happen; a desire accompanied by expectation. Hope usually has a basis or a reason in the background. English poet Alexander Pope, 1688-1744, wrote in an *Essay on Man*:

> Hope springs eternal in the human breast:
> Man never is, but always to be blest.
> The soul, confined and uneasy from home,
> Rests and expatiates in a life to come.

Poets' command of metaphorical language allows them to see what everyone sees but to think and write about what they see or intuit that few others have thought. Alexander Pope could have been referring to an afterlife or hoping for something better in the future. What has yet to be acknowledged in our K-12 public education system and society is, "every human being's central need is to express himself – to show himself to the world as he really is – in word, in gesture, or behavior, in every genuine utterance from the baby's cry to the artist's creation."[229]

People in China, Africa, Asia, the Middle East, and America have been existing under a spell, but now the spell has been broken as the capacity to deal with what leaders throw at them is the opportunity for some countries' people to free themselves, their minds, from illusion and false knowledge, even though they may exchange one despotic leader for others of the same ilk. It's easier to assert our personal power in America, yet many of us have complacently chosen not to get involved in our nation's woes, to let others do our thinking for us. In the meantime, passionate minority voices have overwhelmed reason and human rights so the nation's agenda reflects their beliefs, not our nation's needs for jobs and spending at home not abroad. We have been seduced by fear of terrorist attacks, fear of losing our financial security, and faced with the reality that America is fast becoming a third-world nation with too many uneducated have-nots and an elite class of have-mores. Engaging in hope defuses fear and challenges us to seek information about the founding principles upon which our Western society was built and about ourselves, why we are not a kind, safe, and peaceful country of caring communities and relationships, and how to use our personal power to make a course correction.

"There is power for the owning in every position or condition in the workworld"[250] and in our personal world,[286] but when we don't use our personal power or don't know we have it, then we don't have it.[183] Similarly, not only personal power but hope can make a huge difference in all our lives when, in the absence of optimism, we do not succumb to hopelessness and, instead, engage a sense of the possible that can act as a spur to hope.

Economist Esther Duflo of Massachusetts Institute of Technology is well known for her data-driven analysis of poverty. She and her colleagues evaluated a Bangladeshi microfinance company, BRAC, that invested in extreme poverty-stricken people in West Bengal, India. BRAC gave each family a cow, a couple of goats, or some chickens plus "a small stipend to reduce the temptation to eat or sell the asset immediately, as well as weekly training sessions to teach them how to tend to animals and manage their households. BRAC hoped that there would be a small increase in income from selling the products of the farm animals provided, and that people would become more adept at managing their own finances."[85]

Evidently, the results were dramatic in that a dose of optimism was provided by BRAC that fueled belief in self and hope for more than mere survival. "People think they are in a poverty trap when they are not. Surveys in many countries show that poor parents often believe that a few years of schooling have almost no benefits... So if they cannot ensure that their children can complete school, they tend to keep them out of the classroom altogether... By putting all their investment in the child who they believe to be the brightest, they ensure that their other children never find out what they are good at... these children live down to their parents' expectations,"[85] just as many American schoolchildren are judged, labeled, and live down, instead of up, to society's expectations or their own possibilities.

Dr. Dufolo also found that an Indian law to elect women to head village councils provided the role models for parents to include goals for their daughters, not only for their sons. "Girls were expected to get much less schooling, stay at home and do the bidding of their in-laws."[85] Women in power positions, as role models, "expanded the girls' sense of the possible beyond a life of domestic drudgery. An unexpected consequence, perhaps, but a profoundly hopeful one."[85]

In the United States of America, we don't have many jobs for the uneducated any more. Most such jobs are filled by our guest workers or cheaper labor in poor countries of the world. Their plight today is similar to America's exploited workers before and during the Great Depression of the 1920s and 1930s. Today, we have a huge population of young people who dropped out of high school, those with high school diplomas who cannot pass the U.S. Army's simple ASVAB test, and those who served time in prison for illegal drug using or dealing. All were failed by the K-12 public education system and by our democratic republic. Attention must be paid to educating them to be productive citizens. Blaming and labeling the victims of The Western Intellectual Tradition is not fixing human beings' problems or the public schools' institutional problem that was identified in 1938. Who's in charge? We are! I believe we are attracted to studying, teaching, and writing what we need to learn, and some of us keep looking for the book we have not yet written.

When we reflect upon what we know today of human beings' brains, beginnings, and their institutions' foundations, we learn that his story omits her story and the right-brain's contributions to humanity. Now is an opportunity to contemplate what is missing and what changes in thinking and living would lead to a more harmonious and communication competent nation than we have. It is obvious that we need to heal the hemispheric disconnect within individual selves, to repair the irresponsible relationships between males and females and among diverse human beings, and to heal the cancers within ourselves and our nation.

Only when we heal our genetic disconnect will we be able to be in a sustainable relationship with ourselves, others, animals, and our home, the Earth. Human beings' beginnings, whether through creation, evolution, or intelligent design, is not the issue here. The issue is not to repeat negative human history and current trends away from democracy, but to learn from all of it and to utilize the latest brain, medical, and quantum research so we may upgrade Western society to the 21st century. We have come a long way since the Java Man was discovered, but the past's beliefs and warmongers' practices are alive and well today when our "massaged truths" are getting in the way of humanity's health, education, wisdom, and democracy.

With hope in our hearts, truth in our minds, and meaning in our souls, we experience personal empowerment and initiate true reform within ourselves and with enlightened others. It is hoped that 2012 and the ensuing years will bring about human transformations toward peace, love, understanding, fairness, and collaboration in our nation where some people perceive themselves to be entitled to more than their share of the universal pie.

With a cup half-full perspective and high hopes for America's K-12 public education's future to grow citizens and leaders with full human intelligence and with compassion – not contempt for the undeserving poor – I believe that most Americans have a conscience that will emerge when they are confronted with momentous decisions. To those Americans who do not have adequate humane development, unequal education, and no network opportunities, it's never too late to begin a new life. It's a matter of owning our inherent personal power to be authentic human beings fully connected to our genetic memories, talents, and all living beings and things on Earth. I offer Margaret Mead's words: Never doubt that a small group of thoughtful, committed citizens can change the world; indeed, it's the only thing that ever has. But the process begins with you and with me! Ilya Prigogene wrote about "perturbation" as part of his theory of dissipative structures in all energy systems.[275] For example, Luna moths transform, as butterflies do, from an egg to caterpillar stage, then cocoon or chryslais stage, and birthing to four wings with eye spots on each. Unlike butterflies, Luna moths are nocturnal. We may become perturbed when we are stressed, overwhelmed, or pressured to the point we are so agitated we think we'll explode. Disequilibrium is a sign we're perturbating and growing. If we stay with the agitated state, it's an opportunity for a breakthrough: to arrive on the other side of the agitated state with new ideas and different ways of thinking, feeling, being, and doing. What Ilya Prigogene says about the 2nd law of Thermodynamics is: when we don't lean forward, things and humans don't stay the same; instead, we lean backwards and deteriorate. What we don't use or abuse, we lose. Our nation's democracy is also about learning forward, not backwards, or it will fall apart.

Emily Dickinson's poem is about Hope. Let's hope that The Western Intellectual Tradition will get its "head" out of the past and change its legacy in the near future from Smart versus Wise to Smart and Wise. It is a transformation process with higher levels of consciousness. Hope will not be based on hope alone when we have access to our innate ability to make full and creative use of our human intelligence to restore our genetic memories and to heal ourselves and our society.

"Hope" is the thing with feathers –
That perches in the soul –
And sings the tune without the words -
And never stops – at all –

And sweetest – in the Gale – is heard –
And sore must be the storm –
That could abash the little Bird
That kept so many warm –

I've heard it in the chillest land –
And on the strangest Sea –
Yet – never – in Extremity,
It asked a crumb – of me.

Bibliography Acknowledgment
References (1 - 354)

1. Acemoglu, D. & James A. Robinson, J.A. (2012). *Why Nations Fail: The Origins of Power, Prosperity & Poverty.* New York: Crown Business.
2. Ackerman, D. (2012, 25th March). "The Brain on Love." In *The New York Times*, Sunday Review. pp. SR1, 6.
3. Acton, J.E.E.D., first Baron Acton known as Lord Acton (1877). Letter to Bishop Mandell Creighton on "Power Corrupts..." <http://phrases.org.uk/meanings/absolute-power corrupts-)\>
4. Aguirre, A. (2011, 25th September). "Loan Ranger: Diana Taylor spreads the gospel of microfinance." In *The New York Times*, Style Magazine. pp. 72-73, 118-119.
5. Albrecht, K. (1983). *Organization Development.* Englewood Cliffs, NJ: Prentice Hall. p. 113
6. Albrecht, K. (1983). *Mindex: Your Thinking Style Profile.* San Diego, CA: K. Albrecht.
7. Andrews, A. (2009). *The Noticer: sometimes all a person needs is a little perspective,* Nashville, TN: Thomas Nelson, Inc., p. 65.
8. AP, Washington (2012, 20th March). "Panel Says Schools' Failings Could Threaten Economy and National Security." In *The New York Times*, p. A 12.
9. Appelbaum, B. (2012, 12th June). "For U.S. Families, Net Worth Falls to 1990s Levels." In *The New York Times.* pp. A1, B4.
10. Armario, C. & Turner, D. (2010, 21st December). "SHOCKING: Nearly 1 in 4 High School Graduates Can't Pass Military Entrance Exam." *Associated Press.* <http://www.huffingtonpost.com/2010/12/21/high-chool-grads-fail-mi...>
11. Arnett, J. J. (2004). *Emerging Adulthood: The Winding Road From the Late Teens Through the Twenties,* New York: Oxford University Press.
12. Arntz, W., Chasse, B. & Vicente, M. with Forem, J & Erwin, E. (2005). *What the Bleep Do We Know? Discovering the Endless Possibilities for Altering Your Everyday Reality.* Deerfield Beach, FL: Health Communications, Inc.
13. Assmann, J. (1997). *Moses the Egyptian: The Memory of Egypt in Western Monotheism.* Cambridge, MA: Harvard University Press, p. 14.
14. Bacevich, A.J. (2010). *Washington Rules: America's Path to Permanent War.* New York: H. Holt. pp. 3-4, 25-27, 41, 113, 228.
15. Balmer, R. (2012, 29th April). "Breaking Faith." In *The New York Times* Book Review. p. 13.
16. Baltes, P. B. & Staudinger, U. M. (2000). "Wisdom: A metaheuristic (pragmatic) to orchestrate mind and virtue toward excellence." *American Psychologist* 55 (1). pp. 122-136.

17. Barboza, D. (2010, 30th December). "Shanghai Schools' Approach Pushes Students to Top of Tests." In *The New York Times*. p. A4.
18. Bardwick, J. M. (1979). *In Transition: How feminism, sexual liberation, and the search for self-fulfillment have altered our lives*. New York: Holt, Rinehart & Winston. p. 47.
19. Bellah, R. N. (2011). *Religion in Human Evolution: From the Paleolithic to the Axial Age*. Cambridge, MA: The Belknap Press of Harvard University Press. pp.1, 34, 35, 37, 41-42, 83, 120-121, 212-213, 215, 217-218, 220, 224, 227-228, 269, 283-287.
20. Bellah, R. N. (1985). *Habits of the Heart: Individualism and Commitment in American Life*. New York: Perennial Library, Harper & Row. pp. 231, 232, 324, 493.
21. Bergland, R. (1985). *The Fabric of Mind*. New York: Perennial Library, pp. 1, 109.
22. Berry, W. (2001). *In the Presence of Fear*, Great Barrington, MA: The Orion Society. pp. 9, 17, 28.
23. Blankkinship, D. G. (2010, 12th December). "Parents criticized in education poll." *The Arizona Republic*, p. A21.
24. Bloom, P. & Wynn, K. (2010, 9th May). "The Moral Life of Babies: Can Infants and Toddlers Really Tell Right From Wrong?" In *The New York Times* Magazine. p. 46.
25. Blow, C. M. (2012, 13th January). "Bitter Politics of Envy?" In *The New York Times*. Op-Ed page A.
26. Bono [U2 Band]. (2010, 2nd January). "Ten for the Next Ten." In *The New York Times*, p. WK10.
27. Brizendine, L. (2006). *The Female Brain*. New York: Morgan Road Books. pp. 1, 7, 14, 15, 23.
28. Brody, J. E. (2012, 3rd April). "Burst of Therapy Is Boon for Traumatized Children." In *The New York Times*, Science Times, p. D7.
29. Bronner, E. (2012, 22nd February). "Israeli Court Invalidates a Military Exemption." Middle East. In *The New York Times*.
30. Brooks, D. (2012, 12th June). "The Follower Problem." In *The New York Times*. p. A23.
31. Brooks, D. (2012, 23rd March). "The Relationship School." In *The New York Times*. p. A25.
32. Brooks, D. (2012, 17th February). "The Jeremy Lin Problem." In *The New York Times*. p. A23.
33. Brooks, D. (2011). *The Social Animal: The Hidden Sources of Love, Character, and Achievement*. New York: Random House. pp. x, xv, xii, xi, xiv, 32.
34. Brooks, D. (2011, 8th March). "The New Humanism." In *The New York Times*. p. A23.
35. Brooks, D. (2011, 14th January). "Tree of Failure." In *The New York Times*. p. A23.

36. Brooks, D. (2010, 10th September). "The Genteel Nation," In *The New York Times*, p. A23
37. Brooks, D. (2010, 20th March). "The Return of History." In *The New York Times*. p. A23.
38. Brown, E. R., Arntz, W., Montana, C. & Stewart, R. (2011). *Ghetto Physics: Redefining The Game*. (Download pdf)
39. Brown, E. R. (2002). *Ghetto Physics: Will the Real Pimps and Ho's Please Stand Up!* Movie: DVD
40. Browning, R. (1959). "Andrea Del Sarto." In From *Beowulf to Modern British Writers* by John Ball. New York: The Odyssey Press, Inc. pp.993-995.
41. Browning, R. (1841/1848/1906). *Pippa Passes*. London, UK: Heinemann.
42. Bruni, F. (2012, 25th March). "Rethinking His Religion." In *The New York Times*, Sunday Review.p. SR3.
43. Caldwell, C. (2010, 7th November). "Fantasy Politics: Is it time to awaken from the American dream?" In *The New York Times* Magazine, pp. 19-20.
44. Caldwell, M. (2001, August). "Efficacy of a Decompression Treatment Model in the Clinical Management of Violent Juvenile Offenders. *International Journal of Offender Therapy and Comparative Criminology*. 45: 469-477.
45. Callahan, T. (2010, 21st December). Reaction to "SHOCKING: Nearly 1 in 4 High School Graduates Can't Pass Military Entrance Exam." by representative of the Professional Association of GA Educators. <http://www.huffingtonpost.com/2010/12/21/high-school-grads-fail-mi...>
46. Camping, H. (2008, First Edition). *We Are Almost There!* Oakland, CA: Family Stations, Inc. pp. 12, 19, 25, Cover.
47. Carey, B. (2007, 6th March). "Insufferable Clingingness, Or Health Dependence?" In *The New York Times*. Science Times. pp. D1, 8.
48. Carey, B. (2007, 10th February). "After 28 Years, Princeton Loses ESP Lab to the Relief of Some." In *The New York Times*. pp. A1, A11.
49. Carroll, J. (2006, June). "Who Was Mary Magdalene?" *Smithsonian*. pp. 111, 113, 115, 119.
50. Castner, A. Z. (2003). *The AZCs of Self-Esteem*. Scottsdale, AZ: Cloudbank Creations, Inc.
51. Cauchon, D. (2010, 10th August). "Big gains for federal pay," In *Arizona Republic*. pp. A1. 4.
52. Center for Science in the Public Interest: a nonprofit watchdog and consumer advocacy group for nutrition and health, food safety. Washington, DC, 20005: 1220 L Street, NW., Suite 300.
53. Chabris, C. & Simons, D. (2010, 26th September). "Fight 'The Power'," In *The New York Times* Book Review. p. BR 27.
54. Ciardi, J. (1963, October/1964, April). "How Does A Poem Mean?" Lectures at Latter-day Saints, Utah. (www.lds.org/new-/1987/08/how-does-a-poem-mean?)
55. Ciardi, J. (1959). *How Does A Poem Mean?* New York: Houghton Mifflin.

56. Coffin, W. S. (1989, December). "Making the Spiritual Connection." Article by William Sloane Coffin in *Lear's* (defunct), p. 75.
57. Collins, P. (2001). "If you've got everything, it's good enough: perspectives on successful aging in a Canadian Inuit community." *Journal of Cross-Cultural Gerontology*, 16. pp. 127-155.
58. Coon, C. (2008). "Humanism and the Future of Religion," In *The Evolution of Religion: Stories, Theories, & Critiques*. Eds. J. Bulbulia, R. Sosis, E. Harris, R. & C. Genet, & K. Wyman. Santa Margarita, CA: Collins Foundation Press. p. 139.
59. Cooper, A. (2009, March). "Computing The Cost," *The Sun*, pp. 1, 5, 6, 9.
60. Corbett, S. (2007, 18th March). "The Women's War." In *The New York Times Magazine*. pp. 41-55, 62, 71-72.
61. Creswell, J. & Ahmed, A. (2012, 30th March). "Hedge Fund Managers Fare Well." *The New York Times*, pp. B1, 7.
62. Damasio, A. (1999). *The Feeling of What Happens: Body and Emotion in the Making of Consciousness*. New York: Harcourt Brace & Co. pp. 5, 198-199, 315, 309-310, 312. 332.
63. Damasio, A. (1994). *Descartes' Error*. New York: Grosset/Putnam Book p.160.
64. Dao, J. (2012, 17th May). "Athletes' Brain Disease Is Found in Veterans: Study Says Explosions Injure in Ways Similar to Tackle and Punches." In *The New York Times*. pp. A14, 17.
65. Darwin, C. (1859). *On the Origin of Species by Means of Natural Selection or The Preservation of Favoured Races in the Struggle for Life*. Albemarle Street, London, UK: John Murray.
66. Dean, C. (2009, 10th July). "Views of Scientists and Public in Conflict, Survey Finds." In *The New York Times*. p. A17.
67. Dear Abby Column (2009, 19th February). In *The Arizona Republic*. p. Y10.
68. Delbanco, A. (2012, 9th March). "A Smug Education?" In *The New York Times*, p. A21.
69. Dillon, S. (2010, 10th December). "What works in the classroom? Ask the students." In *The New York Times*. p. A14.
70. Dillon, S. (2010, 7th Dec,). "Top Test Scores From Shanghai Stun Educators."In *The New York Times*. pp. A1, 20.
71. Dilts, R. (1990). *Changing Belief Systems with NLP*, Capitola, CA: Meta Publications, pp. 9, 14, 102, 150.
71. DiSalvo, D. (2012, January). "Why We Forget." The Dana Foundation's *Brain in the News*. pp. 4-5.
73. Doctorow, C., William, Rushkoff, D. & Johnson, B. D. (2011). *The Tomorrow Project Anthology: Conversations About the Future.* © Intel Corporation. Publisher: Richard Bowles. Composition: MPS Ltd., a Macmillan Co., USA. p. 2, 3.

74. Dobbs, D. (2011, October). "Beautiful Brains." *National Geographic*. pp. 36-59.
75. Doidge, N. (2007). *The Brain That Changes Itself*. New York: Penguin Books. pp. xx, 44, 62.
76. Donadio, (2012, 4th June). "As Vatican Manages Crisis, Book Details Infighting." In *The New York Times*. pp. A4, 8
77. Douthat, R. (2012). *Bad Religion: How We Became a Nation of Heretics*. New York: Free Press.
78. Dowd, M. (2012, 20th May). "Here Comes Nobody." In *The New York Times* Sunday Review. p. SR11.
79. Dowd, M. (2011, 14th August). "Power to the Corporation!" In *The New York Times*. p. BW SR 11.
80. Dowd, M. (2010, 18th July). "Rome Fiddles, We Burn." In *The New York Times*. p. wk8.
81. Dowd, M. (2010, 11th April). "Worlds Without Women." In *The New York Times*. p. WK12.
82. Dowd, Michael (2012). *Science, Wisdom, and the Future: Humanity's Quest for a Flourishing Earth*. Genet, C. & R., Palmer, J. & L., Gibler, L.. & Wallen, V. Santa Margarita, CA: Collins Foundation Press. pp. 403, 411.
83. Dreifus, C. (2012, 8th February). "A Conversation with Dr. Janet D. Rowley." In *The New York Times*. p. D2.
84. Drucker, P. F. (1985). *Innovation and Entrepreneurship*. New York: Harper & Row. p. 193.
85. Duflo, E. (2012, 12th May). "Hope springs a trap." *The Economist* p. 83
86. Dye, T. R. & Zeigler, L. H. (1975). *The Irony of Democracy: An Uncommon Introduction to American Politics*. Belmont, CA: Duxbury Press.
87. Economist, The (2012, 5th May). "Shareholder activism and the banks: A new kind of outrage." p. 70.
88. *Economist, The* (2011, 17th December). "Religion in America: The faith (and doubts) of our fathers." pp.35-37
89. Eddy, P. G. (1993). *Who Tampered with the Bible?* Nashville, TN: Winston-Derek Publishers, Inc. p. 81.
90. Edmundson, M. (2012, 1st April). "Education's Hungry Hearts." In *The New York Times*. Sunday Review. p. SR8.
91. Eisler, R. (2012). "Human Nature and Human Possibilities." In *Science, Wisdom, and the Future: Humanity's Quest for a Flourishing Earth*. Eds. C. Genet, et al. Santa Margarita, CA: Collins Foundation Press. pp. 59-61, 65, 67.
92. Eliot, T. S. (1925). *Eliot's Poems: 1909-1925*. London, UK: Faber & Gwyer.
93. Engel, S. (2009, 2nd November). "Teach Your Teachers Well." In *The New York Times*. p. A17.
94. Enright, A. (2012). *Making Babies: Stumbling Into Motherhood*. New York: W. W. Norton & Company.
95. Erikson, E. (1968/1980). *Identity and the Life Cycle*, NY: W. W. Norton. pp. 140, 233.

96. Federal Reserve Board Surveys (1983); (2004)
    <http://www.faculty.fairfield.edu> and
    <http://sociology.ucsc.edu/whorulesamerica/power/wealth>
97. *Federalist Papers, The* (2008). Numbers 1 – 86."The Avalon Project,
    Yale Law School, Lillian Goldman Law Library. Nos. 10, 55, 63.
    <http://avalon.law.yale.edu/subject_menus/fed.asp>
98. Feldenkrais, M. (1977). *Awareness Through Movement*. New York:
    Harper & Row, Publishers. pp. 3, 18.
99. Fields, R. D. (2011, May/June). "Glial cells." *Scientific American Mind*. p. 54
100. Fifer, W. (2010, 24th June). "Infants Capable of Learning While Asleep."
    National Institutes of Health.
    <http://www.nih.gov/news/radio/jun20100624 NICHDinfantlearn...>
101. Foderaro, L. W. (2010, 30th September). "Private Moment Made Public,
    Then a Fatal Jump," In *The New York Times*. pp. A1, 4.
102. Fox, M (1999). *Sins of the Spirit, Blessings of The Flesh*. NY: Three Rivers Press,
    Member of the Crown Publishing Group. pp. 4, 99.
103. Fox, M. (1983). *Original Blessing*. Santa Fe, NM: Bear & Co.
    pp. 48, 120.
104. Franck, F. (1974). *Pilgrimage to Now/Here*. Maryknoll, New York: Orbis
    Books. p. 51.
105. French, J. R. P., Jr. and Raven, B. H. (1959). "The bases of social power."
    In *Studies in Social Power*. D. Cartwright (Ed.). Ann Arbor, MI:
    Institute for Social Research. pp. 150-167.
106. Friedman, R. A. (2010, 23rd March). "Sabotaging Success, but to What End?"
    In *The New York Times*. p. D6.
107. Friedman, T. L. (2012, 1st April). "Why Nations Fail."
    In *The New York Times* Sunday Review. p. SR13.
108. Friedman, T. L. (2009, 30th September). "Where Did We Go?"
    In *The New York Times*. p. A27.
109. Friedman, T. L. (2009, 18th February). "No Way, No How, Not Here."
    In *The New York Times*. p. A27.
110. Friedman, T. L. (2007, 2nd March). "The Silence That Kills."
    In *The New York Times*. p. A21.
111. Friere, P. (2000). *Pedagogy of the Oppressed*. New York:
    Continuum International Publishing Group. p. 47.
112. Gamble, F. (2011). *Thrive: What on Earth Will it Take?* (a DVD
    documentary film). ClearCompass Media. (www.thrivemovement.com)
113. Gardner, A. (2008, September). "Undecided Voters Not so Undecided After
    All." The Dana Foundation's *Brain in the News*.
114. Gardner, H. (1983). *Multiple Intelligences: The Theory in Practice*.
    New York: Basic Books.
115. Gates, B. (2005, 1st March). "America's high schools are obsolete and are
    ruining the lives of millions of Americans every year."
    In *The New York Times*. p. A22.

116. Gazzaniga, M .S. (2011). *Who's in Charge? Free Will and the Science of the Brain*. New York: Harper Collins Publishers. pp. 50, 61, 67, 70, 72, 73, 85, 128, 181, 191, 193, 197-198, 200, 204, 210, 218-219, Jacket.
117. Genet, R. (2012). *Science, Wisdom, and the Future: Humanity's Quest for a Flourishing Earth*. Eds. C. Genet, et al. Santa Margarita, CA: Collins Foundation Press. p. 38.
118. Giberson, K. W. & Stephens, R. J. (2011, 18th October). "The Evangelical Rejection of Reason." In *The New York Times*. p. A21.
119. Gibran, K. (1966). *The Prophet*. New York: Knopf. <http://www-personal.umich.edu/~jrcole/gibran/prophet/html>
120. Gladwell, M. (2008). *Outliers: The Story of Success* NY: Little, Brown and Company. pp. 125, 142.
121. Goleman, D., Boyatzis, R. & McKee, A. (2002). *Primal Leadership. Realizing the Power of Emotional Intelligence*. Boston, MA: Harvard Business School Press. p. 3.
122. Goodstein, L. (2012, 1st June). "American Nuns Vow to Fight Vatican Criticism." In *The New York Times*. p. A11.
123. Goodstein, L. (2011, 23rd July). "Priests Challenge Vatican on Ordaining Women," In *The New York Times*. pp. 1, 3.
124. Gopnik, A. (2009). *The Philosophical Baby: What Children's Minds Tell Us About Truth, Love, and the Meaning of Life*. New York: Farrar, Straus and Giroux pp. 10, 11, 13, 15, 178, 247.
125. Gordon, T. & Burch, N. (1974/1988). *Teacher Effectiveness Training*. New York: Peter H. Wyden.
126. Gordon, T. (1970). *Parent Effectiveness Training: The Proven Program for Raising Responsible Children*. New York: Three Rivers Press/Crown Publishing Group.
127. Gottman, J. (1995). *Why Marriage Succeed or Fail: And How You Can Make Yours Last*. New York: Simon and Schuster
128. Grady, H. (2011, September). *Explore!* Vol. 12, Issue 1. pp. 1-14.
129. Gray, T. (18th century). "Ode on a Distant Prospect of Eton College" The Thomas Gray Archive, University of Oxford, UK. <http://www.thomasgray.org/>
130. Greene, A. (2010, July/August). "Making Connections: The essence of memory is linking one thought to another." *Scientific American Mind*. pp. 22-24.
131. Greenspace (2011, 27th January). "Californians to protest against Koch brothers in Rancho Mirage." Environment, *Los Angeles Times*. <www.latimesblog.latimes.com/greenspace/2011/01/>
132. Grossmann, I. (2012, April 7th - 13th). "Age and Wisdom: Older and wiser?" *The Economist*. p. 91.
133. Grout, M. M. & Budinger, M. (2010). *An Alphabet of Good Health in a Sick World*. Scottsdale, AZ: New Medicine Press. pp. 1, 4, 7, 55.
134. Gunter, H., Meyer, A. & Elbert, T. (2011, 23rd July). "Baby blues." *The Economist*. p. 75.

135. Hafner, F. (2009). "The Mustard Seed Project. Kenilworth, NJ: Personal communication: June 27, 2009.
136. Hagelin, J. (2007). "Beyond Miracles." *Subtle Energies & Energy Medicine*, Vol. 18, No. 1.
137. Haidt, J. (2012, 18th March). "Forget the Money, Follow the Sacredness." In *The New York Times* Sunday Review. p. SR12.
138. Hall, E. T. (1976/1981). *Beyond Culture*. Garden City, New York: Anchor Press/Doubleday. pp. 1, 9, 14.
139. Hall, S. S. (2010). *Wisdom: From Philosophy to Neuroscience*. New York: Alfred A. Knopf. pp. 9, 18, 21, 30, 150, 160, 163.
140. Hamlin, K., Wynn, K., & Bloom, P. (2007, 22nd November). "Social evaluation by preverbal infants." *Nature*. p. 557
141. Hancock, L. (2011, September). "A+ for Finland." *Smithsonian*. pp. 94-100.
142. Hanson, R & Mendius, R. (2009). *Buddha's Brain*. USA: newharbingerpublications, Inc. <www.newharbinger.com> p. 122.
143. Hart, L. A. (1983). *Human Brain and Human Learning*. New York: Longman. p. 53.
144. Hawkins, D. (2009). *Healing and Recovery*. W. Sedona, AZ: Veritas Publishing. pp. 16-17, 20, 41, 59. 201.
145. Hawkins, D. R. (2006). *Transcending The Levels of Consciousness: The Stairway to Enlightenment*. W. Sedona, AZ; Veritas Publishing. p. 116
146. Hawkins, D.R. (2001). *The Eye of I: From Which Nothing Is Hidden*. W. Sedona, AZ: Veritas Publishing, p. 54.
147. Hawkins, D. (2002/1995). *Power vs. Force: The Hidden Determinants of Human Behavior*. W. Sedona, AZ: Veritas Publishing. pp. 90, 271-274.
148. Hebert, B. (2010, 14th September). "A Recovery's Long Odds." In *The New York Times*. p. A 25.
149. Hebert, B. (2010, 31st July). "A Sin And A Shame." In *The New York Times*. p. A15
150. Hebert, B. (2009, 12th January). "A Serious Proposal." In *The New York Times*. p. A 19.
151. Hebert, B. (2009, 8th August). "Women at Risk," In *The New York Times*. p. A 17.
152. Heilbrun, C. G (1997). *The Collected Stories by Carolyn G. Heilbrun*. New York: Ballantine Books. p. 161.
153. Hendrix, H. (1992). *Keeping the Love You Find*. NY: Pocket Books. p. 21.
154. Hillman, J. (1999). *The Power of Character and The Lasting Life*. New York: Random House. p. 91,
155. Hochschild, A. R. (1983). *The Managed Heart: The Commercialization of Human Feeling*. Berkeley, CA: University of California Press.

156. Hock, D. (1999). *Birth of the Chaordic Age*. San Francisco, CA: Berrett-Koehler Publishing, Inc.
157. Hofstadter, R. (1962) *Anti-intellectualism in American Life*. New York: Knopf.
158. Hooper, J. & Teresi, D. (1986). *The 3-Pound Universe*. NY: Dell Publishing Co., Inc. pp. 43, 390.
159. Hornung, E. (1982). *Conceptions of God in Ancient Egypt*. Ithaca, New York: Cornell University Press. p. 251.
160. Howard, C. (2010, 11th June). "Good News! Your Brain is Getting Smarter." *ForbesWoman*. (Forbes.com)
161. Howard, Clare (2012, February). "Downwind: Big Ag at Your Door." 100 Reporters. <http://100r.org/2012/02/downwind/>
162. Howitt, M (1829). Poem: "The Spider and the Fly." <http://en.wikisource.org/wiki/The_Spider_and_the_Fly>
163. Hutchnecker, A. (1974). *The Drive for Power*. New York: M. Evans. p. 242.
164. IBM (2008/2009). "Building a Smarter Planet." <ibm.com/smarterplanet>
165. Isaacson, W. (2011). *Steve Jobs*. NY: Simon & Schuster. pp. 48, 567.
166. Jabr, F. (2010, November/December), "Meeting Your Match," *Scientific American Mind*. pp. 42-45.
167. Jacobsen, T. (1976). *Treasures of Darkness: The History of Mesopotamian Religions*. NY: Yale University Press. p. 114.
168. Jacoby, S. (2008). *The Age of American Unreason*. New York: Pantheon Books.
169. James, E. O. (2004). *The Ancient Gods*. London, UK: Castle Books, Orion Pub. Group, Ltd. pp. 20, 77.
170. Janeway, E. (1980). *Powers of the Weak*. NY: Alfred A. Knopf pp. 51, 108, 110, 148.
171. Kahn, J. (2012, 13th May). "When Is a Problem Child Truly Dangerous?" *The New York Times Magazine*. pp. 32-37, 55, 57).
172. Kahneman, D. (2011). *Thinking, Fast and Slow*. NY: Farrar, Strauss and Giroux. pp. 4, 21, 215, 385.
173. Kahneman, D. (2011, 23rd October). "The Surety of Fools." *The New York Times Magazine*. pp. 30-33. 62.
174. Kaku, M. (2011). *Physics of the Future: How Science Will Shape Human Destiny and Our Daily Lives by the Year 2100*. New York: Doubleday. pp. 174, 304, 347.
175. Kalb, C. (2012, February). "Fetal Armor." *Scientific American*. p. 73.
176. Kanter, R. M. (1989). *When Giants Learn to Dance: Mastering the Challenge of Strategy, Management and Careers in the 1990s*. New York: Simon & Schuster, p.77.

177. Kindlon, D. & Thompson, M. (1999). *Raising Cain: Protecting the Emotional Life of Boys.* NY: Ballantine Books. p.15.
178. Klass, P. (2009, 13th January). "Making Room for Miss Manners Is a Parenting Basic." In *The New York Times.* p. D5.
179. Klein, M. C. (2011, 21st March). "Educated, Unemployed and Frustrated." In *The New York Times.* p. 23.
180. Kleinman, S. & Alexander, M. (2009, 11th March). "Try a Little Tenderness." In *The New York Times.* p. A23.
181. Kochunov, P., Fox, P., Lancaster, J., Tan, L. H., Amunts, K., Zilles, K., Mazziotta, J. & Gao, J. H. (2003, 23rd May). "Localized morphological brain differences between English-speaking Caucasians and Chinese-speaking Asians: new evidence of anatomical plasticity. *Developmental Neuroscience*, Vol. 1, No. 7. pp. 961-964.
182. Kohn, A. (1999, January). *Toward A State of Esteem*, Sacramento, CA: California State Dept. of Education. p. 38
183. Korda. M. (1975). *Power! How to get it, how to use it.* NY: Ballantine Books. pp. 285-286.
184. Kristof, N. D. (2012, 26th April). "Veterans and Brain Disease." In *The New York Times.* p. A23.
185. Kristof, N. D. (2012, 1st March). "Born To Not Get Bullied." In *The New York Times.* p. A27.
186. Kristof, N. D. (2011, 10th October). "Panic of the Plutocrats." In *The New York Times.* p. A21.
187. Kristof, N. D. (2011, 16th June). "Our Lefty Military." In *The New York Times.* p. A33.
188. Kristof, N. D. (2010, 16th July). "Redo That Voodoo." In *The New York Times.* p. A28.
189. Kristof, N. D. (2010. 29th July). 1 Soldier Or 20 Schools?" In *The New York Times.* p. A23.
190. Kristof, N. D. (2010, 10th January). "Religion and Women." In *The New York Times.* p. wk110.
191. Kristof, N. D. (2009, 12h July). "The Joy of Sachs." In *The New York Times.* p. A 19.
192. Kristof, D. D. (2008, 17th April). "Divided We Fall." In *The New York Times.* p. A27.
193. Krugman, P. (2012, 9th March). "Ignorance Is Strength." In *The New York Times.* p. A21.
194. Krugman, P. (2012, 9th January). "America's Unlevel Field." In *The New York Times.* p. A17.
195. Krugman, P. (2011, 9th October). "Panic of the Plutocrats." In *The New York Times.* p. A21.
196. Krugman, 2010, 16th July). "Redo That Voodoo." In *The New York Times.* p. A28.

197. Krugman, P. (2009, 19th October). "The Gold Bug Variations" <http:/www.pkarchive.org/cranks/goldbug.html>
198. Krystal, H. (1988). *Integration & Self-Healing: Affect, Trauma, Alexithymia.* Hillsdale, NJ: Lawrence Erlbaum Associates. pp. 72, 78, 84, 85, 243.
199. Lakoff, G. & Johnson, M. (1999). *Philosophy in the Flesh.* New York: Basic Books.
200. Larson, R. W. (2000, January). "Toward a Psychology of Positive Youth Development." *American Psychologist*, Vol. 55, No. 1. pp. 170-173.
201. Latner, J. (1992). Anton Chekov is quoted in "The Theory of Gestalt Therapy." In *Gestalt Therapy: Perspectives and Applications.* E. Nevins, Ed. Cleveland, OH: The Gestalt Institute of Cleveland Press. p. 30.
202. LeDoux, J. (2002). *Synaptic Self: How Our Brains Become Who We Are.* New York: Viking. pp. 8, 23, 24, 322.
203. LeDoux, J. (1996), *The Emotional Brain.* New York: Houghton Mifflin Harcourt. pp. 9, 11, 191, 231, 236, 238.
204. Lehrer, J. (2012). *IMAGINE: How Creativity Works.* NY: Houghton Mifflin Harcourt. pp. xvii, 8, 9, 11, 231, 236, 238-239, 247.
205. Lehrer, J. (2007, April). "Hearts & Minds- Since Plato, Scholars Have Drawn a Clear Distinction Between Thinking and Feeling. Now Science Suggests That Our Emotions Are What Make Thought Possible." The Dana Foundation's *BRAIN in the NEWS* (ww.dana.org), Vol. 14. No. 4. pp. 3-4.
206. Leonhardt, D. (2009, 1st February). "The Big Fix." In *The New York Times.* Sunday Magazine. pp. 22-29, 48, 50-51.
207. Levitt, S. D. & Dubner, S. J., *Super Freakonomics.* (2009). New York: HarperCollins Publishers Ltd., First Canadian Edition. p. 25.
208. Lipton, B. (2005). *The Biology of Belief.* Santa Rosa, CA: Mountain of Love/Elite Books. pp. 10, 111, 112, 119-120, 128, 151, 153-154, 165, 166, 173, 176, 177, 179.
209. Loewenstein, W. R. (2000). *The Touchstone of Life: Molecular Information, Cell Communication, and the Foundations of Life.* USA: Oxford University Press.
210. Lowrey, A. (2012, 17th April). "French Duo See (Well) Past Tax Rise for Richest." In *The New York Times.* pp. A1, B9.
211. Luntz, F. (2007). *Words That Work: It's Not What You Say, It's What People Hear.* New York: Hyperion.
212. Machiavelli, N. (1519/1903/1935). *The Prince.* NY: Mentor Book.
213. MacLean, P. (1977). "On the Evolution of Three Mentalities," In *New Dimensions in Psychiatry: A World View*, Vol. 2. Eds. Dr. Silvano Arieti & Dr. Gerard Chrzanowski, NewYork: John Wiley & Sons.
214. MacNeilage, P. F., Rogers, L. J., and Vallortigara, G. (2009, July). "The Origins of the Left & Right Brains." *Scientific American.* pp. 60-67.

215. Maddow, R. (2012). *Drift: The Unmooring of American Military Power*. New York: Crown Publishers. pp. 8, 251.
216. Mann, C.C. (2011, June). "The Birth of Religion: The World's First Temple." *National Geographic*, pp. 40, 48, 56, 57-58,
217. Markoff, J. (2009, 24th May). "The Coming Superbrain." In *The New York Times* Week in Review, pp. 1, 4.
218. Marrs, J. (2000). *Rule By Secrecy: The Hidden History that Connects the Trilateral Commission, The Freemasons, and the Great Pyramids*. NY: Perennial, An Imprint of HarperCollins/Publishers. pp. 7, 9, 19, 237, 273, 345, 348, 354, 363-364, 383, 404-405.
219. Maslow, A. H. (1968). *Toward a Psychology of Being*. 3rd Edition. New York: D. Van Nostrand Company. p. 196.
220. Mathison, D. and Finney, M. (2009). *Unlock the Hidden Job Market: 6 steps to a successful job search when times are tough*. Upper Saddle River, NJ: FT Press. Div. Pearson Education, Inc.
221. Maturana, H. (1985). "Ecology of Mind." Interview. <http://www.oikos.org/maten.htm>
222. Matusky, F. & J. (2003). *Healing The Terrorist Within! Self- and Other-Esteem*. Scottsdale, AZ: Cloudbank. p. 65.
223. May, R. (1972). *Power and Innocence: A Search for the Sources of Violence*. NY: Delta. p. 19.
224. McGilchrist, I. (2010, 2nd January). "The Battle Between the Brain's Left and Right Hemispheres." *The Wall Street Journal*. <http://online.wsj.com/article/SB10001424052748704304504574609> Retrieved 3/2010.
225. McGilchrist, I. (2009). *The Master and his Emissary: The Divided Brain and the Making of the Western World*. New Haven, CT: Yale University Press. pp. 1-3, 8-9, 14, 18-19, 28, 35, 185, 206, 277-278, 285-288, 320-321, 323, 331, 343, 359, 393, 461.
226. Medina, J. (2010, 7th February). "An Oasis of Calm, for Young Lives That Need It." In *The New York Times*, p. 29.
227. Mendoza, M. (2010, 14th May). Associated Press: "U.S. War on Drugs Failing." In *The Arizona Republic*, pp.A1, 4.
228. Menzie, N. (2011, 30th October). "Family Radio Founder Harold Camping Repents, Apologizes for False Teachings: Bible Teacher Confesses He Was Wrong to Predict Christ's Return; Says God Has Not Stopped Saving People." U.S.: *The Christian Post*.
229. Miller, A. (1981). *Prisoners of Childhood: The Drama of the Gifted Child and the Search for the True Self*. New York: Basic Books, Inc. pp. 81-82.
230. Mitchell, E. (1992, Winter). "As the Paradigm Shifts Two Decades of Consciousness Research." *Noetic Sciences Review*. No. 24., p. 7.
231. Money, J. & Lamacz, M. (1989). *Vandalized Lovemaps: Paraphilic Outcome of Seven Cases in Pediatric Sexology*. New York: Prometheus.

232. Moore, C. W. (1998). Essay: "Socio-Economic Consequences of the Protestant Reformation." *Canadian Conservative Forum.* <http://www.conservativeforum.org/EssaysForum.asp?ID=6062>
233. Morter, M.T. Jr. (2001). *The Soul Purpose: Unlocking the secrets to health, happiness, and success*. Rogers, AR: Dynamic Life, LLC.
234. Moss, M. (2010, 6th November). "While Warning About Fat, U.S. Pushes Cheese Sales." In *The New York Times.* Home page.
235. Myss, C. (2001). *Sacred Contracts: Awakening Your Divine Potential.* New York: Harmony Books. p. 178, 188.
236. Newberg, A. (2011, 31st May). "Religious Experiences Shrink Part of the Brain." *Scientific American*. p. 67.
237. Nilsen, R. (2008, 3rd August). "Viewpoints." In *The Arizona Republic*. p. V3.
238. Nixon_Shock (1971, 15th August). Economic measures taken by President Richard Nixon canceled the direct convertibility of the U.S. dollar to gold, ending the Bretton Woods system of international financial exchange. <http://en.wikipedia.org/wiki/Nixon_Shock>
239. Nocera, J. (2012, 10th April). "Football And Swahili." In *The New York Times*. p. A21.
240. Nocera, J. (2012, 17th March). "The Good, Bad and Ugly Of Capitalism." In *The New York Times*. p. A19.
241. Nocera, J. (2011, 20th September). "No Extra Credit." In *The New York Times*. p. A2.
242. Nolte, D. L. (1972/1975). "Children Learn What They Live." <http://www.EmpowermentBooks.com>
243. Obama, B. (2011, 12th January). Speech at Memorial in Tucson for Loughans' killing/wounding spree. In *The Arizona Republic*. pp. A 12-14.
244. Ober, C., Sinatra, S. T., & Zucker, M. (2010). *Earthing*. Laguna Beach, CA: Basic Health Publications, Inc. pp. 4, 6, 12-13..
245. Ofri, D. (2012, 28th March). "Doctors Have Feelings, Too." In *The New York Times*. p. A25.
246. Ohanian, S. (1999). *One Size Fits Few: The Folly of Educational Standards.* Portsmouth, NH: Heinemann.
247. Oppenheimer, M (2012, 9th June). "Across Religions, Persistent Battles Over What the Faithful May Read." *The New York Times*. p. A14.
248. Ornstein, R. E. (1972). *The Psychology of Consciousness*, San Francisco, CA: W. H. Freeman. p. 99.
249. Orwell, G. (1946). *Animal Farm*. New York: A Signet Classic/ New American Library. p. x.
250. Oshry, B. (1980). *Middle power*. Power & Systems Training, Inc., P. O. Box 388, Prudential Station, Boston, MA.
251. Overbye, D. (2009, 2nd June). "Wisdom in a Cleric's Garb; Why Not a Lab Coat Too?" In *The New York Times*. p. D2.

252. Pagels, E. (2012). *Revelations: Visions, Prophecy, & Politics in the Book of Revelation*. New York: Viking. pp. 11-13, 16, 37-38, 58, 155, 158-159, 160, 162, 164, 165, 169, 171, 172-173.
253. Pagels, E. (1979). *The Gnostic Gospels*. New York: Vintage Books, A Division of Random House, Inc. pp. 3, 4, 6-8, 10, 13-14, 26, 31, 46-47, 60-61, 66, 71, 75-76, 98, 101.
254. Palmer, P. J. & Zajonc, A. (2010). *The Heart of Higher Education*. San Francisco, CA: JosseyBass. pp. xi, 4, 69, 82-83, 84, 192, 265.
255. Pappano, L. (2012, 22nd January). "How Big-Time Sports Ate College Life." In *The New York Times* Education Life. pp. 22-25.
256. Parker, R. (2008, 9th November). "Essay: The Crisis Last Time." In *The New York Times*. p. 54.
257. Paul, A. M. (2010). *Origins: How the Nine Months Before Birth Shapes the Rest of Our Lives*. New York: Free Press, A Division of Simon & Schuster. pp. 5, 7, 8, 24-27, 28, 46, 195.
258. Paulus, T. (1972/1997). *Hope for the Flowers*. Mahwah, NJ: Paulist Press
259. Peale, N. V. (1952/1956). *The Power of Positive Thinking*. New York: Fawcett Crest. p. 42.
260. Pearce, J.C. (2002). *The Biology of Transcendence*. Rochester, VT: Park Street Press. pp. 27, 42-43, 61, 118, 128, 131, 144, 241, 249, 251-252, 254-255, 261.
261. Perkins, J. (2004). *Confessions of an Economic Hit Man*. New York: Penguin Group (USA), A Plume Book. pp. xi, xiii, xiv, xv, xxii, 180, 181, 182
262. Perry, P. (2003, March/April). "Those who do good, do well." *The Saturday Evening Post*. pp. 61, 66.
263. Pert, C. B. (1997). *Molecules of Emotions: Why You Feel The Way You Feel*. New York: Simon & Schuster. pp. 192-193.
264. Peters, K. (2003, 24th August). "Our Sacred Center," *Unitarian Universalist Society of Boulder*. p. 1.
265. Peters, K. (2002). *Dancing with the Sacred: Evolution, Ecology, and God*. Harrisburg, PA: Trinity Press International. p. 19
266. Peterson, C. & Seligman, M. E. P. (2004). *Character Strengths and Virtues: A Handbook and Classification*. Oxford, UK: Oxford University Press. p. 161-196.
267. Phillips, H. (2006, October 7-13). "Everyday fairytales." *New Scientist*. Vol. 192. No. 2572. pp.32-36.
268. Phillips-Fein, K. (2009). *Invisible Hands: The Making of the Conservative Movement from the New Deal to Reagan*. New York: W. W. Norton & Co.
269. Pink, D. H. (2005). *A Whole New Mind: Moving from the Information Age to the Conceptual Age*. New York: Riverhead Books, Penguin Group (USA), Inc.
270. Pinker, S. (2010, 11th June). "Mind Over Mass Media," In *The New York Times*. p. A 27

271. Plumb, J. H. (1972, Summer). "An epoch...started ten thousand years ago" *Horizon Magazine*. pp. 5, 6.
272. Porter, R. (2003). *Flesh in the Age of Reason: The Modern Foundations of Body and Soul*. New York: W. W. Norton & Co. pp. 3-6, 34, 229, 252, 267, 269, 272, 278, 334, 336, 389, 393, 438.
273. Prescott, D. (1938/1973). Chairman Prescott's transmittal letter with the State-of-Education Report commissioned by the American Council on Education Report (1938). In P. T. Young's *Emotions in Man and Animal* (1973). Melbourne, FL: R. E. Krieger. p. 193.
274. Prescott, D. (1957). *The Child in the Educative Process*. NY: McGraw Hill. Pp 357-358.
275. Prigogene, I. (1997). *The End of Certainty*. New York: The Free Press.
276. Ramachandran, V.S. (1991). *Phantom in the Brain*. New York: Harper Perennial.
277. Rapp, D. J. (2003). *Our Toxic World: A Wake-Up Call – Chemicals Damage Your Body, Brain, Behavior and Sex*. Penryn, CA: Personal Transformation Press. <www.personaltransformationpress..com>
278. Rawcliffe, C. (1999). *Medicine & Society in Later Medieval England*. London, UK: Sandpiper Books, Ltd. p. 174.
279. Reese, S. (2010). *At Wit's End: Is This Thing Working?! A Guide to Better Brain Function*. Scottsdale, AZ: New Education Press.
280. Reinhart, C.M. & Rogoff, K.S. (2009). *This Time Is Different: Eight Centuries of Financial Folly*. Princeton, NJ: Princeton University Press. p. 174.
281. Rich, F. (2010, 29th August), "The Billionaires Bankrolling the Tea Party," In *The New York Times*. p. wk 8.
282. Rich, F. (2009, 12th July). "She broke the G.O.P. and Now She Owns It," Sunday Opinions, *The New York Times*. p. wk 8.
283. Rioch, M. J. (1971). "All We Like Sheep–" (Isaiah 54:6). Followers and Leaders. In *Psychiatry*, 34. pp. 258-273.
284. Robbins, J. (2007). *Healthy at 100: The Scientifically Proven Secrets of the World's Healthiest and Longest Lived Peoples*. New York: Ballantine Books.
285. Rogers, C. with Freiberg, H. (1994). *Freedom To Learn*. Upper Saddle River, New Jersey: Prentice Hall.
286. Rogers, C. (1977). *Carl Rogers on Personal Power: Inner strength and its Revolutionary impact*. New York: Delacorte Press. p. 15.
287. Rogers, C. (1961). *On Becoming A Person*. NY: Houghton Mifflin. p. 37.
288. Rosenow, E. C. (2003). *The Art of Living... The Art of Medicine: The Wit and Wisdom of Life and Medicine – A Physician's Perspective*. Victoria, BC, Canada: Trafford. pp. 52-53.
289. Rosner, H. (2011, 8th November). "Spotted Horses in Cave Art Weren't Just a Figment, DNA Shows." In *The New York Times*. p. D3.
290. Rubenfeld, I. (2000). *The Listening Hand*. NY: Bantam Books. pp. x, xi, 18, 201.
291. Rubenfeld, L. (1995). "Mind Your Body." *CHANGES*. pp. 32-34.

292. Rudoren, J. (2012, 20th May). "The Fight Over Who Fights in Israel." *The New York Times* Sunday Review. p. SR4.
293. Sachs, R. (2012). "Critical Thinking and Wisdom: A Buddhist Perspective." In *Science, Wisdom, and the Future: Humanity's Quest for a Flourishing Earth*. Eds. C. Genet, et al. Santa Margarita, CA: Collins Foundation Press. pp.221-223.
294. Sagan, C. (1977). *The Dragons of Eden*. NY: Random House. p. 238.
295. Salk, J. (1971). *Man Unfolding*, New York: Harper & Row.
296. Samuelson, P. A. (1948/1980). *Economics*. NY: McGraw-Hill.
297. Sarno, J. (2007). *The Divided Mind: The Epidemic of Mindbody Disorders*. NY: HarperCollinsPublishers. pp. 4-5, 8, 58.
298. Saroglou, V. (2012, May/June). "Are We Born to Be Religious? Genes and personality influence our attitudes toward religion. *Scientific American Mind*. pp. 52-57.
299. Scaer, R. (2005). *The Trauma Spectrum: Hidden Wounds and Human Resiliency*. New York: W.W. Norton & Company. pp. 17, 18, 83, 99, 100, 106, 145, 146, 148, 177.
300. Schlesinger, Jr., A. M. (2007, 1st January). "Folly's Antidote." In *The New York Times*. Op-Ed.
301. Schmid, R. E. (2010, 22nd April). AP. "The Research findings are in: Older people are indeed Wiser." In *The Arizona Republic*. pp. E1-2.
302. Schore, A. N. (2003). *Affect Regulation and The Repair of the Self*. New York: W. W. Norton & Co. Inc.
303. Schore, A. N. (1994). *Affect Regulation and the Origin of the Self: The Neurobiology of Emotional Development*. Hillsdale, NJ: Lawrence Erlbaum Associates.
304. Senge, P., Scharmer, C. O., Jaworski, J. & Flowers, B. S. (2004). *Presence: Human Purpose and the Field of the Future*. New York: Doubleday Broadway Publishing Group, a division of Random House, Inc. p. 30.
305. Sharpe, K. (2006). *Science of God: Truth in the Age of Science*. New York: Rowman & Littlefield Publishers, Inc. p. 125.
306. Shlain, L. (2003). *Sex, Time and Power: How Women's Sexuality Shaped Human Evolution*. New York: Viking. pp. 24, 64, 334, 338, 339, 341, 342,347.
307. Shlain, L. (1999). *The Alphabet Versus The Goddess: The Conflict Between Word and Image*. New York: Penguin/Compass. pp. 1, 2, 4, 6, 118, 315.
308. Shlain, L. (1991). *Art & Physics: Parallel Visions in Space, Time & Light*. New York: Perennial, An Imprint of HarperCollins Publishers. p. 431.
309. Shreeve, J. (2010, July). The Evolutionary Road." *National Geographic*. pp. 34-66.
310. Sitchin, Z. (1980). *The Stairway to Heaven: Book II of the Earth Chronicles*. New York: Harper Collins Publishers. pp. vii, 1, 117, 359, 444, 446.
311. Sitchin, Z. (1976). *The 12th Planet: Book 1 of the Earth Chronicles*. New York: Avon Books, An Imprint of HarperCollinsPublishers.
312. Skilling, E. (2009, December). Skilling Institute's Photon Genius. <www.edskilling.com>

313. Smolen, L (2006). *The Trouble with Physics: The Rise of String Theory, the Fall of a Science, and What Comes Next*. New York: Houghton Mifflin Company. pp. 264-265, 267, 314, 329.
314. Stansell, C. (2010, 24th August). "A Forgotten Fight for Suffrage." In *The New York Times*. p. A19.
315. Steinfels, P. (2007). "Beliefs: Lessons for Living Found in Views of the Last Judgment." In *The New York Times*. p. A10.
316. Stern, J. (2010). *Denial: A Memoir of Terror*. New York: Ecco.
317. Sternberg, R. (1998). "A Balance Theory of Wisdom." *Review of General Psychology*. 2:4. pp. 347-365.
318. Steyn, M. (2006). "The future belongs to Islam." [Excerpt from *America Alone: The End of the World As We Know It*, 2010, Series: Playaway Adult Nonfiction]. In *Macleans*, Canada. p. 138, <http://www.macleans.ca/article.jsp?content=20061023_134898>
319. Stoddard, L. & Dallmann-Jones, A. (2010). *Educating for Human Greatness*. Sarasota, FL: Peppertree Press. pp. 76, 107, 157, 159.
320. Stowe, H. B. (1852). *Uncle Tom's Cabin: Life Among the Lowly*. Boston, MA: John P. Jewett & Company.
321. Stray, G. (2009). *Beyond 2012: Catastrophe or Awakening?* Rochester, VT: Bear. pp. 343, 344.
322. Summers, L. H. (2012, 22nd January). "The 21st Century Education." In *The New York Times* Education Life. pp. 26-27, 29.
323. Szent-Gyorgyi, A. (1981, Jan/Feb). Interview. In *Saturday Evening Post*, p. 30. <http://todayinsc.com/S/SzentGyorgyi_Albert/SzentGyorgyi>
324. Tavernise, S. (2009, 16th February). "In Quest for Equal Rights, Muslim Women's Meeting Turns to Islam's Tenets." In *The New York Times*. p. A8.
325. Taylor, J. B. (2006). *My Stroke of Insight*. New York: Viking. pp. 18-19, 34, 124-125, 132-133.
326. Teicher, M. H. (2002, March). "Scars That Won't Heal: The Neurobiology of Child Abuse." *Scientific American*.
327. Tellinger, M. (2010). *Slave Species of god.: The Story of Humankind from the Cradle of Humankind*. 5th edition. Johannesburg, S. Africa: Zulu Planet Publishers, A Music Masters Book. 5th edition. pp. 3, 31.
328. Tennyson, A. (1845). *"Morte D'Arthur." Poems*, 4th Edition. London, UK: Moxon
329. Tennyson, A. (1832), "Oenone. In *From Beowulf to Modern British Writers* (1959). Ball, J. (Ed). p. 940.
330. Theokas, C. (2010, 21st December). "SHOCKING: Nearly 1 in 4 High School Graduates Can't Pass Military Entrance Exam." Report by *The Education Trust*. (Reported by Armario & Turner) <http://www.huffingtonpost.com/2010/12/21>
331. Thompson, W. I (1973, 1974). *Passages About Earth*. New York: Harper Collins. pp. 16, 121-122.

332. Tononi, G. (2010, 21st September). "Sizing Up Consciousness By Its Bits" by Carl Zimmer. In *The New York Times*, Science Times. pp. D1, 4.
333. Treffert, D. (2010). *Islands of Genius*. Philadelphia, PA: Jessica Kingsley Publishers. p. 58.
334. TWIT (The Western Intellectual Tradition): Thompson, W. I. (1973, 1974). *Passages About Earth*. New York: HarperCollins.
335. Van Doren, C. (1991). *The History of Knowledge: The Pivotal Events, People, Achievements of World History*. New York: Ballantine Books. pp. 3, 4, 14, 17, 18, 20, 22, 44, 175.
336. Verghese, A. (2011, 27th February). "Treat the Patient, Not the CT Scan." *The New York Times*. p. A10.
337. Wade, N. (2012, 20th February). "Dead for 32,000 Years, an Arctic Plant Is Revived." In *The New York Times*.
338. Wade, N. (2009). *The Faith Instinct: How Religion Evolved and Why it Endures*. New York: The Penguin Press. p. 2, Jacket
339. Walker, T. (2010, 7th December). "PISA 2009: U.S. Students in the Middle of the Pack." <http://neatoday.org/2010/12/07/pisa2009/>
340. Wallechinsky, D. & Wallace, I., Eds. (1975). *The People's Almanac*. New York: Doubleday & Co., Inc. p. 464.
341. Warner, J. (2010, 11th July). "Egghead Alert." In *The New York Times Magazine*. pp. 11-12.
342. Weber, M. (1954). *Max Weber on Law in Economy and Society*. M. Rheinstein, Editor, Annotator. Cambridge, MA: Harvard University Press
343. Wiesel, E. (1976/1994). *Messengers of God: Biblical Portraits and Legends*. New York: A Touchstone Book, Simon & Schuster. p. 30.
344. Willey, D. (2008, 13th May). "Vatican says aliens could exist." BBC News, Rome, Italy. <http://news.bbc.co.uk/2/hi/7399661.stm>
345. Williams, R. (1967). *You are Extraordinary*. New York: Random House.
346. Wilson, T. D. (2002). *Strangers to Ourselves*. Cambridge, MA: Belknap/Harvard University Press. pp. 22, 24.
347. Winerip, M. (2021, 4th June). "In Lists of Best High Schools, Numbers Don't Tell the Whole Story." In *The New York Times*. p. A13.
348. Wolff, E. N. (2010). "Distribution of net worth and financial wealth in the U.S., 1983-2007." In *Wealth, Income, and Power* by G. William Domhoff (2011). Who Rules America <http:sociologyucsc.edu/whorulesamerica/power/wealth.html>
349. Wong, K. (2012, April). "First of Our Kind." In *Scientific American*. pp. 31-39.
350. Yee, A. (2009, 30th June). "Tibetan Monks and Nuns Turn Their Minds Toward Science." In *The New York Times*. p. D3.
351. Young, P. T. (1973). *Emotions in Man and Animal*. Melbourne, FL: R. E. Krieger. [Re: Daniel Prescott's 1938 commissioned U.S. Department of Education Report and transmittal letter.] p. 193.

352. Young, S. (2004). *Jesus Calling: Devotions for Every Day of the Year. Enjoying Peace in His Presence*. Publisher: Thomas Nelson <thomasnelson.com>
353. Zizek, S. (2007, 24th March). "Knight of the Living Dead." In *The New York Times*. p. A27
354. Zuger, A. (2007, 29th May). "The Brain: Malleable, Capable, Vulnerable." In *The New York Times*. Science Times. p. D5.

Index

-A-

Absurd. 81, 109, 246
Achilles' heel. 147
Agribusiness. 92, 95, 145, 299, 321, 327
Alcoa. 196
Alexithymic. 83
All We Like Sheep. 239
American Council on. 40, 41
American Dream. 27, 39, 91, 146, 154, 169, 184, 318, 359, 399
American Fantasy. 184
American Nuns. 238, 402
America's Secret Societies. 311
America's "Royalty". 311, 313, 324
Amygdala. 10, 115, 137, 158, 293, 381
Annunaki. 328
Anthony of Egypt. 27
Anthropology. . . . . v, 366
Anti-emotional. . . . . vii, 43, 57, 81, 161, 162
Anti-intellectual. . . . . vi, vii, 57, 161, 162
Anu. . . . . ii, 107, 108, 128, 153, 199, 215, 328, 329, 332, 340, 370, 389,
390, 398, 400, 403-409, 411, 412
Apocalyptic Belief. 242
Apostle Peter. 210, 228, 268
Approved Knowledge. . . . . ii, 6, 33, 110, 155, 241, 303, 335, 373
Arctic plant. 328, 412
Ardi. 9, 11, 214, 399
Aristotle. 224, 268
Athletes. 15, 17, 283, 287

-B-

Banking. 27, 102, 183, 262, 271, 272, 307, 312, 314-320, 322, 323,
325, 326, 358
Behaviorism. 148
Beliefs. . . . . i, iv, vi, viii, xii, xv, 1, 9, 10, 13, 22, 24, 26, 29, 32, 36, 42, 51,
56, 73, 74, 76, 78, 79, 81, 87, 88, 96, 98, 99, 102, 103, 105, 113,
115, 117, 143, 147, 158, 160, 168, 171, 178, 184, 186, 188, 198,
200, 202, 205-210, 212, 217-220, 224, 227, 229, 232, 234, 235,
237-240, 242, 243, 247, 249, 256, 259, 261-264, 267-270, 274, 276,
279, 285, 286, 294, 295, 297, 301, 303, 304, 310, 336, 344, 345,
353, 355, 360, 362, 363, 365, 366, 371, 385-387, 392, 395, 411
Bilderbergers. 311, 313, 315

Black Forest, Germany.................................. 334
Black Plague................................... 36
Brothels.. 193
Brown, Dan..................................... 241
Buddhism................................. 219, 250, 254, 255, 257
Butterfly................................... v, xv, 139, 389

-C-

Calvinism............................. 21, 234, 235
Cancer............ 7, ii, xiii-xv, 6, 11, 24, 80, 92, 93, 116, 137, 248, 299, 304,
    311, 325, 336, 339-344, 346, 350, 364, 380, 389, 390
Cancer as Metaphor.............................. ii
Capitalism................. xi, 19, 21, 181, 195, 236, 280, 361, 382, 390, 408
Capitalists............... 16, 19, 44, 92, 181, 190, 195, 196, 198, 204, 258
Carnegie Hall.................................. 17
Cash Cow................................. 185, 322, 353, 364
Cato Institute................................. 196
Causes................... 23, 78, 107, 198, 199, 235, 342, 360, 369, 371
Central Intelligence Agency (CIA)................... 179
Chakras................................... 158, 159
Christianity......... 34, 216, 218, 219, 221, 224-229, 231, 233, 234, 250, 258,
    262, 332, 357, 387
Cognitive science.............................. 2, 81, 300
College Board.................................. 91
Compassion......... iv, xi, 4, 12, 14, 17, 22, 27, 28, 47-49, 56, 58, 59, 75, 81-
    83, 88, 93, 107, 136, 140, 146, 165, 179, 211, 225, 239, 240, 247,
    249, 251, 254, 261, 263, 264, 291, 292, 300, 346, 354, 359, 367,
    395
Compensation................................. 186, 196
Conscious........... iii, iv, vii, xiii, 2, 7, 8, 10-13, 20, 45, 53, 75, 77, 79-81, 95,
    96, 98, 99, 112, 113, 115-117, 119-121, 125, 136, 138, 143, 151,
    157, 159, 160, 162, 171, 179, 194, 206-210, 262, 269, 273, 274,
    285, 293, 294, 344, 346, 371, 372, 386
corpus collosum............................... 369
Cortisol..................................... 95, 127
Council of Arles............................... 231
Council of Nicea........................... 221, 231, 241
Council on Foreign Relations (CFR).............. 311, 313-315
Crusades, The................................. 306
CTE (chronic traumatic encephalopathy)............. 142

-D-

Dalai Lama.................................. 254, 260

Dame. 38
Dear Abby. 56, 400
Dennis. . . . . iii, 139
Dependent. 8, 54, 63, 128, 135, 157, 166, 171, 197, 209, 264, 271,
275-280, 298, 385
Determinism. 148
Disowned Self. 13, 78, 209, 383
Divided Selves. . . . . ii, 148, 162
Divine Chain of Being. 32, 200
Divine Nature of Authority. 8, 33, 100, 186
Divine Right of Kings. 165
Divine Right/Nature. 204, 205, 210, 239, 308, 336
Domino's Pizza. 94
Drug Cartels. 60, 193, 289
Drugs. 15, 24, 42, 43, 53, 56, 59-61, 71, 80, 104, 127, 141, 152, 171,
192-194, 197, 263, 299, 340, 364, 365, 407

-E-

Earthly gods.. 358-361
Economic Hit Men. 84, 324, 359
Economy. 27, 65, 156, 163, 164, 167, 188, 194, 195, 197-199, 201,
202, 273, 317, 318, 346, 348, 353, 397, 413
Ecuador. 323-325
Emerge. . . . . viii, ix, 71, 88, 128, 130, 161, 176, 212, 284, 384, 387, 395
Emerging Adulthood. 173, 174, 397
Emotional Resilience. . . . . vii, 14, 26, 59, 61, 71, 136, 155, 172
Empathy. . . . . iii, 4, 9, 13, 17, 35, 47, 48, 57, 63, 74, 80, 82, 122, 146, 147,
165, 176, 180, 264, 293, 295, 300, 344, 359, 367, 380, 387
Enki.. . . . . 215, 328, 329, 332
Enlil. 215, 328, 329, 332
Epic of Creation. 328
Epigenetics. 132
Epiphany. xiv
Esteem.. . . . . ii, iv, xiii, xv, 13, 17, 22-24, 54, 56, 59, 78, 79, 85, 105, 137,
150, 172, 188, 194, 207, 264, 275, 278-280, 301, 337, 340, 346,
363, 366, 370, 372, 386, 399, 405, 407
Eugenics. 284, 312, 313, 336, 383
Evolution.. . . . . 33, 88, 117, 138, 209-211, 214, 215, 226, 256, 265, 286,
328, 331, 368, 387, 390, 391, 395, 398, 399, 407, 409, 411

-F-

Fairness. 25, 130, 136, 140, 142, 199, 395
Family Radio Stations.. 245
Father Gabriel Funes. 333

Fathers.. . . . . 17, 38, 54, 101, 122, 124, 133, 141, 162, 163, 188, 189, 191,
      218, 224, 225, 237, 273, 285, 297, 360, 364, 383, 387, 401
Fear. . . . . i, ii, iv, vii, 2, 12, 16, 19, 20, 31, 40, 47, 52, 59, 70, 78, 80-82, 84,
     96, 98, 100, 101, 107, 110, 111, 125, 131, 133, 137, 140, 141, 147,
     148, 151, 153, 155, 156, 158, 165, 166, 178, 182, 185, 187, 189,
     195, 205, 209, 210, 225, 233, 235, 239, 242, 244, 249, 252, 257,
     259, 261, 264, 265, 267, 269, 273-276, 280, 281, 287, 293, 300,
     304, 305, 307, 310, 332, 337, 346, 358-360, 381, 386, 393, 398
Federal Employees. 196
Federal Reserve Bank. 315
fetal brain. 124
Fight or Flight Syndrome. 345, 366
financial. . . . . ii, xii, 3, 17, 19, 22, 23, 25, 27-29, 51, 53, 65, 68, 71, 72, 84,
     85, 98, 160, 163-165, 167, 175-177, 181, 183, 184, 186, 190, 195,
financial (cont.)   197-202, 222, 245, 272, 275, 281, 290, 297, 298, 300, 302, 303,
    305, 315-320, 325-327, 336, 344, 353-355, 358-362, 375, 387, 393,
                        408, 410, 413
Finland. 175, 181, 294, 349, 351, 403
Forgiveness. 102, 136, 237
Founding Fathers. 38, 101, 162, 163, 188, 189, 191, 218, 224, 225,
                    297, 360, 364, 383, 387
Fractional Reserve Banking. 316, 317, 325
Free enterprise. 21, 29, 145, 165, 181, 184, 196, 199, 360, 364
Free speech. 59
Freemasonry. 229, 306-310
Functional Magnetic Resonance. 115
Fundamentalism. 30, 210, 253

-G-

Gender Conditioning. 262
Gnostic Christians. 230
Gnostic Gospels. 227, 241, 244, 409
Gold. . . . . . . xiv, 102, 150, 164, 203-205, 319, 325, 329, 333, 361, 387, 406, 408
Gold Rule. 361
Golden Rule. . . . . x, 2, 5, 22, 67, 71, 83, 149, 183, 361, 387, 388
Goldman Sachs. . . . . xi, 200
Gospel of Growth. 322, 323
Gospel of Wealth. 21, 160, 235, 236, 323
Guantanamo. 57

-H-

Halo Effect. 19, 24
Hamlet. 145

Happiness. 78, 122, 128, 155, 192, 198, 199, 210, 248, 261, 275, 382, 408
Haredim. 222, 223
Harkin Energy Company. 324
Haven Academy. 46
Heart Consciousness.. . . . . vii, xi-xiii, 28, 53, 63, 71, 77, 91, 143, 161, 183, 263, 300, 372
Heresy. 102, 103, 155, 229, 230, 299
Hinduism. 219, 250, 253
Hippocampus. 10, 74, 115, 132, 217, 218, 381
Homo Economicus.. . . . . 198, 199
Homo Erectus. 125, 212, 214
Homo Sapiens. 86, 125, 212, 214, 266, 389, 391
Hope. . . . .   ii, ix, xiii, 25, 77, 89, 122, 140, 153, 184, 202, 208, 210, 236, 242, 244, 249, 252, 324, 369, 379, 388, 389, 392, 393, 395, 396, 409
Ho's.. . . . . 107, 290, 398
Human attachment. 129
Human Development.. . . . . v, vii, xi-xiii, 24, 28, 29, 45, 49, 61, 67, 71, 82, 98, 100, 105, 120, 122, 123, 130-132, 139, 142-144, 151, 152, 154,
(Human Dev.)   161, 171-174, 195, 207, 272, 276, 278, 281, 294, 341, 351, 363, 366, 379, 381
Human Development Theories. 174
Human Mind. 36, 75, 114, 214
Hungry Ego.. . . . . 383, 385
Hungry Heart. 385
Hypergraphia.. 235
Hypermasculine.. . . . . 103, 274, 287
Hypnotist. iii

-I-

IBM.. . . . . 62, 63, 146, 404
Illegal Drugs. 53, 59, 194, 197, 364
Illuminati. 309, 310
Imagination. . . . . i, 14, 26, 37, 43, 47, 51, 70, 71, 76, 103, 104, 128, 135, 156
Imaging (fMRI). 115
Immune System. 115, 299, 340, 342-344
in utero. 10, 13, 74, 77-79, 93, 97, 117, 123, 124, 126, 127, 134, 143, 166, 167, 281, 294, 345, 346
Independent.. . . . . 6, 35, 42, 44, 55, 70, 93, 171, 173, 187, 221, 264, 265, 276-280, 315, 316, 326, 385
Industrial Revolution. 36, 38, 200
Inhumane Development. 121, 123, 140

Intel. . . . . viii, ix, 400
Interdependent. 171, 265, 276-278, 281
Invisible Curriculum. 7, 14, 49, 107
Islam. 216, 219, 221, 250-252, 257, 258, 332, 412

-J-
Jekyll Island, Georgia. 313
Jeopardy!. 146
Joan. 339
John of Patmos. 243
Journaling. . . . . v, vi, 151, 388
Judaism. 219, 221, 222, 224, 250

-K-
Karma. 253, 255
Keith. 174
Kimbel, William. 212
Kinesiology. 12, 221, 224
Knights Templar. 36, 305-308
Knots. . . . . xii, xiii, 361
Know Thyself. 369
Koran. 16, 219, 246, 251, 252, 260, 369

-L-
left hemisphere. . . . . iv, 1, 5, 11, 12, 25, 31, 33, 35-37, 78, 105, 125, 142,
149, 159, 176, 234, 236, 300, 303, 373, 383
left-brain. . . . . ii, vi, viii, ix, 2-4, 6, 8-17, 19, 20, 25, 29, 33, 35, 41, 45-49,
53, 62, 68, 70, 71, 73-79, 81-84, 86, 96, 97, 99, 100, 105, 107, 110,
114, 117, 118, 122, 125, 135, 143, 147, 148, 151, 158-161, 163, 165
Left-brain Stroke. 117, 118
Levels. . . . . xv, 12, 17, 24, 31, 53, 78, 90, 106, 120, 127, 129, 162, 196,
200, 209, 211, 217, 218, 241, 243, 246, 276, 284, 286, 294, 317,
342, 350, 361, 396, 397, 403
limbic system. 10, 117, 125, 217, 378
Love. . . . . i, iv, 2, 5, 12, 13, 16, 20, 21, 23, 25-27, 45, 55, 58, 76-82, 89, 94,
97-99, 102-105, 107, 118, 119, 121, 122, 128-130, 133, 134, 136,
138-140, 147, 149, 150, 154, 156, 157, 165, 171, 189, 199, 203,
211, 214, 223, 225, 226, 237, 247, 248, 257, 259, 263-265, 269,
270, 274, 275, 278, 280-285, 287, 288, 291, 300, 346, 358, 366,
370, 376, 377, 381, 382, 386, 388-391, 395, 397, 398, 402, 404,
406
Lowered Expectations. 349
Lucy. 6, 212
Luna Moth. . . . . xv, 395

-M-

Main Street. . . . . xvi, 164, 188
Manhood. 290
Mary Magdalene. 227, 228, 232, 233, 268, 306, 399
MaryBeth. 77
Mayan Calendar. 18, 31, 338
Mesoamerica. 18, 334
Mesopotamia. 34, 215, 216, 220, 221, 331-333, 404
Metaphor. . . . . ii, xv, 35, 37, 71, 77, 110, 159, 162, 343, 344, 350, 361, 364, 389, 390
Meyer, A.. 403
Misogyny. 224, 262, 268, 276, 282, 284, 285, 288, 291
Moltmann, Jurgen. 261
Monte Verde, Chile. 330
moral. . . . . xi, 16, 25, 27, 35, 43, 48, 57, 84, 85, 87, 90, 98, 111, 136-138, 142, 150, 166-168, 177, 187, 201, 202, 211, 212, 218, 237, 239, 250, 253, 256, 258, 260, 274, 280, 283, 289, 292, 297, 346, 350, 353, 359, 361, 382, 389, 398
Muhammad. 217, 218, 250, 252, 258, 259, 307
Multicultural America. 192, 250

-N-

Nag Hammadi. 227, 239, 241, 244
Nancy. 160
National Institutes of Health (NIH). 6
Native American Elder. 89, 121
Neanderthal.. 125
neocortex. 10, 74, 115, 117, 125, 136
New American Academy. 377
New World Order, A. 315
Newtonian Physics. 198
Ninhursaga. 215, 329, 332
Norway. . . . . xii, 181, 294

-O-

Occupy Wall Street. 154, 189
of Authority. 8, 33, 100, 178, 186, 204, 205, 210, 239, 247, 308, 336, 353-356, 358, 364
Old Wives' Tales. 123
Online Education. 67
Optimism. 112, 141, 259, 281, 384, 393
Original Sin. 21, 34, 232, 233, 240, 242, 263, 268, 285, 333, 334, 336
Oxytocin. 24, 130

-P-

Passion submerges Reason. 30, 97
Patriarchy. 224, 237, 251, 256, 262, 268, 282, 285, 286, 386
Paul. 117, 136, 141, 201, 224, 232, 315, 318, 319, 326, 409
Pentagon, The. 179
Permanent War. 166, 180, 226, 296
Personal. . . . . ii, iv, vii, ix, 8, 9, 21, 31, 46, 59, 62, 68, 69, 72, 76, 83, 87,
90, 103, 105-107, 120, 125, 140, 144, 147, 152-154, 157, 167, 178,
179, 182, 185-187, 189, 207, 209, 221, 231, 247, 248, 263, 278-
281, 288, 295, 301, 353-355, 364, 367, 369, 371, 391-393, 395,
402, 403, 410
Perturbation. . . . . xv, 388
Pew Research Center. 89
Physiology. . . . . v, 20, 79, 96, 124
Pimp. 290
Plato. 35, 224, 268, 379, 406
Pope Benedict XVI. 98, 315
Pornography. 285, 289, 291
Positive Psychology. 56, 87, 109
Poverty. 3, 7, 21, 25, 30, 65, 80, 137, 149, 167, 171, 185, 190, 202,
203, 248, 273, 285, 316, 320-322, 349, 350, 383, 384, 393, 397
Power and Politics. 162, 177
Power:. 233, 358, 410, 411
prefrontal cortex.. . . . . 105, 115, 134, 135, 172, 173
Prefrontal Lobes. . . . . ix, 10, 26, 62, 119, 134, 135, 152, 274, 352
Private Sector. . . . . x, 196
Prostitution. 285, 289, 290, 293
Psychology.. . . . . ii, iii, v, 56, 67, 77, 87, 109, 110, 116, 257, 272, 366, 370,
406-408, 411
Psychopaths. 57, 122
PTSD (post-traumatic stress disorder). 112

-Q-

Quakers. 234, 235, 241
Quantum Physics. 9, 80, 104, 114

-R-

Redfield, James. 241

Relationships............ v, vii, x, xii, 4, 10, 14, 24, 43, 61, 68, 71, 77-81, 83, 98, 99, 106, 107, 112, 128, 131, 133, 134, 137, 138, 141, 144, 153, 157, 158, 171, 173, 178, 189, 195, 208, 248, 256, 262, 266, 267, 269, 271, 277, 279, 281, 284, 302, 354, 357, 367, 377, 378, 381, 386, 388, 390, 391, 393, 394
Religions' Common Denominators.................................. 255
reptilian brain. 10, 125
Resistance to Change..................... 7, 103-105, 209, 223
right hemisphere. .... iv, 10-12, 35, 37, 40, 42, 49, 77, 78, 106, 107, 125, 142, 149, 208, 300, 303, 346, 379, 383
right-brain.......... v-vii, ix, xi, 2-4, 9-12, 14, 17, 19, 20, 24-30, 33, 35, 41, 43, 45, 47-49, 52, 59, 62, 71-78, 81, 84, 86, 90, 91, 95-97, 100, 101, 105, 107, 110, 114, 118, 121, 122, 124, 129, 130, 134, 136, 141, 143, 147, 148, 151-155, 158-161, 163
Roots of Violence.. 58
Rosicrucians.. 309
Roswell, New Mexico...................................... 334

-S-

Savants. 87, 176
Scandinavian. 364
Schenck, Sister Christine.. 228
Schizophrenia........................... 25, 105, 176, 249, 300
Shaman. xii
Shell Oil Company...................................... 311
society............ vi, viii, xi, xii, xiv, xv, 1, 2, 4, 6, 7, 12, 14, 15, 22, 24, 25, 30, 33-35, 45, 49, 52-55, 59, 61, 67, 69, 71, 73, 78, 80-83, 86, 87, 90, 91, 100, 102, 103, 107, 112, 130, 131, 135, 137, 141-143, 147, 154, 155, 160, 166, 169, 170, 172, 173, 175, 177, 179, 187, 190, 193, 194, 199, 201, 210, 215, 217, 224, 235, 237, 247, 248, 251, 256, 258, 261-264, 273, 277, 282-286, 288-290, 292, 294, 295, 297, 300, 301, 304-306, 308, 309, 313-315, 334, 344, 349, 366, 370, 371, 379, 382, 383, 390, 392, 393, 395, 396, 398, 409, 410, 413
Sociology.................................. v, 104, 366, 401
Socrates................................. 7, 35, 81, 118, 216, 268
Sovereignty. 99, 100, 162, 233, 315, 316
Special Education................................... 42, 348
Standard Oil Company................................... 312
Status quo. .... vi, viii, ix, xii, xv, xvi, 6, 9, 12, 24, 29, 31, 101, 102, 105, 106, 110, 111, 142, 147, 156, 182, 190, 200, 209, 249, 298, 301, 303, 304, 319, 324, 325, 331, 334, 337, 369, 379, 389
Story of Human, Humane, and Inhumane Development.................. 140
Strategic Air Command (SAC)............................ 179
Sumerian Civilization................................. 238, 358

Sumerian Tablets. 241, 242, 247, 332, 335, 355
SuperPacs. 169, 181, 204, 325, 352, 360, 362
Susan. . . . . xii, xiii, 183, 271
System. . . . . ii, ii, iv, vii, xi, xiv, xv, 4, 6, 7, 9, 10, 12, 23, 24, 27, 28, 31, 34, 37-40, 42-44, 46, 48-54, 61, 71, 73, 75, 76, 81, 91, 93, 95-98, 100, 101, 103, 115, 117, 120, 122, 123, 125, 137, 140, 142-145, 147-150, 154-156, 158, 159, 162, 165, 169, 170, 175, 181, 186, 188, 189, 191, 196-198, 200-202, 211, 217, 218, 222, 224, 234, 239, 250, 251, 253, 262, 265, 276, 278, 281, 294, 295, 297, 299, 300, 304, 307, 315-320, 322, 326-329, 335, 336, 340-345, 347, 349, 351, 353-355, 360, 363, 364, 370-372, 376, 378, 379, 382, 385, 392, 394, 408

-T-

Tavistock. 175, 356
Taylor, Diane. 320
Tea Party. 73, 189, 199, 315, 316, 318, 319, 410
Teach for America (TFA). 55
Teachable Moment. 139, 339
Templeton, St. John. 261
Testosterone. 10, 24, 74, 77, 97, 124, 126, 130, 281, 284, 294
Thalidomide. 127, 340
Thinking Purple. . . . . i, 109, 158-161
Torture. 34, 57, 185, 244, 249, 283, 285, 292, 293, 298, 384
Town. 38, 50
Toxic Memories. 23
Toxic Soup. 123, 263
Transformation. . . . . 3, 5, 6, i, ii, vii, xiv, xv, 31, 106, 290, 292, 327, 340, 342, 343, 396, 410
Traumatized Children. 152, 153
Trilateral Commission, The. 315, 407
Truthful Knowledge. 30, 31, 155, 295, 297, 300, 383, 384
Twitter. 61, 62, 66, 67

-U-

U.S. Army. . . . . iii, xii, 116, 143, 349, 351
U.S. Supreme Court. 59, 183, 196, 360, 362
Ugly American. 180
Unconscious. . . . . iv, vii, xiii, 7, 8, 10-13, 20, 45, 75, 77, 79-81, 96, 98, 99, 112, 113, 115-117, 120, 121, 125, 136, 143, 151, 157, 159, 160, 162, 171, 194, 206-208, 210, 262, 269, 273, 274, 285, 293, 294, 344, 346, 371, 372, 386
unisex brain. 10, 97, 124

-V-

Vick, Michael.. 292
Vietnam. 141, 142, 180, 319
Violence as Entertainment. 144
Virtues.. . . . . iv, vii, xi, 2, 5, 7, 12, 14, 17, 24, 25, 28-30, 33, 45, 49, 52, 69, 71, 72, 89, 100, 122, 142, 143, 154, 163, 165, 177, 217, 264, 286, 300, 310, 345, 346, 354, 358, 359, 380, 387, 409
Voodoo Economics.. . . . . 201, 202

-W-

Wahhabism.. 258
Walking Wounded. 141, 142, 369
Wars on.. 61
Watson. 14, 146, 147, 153, 300
Wealth versus Income. 320
weight.. . . . . 125, 134, 137, 186, 197
Whistleblowers. 65, 238, 297
whole-brain.. . . . . vi, xii, xiv, 5, 13, 14, 29-31, 52, 68, 69, 78, 87, 90, 101, 103, 106, 121, 142, 150, 157
Wikileaks. 65
Women's Rights. . . . . ix, x, xiv, 43, 73, 98, 164, 252, 258-260, 263, 265, 267, 270, 273, 274, 315, 360, 372